MW01284431

THE
COLLEGE
PRESS
NIV
COMMENTARY

HEBREWS

THE COLLEGE PRESS NIV COMMENTARY

HEBREWS

JIM GIRDWOOD & PETER VERKRUYSE

New Testament Series Co-Editors:

Jack Cottrell, Ph.D.
Cincinnati Bible Seminary

Tony Ash, Ph.D.
Abilene Christian University

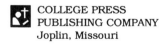
COLLEGE PRESS
PUBLISHING COMPANY
Joplin, Missouri

Library of Congress Cataloging-in-Publication Data

Girdwood, James.
    Hebrews / Jim Girdwood & Peter Verkruyse.
      p.   cm. — (The College Press NIV commentary)
    Includes bibliographical references.
    ISBN 0-89900-637-X (hardcover)
    1. Bible. N.T. Hebrews—Commentaries. I. Verkruyse, Peter,
  1959-   . II. Bible. N.T. Hebrews. English. New International.
  1997. III. Title. IV. Series.
BS2775.3.G57 1997
227'.87077—dc21   97-9139
                                                  CIP

A WORD
FROM THE PUBLISHER

Years ago a movement was begun with the dream of uniting all Christians on the basis of a common purpose (world evangelism) under a common authority (The Word of God). The College Press NIV Commentary Series is a serious effort to join the scholarship of two branches of this unity movement so as to speak with one voice concerning the Word of God. Our desire is to provide a resource for your study of the New Testament that will benefit you whether you are preparing a Bible School lesson, a sermon, a college course or your own personal devotions. Today as we survey the wreckage of a broken world, we must turn again to the Lord and his Word, unite under his banner and communicate the life-giving message to those who are in desperate need. This is our purpose.

ABBREVIATIONS

ABD......................Anchor Bible Dictionary
BAGD................Bauer-Arndt-Gingrich-Danker Greek Lexicon (2nd. ed.)
BDB....................New Brown-Driver-Briggs-Gesenius Hebrew and English
                       Lexicon
BDF.....................Blass-Debrunner-Funk Greek Grammar
ISBE...................International Standard Bible Encyclopedia (Bromiley)
KJV.....................King James Version
LN.....................Louw & Nida's Lexicon Based on Semantic Domains
LSJ....................Liddell-Scott-Jones Greek Lexicon
LXX.....................Septuagint
MHT.................Moulton-Howard-Turner Greek Grammar
MM....................Moulton & Milligan's Vocabulary of Greek Testament
NASB................New American Standard Bible
NIDNTT...........New International Dictionary of New Testament
                       Theology
NJB.....................New Jerusalem Bible
RSV....................Revised Standard Version
TDNT................Theological Dictionary of the New Testament, ed. by
                       Gerhard Kittel and Gerhard Friedrich
ZPED.................Zondervan Pictorial Encyclopedia of the Bible

INTRODUCTION

It is difficult to overestimate the significance of Hebrews for understanding the nature of the new covenant. No other document in the New Testament canon comments as directly and extensively upon this covenant as does Hebrews. Its description of Jesus as the great high priest of the believer is a unique contribution to New Testament Christology.

Yet Hebrews is perhaps as well known for the difficulties it presents as it is for its distinctive contributions to our understanding of the ministry of Jesus and the nature of our salvation. It is difficult to be certain about who wrote it, when and to whom. It is a letter and not quite a letter. Many find its line of argument intricate and complex, its theology abstract and obscure, and its use of the Old Testament puzzling if not problematic. This commentary will begin by addressing some of these considerations.

AUTHORSHIP

Over the years, most of the debate about the authorship of Hebrews has focused on whether or not Paul wrote this letter. Arguments have been made for other possible authors as well. What we can know for certain about the author is best gleaned from the letter itself, but many will want to know how this debate affects our confidence in the authority and inspiration of the letter.

Did Paul write the Letter to the Hebrews?

Though few defend Pauline authorship of Hebrews today,[1] in the past this view has enjoyed the support of significant church leaders and traditions. The earliest extant copy of Hebrews (early third century) has been received as part of a collection of Paul's letters, in which it was placed after Romans. Pauline authorship was defended by notable church fathers in the East, e.g., Clement of Alexandria (c.150-c.215) and Origen (185-253) who, despite reservations, defended it as essentially Pauline, at least in part on the weight of what was then received tradition. Later, Jerome and Augustine helped to shift opinion in the West and the Sixth Synod of Carthage (419) established a tradition of support for Pauline authorship which lasted until the Reformation.

However, the weight of the evidence — both historical and texual — is far from clear. Early church opinion was far from universal. In the West, prior to Jerome and Augustine, such leaders as Irenaeus and Hippolytus of Rome did not accept Hebrews as Pauline. The *Muratorian Canon* (a list of documents accepted as New Testament Scripture, c. 170) included thirteen letters identified as Pauline but excluded Hebrews. When reformers such as Calvin and Luther reexamined the question centuries later, neither concluded that Paul was its author. Contemporary critics consider Pauline authorship implausible in light of clear differences between the vocabulary and style of Hebrews and epistles known to be Pauline. Further, it has been argued as improbable for Paul to refer to himself as the author does in 2:3 ("This salvation, which was first announced by the Lord, was confirmed to us by those who heard him") in light of what he says of himself in Galatians 1:11-12 ("I did not receive it from any man, nor was I taught it; rather, I received it by revelation from Jesus Christ").

---

[1]Carson, Moo and Morris note that the last major defense of Pauline authorship was written more than fifty years ago. *An Introduction to the New Testament* (Grand Rapids: Zondervan, 1992), p. 395.

Who else could have written the letter to the Hebrews?

As early as the second century, Tertullian identified Barnabas as the author of the letter. Barnabas was a Levite (Acts 4:26), and there is much about levitical ritual in the epistle. He was also a Hellenistic Jew, a member of the Jerusalem church and a missionary partner of Paul (Acts 9:27; 11:30; 12:1-14:28). All of this evidence is circumstantial, however, and nothing but Tertullian's opinion connects him to the letter directly.

Clement of Alexandria first suggested that Luke translated a Hebrew text written by Paul. Calvin affirmed this possiblity centuries later. There are some similarities in the Greek style of Luke-Acts and Hebrews. But there is little other evidence and there are also some differences in style. Calvin also suggested Clement of Rome as a possibility. However, Clement of Rome widely quoted from the letter himself. It is unlikely that he would quote himself and his use of the Old Testament is often at variance with that in Hebrews.

Luther was the first to suggest Apollos as the possible author of Hebrews, a view which continues to enjoy some popularity. He was a "learned man, with a thorough knowledge of the Scriptures" who "vigorously refuted the Jews in public debate, proving from the Scriptures that Jesus was the Christ" (Acts 18:24-28). Presumably, he would have been capable of the careful handling of the LXX found in Hebrews. Also, he probably had some connection to the Pauline mission (1 Corinthians 1-4). But concluding that he was therefore the author of Hebrews is, at best, conjecture.

Among others, arguments have been made for Peter, Jude, Stephen, Aristion, Priscilla, Silas, Timothy, Epaphras, Philip and Mary the mother of Jesus as possible authors of Hebrews. Two other possibilities remain. An associate of Paul could have written the letter for him (a view first suggested by Origen in 220). It is also possible that Hebrews was written by some other anonymous Christian unknown to us. The letter itself does not clearly identify its author. Perhaps the fairest conclusion is that advanced by Origen, in spite of his inclination to defend Pauline authorship: "who wrote the Epistle, God only knows the truth."[2]

How does the debate about authorship affect our view of the letter?

It is important to note that, although the debate over authorship has extended over the centuries, the question of the letter's canonicity (i.e., its inspiration and authority) has not. Even though church fathers in the East may have had doubts about its authorship, there is no evidence that they ever questioned its canonicity. Though the Muratorian Canon excluded Hebrews (as well as James and 1-2 Peter), all four books were included in the New Testament canon by the Synod of Hippo (393) and the Third (397) and Sixth (419) Synods of Carthage. Subsequent questions about its authorship during the Reformation had no effect at all upon the reformers' view of its authority or inspiration.

It is clear that apostolicity, as well as other issues such as universality and the "rule of faith," were important in the early decisions about the New Testament canon. We must keep in mind, however, that a document's "canonical" status is the result of a human process which does not bestow divine authority or inspiration upon a document but recognizes the authority and inspiration which it inherently possesses because it has been "God-breathed" (2 Tim 3:16). In other words, if it is true that Hebrews is a divinely inspired and authoritative document, its inspiration and authority remain factual in an objective sense apart from our own inability to clearly discern the identity of its author. In his providence, God bore witness to the inspiration and authority of this letter in a manner that left little room for doubt, as Hebrews persistently silenced the questions of men who soon found that it "is useful for teaching, rebuking, correcting and training in righteousness, so that the man of God may be thoroughly equipped for every good work" (2 Tim 3:16-17).

---

[2]Eusebius, *Ecclesiastical History*, 6.25.14.

What do we know about the author?

Though the question of authorship is not determinative of either the letter's inspiration or authority, it is significant for our interpretation of Hebrews. Knowing as much as we can about the author can be helpful for discerning the meaning of a text. We may not be able to know the identify of our author with any degree of certainty, but there is much that we can know about him.

He was probably a Hellenistic Jew for he was both steeped in the LXX and possessed of an excellent vocabulary and a polished style for writing in the Greek language. Presumably, then, he was well educated. He was probably a second generation Christian (2:3) but one with direct connection to apostolic influence since he was a companion of Timothy (13:23) and thus possibly an associate of Paul. It is possible that he wrote from Italy, although 13:24 could also be taken to mean that the recipients were in Italy and some in his own party were from there as well. The rhetoric of the letter and his description of it as "my word of exhortation" (13:22) suggest that he was probably a preacher. His "short letter" reveals a compassionate pastor, a keen theologian and a superior logician who applies all the resources of revelation and rhetoric at his command so that his dear friends will "not drift away" (2:1).

DATE, DESTINATION AND PURPOSE

Three important facts suggest at least a general date for the letter. First, Clement of Rome cited Hebrews frequently. 1 Clement was written in A.D. 95 or 96 and thus Hebrews would not only have been completed but well circulated by this date. Second, there is thus little reason to doubt that the Timothy of 13:23 was the associate of Paul referred to elsewhere in the New Testament. Though we do not know how old Timothy was when he joined Paul in his work, it is unlikely that this reference would place the letter very late in the first century. Finally, much is made of the destruction of the Jerusalem temple in A.D. 70. Although it is possible that the author would not have referred to this event if it had happened by the time of writing, it seems improbable that he would omit reference to an event that not only had a significant effect on the lives of first-century Jews (including Christians) but would have added great force to his own argument. Further, he refers to old covenant worship rituals in the present tense (8:4-5; 10:1-3).

Other considerations as to the probable date of the letter pertain to the identity and location of its recipients. The title "To the Hebrews" may have been added later and reflect later opinions about its contents but it accompanies the letter in all of the oldest Greek manuscripts and there is no evidence that the letter ever bore any other title. Some suggest that the phrase could be translated "against the Hebrews" but it is the same formula used in Paul's letters which were hardly "against" the Romans, Galatians, etc. The title of the letter thus suggests that its recipients were Jewish, and the content that they were both Jewish and Christian.

The letter itself indicates that its recipients were enduring persecution (10:33-34; 12:4; 13:3, 23). The more natural reading of 13:24 suggests that the author wrote *to* Italy rather than *from* Italy (for which the expression "those *in* Italy send you their greetings" would have been more appropriate). The Edict of Claudius had expelled Jews from Rome in 49 but many had returned by the time of the persecution begun by Nero in 64. Since our earliest quotes of Hebrews come to us from Clement of Rome, its circulation there was likely at an early date. The cumulative evidence thus suggests that the letter was addressed to Jewish Christians in Rome who suffered under the persecutions of Nero.

The combination of these circumstances and statements in the letter suggest its purpose. Though some have suggested that Hebrews was written foremost to combat an early Jewish perversion of Christian doctrine or as a generic tract to demonstrate the superiority of Christianity, key verses in the letter suggest that it was addressed to a particular community with a view to responding to an urgent need. The following verses are all suggestive:

Passage	Exhortation	End in View
2:1	We must pay more careful attention . . . to what we have heard	so that we do not drift away
3:1	fix your thoughts on Jesus (cp. 12:2)	
3:6	hold on to our courage and the hope of which we boast	
3:12	See to it . . . that none of you has a . . . heart that turns away from the living God	
3:13	encourage one another daily	so that none of you may be hardened by sin's deceitfulness
3:14	. . . if we hold firmly till the end the confidence we had at first	We have come to share in Christ . . .
4:1	let us be careful	that none of you be found to have fallen short of it [rest]
4:11	Let us . . . make every effort to enter that rest	so that no one will fall
4:14	let us hold firmly to the faith we profess	
6:11	show this same diligence to the very end	in order to make your hope sure
10:23	Let us hold unswervingly to the hope we profess	
10:35	So do not throw away your confidence	it will be richly rewarded
10:36	You need to persevere	so that when you have done the will of God, you will receive what he has promised.
12:1	Let us run with perseverance the race marked out for us	
12:2	Let us fix our eyes on Jesus (cp. 3:1)	
12:3	Consider him who endured such opposition from sinful men	so that you will not grow weary and lose heart

Hebrews is, without doubt, a theologically valuable document which presents a well arranged argument in defense of the superiority of the new covenant. Yet these verses suggest that the author had an immediate purpose in mind for his theology and his rhetoric — the encouragement of Christian brothers and sisters who, suffering under persecutions which threatened even martyrdom, were tempted to abandon their strength. In the midst of their suffering, our author sends his "short letter" and "word of exhortation" (13:22) that they might fix their eyes on Jesus (3:1; 12:2), whose greatness he demonstrates from their own beloved Scriptures and cherished heritage.

FORM AND STRUCTURE

Since Hebrews includes some of the formal features of an epistle (e.g., personal greetings and closing formula) but not others (e.g., typical introductory greeting or address), there has been much debate as to whether it is more of a letter or a sermon. However, this particular formulation of the *genre* question probably reads a sharper distinction between written and oral communication back into an era when rhetoric rarely made such a rigid separation. Other epistles in the New Testament were clearly written in the knowledge that they would be read in the presence of congregations. It is thus possible to argue that, though written, they should be viewed primarily as oral documents. Writing lengthy treatises with significant oral features was a typical "rhetorical" practice for the ancients (e.g., the "template" or model speeches of Isocrates and others). Hence, Hebrews could well have been constructed as a "written homily," i.e., a letter with sermonic features.

This is to propose a variation of Deissmann's suggestion that Hebrews could have been an example of Christian literary art (i.e., a kind of treatise). Guthrie's criticism — that the writer's purpose was too serious to be regarded in this light[3] —

---

[3]See Donald Guthrie, "Hebrews, Epistle to" in *International Standard Bible Encyclopedia*, Vol. 2. Ed. by G. Bromiley (Grand Rapids: Eerdmans, 1979), p. 664.

assumes that literary art cannot be addressed to particular communities and urgent occasions, when in fact, rhetoric is chiefly defined by (1) its "addressed" nature and (2) its "contingent" character. The fact that it is addressed to specific communities, their circumstances and the demands of those circumstances is precisely what, according to Aristotle, distinguishes "rhetoric" from its counterpart "dialect." It is quite in keeping with at least one significant ancient rhetorical tradition to regard Hebrews as a written homily — an extended written treatise with significant oral features, addressed to a particular community with a view to responding to an urgent need.

Of what import is this conclusion? There is little value in examining Hebrews for exact correspondence to any particular classical scheme of rhetoric as some have done[4] for (1) a strong case has been made that there is no single classical tradition of rhetoric[5] and (2) our uncertainty about the identity of the author makes it impossible for us to do anything more than speculate about the possible significance of any such similarities.

There are several values, however, in recognizing the "rhetorical" nature of the document. First, this encourages us to keep in mind that, above all, Hebrews is an attempt to *persuade* its recipients (to take action, i.e., a case of deliberative rhetoric). Close attention should thus be paid to its argumentative dimensions. Also, as we attempt to follow the writer's development of thought, we should be alert for the use of rhetorical devices which signal transitions from argumentative sections to hortatory sections that address the contingiences of the community's situation. Further, apart from the complexities which separated competing rhetorical traditions in the ancient world, it is not inappropriate to look for evidence of the kinds of *topoi* (argumentative commonplaces) more

---

[4]Lindars describes the work of C. Spicq (*L'Epitre aux Hebreux*) in his "The Rhetorical Structure of Hebrews." New Testament Studies Vol. 35 (1989), p. 383.

[5]See Thomas Conley's *Rhetoric in the European Tradition* (New York: Longman Press, 1990).

widely employed and with which a well educated author was likely to be familiar. This should aid our understanding of the nature of the proofs employed by our author. Finally, it reminds us to seek the relevance of the subject matter of Hebrews in relationship to particular sets of life circumstances (persecution, suffering, temptation, and discouragement among them).

Hebrews is organized around a series of quotations from the Old Testament which are not only presented as argument but also developed with a variety of exegetical procedures (see below). If we use these quotations as a guideline for discerning its structure, the following picture of Hebrews emerges.

Chapter One is an introduction. This chapter is full of Old Testament quotations demonstrating Jesus' superiority over angels.

Chapter Two appeals to Psalm 8. Jesus rescues man by coming down beneath angels, joining man in flesh and blood, dying, and then returning to his place of exaltation above the angels. All who cling to him in faith return with him to the throne.

Chapters Three and Four deal with Psalm 95. God offers rest to all who trust him. The land of Canaan was not that rest, for this Psalm spoke of a rest long after the Israelites who wandered in the desert hardened their hearts and lost the rest which God offered to them. God's rest is still available for all who believe him.

Chapters Five, Six and Seven are organized around Psalm 110. Jesus is a priest like Melchizedek, who was also superior to the priesthood of the old covenant. Jesus, in fact, is a priest forever by God's oath.

Chapter Eight introduces Jeremiah 31. The new covenant, created by Jesus our great high priest, is superior to the old covenant. It is founded on better promises than the old covenant, which was a mere copy and shadow of this new covenant.

Chapters Nine and Ten treat Psalm 40. Jesus' living sacrifice of himself through obedience is far superior to the Old Testament sacrifices of dead bulls and goats repeatedly offered in the old tabernacle. Jesus took this sacrifice into the very presence of God, thus fully taking away sins and cleansing our consciences.

Chapter Eleven develops a theme from Habakkuk 2, that the righteous will live by faith. This principle by which we live is illustrated by numerous examples of people living by faith.

Chapter Twelve treats Proverbs 3. We must accept the discipline God brings upon us, for God disciplines those he loves.

Chapter Thirteen is the conclusion. It is full of exhortations on how to give ourselves to God in the life of faith.

Remove the introductory and concluding chapters for a moment and an interesting picture of the structure of the main body of thought emerges. The new covenant (chapter 8) is central, tying together his priesthood (chapters 5-7) and his sacrifice (chapters 9-10). This is prepared for by the offer of rescue (chapter 2) and rest (chapters 3-4) and followed by the response of faith (chapter 11) and the endurance of discipline (chapter 12) which he expects from us.

There are many other uses of the Old Testament woven into this main structure of the book but the central focus is on Jesus the superior priest who brings his superior sacrifice to God. This is the core of the new covenant. By this means he offers rescue and rest. From us he expects faith and endurance.

In a homespun way the structure of the letter may be compared to a wide-brimmed Texas hat or a sombrero. The high sides of the hat are his priesthood (chapters 5-7) and his sacrifice (chapter 10). The crown tying all together is the new covenant (chapter 8). The wide brim on one side is his offer of rescue (chapter 2) and rest (chapters 3-4). The wide brim on the other side is our expected faith (chapter 11) and endurance (chapter 12). The whole treatise is introduced (chapter 1) and concluded (chapter 13) with a generous collection of Old Testament connections.

USE OF THE OLD TESTAMENT

The author draws his quotations of the Old Testament not from any Hebrew text but from the Septuagint (LXX), a Greek translation which was read by Jews and Christians throughout the world in the first century and which he regarded as an accurate expression of the word of God. There is little conclusive evidence as to whether he followed any particular manuscript or tradition of the LXX.[6]

His methods of interpretation are varied. They include:[7]

- Etymology (determining the meaning or significance of a word by dividing it into its constituent parts) and/or the literal sense of a word of phrase
- *qal wa-homer*, a rabbinical method of arguing from lesser to greater
- *gezerah shawah*, another rabbinical method which established a relationship between two passages of Scripture on the basis of similar wording, using one passage to expand the meaning of the other
- Typology, a method of viewing a place, person, event, etc. in the Bible as a pattern (or "type") of a later place, person, event, etc. ("antitype"). The "type" takes on a significance beyond its historical referent which is later recognized as a result of its similarities with the "antitype"
- Homiletical Midrash, a kind of hortatory running commentary which applies a passage to the experience of an audience

---

[6]See Ellingworth, *Commentary on Hebrews*, New International Greek Testament Commentary (Grand Rapids: Eerdmans, 1993), p. 38.

[7]See Andrew Trotter, *Interpreting the Epistle to the Hebrews* (Grand Rapids: Baker), pp. 187-196.

OUTLINE

I. JESUS IS SUPERIOR TO THE ANGELS — 1:1-14

A. The Preeminence of the Son — 1:1-4

B. The Son Superior to the Angels — 1:5-14

II. JESUS RESCUES MAN — 2:1-18

A. Warning Not to Ignore Such a Great Salvation — 2:1-4

B. Jesus Became a Man to Bring Men to Glory — 2:5-18

III. GOD OFFERS REST TO ALL WHO TRUST HIM — 3:1–4:16

A. Jesus Is Superior to Moses — 3:1-6

B. Psalm 95:7-11 — 3:7-11

C. Hold Firm to the End — 3:12-15

D. Unbelieving Israelites Fell in the Desert — 3:16-19

E. A Sabbath-Rest for the People of God — 4:1-5

F. A Sabbath-Rest Remains — 4:6-11

G. The Message from God Does Its Part to Save Us — 4:12-13

H. Jesus, the Great High Priest — 4:14-16

IV. JESUS IS SUPERIOR TO THE PRIESTHOOD OF THE OLD COVENANT AND A PRIEST FOREVER BY GOD'S OATH — 5:1-7:28

A. Requirements of the High Priest — 5:1-4

B. Jesus Fulfills the Requirements and Offers Eternal Salvation — 5:5-10

C. [Excursus: Responding to God] — 5:11–6:12

    1. Still Infants — 5:11-14

    2. On to Maturity — 6:1-3

    3. Those Who Fall Away — 6:4-8

    4. Confident of Better Things — 6:9-12

D. God's Oath Makes His Purpose Sure — 6:13-20

E. Melchizedek Like the Son of God — 7:1-3

F. Melchizedek Greater than Abraham — 7:4-10

G. Jesus Is High Priest Based on His Resurrection which Introduces a Better Hope — 7:11-19

H. Jesus Is High Priest Based on God's Oath which Produces a Better Covenant — 7:20-22

I. Jesus' Resurrection Creates a Permanent Priesthood — 7:23-25

J. Jesus' Death Provides the Perfect Sacrifice — 7:26-28

V. THE NEW COVENANT BROUGHT BY JESUS OUR HIGH PRIEST IS SUPERIOR TO THE OLD COVENANT — 8:1-13

A. Our High Priest Reigns and Serves in the True Tabernacle, Prefigured by Old Testament Shadows — 8:1-5

B. Our High Priest Is Mediator of the New Covenant, Promised through the Prophet Jeremiah — 8:6-13

VI. JESUS' SACRIFICE OF HIMSELF IS SUPERIOR TO THE SACRIFICES OF THE OLD COVENANT AND SETS US FREE FROM SIN — 9:1-10:39

A. The Tabernacle and Its Tools — 9:1-5

B. The Day of Atonement — 9:6-10

C. Jesus' Sacrifice Cleanses Our Conscience — 9:11-14

D. Jesus' Death Inaugurates the New Covenant — 9:15-22

E. Jesus' Sacrifice Was Once for All — 9:23-28

F. Old Covenant Sacrifices Could Not Take Away
   Sin — 10:1-4

G. Christ Offered His Body to Make Us Holy — 10:5-10

H. Our High Priest Now Reigns — 10:11-14

I. Witness of the Holy Spirit through Jeremiah — 10:15-18

J. Let Us Draw Near to God and Spur
   One Another On — 10:19-25

K. The Judgment of God on Those Who Keep
   Sinning — 10:26-31

L. Reminder of Earlier Suffering — 10:32-34

M. The Need to Persevere — 10:35-39

VII. GOD EXPECTS US TO SHOW FAITH — 11:1-40

A. The Nature of Faith — 11:1-3

B. Faith Illustrated by Abel, Enoch, and Noah — 11:4-7

C. Faith Illustrated by Abraham — 11:8-19

D. Faith Illustrated by Isaac, Jacob, and Joseph— 11:20-22

E. Faith Illustrated by Moses — 11:23-28

F. Faith Illustrated in Israel — 11:29-38

G. God Planned to Make Them Perfect with Us — 11:39-40

VIII. GOD EXPECTS US TO ENDURE
    DISCIPLINE — 12:1-29

A. A Call to Perseverance — 12:1-3

B. The Word of Encouragement — 12:4-6

C. God Disciplines His Children — 12:7-11

D. Practical Actions — 12:12-17

E. Terrifying Mt. Sinai — 12:18-21

F. Mt. Zion, the Heavenly Jerusalem — 12:22-24

G. A Kingdom which Cannot Be Shaken — 12:25-29

IX. CONCLUDING EXHORTATIONS — 13:1-25

A. Keep Loving Each Other — 13:1-3

B. Stay Pure — 13:4-6

C. Remember Your Leaders — 13:7-8

D. Counterparts to Old Covenant Practices — 13:9-16

E. Obey Your Leaders and Pray for Us — 13:17-19

F. Benediction and Closing Exhortations — 13:20-22

G. Personal Greetings — 13:23-25

BIBLIOGRAPHY

Aristotle. *The "Art" of Rhetoric.* Loeb Classical Library. Translated by J. H. Freese. Cambridge: Harvard University Press, 1926.

_____. *On Rhetoric.* Edited and translated by George A. Kennedy. New York, Oxford: Oxford University Press, 1991.

Attridge, Harold W. *Hebrews.* Hermeneia Commentaries. Edited by Helmut Koester. Philadelphia: Fortress Press, 1989.

Bauer, Walter. *A Greek-English Lexicon of the New Testament and Other Early Christian Literature.* Translated by William Arndt and F.W. Gingrich. 2nd ed. Revised and augmented by F.W. Gingrich and F.W. Danker. Chicago: University of Chicago Press, 1979.

Beasley-Murray, G.R. "Baptism." *The New International Dictionary of New Testament Theology.* Vol. 1. Edited by Colin Brown. Grand Rapids: Zondervan, 1975.

Bietenhard, H. "Name." *The New International Dictionary of New Testament Theology.* Vol. 2. Edited by Colin Brown. Grand Rapids: Zondervan, 1975.

Blass, F., A. Debrunner, and Robert W. Funk. *A Greek Grammar of the New Testament and Other Early Christian Literature.* Chicago: University of Chicago Press, 1961.

Blowers, Paul. "Patterns of Perfection in Hebrews." Unpublished paper presented to a Fellowship of Professors at

Johnson Bible College in Knoxville, Tennessee, September. 21, 1990.

Boatman, Don Earl. *Helps From Hebrews*. Bible Study Textbook. Joplin, MO: College Press, 1960.

Bromiley, Geoffery, ed. *International Standard Bible Encyclopedia*. 4 Vols. Rev. ed. Grand Rapids: Eerdmans, 1979.

Brown, Colin, ed. *The New International Dictionary of New Testament Theology*. 3 Vols. Grand Rapids: Zondervan, 1975.

Brown, Francis, *et al*. *The New Brown-Driver-Briggs-Gesenius Hebrew and English Lexicon*. Lafayette, IN: Associated Publishers and Authors, Inc., 1980.

Bruce, F.F. *The Epistle to the Hebrews*. New International Critical Commentary on the New Testament. Grand Rapids: Eerdmans, 1964.

Calvin, John. *The Epistle of Paul the Apostle to the Hebrews*. Trans. by William B. Johnston. Grand Rapids: Eerdmans, 1963.

Carson, D.A., Douglas J. Moo and Leon Morris. *An Introduction to the New Testament*. Grand Rapids: Zondervan, 1992.

Chamberlain, William. *An Exegetical Grammar of the Greek New Testament*. Grand Rapids: Baker, 1941. Reprinted 1979.

Crouch, Owen. *God Has Spoken: Expository Preaching and Teaching – Hebrews*. Joplin, MO: College Press, 1983. Reprinted 1990.

Davidson, A.B. *The Epistle to the Hebrews*. Edinburgh: T. & T. Clark, n.d.

Dods, Marcus. *The Epistle to the Hebrews*. Vol. IV in The Expositor's Greek Testament. Edited by W. Robertson Nicoll. Grand Rapids: Eerdmans, 1910.

Douglas, J.D., ed. *The New Bible Dictionary*. 2nd. Ed. Leicester, England: InterVarsity, 1992.

Ellingworth, Paul. *Commentary on Hebrews*. New International Greek Testament Commentary. Grand Rapids: Eerdmans, 1993.

Elwell, Walter, ed. *Evangelical Dictionary of Theology*. Grand Rapids: Baker, 1984.

Enos, Theresa, ed. *Encyclopedia of Rhetoric and Composition: Communication From Ancient Times to the Information Age*. New York: Garland Pub., 1996.

Fant, Clyde E. and Pinson, William E., eds. *Twenty Centuries of Great Preaching: An Encyclopedia of Preaching*. 23 Vols. Waco, TX: Word Books, 1971.

Feinberg, C.L. "Tithe." *The Zondervan Pictorial Encyclopedia of the Bible*. Vol. 5. Edited by Merrill C. Tenney. Grand Rapids: Eerdmans, 1974-76.

Fensham, F.C. "Oath." *International Standard Bible Encyclopedia*, Vol. III, ed. by G. Bromiley. Grand Rapids: Eerdmans, 1979.

Fiensy, David. *New Testament Introduction*. The College Press NIV Commentary. Joplin, MO: College Press, 1994.

Gooding, D.W. and D.J. Wiseman. "Censer." *The New Bible Dictionary*. 2nd ed. Edited by J.D. Douglas. Leicester, England: InterVarsity, 1982.

Gregory, T.M. "Oath." *The Zondervan Pictorial Encyclopedia of the Bible*. Vol. 4. Edited by Merrill C. Tenney. Grand Rapids: Eerdmans, 1974-76.

Guthrie, Donald. "Epistle to the Hebrews," *International Standard Bible Encyclopedia*, Vol. 2. Edited by G. Bromiley. Grand Rapids: Eerdmans, 1979.

_____. *Hebrews*. Tyndale New Testament Commentary. Grand Rapids: Eerdmans, 1983.

_____. *New Testament Introduction.* 3rd ed. rev. Downers Grove, IL: Intervarsity Press, 1970.

Hatch, Edwin and Henry Redpath. *A Concordance to the Septuagint.* Two Volumes including supplement. Graz, Austria: Akademische Druck –Univ. Verlagstalt, 1954.

Héring, Jean. *The Epistle to the Hebrews.* London: Epworth Press, 1970.

Josephus. *Jewish Antiquities.* Books I-IV. Loeb Classical Library. Translated by H. St. J. Thackeray. Cambridge: Harvard University Press, 1930.

_____. *The Jewish War.* Books IV-VII. Loeb Classical Library. Translated by H. St. J. Thackeray. Cambridge: Harvard University Press, 1928.

Kittel, Gerhard and Gerhard Friedrich, eds. *Theological Dictionary of the New Testament.* 10 Vols. Translated and edited by Geoffrey Bromiley. Grand Rapids: Eerdmans, 1964-76.

Kistemaker, Simon. *Exposition of the Epistle to the Hebrews.* New Testament Commentary. Grand Rapids: Baker, 1984.

Konig, Eduard. "Tabernacle." *The Jewish Encyclopedia.* Ed. by Isadore Singer. New York: KTAV Publishing House, Inc., n.d.

Lane, William L. *Hebrews 1-8.* Word Biblical Commentary, Vol. 47A. Edited by David A. Hubbard, John D. W. Watts and Ralph P. Martin. Dallas: Word Books, 1991.

_____. *Hebrews 9-13.* Word Biblical Commentary, Vol. 47A. Edited by David A. Hubbard, John D.W. Watts and Ralph P. Martin. Dallas: Word Books, 1991.

Lenski, R.C.H. *The Interpretation of the Epistle to the Hebrews and the Epistle of James.* Minneapolis: Augsburg Press, 1966.

Liddell, Henry George and Robert Scott. *A Greek-English Lexicon.* 9th ed. Rev. and augmented by Sir Henry Stuart Jones. Oxford: Clarendon Press, 1940.

Lindars, Barnabas. "The Rhetorical Structure of Hebrews." *New Testament Studies* Vol. 35 (1989), pp. 382-406.

Louw, Johannes and Eugene A. Nida, eds. *Greek-English Lexicon of the New Testament Based on Semantic Domains.* 2 Vols. New York: United Bible Societies, 1988.

Martin, Ralph P. *New Testament Foundations: A Guide for Christian Students.* 2 Vols. Grand Rapids: Eerdmans, 1978.

Metzger, Bruce M. *A Textual Commentary on the Greek Testament.* New York, London: United Bible Societies, 1971, corrected edition, 1975.

Meyer, F.B. *The Way into the Holiest: Expositions of the Epistle to the Hebrews.* Fort Washington, PA: Christian Literature Crusade, 1982.

Milligan, R. *Epistle to the Hebrews.* The New Testament Commentary, Vol. IX. Cincinnati: Standard Pub., n.d.

Moffat, James. *A Critical and Exegetical Commentary on the Epistle to the Hebrews.* The International Critical Commentary. Edinburgh: T. & T. Clark, 1924. Reprinted 1968.

Montefiore, Hugh. *The Epistle to the Hebrews.* Peabody, MA: Hendrickson Publishers, 1964. Reprinted 1987.

Morris, Leon, *et al. The Expositor's Bible Commentary*, Volume 12. Edited by Frank E. Gaebelein. Grand Rapids: Zondervan, 1981.

Moule, Charles F. *Idiom Book of New Testament Greek.* 2nd ed. Cambridge: Cambridge University Press, 1959.

Moulton, James H. and George Milligan. *The Vocabulary of the Greek Testament: Illustrated from the Papyri and Other Non-Literary Sources.* Grand Rapids: Eerdmans, 1930. Reprinted 1980.

Moulton, James H., Wilbert F. Howard and Nigel Turner. *A Grammar of New Testament Greek.* 4 Vols. Edinburgh: T. & T. Clark, 1963-79.

Moulton, W.F. and A.S. Geden. *A Concordance to the Greek Testament*. Edinburgh: T. & T. Clark, 1897. 5th ed., 1978.

Nairne, A. *The Epistle to the Hebrews*. Cambridge: Cambridge University Press, 1921.

Paterson, J. H. "Sea." *The Zondervan Pictorial Encyclopedia of the Bible*. Vol. 5. Edited by Merrill C. Tenney. Grand Rapids: Eerdmans, 1974-76.

Rahlfs, Alfred, ed. *Septuaginta*. 2 vols. in 1. Stuttgart: Deutsche Bibel Stiftung, 1935.

Schiappa, Edward. "Protagoras." *Encyclopedia of Rhetoric and Composition: Communication*. ed. by Theresa Enos. New York: Garland Pub., 1996.

Silva, Moises. "Perfection and Eschatology in Hebrews." *Westminster Theological Journal*. Vol. 39 (1976), pp. 60-71.

Singer, Isadore, ed. *The Jewish Encyclopedia*. New York: Ktav Publishing House, Inc., n.d.

Spicq, C. *L'Épitre Aux Hebreux*. Paris: Librairie Lecoffre, 1952.

Soulen, Richard. *Handbook of Biblical Criticism*. 2nd ed. Atlanta: John Knox Press, 1976, 1981.

Swetnam, J. "Sacrifice and Revelation in the Epistle to the Hebrews: Observations and Surmises on Hebrew 9, 26." *Catholic Biblical Quarterly* Vol. 30 (1968), pp. 227-254.

Tenney, Merrill C., ed. *The Zondervan Pictorial Encyclopedia of the Bible*. 5 Vols. Grand Rapids: Zondervan, 1974-76.

Thayer, Joseph. *A Greek-English Lexicon of the New Testament*. 4th Edition. Edinburgh: T. & T. Clark, 1901.

Thompson, James. *The Letter to the Hebrews*. The Living Word Commentary. Edited by Everett Ferguson. Austin, TX: R.B. Sweet Co., 1971.

Trotter, Andrew H., Jr. *Interpeting the Epistle to the Hebrews.* Guides to New Testament Exegesis. Edited by Scot McKnight. Grand Rapids: Baker, 1996.

Waltke, B.K. "Melchizedek." *The Zondervan Pictorial Encyclopedia of the Bible.* Vol. 4. Edited by Merrill C. Tenney. Grand Rapids: Zondervan, 1975-76.

Westcott, B.F. *The Epistle to the Hebrews.* 2nd Edition. 1892. Reprint, Grand Rapids: Eerdmans. 1994.

Wiseman, D.J. "Weights and Measures." *The New Bible Dictionary.* 2nd ed. Ed. By J.D. Douglas. Leicester, England: InterVarsity, 1982.

Zodhiates, Spiros. *The Complete Word Study Dictionary: New Testament.* Rev. ed. Chattanooga, TN: AMG Press, 1993.

HEBREWS 1

I. JESUS IS SUPERIOR TO THE ANGELS (1:1-14)

A. THE PREEMINENCE OF THE SON (1:1-4)

[1]In the past God spoke to our forefathers through the prophets at many times and in various ways, [2]but in these last days he has spoken to us by his Son, whom he appointed heir of all things, and through whom he made the universe. [3]The Son is the radiance of God's glory and the exact representation of his being, sustaining all things by his powerful word. After he had provided purification for sins, he sat down at the right hand of the Majesty in heaven. [4]So he became as much superior to the angels as the name he has inherited is superior to theirs.

Meet Jesus. The opening chapter of Hebrews leaps immediately into a presentation of Jesus in his glorious superiority. All previous communications from God find their climax in God's message through him (1:1-2). All of redemption is dominated by him (1:2-4). All angelic hosts bow before him (1:5-14).[1]

The central message of the book of Hebrews is that in the new covenant, Jesus, as a superior priest, has offered himself as a superior sacrifice for fallen man (Heb 5-10). Jesus' superiority to angels (1:5-14), his joining man to rescue him (Heb 2), and God's offer of divine rest (Heb 3-4) all lead up to this

---

[1]John began his first epistle with similar abruptness before settling into its steady cycles (1 John 1:1-4, then 1:5ff.).

majestic message. His faithfulness (12:1-2) climaxes the master list of believers (Heb 11) and sets the pace for our surviving God's discipline (Heb 12). His example of separating from the world becomes our motivation for separating from the world (Heb 13).

To place the work of Jesus in its proper preeminent position the book of Hebrews introduces Jesus by reviewing his central role in all of the history of redemption (1:1-4). The seven items presented in this history (1:2b-3) are themselves introduced by showing Jesus' dominance over revelation (1:1-2a) and concluded with the superior name subsequently given to him (1:4).

Whereas the prophets of old had received their messages from God only in small portions, Jesus showed us fully what God is like (John 1:14-18; 14:8-10). Their message came at a distance by words and visions and dreams. He stood before us. In their holy rites and institutions, in their ennobling laws, even in their special history, they saw the shadow of God. Jesus was God, visible before us.

Notice the contrasts with which the book begins. 1. "These last days" are contrasted with "the past." 2. "We" are contrasted with "the fathers." 3. "The Son" stands over against "the prophets." 4. The following chart shows these contrasts clearly in tabular form.

Old Testament messages	New Testament messages
1. In the past	6. but in these last days
2. God spoke	7. he has spoken
3. to our forefathers	8. to us
4. through the prophets	9. by his Son
5. at many times and in various ways	

1:1 In the past God spoke to our forefathers through the prophets at many times and in various ways,

God shared tiny bits of his message with various people before Jesus in a wide variety of ways: direct speech, proverbs, prophecy, various laws, dreams, visions, guidance, testing, providential plagues, providential provisions, heightened abilities (to the Jews in general — Deut 8:17-18; and to tabernacle builders in particular — Exod 31:1-11; 35:30-36:1), sending good or bad spirits (1 Sam 10:9-13; 16:14), stirring one's heart by a noble theme (Ps 45:1), symbolic action or ritual (use of blood — Heb 9:16-25; cf. Ezekiel's many symbolic deeds), symbolic office (high priest, king, family structure, judicial deliverer), symbolic buildings and utensils (altars, ark, veil of tabernacle — 9:8), miracles of healings and control of nature, etc.

All of these were partial. By contrast, the message Jesus brought was full and final (1:1-2; 2:1-4). Who is this One who could tower over the voice of prophets? Hebrews 1:2-3 proceeds to describe him with seven statements that survey the whole history of redemption. These seven items fill out the opening paragraph.

At many times and in various ways. In the opening statement each description of the OT message finds its counterpart in the parallel description of the NT message from God, except the phrase, "at many times and in various ways." The Greek text puts this phrase as the first words of the book. It seems peculiar to begin a work about the totally sufficient preeminence of Christ with words that could almost be translated, "By scattered bits and pieces!"

A second characteristic of the first words adds to this disarmingly inauspicious beginning. They form a double alliteration repeated three times by beginning each group of sounds with "p" and ending with "s," thus p..s, p..s, p..s, "*PolymerōS kai PolytropoS Palai-ho-theoS*" (πολυμερῶς καί πολυτρόπως πάλαι ὁ θεός).[2] An English translation does not catch this alliteration at all.

The grand display of the rest of the book is clearly designed to show the majestic work of Christ, not the minuscule word-

---

[2]Neither of the alliterated pair of words in the text appear elsewhere in the NT, and in the LXX they are only in IV Macc 3.21; though BAGD finds them a few times here and there in the classics and twice together in statements of Maximus (second century AD).

play of men. By avoiding a contrasting statement for this first phrase, he leaves the thought of Christ's full revelation open for the whole epistle to develop.

Did the writer want his readers to be charmed at the outset with his literary devices so that he could slip in these seven awesome traits of Jesus before they could stop their ears? In the Greek text the first four verses of Hebrews form a single sentence. When his long opening Greek sentence ends, he immediately begins quoting Scripture. A Jew, caught off guard, may feel compelled now to listen reverently to Scripture.

God spoke. God took the initiative. The primary perspective of the Bible is that God has spoken to man. It is not a collection of men's musings about God, nor sages' finest thoughts on the good life or the afterlife or deity. One's fundamental *approach* to the book of Hebrews, indeed, to the whole Bible, makes so much difference in how we hear its message.

Missing this beginning point produces writings that are full of discussions on the natural sources and capabilities of the author of Hebrews, but devoid of a sense of God's overriding influence. Perhaps one should rather say they are devoid of a sense of how biblical authors were "carried along by the Holy Spirit" (2 Pet 1:21).

Recognizing the work of the Holy Spirit in generating the Bible writings does not erase the human participation in presenting a passage. But in struggling with the human side, we must never lose sight of the divine side. This assessment may sound embarrassingly naive in the presence of books that collect massive amounts of material from innumerable obscure sources assembled over many years by highly skilled scholars. We must never forget. If one's aim is wrong, no amount of craftsmanship in rifle-building can make a marksman hit the center of the target.

God **spoke**. He chose language as his primary medium of communication. This was true of the bits and pieces "in the past" as well as the final message by the Son "in these last days." Hebrews, like other biblical literature, is a revelation of propositions God selected, of information God chose, of assessments God made that he as creator wanted to make known to mankind, his noblest creatures. His thoughts and feelings, his heart and character, his plans and deeds are reported here. The thoughts, feelings and deeds of others are recorded which God wanted men to see. But the main point is that this book expresses God's messages to man.

The message of God is linguistic, often propositional. He spoke. He did not limit himself to foggy visions, fleeting feelings or veiled signs which could be easily misunderstood. He communicated to man with words of human language. The Old Testament is full of statements like, "declares the Sovereign Lord;" or "This is what the Lord says;" or "The Lord called to Moses and spoke to him saying." Of course there are many other kinds of ways God delivered different facets of his message — dreams, symbolic acts, signs, allegories, events of history, rituals, sacred places, building structures, vocations, etc. His usual way of communicating was in ordinary speech with its ordinary linguistic devices including plain statements as well as figures of speech like commands, descriptions, metaphors, similes, rhetorical questions, hyperbole or irony. The heritage of the people of God is centered in a book, that is, in human language in written form.

It is interesting to contemplate the place of the spoken word in God's overall plan for man's own activity: in worship, evangelism, song, intimacy, communication. Speech is the action most frequently attributed to God in the first chapter of Genesis. God spoke the fully adorned world into existence.[3]

---

[3]In the New International Version Genesis 1 reports God's *speaking* with the phrase, "God said," verses 3, 6, 9, 11, 14, 20, 24, 26 and 29. "God blessed and said," is in verses 22 and 28. Speech is indicated also by the word "called," verses 5(twice), 8 and 10(twice).

Descriptions of God's *other activity* in creation according to Gen 1 include "created," verses 1, 21 and 27(three times); "separated," verses 4 and 7; "made," verses 7, 16(twice), 25, [26] and 31; and "set," verse 17. In verse 2 the Spirit of God "was hovering." God also said he would "give," verse 30.

More

Speech is one of the primary differences between man and animals. All creatures seem to have some kind of communication within each species. No creature approaches the high level of verbal communication found in man, who was created in the image of God. Using speech man builds a culture and a history. He becomes educated by building a thought-bank of abstract concepts and knowledge dependent on the patterns of speech. Man was made in the image of God to interrelate with him. In this opening statement God is shown to use the vehicle of speech to address his messages to man.

Jesus is the last word. All other messages from God were only partial and sporadic. Final full truth came from Jesus, for he is the truth (John 1:17; 14:6).

"**The past**" is contrasted with "these last days." All history is here divided into two parts. There are other ways of viewing history. It may be seen as spiraling events, as seven dispensations, or as ages of starlight, moonlight, then sunlight. For the purposes of the book of Hebrews Jesus' presentation of God's message of salvation stands at the fulcrum of history. It marks the change, the turning point, the beginning of a new era. All that came before him is "the past." All that has come since is "the last days." This is reflected in the widespread dating system that uses BC and AD, or the alternate designations, BCE and CE.

1:2 but in these last days he has spoken to us by his Son, whom he appointed heir of all things, and through whom he made the universe.

God has spoken to us by his Son "**in these last days**." There is only a handful of passages that use the exact phrase "in the last days" (Isa 2:2 = Mic 4:1; Hos 3:5; Acts 2:17; 2 Tim 3:1; Heb 1:2; James 5:3; and 2 Pet 3:3). Heb 1:2 actually has a fuller

---

The creator's *observation* of his work is shown with the word "saw," in verses 4, 10, 12, 18, 21, 25 and 31.

Speech as the predominant creation activity is indicated in numerous other Bible passages which use God's speaking as a summary of his creation activity, for example, Ps 33:6, 9; Heb 11:3; 2 Pet 3:5.

phrase "in these last days." Acts 2:17 substitutes the phrase "in the last days" in quoting Joel 2:28 which actually said "afterward."[4] Several similar phrases speak of "last" things: "the last time" (1 Pet 1:5); "the last times" (Jude 18); "in these last times" (1 Pet 1:20); "the last day" (John 6:39, 40, 41, 54; 11:24; 12:48; no OT ref.); even "the last hour" (1 John 2:18 [twice]). One should examine the phrase "the end of the age" (Matt 13:39, 40, 49; 24:3; 28:20) or "the end of the ages" (Heb 9:26).

Aside from a few scattered passages, the only certainly authentic words of Jesus which we have are those recorded in the four Gospels. See Acts 1:3-8; 9:4-16; 20:35; 22:7-10; 26:14-18; 1 Cor 11:23-25; 2 Cor 12:9; Heb 5:7; 7:25. Therefore, the communication of God through Jesus "in these last days" surely included the time of the earthly ministry of Jesus when he spoke the words from God to us. Jesus said the words that he spoke were God's words (John 3:34; 14:10, 24; 17:8). Belief in Jesus' words accompanies belief in God (John 5:24). By his ministry, climaxing in his death and resurrection, Jesus began a new era, called "the last days." This new era is here characterized neither by his functioning as high priest, nor by his offering his own blood as the perfect sacrifice, nor even by his inaugurating the new covenant. These will be developed later in the heart of the book of Hebrews. Here as the book begins, the message from Jesus is central, as though the "last days" is the time when the words of Jesus are predominant, replacing the partial messages of "the past" which found their completion in his new message about his new work in his new era. If this reasoning is correct, then we have been in the "last days" since Jesus walked the earth. Since Jesus' words have not been replaced by any other words, we are still in the last days.

"The past" would logically be the other era leading up to the new era which Jesus brought. Dividing history this way makes "the last days" the whole era from the time of Jesus' ministry on into the future until Jesus changes the new covenant.

---

[4]In Acts 15:16 James used the phrase "After this" as equivalent to "In that day," which appears in Amos 9:11.

There is an interesting statement in Acts 1:3, "After his suffering, he showed himself to these men and gave many convincing proofs that he was alive. He appeared to them over a period of forty days and spoke about the kingdom of God." The only things we know that Jesus said during the forty days between his resurrection and his ascension are those reported in Matthew 28, Mark 16, Luke 24, John 20-21 and Acts 1. There were seven major items. (1) He confirmed that he really had raised from death. (2) He explained how he fulfilled the OT Scriptures, "the law of Moses, the prophets, and the psalms." (3) He gave the great commission to preach the gospel to the whole world. (4) He promised that power would be sent from the Father. (5) He reinstated Peter so he would feed Jesus' sheep. (6) He predicted the manner of Peter's death. (7) He uttered various ordinary greetings in general conversation.

What do these seven things teach us about the kingdom? From its beginning the church has accepted (3) as central to her mission. Her mouth was full of (1) and (2). At his ascension Jesus said (4) would be "in a few days" (Acts 1:5). The special empowering events of Pentecost, recorded in Acts 2, were just ten days after his ascension. Peter certainly aligned his energies with the new Christian community in preaching the gospel and building up the church, (5) and (6). Ordinary greetings, (7), have nothing distinctive about the kingdom.

If Jesus talked about central church concerns, when Luke said he was talking about the kingdom, then the church is operating at the same time as the kingdom with the same message and empowering of the Holy Spirit as the kingdom. The church appears either to be the same as the kingdom or indistinguishably aligned with it.

The "last days" therefore must include the time of Jesus' ministry, when he spoke the words from God to us.[5] By his ministry, climaxing in his death and resurrection, Jesus began

---

[5]Jesus said the words he spoke were God's words (John 3:34; 14:10, 24; 17:8). Belief in Jesus' words accompanies belief in God (John 5:24).

a new era, called "the last days." The new era, the last days, is
presented here but not described here. Later in the book we
will learn of his functioning as high priest, his offering his
own blood as the perfect sacrifice, and his inaugurating the
new covenant. Here as the book begins, the message from
Jesus is central. The "last days" is the time when his words
predominate, replacing the partial messages of "the past."
They found their completion in his new message about his
new work in his new era. If this reasoning is correct, then we
have been in the "last days" since Jesus walked the earth, and
we are still in them.

Hebrews later reaffirms the idea that Jesus' first coming
marked the beginning of the last age of earth history, i.e.,
"the last days." Jesus did not enter heaven to offer himself
again and again like the OT high priests entered the Most
Holy Place (Holy of Holies) again and again. "Then Christ
would have had to suffer many times since the creation of the
world. But now he has appeared once for all *at the end of the
ages* to do away with sin by the sacrifice of himself" (9:26,
emphasis added).

"We" are contrasted with "**our forefathers**" (lit., "the
fathers"). In Christ there are much greater privileges than
what the fathers enjoyed. Ours is a better revelation offering
better promises in a better era. This gives no justification for
arrogant boasting. The fathers are made models of faith in
this very book. They did well with what was available to them.
Our question is, how well we do with what is available to us?
Abraham is presented as the man of faith *par excellence* in
Romans 4:1-25. James said Rahab's deeds should be copied
(2:25). The Believers' Hall of Fame is full of examples of the
fathers who pleased God (Hebrews 11).

Like other cultures on the Mediterranean shores, the
Middle East and the Far East, the Jews were inclined to think
in terms of family solidarity. This perspective made the Jews
of NT times embrace as one the Jews in other times and other
places. The NIV is a bit misleading when it translates the
same word πατήρ (*patēr*) as "father(s)" 452 times and as "fore-

fathers" 16 times. It is the same word. At the same time the NIV translated the Hebrew word אב (*'ab,* father) in the Old Testament as "father(s)" 1160 times and "forefather(s)" 96 times. Jeremiah 11:10 has the fuller expression *'abot hari'shonim,* "their first fathers."

Jesus stands over against all **the prophets**. Before Jesus came, the messages from God were partial and scattered. The message he brought was whole, climactic, synthesizing, exhaustive. There is a similar contrast in the beginning of the Gospel of John between the law given by Moses, whereas grace and truth have come from Jesus (John 1:14-18). Philip correctly saw that the primary role of Moses and the prophets was to point to Jesus (John 1:43-46). This was the same perspective that Jesus presented to the two disciples who were approaching Emmaus (Luke 24:25-27). Peter said the same to his temple listeners (Acts 3:17-25).

The sequence of these seven facets of Jesus' greatness spans all of history. First, God decided where he wanted history to end. He planned the final outcome before he took the first step. In the beginning, before the creation of the world, God decided he wanted Jesus to end up as **heir**. Once he began the universe and started history, it would all lead up to this final end in which Jesus would be "heir of all things." Many other Scriptures fill in this picture. For example, redeemed believers will sit on the throne with him forever (Eph 2:6-7). All wickedness will be removed from God and his people, being thoroughly destroyed forever (Rev 20:11-15; 21:1-8, 27; 22:14-15).

Second, once the outcome was established, God gave his attention to getting it started. Genesis 1-2 says that God **created the universe** and everything in it. Other passages amplify this to indicate that God probably made the overall plan, but Jesus did the actual "hands-on" creating (John 1:1-5; Col 1:15-17; etc.). It was certainly a prime place for an important person. Hebrews moves from one end of history to the other to describe Jesus.

1:3 The Son is the radiance of God's glory and the exact representation of his being, sustaining all things by his powerful word. After he had provided purification for sins, he sat down at the right hand of the Majesty in heaven.

The third and fourth traits are closely related. Jesus is so intimately linked to the Father that upon seeing Jesus, one sees the Father. So John 14:9. BAGD says the first word, ἀπαύγασμα (*apaugasma*, NIV **"radiance"**) may be understood actively "radiance, effulgence"; or passively "reflection"; then adds, "The mng. cannot always be determined w. certainty" though the Greek fathers prefer the active meaning.

The second word in the pair of expressions, χαρακτήρ (*charaktēr*, NIV **"exact representation"**) is used of the impression stamped on coins. The idea is clear that the Son and the Father are as much alike as a die and the coin it stamps. Jesus is so much like the "being" (ὑπόστασις, *hypostasis*) of God that to understand the nature and behavior of Jesus is to understand the nature and behavior of God.

Fifth, our eyes are drawn across history to witness the predictability of stable laws that keep the universe functioning. It is nothing less than the power of Jesus' own words that are **sustaining all things**. The gospel writers present Jesus out front performing miracles, interrupting or controlling the laws of nature. They do not show this side of his work, behind the scenes sustaining and holding all together as in this passage and Colossians 1:17.

Sixth, his finest work of all is presented next. Jesus **provided purification for sins**. This work centers in the cross. Hebrews will explain much about the significance of what Jesus did in the heavenly tabernacle as high priest with the blood he poured out when he died on the cross. In terms of chronological sequence that heavenly work was completed before Jesus sat down. This is expressed by the grammatical structure here. The word "provided" is an aorist participle. The word "sat down" is an indicative verb. The action of an aorist participle normally precedes the action of the main verb. Hence, the NIV is correct, "After he had provided purification for sins, he sat down at the right hand of the Majesty in heaven."

Seventh, Jesus **sat down** beside God. The image may indicate his finished work as high priest or his role as reigning king. The first is the major idea of Hebrews, associating his sitting down with providing purification (1:3), with his ministry as high priest (8:1) or victory after the cross (12:2). His work of the cross is over, hence he can sit (as Heb 12:2 says); but his interceding continues while he sits. The present tense of "intercede" is used in both Romans 8:34 and Hebrews 7:25. His rule as king appears to be primary in 1:13. Both sacrificing and conquest are joined to his sitting down in 10:12; both roles of prince and savior in Acts 5:31. Except for Romans 8:34 where Jesus is at God's right hand interceding for us, most NT references to Jesus' sitting at God's right hand relate more to power over enemies than purifying of sins.[6]

The wide variety of expressions used in Hebrews may be sampled by looking at the way he describes Jesus' sitting beside God. God told Jesus to "sit at my right hand" (1:13). He "sat down at the right hand of God" (10:12). He "sat down at the right hand of the Majesty in heaven" (1:3). He "sat down at the right hand of the throne of God" (12:2). He "sat down at the right hand of the throne of the Majesty in heaven" (8:1). The rest of the NT does not show this much variety. Matthew (26:64) writes of Jesus' sitting at the right hand "of the Mighty One." In the parallel passage Luke (22:69) said, "of the Mighty God." Outside Hebrews only these two parallel passages in the NT use a substitute for the name of God. It is interesting that Hebrews uses a substitute name twice in this group of passages, calling God "the Majesty in heaven" (1:3; 8:1).

---

[6]His sitting down at the right hand of God (or "the Majesty in heaven" Heb 1:3) is taken from Ps 110:4. It appears also in Matt 22:44; Mark 12:36; Luke 20:42 (specifically quoting Ps 110:4 as Acts 2:34 and Heb 1:13 also do); and in Matt 26:64; Mark 14:62; Luke 22:69; as well as Mark 16:19; Acts 2:33-34; (7:55-56); Eph 1:20; Col 3:1 and 1 Pet 3:22.

The two descriptions that climax the opening paragraph touch the two central issues in Hebrews: Jesus' sacrifice of himself on the cross providing purification for our sins and Jesus' finished work as high priest in the heavenly tabernacle, allowing him to sit in authority beside the Father and intercede for us. In Hebrews 10:11-14 the contrast is specifically stated. OT priests continually stood daily ministering about their unending offerings, whereas Jesus made one totally sufficient offering and with his work finished sat down at the right hand of God.

What are the most important *events* in all of history? If the answer is that 1) Jesus' will end up as heir of all, 2) he created all, 3) he died once for all, and 4) he sat down beside God; then the answer sounds like the opening paragraph of Hebrews. Jesus stands supreme among all.

1:4 So he became as much superior to the angels as the name he has inherited is superior to theirs.

There is one more magnificent idea with which Hebrews summarizes this opening declaration of Jesus' preeminence. Having become so much greater than the angels it fitting that he has won a name much more significant than theirs. It may be too pedantic to inquire whether the name is "son" (as in 1:2; twice in 1:5 [both from OT quotations]; 1:8 [from an OT quotation]; 3:6; 5:5 [from an OT quotation]; 5:8; 7:28); more specifically "son of God" (2:6; 4:14; 6:6; 10:29); "God" (as in Heb 1:8); "Lord" (as in Heb 1:10 and Phil 2:9-11); "Savior" (as in Matt 1:21); or simply a metaphorical term meaning a person or position the "name" would represent, i.e., all a person would represent in his exalted position. Whatever the specific idea that is intended here, the general idea is clear, that Jesus is far superior to angels. The rest of the chapter will undergird this idea of superiority more fully. Some scholars think Jesus' superiority over angels is presented to deter a tendency to worship angels.

The finished work of Christ brought him the highest exaltation. This concluding statement of superiority of position balances the opening statement of superiority of communication (1:1-2a), and with it showcases the seven brilliant gems set in this redemptive string of jewelry.

The word "superior" is written all across the epistle. Hebrews calls many things "better" or "superior:" Jesus' ministry (8:6); his new covenant (8:6); a better hope (7:19), a better covenant (7:22; 8:6); a better resurrection (11:35); a better country (11:16); better possessions (10:34); a better sacrifice that purifies the heavenly things (9:22). It is fitting that God expects better things of us (6:9). These all become possible through the one who obtained a better name (1:4).

B. THE SON SUPERIOR TO THE ANGELS (1:5-14)

[5]For to which of the angels did God ever say,
"You are my Son; today I have become your Father[a]"[b]?
Or again,
"I will be his Father, and he will be my Son"[c]?
[6]And again, when God brings his firstborn into the world, he says,
"Let all God's angels worship him."[d]
[7]In speaking of the angels he says,
"He makes his angels winds,
his servants flames of fire."[e]
[8]But about the Son he says,
"Your throne, O God, will last for ever and ever,
and righteousness will be the scepter of your kingdom.
[9]You have loved righteousness and hated wickedness;
therefore God, your God, has set you above your companions
by anointing you with the oil of joy."[f]
[10]He also says,
"In the beginning, O Lord, you laid the foundations of the earth,
and the heavens are the work of your hands.

¹¹**They will perish, but you remain;**
they will all wear out like a garment.
¹²**You will roll them up like a robe;**
like a garment they will be changed.
But you remain the same,
and your years will never end."^g
¹³**To which of the angels did God ever say,**
"Sit at my right hand until I make your enemies
a footstool for your feet"^h?
¹⁴**Are not all angels ministering spirits sent to serve those**
who will inherit salvation?

^a5 Or *have begotten you*   ^b5 Psalm 2:7   ^c5 2 Samuel 7:14; 1 Chron. 17:13
^d6 Deut. 32:43 (see Dead Sea Scrolls and Septuagint)   ^e7 Psalm 104:4
^f9 Psalm 45:6,7   ^g12 Psalm 102:25-27   ^h13 Psalm 110:1

The rest of the chapter is primarily comprised of quotations from the Old Testament. Like the opening paragraph (1:1-4), they range all over the history of redemption. There are seven quotations, just as there were seven major facets of Christ shown in that first paragraph. However, the quotations do not correspond item for item with the earlier list. The author probably wanted to undergird the general idea of Jesus' superiority rather than to secure the certainty of each item by itself.

1:5 For to which of the angels did God ever say, "You are my Son; today I have become your Father"? Or again, "I will be his Father, and he will be my Son"?
The conjunction "for" (γάρ, *gar*) ties the two halves of the chapter tightly together. It indicates the cause or reason for something just stated. The reason we know that Jesus holds the exalted position stated in the opening paragraph will be found in the following quotations from Scripture. The first half of the chapter presented Jesus' supremacy; the last half will prove it. Fortunately, the NIV translated the word "for" here. For whatever reasons, it left untranslated 46 of the 91 appearances of the conjunction *gar* in Hebrews. See further information at 2:5.

1:6 And again, when God brings his firstborn into the world, he says, "Let all God's angels worship him." 1:7 In speaking of the angels he says, "He makes his angels winds, his servants flames of fire."

In general, the quotations show Jesus' preeminence by viewing his sonship with the father and his rule over creation. The first three quotes focus on his sonship; the last four on his rule in creation. The first three quotations are tied together: A (v. 5a) "or again" B (v. 5b) "and again" C (v. 6). God called Jesus "son" (A, B), whereas when he brought him into the world, angels were to worship him (C). The last four passages are presented as two contrasting pairs. "In speaking of angels he says" D (v. 7), "but about the Son he says" E (vv. 8-9). "He also says" F (vv. 10-12); but "to which of the angels did God ever say" G (v. 13)?

Seven OT passages quoted to exhibit the supremacy of the Son (1:5-13).	
Ps 2:7	Jesus is proclaimed "SON" at some event called "today."
2 Sam 7:14	God promised to be his Father and he his Son.
Deut 32:43	Angels were told to worship him when Jesus entered the world.
Ps 104:4	God makes his angels winds and fire in serving.
Ps 45:6-7	The Son reigns forever with righteousness and joy.
Ps 102:25-27	The Son made heaven and earth & eventually will discard them.
Ps 110:1	God made the Son sit at right hand till all enemies are subdued

An examination of the central thought of these quotations will lay the steps of his argument more plainly before us.

The central thought	*The NIV Text including Old Testament passages quoted*
1. God's pride in Jesus' work. (the cross?)	1. (1:5a) To which of the angels did God ever say, "You are my Son; today I have become your Father "? (Ps 2:7)
2. God's promise/ pledge to the Son-Father relationship	2. (1:5b) Or again, "I will be his Father, and he will be my Son"? (2 Sam 7:14)
3. Incarnation: angels are assigned to worship the Son	3. (1:6) And again, when God brings his firstborn into the world, he says, "Let all God's angels worship him." (Deut 32:43)
4. Incarnation or general role: angels serve (the Son)	4. (1:7) In speaking of the angels he says, "He makes his angels winds, his servants flames of fire." (Ps 104:4)
5. The Son's righteous rule	5.(1:8-9) But about the Son he says, "Your throne, O God, will last for ever and ever, and righteousness will be the scepter of your kingdom. You have loved righteousness and hated wickedness; therefore God, your God, has set you above your companions by anointing you with the oil of joy." (Ps 45:6-7)
6. The Son created the universe and will bring it to an end; but he remains the same forever	6. (1:10-12) He also says, "In the beginning, O Lord, you laid the foundations of the earth, and the heavens are the work of your hands. They will perish, but you remain; they will all wear out like a garment. You will roll them up like a robe; like a garment they will be changed. But you remain the same, and your years will never end." (Ps 102:25-27)
7. The Son reigns, and God subdues his enemies.	7. (1:13) To which of the angels did God ever say, "Sit at my right hand until I make your enemies a footstool for your feet"? (Ps 110:1)

After the series of quotations our author makes one closing statement concerning the angels' place (1:14). They are to serve those who will inherit salvation. Instead of being above mankind, angels find themselves beneath mankind, serving those who by the power of this marvelous Son Jesus are now destined to inherit salvation. By his work believers become heirs with Jesus. He is heir of all things; they are heirs of salvation.[7] Chapter two will explain how Jesus joined mankind to provide this inheritance for all his brothers in the human family.

1:8 But about the Son he says, "Your throne, O God, will last for ever and ever, and righteousness will be the scepter of your kingdom.

In the longer quotations more than a single idea appears. This is particularly true of the fifth and sixth quotations. Simply put, he rules. The text elaborates by introducing a **throne**, a **scepter** and a **kingdom**. His **throne** will last **forever**.

The **throne** is mentioned in Hebrews only four times. In two passages Jesus has finished the work of atonement and has sat down at the right hand of God (8:1; 12:2). The one before us exalts the Son by quoting OT verses which show that his throne lasts for ever. The other passage invites us to approach his throne for assistance when we have needs, calling it "the throne of grace" (4:16). It, too, is preceded by verses that show Jesus' finished work of atonement (4:14-15). Hebrews does not connect the throne of the Messiah with any physical earthly reign.

If he currently has a throne and this throne is eternal, what room is there for a different future throne? More specifically, if this throne is "David's throne" which had been prophesied, and God has already seated Jesus on it, as Mark 16:19; Acts 2:22-36; Romans 8:34; Colossians 3:1, and other

---

[7]The phrase "fellow heirs of Christ" in Rom 8:17 is not clear. It may mean (1) fellow heirs with Christ as an equal heir, or (2) fellow heirs with other believers, all of whom belong to Christ.

From a variant reading in Rev 21:7 the King James Version says that he who overcomes will inherit "all things." The NIV says he who overcomes will inherit "all this," whereas the Greek has simply "these things" (ταῦτα, *tauta*). The NIV is not dependable for this differentiation. For *tauta* it has "this" in 1 John 1:4 and 2:1, but "these things" in 1 John 2:26 and 5:13. Hebrews only uses this neuter plural pronoun "these things" five times (4:8; 7:13; 9:6; 11:12; 13:11).

passages indicate, how can some say he is not on it now, but will be placed upon it in some future time?[8]

1:9 You have loved righteousness and hated wickedness; therefore God, your God, has set you above your companions by anointing you with the oil of joy."

He rules with **righteousness** not with might. His kingdom is "not of this world" as he told Pilate (John 18:36) and the Jews (John 8:23). It is not a kingdom at all in the ordinary sense of the word. There are no plush palaces, no visible royal regalia, no elaborate political negotiations with other kingdoms. Yet in some special way he rules in the hearts of his people more thoroughly than any earthly king rules his subjects. He rules with righteousness. He loves righteousness. He **hates wickedness**. If the principle of physics is true also in the moral realm, one could expect that for every force there would be an equal and opposite force. He hates sin with the same strength with which he loves righteousness. He pushes as hard in one direction as the other. That is a harsh thought in a world that does not even like to think about sin.

Because of this scenerio (διὰ τοῦτο, *dia touto*, i.e.,"on account of this", "therefore") in which Jesus loves righteousness and hates wickedness, God has **set** him **above his companions**. Outside of Hebrews, the word "companion" (μέτο–χος, *metochos*), occurs in the NT only in Luke 5:7 of fishing-partners. Hebrews 12:8 uses it of the physical fatherly disci-

---

[8]God promised to place a son of David on his throne forever (2 Sam 7:11-16 ; 1 Chr 17:7-14; Ps 89:3-4). The promise for earthly kings to rule on David's throne was conditional (1 Kgs 9:3-9; Ps 132:11-18 cited in Acts 2:30; Jer 17:24-25; 22:2-5, 30). Because of his mercy God did not abort their rule long after they had broken the covenant (Ps 89:1-52).

Many prophecies anticipate a Messianic king. Isa 9:6-7; Jer 3:14-18; 33:17-22; Ezek 34:23-24; 37:24-25; Hos 3:5; Zech 6:13; 9:9; Luke 1:32. The NT indicates that Jesus was that Messiah who, after his death and resurrection, now sits on his throne (Acts 2:29-36; 5:31; 17:7; Heb 8;1; 12:2). Jesus often compared himself to a king (Matt 18:23ff.; 22:2ff.; 25:34, 40). He did not deny it when called a king (John 1:49; John 18:33-37). See being a king as a major issue in the trial and condemnation (Matt 26-27; John 18-19).

pline in which all of us are participants. The other uses in
Hebrews are religious. We become companions of the Holy
Spirit at our conversion (6:4), participants in the heavenly calling (3:1), and remain so by continuing to be faithful (3:14).
Hebrews 1:9 alone applies the designation to Christ. He is
honored **above** (παρά, *para*) his companions as his exalted
name is above (*para*) that of the angels (1:4). This leaves
unclear whether the word "companions" is intended to signify
angels or men. The whole force of the first chapter points
toward angels.

Anointing. The adjective χριστός (*christos*, "anointed")
appears so frequently with the name Jesus that BAGD can
write of "certain passages in which χριστός does not mean the
Messiah in general (even when the reference is to Jesus), but a
very definite Messiah, Jesus, who now is called *Christ* not as a
title but as a name" and then list dozens of passages used "as
a personal name."[9]

Jesus applied Isaiah 61:1 to himself in Nazareth at the
beginning of his ministry.

> The Spirit of the Sovereign LORD is on me, because the LORD
> has **anointed** me to preach good news to the poor. He has sent
> me to bind up the brokenhearted, to proclaim freedom for the
> captives and release from darkness for the prisoners, to pro-

---

[9]Walter Bauer, *A Greek English Lexicon of the New Testament and Other Early
Christian Literature*, trans. by William Arndt and F.W. Gingrich. 2nd ed.
Revised and Augmented by F.W. Gingrich and F.W. Danker (Chicago:
University of Chicago Press, 1979), p.887. Although the name "Christ"
appears so much in the NT, its cognate verb χρίω ("I anoint") is seen only
five times (Luke 4:18; Acts 4:27; 10:38; 2 Cor 1:21; and Heb 1:9). Two of
these are in quotations from the OT (Luke 4:18 from Isa 61:1; and Heb 1:9
from Ps 45:8).

Another one of the five, 2 Cor 1:21, is not even pointing to Jesus, but to
his followers! If the Christians in their prayer in Acts 4 (verse 27) used the
verb χρίω because they had just prayed the words of Psalm 2 which called
Jesus God's χριστός, then we are indeed left with remarkably little NT
attachment to this verb. It does not appear nearly as often as one might
expect based on its LXX frequency.

> claim the year of the Lord's favor and the day of vengeance of
> our God, to comfort all who mourn, . . . (Isa 61:1-2)

Peter told Cornelius (Acts 10:38) that after he was anointed with the Holy Spirit *and power,* Jesus then went around doing good and healing those oppressed by Satan. His words may imply that the anointing happened at Jesus' baptism. God certainly reassured Jesus of his mission at that time by means of the voice and the dove. On the other hand, the anointing may have occured in heaven before Jesus came to earth. He was "chosen before the creation of the world" (1 Pet 1:20). He was the lamb "slain from the creation of the world" (Rev 13:8; see Rev 5:6, 12). It is possible that the whole terminology is not intended to tell the time but the fact of the matter.

There is something wonderfully refreshing in the image of joy as the medium when Jesus was "anointed with the oil of **joy.**" We are not surprised to find Jesus "full of joy through the Holy Spirit" (Luke 10:21), nor to find the seventy-two "return with joy" from a victorious mission for him (Luke 10:17). The happiness surrounding his birth anticipated the joy of his ministry. Like Mary (Luke 1:47) and the angels (Luke 2:10), the pre-born forerunner (Luke 1:44) rejoiced at his coming.

He announced his ministry with a message of joy from Isaiah 61 (Luke 4:16-22). His parables reminded people of the joy of receiving his message (Matt 13:20,40) and the joy of finding a lost sheep, a lost coin or a lost son (Luke 15:6, 9, 20-24). Even heaven rang with joy at earth's victories (Luke 15:7 and 10). He promised the disciples that their grief at his death would soon be turned into joy (John 16:20,22). It was (Matt 28:8; Luke 24:41, 52). The joy he promised for their faithfulness (Matt 5:12; Luke 10:20), he pictured for their helpfulness when he would return and say, "Come and share your master's happiness!" (Matt 25:21,23. See 25:34). He intended that his followers' joy would be complete (John 16:24). As he said, "I have told you this so that my joy may be in you and that your joy may be complete" (John 15:11. See

17:13). Though he was "a man of sorrows" (Isa 53:3), sorrow was certainly not the only feature of his person and ministry.

He is also called "**God**," a name customarily reserved for the Father. Compare Isaiah's description of him in Isaiah 9:5-6. Also note that Jesus is called "Lord" in verse 10. Several passages attribute divine names to Jesus, for example, John 8:58; Acts 2:36 and Philippians 2:11. Jesus suggested that some OT passages ascribed divine names to him when he asked about whose son the Christ was (Matt 22:41-46). His own reply shows that David called him "Lord," i.e., Greek κύριος (*kurios*), where the OT had the Hebrew word for "Lord," אדני (*adonai*, Ps 110:1). This Psalm will be used repeatedly throughout the book of Hebrews. Psalm 110:1 is used in 1:3, 13; 8:1 and 10:12; while Psalm 110:4 is in Hebrews 5:6, 10; 6:20; 7:3, 11, 15, 17 and 21. John 12:37-41 says the "Lord" (*adonai*) of Isaiah 6, who was high and exalted, seated on a throne, was actually Jesus.

1:10 He also says, "In the beginning, O Lord, you laid the foundations of the earth, and the heavens are the work of your hands.

Besides having divine names applied to him, Jesus also performed deeds which only deity could do. He forgave sins, performed miracles and spoke flawlessly. He created heaven and earth. See 1:2. Here the idea from 1:2 that he created the universe (τοὺς αἰῶνας, *tous aiōnas*, "the ages") is expanded to include taking charge of the founding and finishing of both the heavens (οὐρανοί, *ouranoi*) and earth (γῆ, *gē*).

1:11 They will perish, but you remain; they will all wear out like a garment.

The idea is very clear that he is not a part of this universe. In some way he is outside of it. He created it, though he existed before it existed. He will roll it all up like a worn-out garment when it has finished its usefulness. He does not roll himself up in it. Rather, he remains unending when it ends. A similar idea rises in 9:11. The tabernacle in which Jesus performs his high priestly duties is "not a part of this creation."

1:12 You will roll them up like a robe; like a garment they will be changed. But you remain the same, and your years will never end."

Though all heaven and earth will perish, he will **remain the same** (1:11-12). Jesus' permanence will be asserted several more times in the book. His is "an indestructible life" (7:16, 25). His is "a permanent priesthood" (7:24) to last "forever" (5:6; 7:17, 21). His sacrifice was "once for all time" (7:27; 9:25-28; 10:12-14). He is the same yesterday and today and forever (13:8).

1:13 To which of the angels did God ever say, "Sit at my right hand until I make your enemies a footstool for your feet"?

God never spoke to angels the remarkable words of Psalm 110:1. The Son alone was summoned to **sit at God's right hand**. This was the place of greatest honor and authority. The sheep were gathered at Jesus' right hand to be blessed, while the goats were gathered at his left hand to be destroyed (Matt 25:31-46). The scepter was held in a king's right hand (Matt 27:29), which was his hand of authority (Ps 89:25). Preferential blessing was done with the right hand (Gen 48:12-20). God swore by his right hand (Isa 62:8). Solomon seated his mother Bathsheba at his right hand when she approached him with a request (1 Kgs 2:19). Asaph served Heman faithfully "at his right hand" (1 Chr 6:39). The royal bride was at the king's right hand (Ps 45:9). It is a right hand of fellowship (Gal 2:9).

Since most people are right-handed, the right hand is the one customarily grasping the sword. Thus to call for God's right hand to act in defense or aggression on one's behalf may be a metonymy for asking God himself to act. One who stands at the right hand stands to serve (Ps 109:31). Though the Messiah is seated at God's right hand (Ps 110:1), the Lord is pictured as being at the Messiah's right hand to serve and protect him (Ps 110:5). The Psalm verse (110:1) implies this reversal of roles. The Son is invited to sit at God's right hand. Then God acts as the Son's "right hand man" by subduing the Son's enemies for him.

God promised to subdue Jesus' **enemies**. Setting one's enemies as a **footstool** (ὑποπόδιον, *hypopodion*) may be seen in
Joshua's treatment of the five Amorite kings whom he defeated.
He instructed his army commanders to "put your feet on the
necks of these kings" (Josh 10:24). The word appears only nine
times in the NT. Psalm 110:1 is quoted again including this
imagery in Matthew 22:44; Mark 12:36; Luke 20:41; Acts 2:35;
Hebrews 1:13; and an allusion in Hebrews 10:13. A literal footstool is intended in James 2:3. Twice the earth is called God's
footstool (Matt 5:35 and Acts 7:49), probably pointing to Isaiah
66:1. The image of putting enemies under his feet clearly means
that Jesus will gain total control (1 Cor 15:25-28; see Matt
28:18). Subduing enemies was putting them under one's feet
(1 Kgs 5:3; Ps 18:37-40). Compare the image of crushing enemies as dust beneath one's feet (2 Sam 22:38-43). The image is
more severe than simply bowing at one's feet (Deut 33:3; 1 Sam
25:24; Esth 8:3; Isa 60:14) or holding one's feet in supplication
(2 Kgs 4:27,37) or even licking the dust at one's feet (Isa 49:23).

Having control over something is having it under ones'
feet. The top place in creation is given to man, "You made
him ruler over the works of your hands; you put everything
under his feet" (Ps 8:6; see also 45:5). The eighth Psalm will
be used in the argument of Hebrews chapter two, but it puts
creatures — flocks, herds, fish, etc. — not enemies, beneath
man's feet.

It should be noted that even Jesus has enemies. But they
did not deter him from doing what he needed to do for the
Father. He came to destroy Satan, his principle enemy, and
death, Satan's major weapon against man (Heb 2:14-16;
1 John 3:8). Satan is called "the enemy" in the parable of the
weeds (Matt 13:25,28,39) and when the seventy-two returned
from their mission (Luke 10:17-20). Those who resist Jesus'
rule in their lives position themselves as his enemies (Luke
19:27; Rom 5:10; Phil 3:18; Col 1:21; James 4:4). He warned,
"Woe to you when all men speak well of you, for that is how
their fathers treated the false prophets" (Luke 6:26).

1:14 Are not all angels ministering spirits sent to serve those who will inherit salvation?

In this verse, suddenly the contrast changes. It is no longer Jesus above the angels. It is Jesus and his redeemed followers above the angels. When Jesus entered the world, **angels** were told to worship him (Heb 1:6). Now their task seems to center on serving redeemed mankind, "those who will inherit salvation." Nor will they rule in the world to come (2:5), though they are stronger than men (2 Pet 2:11).

The most common service angels give to men is to bring messages from God. Angels so thoroughly represent God that an angel appeared to Moses in the burning bush, but it was God who spoke from the bush (Exod 3:1-4; Acts 7:30,35). They assisted in the giving of the law at Mt. Sinai (Acts 7:38, 53; Gal 3:19; Heb 2:2).

Other ways of helping are not so visible. Angels guarded Jesus against mishaps (Matt 4:6 citing Ps 91:11-12). They may do the same for others. Jesus talked about children as having "their angels" (Matt 18:10). If this is a one-to-one ratio, and if they do not terminate their care at age twelve or fifteen or twenty, each person may have a personal "guardian angel" until death. Evidently there is also an angel assigned to each church (Rev 1:20; 2:1; etc.) and to each nation (Dan 10:12-14; 12:1), as well as generally in the world (Rev 7:1; Zech 6:5).

Angels sang at Jesus' birth (Luke 2:13-15). Angels "served" or "attended" Jesus after his temptation (Matt 4:11) and when he wrestled in Gethsemane (Luke 22:43). It is not clear whether they were visibly present or in some way simply refreshed his spirit. Jesus could have had twelve legions of angels rescue him from arrest if he had called for them (Matt 26:50-54). How many might be available for us in an emergency if we are doing the work of God? An angel rolled back the stone from Jesus' tomb (Matt 28:2).

Angels want to understand more of God's plans and God's words than they are allowed to know (1 Pet 1:12). Angels are not allowed to tell the gospel story. That privilege belongs to Christians. Nevertheless, they help in many ways. An angel guided Philip to the Ethiopian eunuch (Acts 8:26). Similar assistance was given to Cornelius to get the message of God from Peter (Acts 10:3, 7, 10; 11:13). Angels opened prison doors to free the apostles, while keeping the guards blinded about their escape (Acts 5:19-24; 12:1-12; probably 16:22-27).

At death angels carried Lazarus to Abraham's bosom (Luke 16:22). At the end of the world they will separate the wicked from the righteous (Matt 13:36-43, 47-50). They form the great watch tribunal of heaven before whom Jesus will either acknowledge or disown each person (Luke 12:8-10; Rev 14:10).

Men will eventually judge angels (1 Cor 6:3). Angels apparently still have the capability of turning from God as Satan and other angels have already done (Matt 25:41; Gal 1:8; 2 Pet 2:4, 9; Jude 6; Rev 12:7-9). There are evidently many levels of angels, all in submission to Christ (1 Pet 3:22). The book of Revelation is full of reports of the activities of angels in serving God and man. So very little is said in the Scripture directly about angels. They may well play a much larger role in our safety and in carrying out our plans than we know.

We **will** (or "are about to;" μέλλοντας, *mellontas*) inherit salvation. The verb is used ten times in Hebrews. The law was only a shadow of the "good things that are coming" (10:1). Abraham went to a place "he would later receive as his inheritance" (11:8). Isaac blessed Jacob and Esau "in regard to their future" (11:20). Moses was warned "when he was about to build the tabernacle" (8:5). Believers' supreme position will be realized in the future, in "the world to come" (2:5), where they will (or are about to) inherit salvation (1:14). The powers of this "coming" age are already tasted by believers now (6:5). We do not have an enduring city here, but are looking for the city "that is to come" (13:14). There will be severe punishment for backsliders with fire that will (or "is about to") consume the enemies of God (10:27). One appearance is in a variant reading in 9:11. Christ is high priest of good things that have (already) come. A variant reading has "good things that are about to be."

As Christ has already **inherited** a superior name (1:4), and will inherit all things (1:2), believers will inherit salvation. Elsewhere this promised inheritance (6:12; 9:18) is identified as eternal life (Matt 19:29; Titus 3:7) or a kingdom (Matt 25:34; James 2:5). Of course it is kept safely in heaven (1 Pet 1:4).

Dods suggests that by the time Hebrews was written the term "**salvation**" had come to be used "as the semi-technical term for the deliverance from sin and entrance into permanent wellbeing effected by Christ."[10] The word may be introduced here to prepare us for the discussion about it which will follow in chapter two. It will be the focus of the warning in 2:1-4, and Jesus is seen as the author of this salvation in 2:10.

---

[10]Marcus Dods, *The Epistle to the Hebrews*, volume IV in *The Expositor's Greek Testament*, edited by W. Robertson Nicoll (Grand Rapids: Eerdmans, 1910), IV:258.

HEBREWS 2

II. JESUS RESCUES MAN (2:1-18)

Chapter one introduced Jesus as towering over all of redemption history, far superior to angels. Chapter two shows how he joined the human race to rescue man. In two parts, the chapter warns us not to neglect his offer of salvation (2:1-4), then informs us how he achieved it (2:5-18). He who was far above angels came beneath them to unite fully with mankind (2:5-8). Then God crowned him with glory and honor, and through him is bringing many sons to glory (2:9-10). Jesus became like his brothers in every way including suffering and death. Some OT verses indicate this equality (2:11-14a). By his death he destroyed Satan, ended man's fear of death, and earned his status as our high priest (2:14-18).

A. WARNING NOT TO IGNORE SUCH A GREAT SALVATION (2:1-4)

¹We must pay more careful attention, therefore, to what we have heard, so that we do not drift away. ²For if the message spoken by angels was binding, and every violation and disobedience received its just punishment, ³how shall we escape if we ignore such a great salvation? This salvation, which was first announced by the Lord, was confirmed to us by those who heard him. ⁴God also testified to it by signs, wonders and various miracles, and gifts of the Holy Spirit distributed according to his will.

After presenting the glory of the Son, our author pauses to warn about the practical consequences of our response to what he has done. The message of the OT covenant spoken by angels was sure and its punishments sure. The greater salvation Jesus brought was more secure, so its punishment was more severe. Jesus announced it; his hearers confirmed it; God added his witness to it. The system of Mt. Sinai brought a just punishment for violation. There is likewise no escape if we neglect this greater salvation personally brought by Jesus himself. The author is so elated at who Jesus is and what he has done (chapter one) that his literary skills are greatly elevated in the opening paragraph of chapter two. His descriptions use several rare words, heavy alliteration, a complicated sentence and an embellished list.

The paragraph contrasts the two systems. The Sinai covenant was (a) a message spoken by angels; (b) it was binding; and (c) it included a just punishment for every infraction. The covenant Christ brought was (a) announced by the Lord himself; (b) confirmed by hearers and by God himself; and (c) included no escape for ignoring or even drifting away.

In the first chapter all previous revelation from God was contrasted with the final revelation of God in his Son. In chapter two our author narrows this view to put the NT over against the single finest, fullest pinnacle of OT revelation, i.e., the covenant of Mt. Sinai. He says that the Sinai revelation was spoken through angels (2:2, δι' ἀγγέλων, *di' angelōn*). Stephen mentioned this (Acts 7:53) and so did Paul (Gal 3:19; see 3:38), although it was only suggested in the Pentateuch (Deut 33:2). The thirteenth century rabbi, Nachmanides, claimed, "Though myriads of angels were present, the Torah was communicated to Israel directly by God."[1] By contrast, the new message was much more significant, because it was given by the Son, who is much more significant than the angels.

2:1 We must pay more careful attention, therefore, to what we have heard, so that we do not drift away.

This is the first of many exhortations in the book of

---

[1]Nachmanides as quoted by S. Fisch in *The Soncino Chumash*, edited by A. Cohen (London: Soncino Press, 1947), p. 1176.

Hebrews. Sometimes they appear in the second person plural, "you," where the readers are directly addressed. Sometimes the author stands beside his readers by using the first person plural, "we" or "us." One should especially notice the exhortations in 2:1-4; 3:6, 7-19; 4:1, 11, 14-16; 5:11-14; 6:1-12, 18-20; 10:19-39; 12:1-17, 25-28; 13:1-22.

We **must** pay more careful attention to what we have heard. We are prone to forget. Henry compares our minds and memories to a leaky vessel, "They do not without much care retain what is poured into them." What Jesus offers is far superior to what the OT system offered. Once we have heard this message, there are no other alternatives. There is no higher court to which we may appeal. We either live faithful to this offer or suffer a fate far worse than that of OT violators. Hebrews uses four different words to indicate necessity: ἀνάγκη (*anagkē*) and cognates ("compulsion;" 7:12, 27; 9:16, 23), δεῖ (*dei*, "must;" 2:1; 9:26; 11:6), ὀφείλω (*opheilō*) and cognates ("to owe;" 2:17; 5:3, 12) and πρέπω (*prepō*, "to be fitting;" 2:10; 7:26). The third word evidently came from the financial world, and indicated owing a debt. The fourth carries the idea of necessity only in that something is most appropriate. The first two are more difficult to distinguish.

In view of the greater offer from a greater person with greater confirmation at a greater point in the history of redemption and greater evident consequences of improper response the author would certainly use the most powerful word he could to show the necessity of paying attention. We **must** (*dei*) pay attention. The same word will be used twice later. If Christ were to offer himself again and again like the repeated animal sacrifices, he "**would have to** suffer many times since the creation of the world" (9:26). Similarly anyone who comes to God "**must** believe that he exists and that he rewards those who earnestly seek him" (11:6). In both of these instances there is not the tiniest possibility that either could be avoided. Compare other absolute necessities, "The Son of Man *must* suffer many things" (Mark 8:31), and "You *must* be born again" (John 3:7). Tiedtke finds the NT using this word to focus on three areas: apocalyptic contexts, Jesus' life and way as salvation history, and necessities in the life of the Christian.[2]

The author of Hebrews finds that the law *must* (ἀνάγκη, *anangkē*) change when the priesthood changed (7:12); that unlike Christ OT priests *had to* offer sacrifices first for their own sins, then for the people (7:27); that the death of one making a will *must* be proven for a will to be put in force (9:16); and that the earthly tabernacle *must* be purified indicating that the heavenly things needed even better sacrifices for purification (9:23).

Accepting the task of becoming man's high priest carried with it the obligation (ὀφείλω, *opheilō*, "to owe") that Jesus be made like his brothers in every way (2:17). He owed that to them if he would become a merciful and faithful high priest. Without this total identification, he would still have been able to purify the heavens with his blood. He would still have been perfect. But we would not have understood that he understood. We would not have had immediate evidence of his caring or his ability to help. He may have performed his office satisfactorily, but we are more inclined to respond because of his total identification with us. This was unlike the OT priests who, because of their own sins, were *obligated* to make an offering for themselves before they could make the offering for the people (5:3). In a third application, the author states that his readers had been Christians long enough that the time alone *obligated* them to be teachers. Something was terribly wrong when in fact they still needed to be taught (5:12).

It was appropriate (πρέπω, *prepō*) that God should make Jesus complete through suffering, since he was the author of our salvation (2:10). Some things are appropriate for God. Some things are also proper and fitting for man. The NIV misses the idea of this word entirely in 7:26, "Such a high priest meets our need." The NRSV is better here, "For it was fitting that we should have such a high priest." The KJV

---

[2]E. Tiedtke, et al, "Necessity, Must, Obligation," in NIDNTT, 2:665-666.

phrase is old enough to be awkward today, "Such an high priest *became* us."

The word "better" could be written across the book of Hebrews; the word "**more** should be written across our response. Some things require greater (περισσοτέρως, *perissoterōs*, "far more, to a much greater degree") diligence. We are prone to dangerous carelessness. Does he say to pay closer attention (1) than you have been paying; (2) than the Israelites paid (3:16-4:2); or (3) than anyone is normally inclined to do? The author also urged his readers to pray "*particularly*" (NIV; NRSV has "all the more;" KJV, "the rather") in order that he may be with them very soon (13:19). Likewise, they needed especially to pay *more careful* attention to the gospel (2:1). God's oath makes *even clearer* to us that he is totally committed to the universal promise he made to Abraham (6:17). Likewise, the unique priesthood of Melchizedek made Jesus' unique priesthood *even clearer* to us (7:15).

The phrase, "**what we have heard,**" is a single word, an aorist participle (lit., "what was heard"). The whole message is evidently in mind. "To hear" implies "to obey." The big problem lay not with the simplicity of the beginning, but with the difficulty of remaining faithful.

The author worries about his readers, afraid that they might **drift away.** Dods suggests that since προσέχω (*prosechō*, "to pay attention") "is commonly used of bringing a ship to land, this sense may have suggested the [use of] παραρυῶμεν" ("to drift away"). Liddell and Scott defines the verb παραρρέω (*pararreō*,) "*To flow beside, by* or *past;* II. *to slip away, to slip* from one's memory; III. *to slip in unawares.*" Westcott found it used of things which slip away, as a ring from the finger, or of taking a wrong course, as a crumb of food entering the windpipe, or of an embarrassing subject arising among company. Then he observed, "We are all continuously exposed to the action of currents of opinion, habit, action, which tend to carry us away insensibly from the position which we ought to maintain."[3]

---

[3]Westcott, *The Epistle to the Hebrews* (Grand Rapids: Eerdmans, 1994, Reprint of 2nd Edition, 1892), p. 37.

Regularly meeting together with other Christians (10:25) and daily encouragement from other Christians (3:13) combined with daily prayer and Bible reading (4:12-16) will greatly reduce the risk of drifting away.

BAGD says the word means, "flow by, slip away" or figuratively, "be washed away, drift away." Proverbs 3:21 says, "Son, do not let slip away, but keep my counsel and understanding." Isaiah 44:4 wrote of "running" water. Without the prefix *para-*, the verb *rheō* ("to flow") is found in John 7:38 to describe the abundant inner supply of the Holy Spirit, "Streams of living water will flow from within him." It is part of the common OT phrase describing the promised land as a land "flowing" with milk and honey. The main idea in our verse seems to be the unnoticed, gradual slipping away of one's salvation because of inattention.

In 13:22 our author calls the whole epistle "a word of exhortation." It may seem odd that the first exhortation of the epistle should warn against negligence. Does he have some reason to think that his readers have begun to let their first vigor as Christians diminish? It is a major emphasis of the book (3:12-14; 4:1-2, 11, 15; 5:11-6:12; 10:19-11:3, 6; 12:1-13:25). It is a perpetual concern in the church today. Nairne records that "In an ancient prologue to the Pauline epistles (in an Irish MS. of the Vulgate) Hebrews is described simply thus — 'To the Hebrews whom he exhorts like the Thessalonians that in the commandments of God they should more readily endure persecutions.'"[4] With so many blessings available both now and later, it would be tragic for anyone to just drift away from them all.

2:2 For if the message spoken by angels was binding, and every violation and disobedience received its just punishment,

"**If** the message spoken by angels was binding . . ." Bruce

---

[4]Alexander Nairne, *The Epistle to the Hebrews* (Cambridge: At the University Press, 1921 [In the Series: *The Cambridge Bible for Schools and Colleges*, gen ed, R. St John Parry]), p.13.

reminds us that Hebrews reasons from the law to the gospel here and in 7:21f; 9:14 and 10:28f.[5] Verse two begins with a condition that is assumed to be true. There are twelve such conditional statements in Hebrews (2:2; 3:11, 18; 4:3, 5, 8; 6:9, 14; 7:11, 15; 8:4, 7; 9:13; 11:15; 12:8, 25).[6]

The message spoken by angels was binding. "If the message spoken by angels was binding, *and it was*, then . . ." Stephen (Acts 7:53) and Paul (Gal 3:19) explain that the law was "put into effect" by angels. Josephus has the same idea in *Antiquities*, XV. 136 (XV.v.3).[7] Deuteronomy 33:2 indicates that angels were at Mt. Sinai with God, but does not specify what they did. Stephen said "the angel" spoke to Moses on

---

[5]F.F. Bruce, *The Epistle to the Hebrews*, revised edition (Grand Rapids: Eerdmans, 1990), p. 68. The other three passages compare OT priests entering office without an oath, but Jesus entering with an oath (7:21f.); OT blood making bodies outwardly clean, but the blood of Jesus cleansing the conscience (9:14); and death being inflicted without mercy for rejecting the law, but a much greater penalty given for rejecting the Son of God, his blood and the Holy Spirit (10:28f.). This *a fortiori* reasoning, i.e., from lesser case to greater, was called *qal wa-homer* ("light and heavy") by the Rabbis.

[6]Four of these twelve instances in Hebrews are in quotations from the OT where they translate a way of making an oath statement in the Hebrew language (3:11; 4:3, 5; 6:14). For example, 3:11 literally says, "If they will enter my rest." The terrible thing that would happen if they did enter is not stated. The idea is expressed better in English by not translating literally, but in a manner we use for an oath statement, as in the NIV "They shall never enter my rest." In two of these conditional statements the certainty of the condition is virtually invisible in the NIV: "If we speak like this" (6:9), and "If the blood of goats and bulls" (9:13). The NIV translation of 9:13 is particularly unfortunate, because it destroys the grammatical link with the next verse.

[7]Marcus simply translates, "We have learned the noblest of our doctrines and the holiest of our laws from the messengers sent by God." Then he adds this note, "Most scholars take αγγελοι here to mean "angels" but it seems to me that the prophets (or priests) are meant, cf. Ap. I.37."'His note adds further defense of his view "that Hecataeus of Abdera (ap. Diodorus xl.3) speaks of the high priest as αγγελον των του θεου προσταγματων, and that in the LXX of Malachi ii.7 the high priest, as interpreter of the Torah, is called αγγελον του κυριου." Ralph Marcus, translator, *Josephus*, in nine volumes, in the *Loeb Classical Library*, edited by T. E. Page, et al.; (Cambridge: Harvard University Press, 1963), VIII:66-67 (Ant. XV.136 [XV.v.3]). Extrabiblical material greatly embellished the role of angels in the giving of the law.

Mt. Sinai and with our fathers "and he received living words
to pass on to us" (Acts 7:38). This is one place where the NT
adds further information about an OT event beyond the
information recorded in the OT. A person's view of Scripture
will greatly affect how this additional information is per-
ceived.

The OT law **was binding**. BAGD calls βέβαιος (*bebaios*)
"firm, permanent." The word is more frequent in Hebrews
than in all the rest of the NT (2:2; 3:6, 14; 6:19; 9:17; Rom
4:16; 2 Cor 1:7; 2 Pet 1:10, 19). Cf. The verb βεβαιόω (*bebaioō*,
"to make firm, establish" — 2:3; 13:9) and the noun βεβαίωσις
(*bebaiōsis*, "confirmation" — 6:16). Moulton and Milligan claim
that the verb *bebaioō* is a very common legal term, and assert
that "Deissman has shown very fully how much force the technical use of this word and its cognates to denote legally guaranteed security adds to their occurrence in the NT."[8] For
example, a will is "in force" only when somebody has died
(9:17).

Every **violation and disobedience** received its just punishment. Spicq considers παράβασις (*parabasis*, "violation") a
positive and παρακοή (*parakoē*, "disobedience") a negative
infraction, both of which involve one's will. These may come
from either weakness or rebellion. Man cannot keep the law
perfectly, but often he does not want to keep it. Louw and
Nida caution that "For terms involving 'disobedience' or
'transgression,' there are often a number of subtle distinctions [in different languages] reflecting several different types
of contrasts."[9] Adam's sin in the garden of Eden is called both

---

[8]Deissman is cited by James H. Moulton and George Milligan, *The
Vocabulary of the Greek Testament: Illustrated from the Papyri and Other Non-
Literary Sources* (Grand Rapids: Eerdmans, 1930), p. 107. They add an example where a lease is "guaranteed" for five years, and quote another source
who wrote, "and I will further guarantee the property always against all
claims with every guarantee."

[9]Johannes Louw and Eugene A. Nida, eds. *Greek-English Lexicon of the New
Testament Based on Semantic Domains.* 2 Vols. (New York: United Bible
Societies, 1988), 1:469.

a *parabasis* and a *parakoē* in Romans 5:14 and 19. By using alliterations and rare words the very sounds of the words make the passage appear more ominous. Note the alliteration in verse one, *PeRiSSoterōs PRoSechein . . . PaRaruōmen* ("we must pay more careful attention"), and in verse two, *PAsa PARAbasis kai PARAkoē* ("every violation and disobedience").

Punishment from God is always **just**. Dods says classical writers use the simpler form μισθοδοσία (*misthodosia*, "payment of wages") whereas Hebrews (2:2; 10:35; and 11:26) has the longer form μισθαποδοσία (*misthapodosia*, "payment of wages"). Here it is a penalty; in 10:35 and 11:26 it is a reward. Hebrews also uses the longer μισθαποδότης (*misthapodotēs*, "one who pays wages, a rewarder") in 11:6 rather than the shorter μισθοδότης (*misthodotēs*, "one who pays wages, a paymaster"). None of these four words occur elsewhere in the NT. The OT law gave proper rewards (2:2). The NT way will bring a rich reward (10:36). Moses knew enough of God's eventual reward to prefer it rather than to retain his high status in Egypt (11:26). Of course, in this imagery God is seen as the paymaster. The word **"just"** (ἔνδικος, *endikos*) does not appear at all in the LXX, and only in the NT here and in Romans 3:8. Paul said the condemnation of the sinful world, who misrepresented the message of grace as one of license, was a "just" (NIV, "deserved") sentence. The prefix *en-* ("in") in the word *en-dikos* implies that the punishment is just in and of itself. No external authority is needed to endorse its validity.[10]

2:3 how shall we escape if we ignore such a great salvation? This salvation, which was first announced by the Lord, was confirmed to us by those who heard him.

There is no other sacrifice (Heb 10:26). There will be no escape. One might escape from a guarded city (2 Cor 11:32-

---

[10]Thayer describes the word ἐν (*en*, "in") this way: "III. In Composition. Prefixed to Adjectives ἐν denotes lying or situated in some place or condition, possessed of or noted for something." Joseph Thayer, *A Greek-English Lexicon of the New Testament*, fourth edition (Edinburgh: T. & T. Clark, 1901), p. 213.

33). One might escape from prison (Acts 12:1-19; 16:27).
None will escape from an angry God who has been ignored
(10:26-31; 12:29). Jesus told a parable of people who ignored
a king's invitation to a wedding banquet for his son. He did
not take this insult lightly (Matt 22:1-7). The verb ἀμελέω
(*ameleō*, "to ignore, to not care") only occurs five times in the
NT (Matt 22:5; 1 Tim 4:14; Heb 2:3; 8:9; and 2 Pet 1:12) and
four times in the LXX (Jer 4:17; 38[31]:32 [quoted in Heb
8:9]; Wisdom 3:10; and 2 Macc 4:14). Because Judah ignored
God, she would be punished (Jer 4:17). In fact, God then
ignored her for breaking his covenant (Jer 38[31]:32). In the
Maccabean era priests ignored the sacrifices, turning to the
Greek culture (2 Macc 4:14).

It is **such a great** (τηλικαύτης, *telikautes*) salvation, too
great to be carelessly ignored. Paul used this word to describe
his being delivered from "such a deadly" peril in Asia Minor
when he nearly died fighting "wild beasts" (2 Cor 1:8-10; cf.
1 Cor 15:30-32). James contrasted the tiny rudders with "so
large" ships which they steer (James 3:4). In his visions in
Revelation John saw "so tremendous" an earthquake that
none like it had ever occurred before (Rev 16:18).

The paragraph shows the greatness of this salvation by
specifying its source and its confirmation. To these Dods adds
the greatness of Him who mediates it (1:4), the method
employed (2:10) and the results, i.e., bringing *many* sons to
glory (2:10).[11] The phrase "by the Lord" (διά, *dia* with a genitive case) matches the phrase in 1:2, "by his Son" (also *dia*
with a genitive). Jesus was God's agent in bringing the final
revelation and the great salvation. Dods remarks that this
message was not delivered by angels or other delegates who
might have misunderstood the message but by the Lord himself. The source is unquestionably pure.

Jesus **first announced** this salvation.[12] Introduced by John
the Baptist as the lamb of God who takes away the sin of the

---

[11]Marcus Dods, IV:259.
[12]Compare Jesus' announcement to the spirits in prison (1 Pet 3:19).

world, Jesus then spent three years explaining what this meant
and preparing people for the greatest enterprise on earth.
Believers and non-believers alike who heard him were
enthralled at his words. Jesus himself said, "I have spoken
openly to the world. I always taught in synagogues or at the
temple, where all the Jews come together. I said nothing in
secret. Why question me? Ask those who heard me. Surely
they know what I said" (John 18:20-21). During his ministry
Jesus used twelve (Matt 10:5ff.), later seventy-two (Luke
10:1ff.) to speak *his* message. He explained, "He who listens to
you listens to me; he who rejects you rejects me" (Luke 10:16).

This salvation **was confirmed to us by those who heard him**.
These words are understood by some to indicate that the author
of Hebrews must have been a second generation Christian.
How else could he say the message of Christ "was confirmed to
us by those who heard him?" These scholars remind us that
Paul, by contrast, strongly defended his firsthand information
which he received directly from the Lord himself because he
was an apostle. See 1 Cor 11:23; 15:1-3; 2 Cor 10:8, 13; 11:5-6,
10-12; 12:1-13; 13:2-3; Gal 1:1, 11-12, 16-17; 2:6-15.

However, Paul often used the editorial "we" (Rom 3:8; 4:9;
etc.). Just as clearly some "we's" are not editorial, but include
the perspective of all readers as he stood beside them speaking as one of them. For example, "*We* died to sin" (Rom 6:2);
or, "*We* will judge angels" (1 Cor 2:12); or, "Because of his
great love for *us*" (Eph 2:4). These and dozens of other examples show that Paul often placed himself among his readers as
an equal. Similarly, the author of Hebrews used the editorial
"we" (Heb 5:11; 6:9; 7:15; etc.). He also sometimes stood
beside his readers and spoke from their perspective as one of
them. For example, "*We* are his house" (3:6); or "the hope
offered to *us*" (6:18); or, "a better hope . . . by which *we* draw
near to God" (7:19).[13] The statement in 2:3 does not close the

---

[13]The contrast of "we" versus "you" in Heb 6:11-12 and elsewhere also
appears in Paul's epistles, for example, "We are weak, but you are strong!"
(1 Cor 4:8). See also other places in his writings.

door to apostolic authorship of the book of Hebrews.[14]

2:4 God also testified to it by signs, wonders and various miracles, and gifts of the Holy Spirit distributed according to his will.

Confirmation by men assures the truth of the message (1 Cor 1:6); the testimony of God[15] is far more assuring. Concerning the verb, συνεπιμαρτυρέω, (*synepimartyreō,* "to testify at the same time") Ellingworth asserts that "both prefixes are to be given their due weight: the witness of events accompanies (*syn-*) and adds to (*-epi-*) the witness of words."[16] God undergirded the message from Jesus with **signs, wonders and various miracles**, and gifts of the Holy Spirit. To the testimony of eyewitnesses God himself added supernatural activity to make the message certain beyond doubt.

All three words may describe the same phenomenon, but from three different angles. As a "miracle" (δύναμις, *dynamis,* "power") the event is an unusual display of might. As a "wonder" (τέρας, *teras,* "prodigy, wonder") it excites the admiration of those who watch. As a "sign" (σημεῖον, *sēmeion,* "sign, indication") it points to something beyond itself. By putting these

---

[14]Ellingworth also concludes that "It is too much to read into this verse that the writer and his readers belonged to a second generation of Christians."

[15]Coenen remarks that God is usually "concealed behind the passive verbs" of giving testimony in Hebrews (11:2, 4, 5, 39). See L. Coenen, "Witness," in *The New International Dictionary of New Testament Theology* (Grand Rapids: Zondervan, 1975), 3:1038-1047, p. 1047. He is not concealed in 2:4.

[16]Peter *adds* his testimony (ἐπιμαρτυρέω, *epi-martyreō*) that the true grace of God will help his readers remain strong during their suffering (1 Pet 5:10-12). This compound form of *martyreō* appears nine times in the LXX, but never in the church fathers. Paul said the Holy Spirit *agrees with* (*sum-martyreō*) our spirit that we are children of God (Rom 8:16). Pagans' consciences *agree* that the OT law is right (Rom 2:15). Paul's own conscience *agrees with* the Holy Spirit that he is telling his readers the truth (Rom 9:1). This compound form of *martyreō* appears nowhere in the LXX and seldom in the church fathers. Lampe lists only one instance of the double compound *sun-epi-martyreō* in a fragment from Philostorgius (early fifth century A.D.).

together an event called a "miracle" would be an unusual display of power which is admired by beholders and points to something beyond itself. It is unfortunate that the word "miracle" has come to be used for wonder alone, i.e., anything which excites man's wonder, like a sunset or a birth or one's transformation at conversion. While these are certainly admirable events, they are in a totally different class from the events mentioned in the Bible as miracles.

It should be noted that in the beginning church miracles never replaced the telling of the gospel message. Instead, miracles drew attention to the human messengers and indicated that they had supernatural endorsement for what they said. In a similar fashion angels, as supernatural messengers, were never allowed to tell the story about Jesus. They could only bring together those seeking and those carrying the news of redemption.

To these three words for miracle our paragraph adds "gifts (μερισμός, *merismos*, "apportionment") of the Holy Spirit distributed according to his will." The ordinary word for these gifts would be *charisma*. ("gift"). Here the idea is rather that the Holy Spirit has given various people various assistance, "parting" or "distributing" to each as he chose. Cf. 1 Cor 12:11.

B. JESUS BECAME A MAN TO BRING MEN TO GLORY (2:5-18)

[5]It is not to angels that he has subjected the world to come, about which we are speaking. [6]But there is a place where someone has testified:
"What is man that you are mindful of him,
the son of man that you care for him?
[7]You made him a little[a] lower than the angels;
you crowned him with glory and honor
[8]and put everything under his feet."[b]
In putting everything under him, God left nothing that is

not subject to him. Yet at present we do not see everything subject to him. ⁹But we see Jesus, who was made a little lower than the angels, now crowned with glory and honor because he suffered death, so that by the grace of God he might taste death for everyone.

ᵃ7 Or *him for a little while*; **also in verse 9   ᵇ8 Psalm 8:4-6**

The first chapter established Jesus' deity, far above angels. The second chapter establishes his humanity, equal with man. He even suffered (2:9-10, 18) and died (2:9, 14-15). His superiority is seen in a new way. He who is rightfully above the angels came down beneath the angels to become fully identified with man. His newly created nature of god-man made Jesus able to perform a new role. He would be the high priest in this great salvation plan. When he returned to his rightful place above the angels he would "bring many sons to glory" with him.

Who has ever read this chapter for the Christmas story? Matthew chapter one and Luke chapter two are used. Rarely will anyone read Philippians two, though for variety some might dare to use John chapter one. But Hebrews two demonstrates its value to us in that while we were lower than the angels he came to rescue us. If Hebrews one is titled the grandeur of the Son, Hebrews two should be called the grandeur of the Savior.

2:5 It is not to angels that he has subjected the world to come, about which we are speaking.

"**Not to angels.**" In 1:14 angels were seen as servants of those who will inherit salvation. Next the readers were warned not to miss out on this salvation, which is greater than the OT offer brought by angels (2:1-4). Now it is explained that angels will not rule the world to come. Man is destined for that exalted position. Man will find his way to glory through The Perfect Man, Jesus, who entered the human race to rescue us. He earned this top position in the afterlife for us.

Jesus was no mere man of flesh and blood (v.14), inferior
to angels (v.7), tempted (v.18), suffering (vv.10, 18), dying
(vv.9, 14). There is something revulsive about one who
demeans himself to live beneath his capabilities. There is
something fascinating about a creator-God who demeans himself to join and lift his creatures who are incapable of lifting
themselves. He identified so fully with his inferior creatures
that he could lift them up out of their fear-filled frailty and
bring them to glory with him. This is the story of chapter two.

It is interesting that the warning against neglecting this
great salvation appears before the salvation is even described.
The author has kept his audience gazing off into the distance
at a person far superior to angels. Only a few loose strands
have tied us to him. (a) We are related to the fathers through
whom God spoke bits and pieces (1:1). (b) God's culminating
message through Jesus was given to us (1:2). (c) Jesus made
purification for our sins (1:3). He sternly admonished us not
to ignore this great salvation (2:1-4). In 2:5 he says it is **the
world to come, about which we are speaking**. What was only
hinted before is now plainly stated. Heaven is the bottom line.

Flender says the word "world" (οἰκουμένη, *oikoumene*) was
used (a) for the lands inhabited by the Greeks as opposed to
lands of the barbarians, then (b) for the whole inhabited
world including lands of barbarians, finally, (c) by the second
century B.C. for lands under the Roman rule.[17] This geo-
graphical political image is used twice in Hebrews: in 1:6 of
this world into which Christ entered; and in 2:5 of the world
to come into which he will bring believers. Κόσμος (*kosmos*),
the usual word for "world" in the NT, is used in Hebrews of
the physical world which he created (4:3; 9:26) and of "the
world as mankind" [LS] (10:5; 11:7, 38).

God controls the future. He has already **subjected** (ὑπο–
τάσσω, *hypotassō*, "to subject, subordinate") the world to come
to mankind, not to angels. One who can speak the world into
existence (Gen 1:3, 6, 9, etc.) or one who can sustain it by his

---

[17]O. Flender, "Earth, Land, World," in NIDNTT, 1:518-519.

powerful word (1:3) can certainly determine the future of that world and all that is in it. God is orderly (1 Cor 14:34, 40). His creation is orderly.[18] His law was designed to help people live orderly lives (1 Tim 1:8-11). He has appointed governments to enforce order (Rom 13:1-7). Lack of order leads to frustration (Rom 8:18-21). Eventually everything will once again be subjected to Christ (1 Cor 15:27-28; Eph 1:22; Phil 3:21; Heb 1:2; 1 Pet 3:22). Man will take his place beside the exalted Christ.

2:6 But there is a place where someone has testified: "What is man that you are mindful of him, the son of man that you care for him?

There is a place where someone has testified. Dods says the uniquely vague way of introducing this quotation is not because of doubt about authorship of the psalm nor because of quoting from memory, but is instead "a rhetorical mode of suggesting that his readers knew the passage well enough." Then he claims that Philo frequently used an indefinite form of quotation, and even this exact phrasing. This is the only OT quotation in Hebrews which refers to the human author. For example, "To which of the angels did God ever say" (1:5); or "Jesus . . . says" (2:11-12); or "as the Holy Spirit says" (3:7); or "just as God has said" (4:3). Even when David is mentioned in 4:7, God is the author of his words, "God . . . spoke through David" (4:7). Habakkuk 2:3-4 (in Heb 10:37-38) and Proverbs 3:11-12 (in Heb 12:5-6) are introduced without specifying either a divine or a human author. In 13:6 the author of Hebrews simply uses the words of Psalm 118:6-7 without naming its author to verbalize his own confidence in God.

---

[18]All created things, including demons, are subject to man (Heb 2:8; Luke 10:17, 20). The church is subject to Christ and to God (Eph 5:24; Heb 12:9). In general Christians are to submit to one another (Eph 5:21). Specifically, wives submit to husbands (Eph 5:22; Col 3:18; Titus 2:5; 1 Pet 3:1, 5; see 1 Tim 2:11); children to parents (Luke 2:51; Eph 6:1-3; Col 3:20; 1 Tim 3:4; Heb 12:9); servants to masters (Eph 6:5-8; Col 3:22-25; Titus 2:9; 1 Pet 2:18-25); young men to older men (1 Pet 5:5). All Christians are to be submissive to governmental authorities (Rom 13:1-7; Titus 3:1; 1 Pet 2:13-17).

Seybold notes the significance of the eighth Psalm, "After the Imago-Dei text of Gen. 1,26f. and the Yahwistic cornerstone, Gen. 2,7, Ps. 8 is the most important statement in the Old Testament on the position of humanity within the created order."[19] Kirkpatrick refers to Paul's use of the terminology from Psalm 8:6 in 1 Corinthians 15:27 and Ephesians 1:22, then concludes, "If all things were subjected to the first Adam who failed through sin, not less must they be subjected to the second Adam who triumphs through obedience, and fulfils the destiny of the race."[20] The text of Hebrews indicates that Psalm 8 was not intended to describe the exalted position of man in this world only, but also in the world to come.

In its customary parallelism the Hebrew poetry of Psalm 8 says the same thought twice. **"What is man that you are mindful of him,"** means the same as "[What is] the son of man that you care for him."[21] The next lines describe the astonishingly high position in which God has assigned man, his most honored creature. Dods sees in this quotation three particular ways that illustrate the greatness of man: (1) God made him a little lower than the angels; (2) God crowned him with glory and honor; and (3) God put everything under his feet.

2:7 You made him a little lower than the angels; you crowned him with glory and honor

The word βραχύς (*brachys*, "a **little**") may be used of (1) a little space, *a little further on* (Acts 27:28); (2) a little time, *a little later* (Luke 22:38); or (3) a little quantity, *a small amount* of food (John 6:7) or even *a few* words (Heb 13:22). The flexibility of this word opens the door to the commentaries' vacillation.

---

[19]Klaus Seybold, *Introducing the Psalms*, translated by R. Graeme Dunphy (Edinburgh: T. & T. Clark, 1990), p. 153.

[20]A.F. Kirkpatrick, editor, *The Book of Psalms* (Cambridge, England: University Press, 1906), p. 36.

[21]The Talmud applied this Psalm to Moses rather than to the Messiah. See Shabbath 88b (p.422); Rosh haShannah 21b (p. 90); Nedarim 38a (p. 119). The page numbers are in *The Soncino Talmud*, edited by I. Epstein, eighteen double volumes (London: The Soncino Press, 1938).

Does the text mean that Jesus was lower than angels in degree or time? By entering the world of time he was "for a little while" lower. By descending from heaven to earthbound humanity he was "a little degree" lower. The Hebrew words in the Psalm are clear, "you made him lack a little." The Psalm is very physically oriented. It sees God's glory "above the heavens" in a world of praise and splendid power (Ps 8:1-3). But it sees man's puny place beneath majestic stars, ruling over flocks and herds, beasts and birds, and fish that swim the seas (Ps 8:4-8). This is the world Jesus entered when he became a man.

The LXX has "a little lower than **angels**" (ἄγγελοι, *angeloi*) where the Hebrew text had "a little lower than God" (אֱלוֹהִים, *'elohim*). Though the word *'elohim* normally means Jahweh, the creator-god of the Old Testament, sometimes it is used differently. BDB gives references where *'elohim* may mean angels.[22] This is how the LXX translators understood Psalm 8:5. The author of Hebrews follows the LXX text. The NIV translates Psalm 8:5 "a little lower than the heavenly beings" and adds a note in its margin, "Or *than God*." From the perspective of earthly things, either idea of heavenly beings, whether "God" or "angels," would show man's relative position. On earth man is above everything else which is on the earth. The only thing higher would be heaven and its inhabi-

---

[22]BDB gives references where *'elohim* means (1) "*rulers, judges,* either as divine representatives at sacred places or as reflecting divine majesty and power" (Exod 21:6; 22:7, 8, 27; 1 Sam 2:25; Judg 5:8; Ps 82:1, 6; 138:1); (2) "*divine ones,* superhuman beings including God and angels" (Ps 8:6; Gen 1:27; cf. Job 38:7); (3) "*angels*" (Ps 97:7; cf. "The sons of God, or sons of gods=angels Job 1:6; 2:1; 38:7; Gen 6:24); (4) "*gods*" (Exod 18:11; 22:16; 1 Sam 4:8; 2 Chr 2:4; Ps 86:8); cf. "*The God of gods,* supreme God" (Deut 31:10:17; etc.); "*other gods*" (Exod 20:3; 23:18; etc.); "*foreign gods*" (Gen 35:2, 4; Josh 24:20, 23; etc.); "*gods of the nations*" (2 Kgs 18:38; 19:12; etc.); (5) "*god or goddess*" — Dagon (1 Sam 5:7); Chemosh (Judg 11:24; 1 Kgs 11:33) Baal (1 Kgs 18:24); Ashtereth goddess of the Zidonians (Judg 9:27; Dan 1:2); the god of the land (1 Kgs 20:28; 2 Kgs 17:26-27); (6) "*godlike one*" — of Moses (Exod 4:16; 7:1), of the shade of Samuel (1 Sam 28:13), of the Messianic king (Ps 45:7). Francis Brown, et al, *The New Brown-Driver-Briggs-Gesenius Hebrew and English Lexicon* (Lafayette, IN: Associated Publishers and Authors, Inc., 1980), p. 43.

tants. A hint of the future world was seen in Hebrews 1:14 where angels are subservient to man. It is clear from 2:8 that mortals have not yet fully reached their promised potential. It will soon be explained that this full potential will only be achieved in Christ.

2:8 and put everything under his feet." In putting everything under him, God left nothing that is not subject to him. Yet at present we do not see everything subject to him.

The exalted position of mankind on earth is a preparation for a similarly exalted position in the world to come. Man and woman are set above all other creatures. Three passages describe man as made in the image of God (Gen 1:26-28; 5:1-3; 9:6). The first passage comes as a climax of creation. The second begins the genealogical list. The third makes this nature the reason for the death sentence on every murderer. Thus, the crowning of creation, the linking of all family heritage and the honoring of the sanctity of life are all traced to the image of God in man. C.F.H. Henry says, "Man is made for personal and endless fellowship with God, involving rational understanding (Gen. 1:28ff.), moral obedience (2:16-17), and religious communion (3:3)."[23] Not even angels have this distinction. Henry explains further, "The creation-image was probationary; the redemption-image is not;" and again, "the NT also speaks of the divine image in the natural man (I Cor. 11:7; James 3:9). But its central message is redeemed man's renewal in the image of Christ."[24] We have been recreated in the likeness of Christ through the new birth (Eph 2:10; John 3:3-5) with the capacity of copying his character and his deeds (1 Cor 11:1; Eph 5:1). Hebrews also urges the mimicking of the leaders whom God has set in the church (6:12; 13:7). This is like the exhortation from Paul in 1 Corinthians 11:1, "Follow my example, as I follow the example of Christ."

---

[23]C.F.H. Henry, "Image of God," in *Evangelical Dictionary of Theology*, edited by Walter Elwell (Grand Rapids: Baker, 1984), pp. 545-548.

[24]Ibid., p. 547.

The problem is that **at present we do not see everything subject to** man. Because of his sin, man's original position has been lost. Even his own impulses are as uncontrollable as a wild animal. His potential position, never attained, can only be realized in Christ (Rom 5:12-21; Rev 3:21; 22:4-5).

2:9 But we see Jesus, who was made a little lower than the angels, now crowned with glory and honor because he suffered death, so that by the grace of God he might taste death for everyone.

This is the first mention of the name "Jesus" in Hebrews. When the church was first begun, Peter said Jesus was already reigning on the throne of David[25] (Acts 2:29-36; 5:30-31. Cf. Ps 132:11; Isa 9:7; Mark 16:19; Luke 1:31-32; Rom 8:34; Phil 2:9; Col 3:1. See also Rev 3:21; 5:6; 7:17; 11:15; 22:1, 3, 5). Jesus did what we were supposed to do. Jesus became what we were supposed to become. We could almost call Jesus "the capital M man." Paul called him the "last Adam" (1 Cor 15:45; cf. Rom 5:12-21), for like the first Adam, he headed up a whole new world. How and why Jesus did what he did are explained in the rest of the chapter.

The word "**crowned**" (στεφανόω, *stephanoō*, "to wreath with a crown, to crown") is a perfect participle. BAGD says the verb literally means "to crown the winner in an athletic contest." Jesus won. He was crowned as victor. **Now** he enjoys the glory of that new status. Many passages in the NT associate Jesus with glory and honor. Isaiah so often associated the glory of God with the Messiah that one could almost write "Jesus" every time "glory" is mentioned in his book. As a country basks in the glory that her athletes win in the Olympic games, so all men, as brothers of Christ (2:10-17), can enjoy the victory he won for mankind.

Jesus' rescue mission, though available for everyone, became available only **by the grace of God**. Using Esser's

---

[25]The "throne of David" is also called "the throne of Israel" (1 Kgs 8:20, 25; 9:5; 2 Chr 6:10, 16; Jer 33:17) and even the "throne of the LORD" (1 Chr 29:23).

phrases one might say that the grace of God, as the undeserved gift of God, anchored in the purpose of God, and flowing from the power of God, makes the new man in Christ
what he is.[26] In the macro-history of redemption (Rom 5:15)
the grace of God defines the mission of Christ (1 Cor 1:4;
15:10) so that it can reach every person in the entire world
(Heb 2:9; Matt 28:18-20; 2 Cor 4:15). In the micro-history of
redemption the grace of God justifies each individual freely
(Acts 15:11; Rom 3:23-24; Titus 2:11) bringing him into a new
way of life (Acts 13:43; 14:26; 2 Cor 8:7; Eph 2:5) where he
finds whatever help is needed (Heb 4:16) to bring him to eternal glory (1 Pet 5:10).

When Jesus **"tasted" death**, he did not merely touch
against it as though with his tongue only. This is a figurative
expression for partaking of or enjoying something. Thus
"tasting the supper" in Luke 14:24 means eating the whole
meal. So Acts 10:10 and 20:11. To "taste death" in Matthew
16:28; Mark 9:1; Luke 9:27 and John 8:52 means to experience death or as Liddell and Scott says, "to come to know
something." Hence, in 6:4-5 "tasting" the heavenly gift, the
goodness of the word of God and the powers of the coming
age means coming to know them. In this sense, Liddell and
Scott mentions tasting the spear. This does not mean that
Christ only sampled death, as Chrysostom suggested, by only
remaining dead briefly before his resurrection. No. With a
similarly powerful imagery one may say he fully "drank the
cup" which the Father had given him (Matt 10:22-23; 26:39-
42). BAGD says, *"drink the cup* = submit to a severe trial, or
death," and claims that Matt 20:22f refers to "those who suffer the same fate." The concept of the substitutionary atonement is very important in the book of Hebrews.

**[10]In bringing many sons to glory, it was fitting that God,
for whom and through whom everything exists, should make
the author of their salvation perfect through suffering.**

---

[26]H.H. Esser, "Grace, Spiritual Gifts," in NIDNTT, 2:115-124.

¹¹Both the one who makes men holy and those who are made holy are of the same family. So Jesus is not ashamed to call them brothers. ¹²He says,

"I will declare your name to my brothers;

in the presence of the congregation I will sing your praises."ᵃ

¹³And again,

"I will put my trust in him."ᵇ

And again he says,

"Here am I, and the children God has given me."ᶜ

ᵃ12 Psalm 22:22   ᵇ13 Isaiah 8:17   ᶜ13 Isaiah 8:18

A new problem was introduced in 2:9. Jesus died. His death seemed to be clear evidence to the Jews that Jesus could not be the Messiah (1 Cor 1:23). Christians understand that the substitutionary death of the god-man Jesus frees man from sin. Jews in general do not accept this idea. For them the "Messiah" in Isaiah 53 must be someone else: the author, some other holy man, an idealized person, a holy remnant, or the entire Jewish nation.

The explanation in Hebrews 2 of the work of Jesus is that the Messiah comes to rescue fallen man, to bring "many sons to glory." He descended beneath the angels and became a full flesh and blood brother with the human family. While among them, he was tempted, suffered and died. His temptation and suffering made him able to help others who suffer and are being tempted. His death permitted him to break the fear and power of death, and Satan with it. Having finished his work on earth, he has been crowned with glory and honor, and now functions as our high priest in heaven making atonement for our sins.

Jewish ideas of the Messiah are very different from these. Cohen put his finger on the central issue, "The Talmud nowhere indicates a belief in a superhuman Deliverer as the Messiah."[27] Jewish interpretations of OT prophecies about the

---

[27]A. Cohen, *Everyman's Talmud* (New York: E.P. Dutton & Co., Inc., 1949), p. 437.

Messiah and the Messianic era fluctuate widely. On the one side there is a virtual historico-grammatical rigidity that sees its meaning exhausted in the prophet's own day according to his human ability to see the future and understand it. Rabbi Hillel, not one of the famous pair, said the Messiah had already come in the days of King Hezekiah (Sanhedrin 98b).[28] On the other side there is a fantastic literalism that washes out all figurative language of prophecy into a detailed pre-written history. This rivals the elaborate modern schemes of understanding prophecy as detailed pre-written history of the end times, which is always only weeks or months from beginning to unfold before us. There are all kinds of varieties between these two.

Speculations about the Messiah mushroomed among the Jews. The more they were persecuted, the more they longed for the promised mysterious deliverer. Unable to harmonize all the information from the numerous OT Messianic passages into a single person, some concluded that there must be two Messiahs. Thus we read of Messiah ben David, and later of Messiah ben Joseph as well.[29]

God overcame many obstacles **in bringing many sons to glory**. (1) Man fell. (2) Man was inclined toward heavy sinfulness (Gen 6:5-7; Rom 3:10-20). (3) God's own holiness prevented his simply brushing man's guilt aside. (4) His unique son Jesus must die in man's place to bear the brunt of this wickedness. (5) Satan lured many angels away from God and encouraged man's sinfulness. Yet God was not content to lose man or even let him sink to a lesser role. He was determined to bring him all the way to the throne to be with him for all ages to come (Eph 1:3-2:10).

He persisted in his plan, doing what was **fitting** for God. Man fell? He would lift him. Man was inclined to sin? He would start him over in a new birth. He could not allow sin in

---

[28]Sanhedrin 98b, in the Soncino edition of Sanhedrin 98b, p.667.

[29]Sukkah 52a [Soncino edition of Sukkah, p. 248-249, 251]. See also Moses Buttenweiser, "Messiah," in *The Jewish Encyclopedia*, edited by Isidore Singer (New York: Ktav Publishing House, n.d.), VIII:505-512.

his holy presence? He would wash away man's sin. There was
no one to achieve all this? Yes, there was his Son Jesus. Satan
stood in the way? Let him be destroyed forever. This would
solve both man's sins and his sinfulness. This would pay for
the past and safeguard the future. This would purge man's
guilt and his nature. The first part was solved by sending Jesus
to die for us. The second part was solved by recreating us in
the image of Christ. It was a resolution fit for God. Bruce says
we will learn what is worthy of God by considering what God
has actually done. One who says he would have a high opinion of God who would or would not do this or that is not
telling us about God, but about himself.[30]

Everything (τὰ πάντα, *ta panta*) **exists for God and
through God** (2:10), who is the builder of everything (3:4).
Everything is open before him (4:13). Jesus made everything,
sustains everything and will be the heir of everything (1:2-3).
Everything is forgiven and cleansed through his blood (9:22-
28). Man was supposed to be over all of creation (2:6-8).
Because man fell, Jesus entered the human race to become a
man and rescue man. Like man he suffered and died. Unlike
man his death broke the devil's death-grip on man. Like man
he suffered when he was tempted. Unlike man he remained
sinless and became able to help others who are being tempted. Like man he died. Unlike man he died for others.

At the center of his plan God would **make the author of
their salvation perfect through suffering**. Ellingworth collects
much useful information about the word ἀρχηγός (*archēgos*,
"author"). It only appears four times in the NT, but always of
Jesus (Acts 3:15; 5:31; Heb 2:10 and 12:2). Elsewhere it is
used of a leader or ruler, of the founder of a kingdom, of the
originator of an art, and of a pioneer opening a path for others to follow. Ellingworth reminds us of Jesus' practice of calling disciples to follow him and of walking ahead of them.
Bruce says, "The pathway of perfection which his people must

---

[30]F.F. Bruce, p. 79.

tread must first be trodden by the Pathfinder."[31] Hebrews also calls Jesus the source (αἴτιος, *aitios*, "cause, reason," 5:9) of eternal salvation.

In what sense was Jesus "**made perfect**?"[32] It certainly does not mean "flawless" as though he had faults or fractures making him blameworthy. He was without sin (4:15). Yet he added something to himself by becoming flesh and blood. In the incarnation Jesus became fully human. He was also divine, as his divine behavior during his ministry showed. Thus he became the only one who was both God and man at the same time. The church fathers struggled in trying to define exactly how these two natures were related in one person. He could participate in death fully, for he was man. At the same time, in his death he could carry the sins of all other men, for he was God. One could say that neither God the Father nor the Holy Spirit could die for man. They remained only God. No human being could perform this function. They remained only men. Jesus was made perfect, i.e., made complete, through suffering — death being only one form of suffering, though perhaps the worst form.

---

[31]Ibid., p. 80. Bruce reminds us that C.J.A. Hickling suggested that the phrase "the pioneer of their salvation" summarizes Jesus' distinctive use of the title "Son of Man."

[32]It would be helpful to examine Ellingworth's careful analysis of the semantic components of τελειόω (*teleioō*) in Hebrews. The word appears in 2:10; 5:9; 7:19, 28; 9:9; 10:1, 14; 11:40 and 12:23. There are six varied definitions of the word which he examines. (1) telic: to bring something to its goal or completion (2 Chr 8:16 of the completion of a building; John 17:4 of a task); (2) cultic: to qualify someone for participation in worship; (3) ethical: to remove imperfections; (4) organic: to make mature (cf. 1 Cor 14:20); (5) temporal: to complete (a period, e.g., Luke 2:43); and (6) human: to die (e.g., Luke 13:22). His analysis finds each of the first three definitions represented in several of the passages in Hebrews, but the last three definitions only "doubtfully relevant to Hebrews." LS and BAGD do not divide the meanings of τελειόω this way. One should also consider τέλειος ("complete, perfect," 5:14; 9:11); τελειότης ("perfection, completeness," 6:1); τελείωσις ("perfection, fulfillment of a promise," 7:11); τελειώτης ("perfecter," 12:2); and even τελευτάω ("to come to an end, die," 11:22). Except for τελειώτης these occur elsewhere in the NT besides a few other cognates.

The word "sufferings" (παθημάτων, *pathēmatōn*) is plural, perhaps to indicate the many different kinds of suffering which he endured besides his death. He faced exhaustion, loneliness, frustration, misrepresentation, in short, all the limitations of the human frame. He was tempted in every way just as we are (4:15). Perhaps it is plural here to match the many failures of the people (verse 17). Perhaps it simply expands on the singular of 2:9. The NIV of 2:9, "because he suffered death," is literally "on account of the suffering of death."

2:11 Both the one who makes men holy and those who are made holy are of the same family. So Jesus is not ashamed to call them brothers.

It is a unique unity — God and man bonded together in one family. **Both the one who makes men holy and those who are made holy are of the same family**. There is some uncertainty about the precise meaning of the phrase, "**of the same family**" (ἐξ ἑνός, *ex henos*). The KJV has "of one;" NASB "from one *Father*;" NRSV "have one Father;" NRSVmg "Gk *are all of one.*" The problem is that the word *henos* is spelled the same whether masculine or neuter. If it is masculine, it may point to a person — (1) God, (2) Adam, (3) Abraham, (4) some unspecified person, (5) an idealized person, i.e., human origin in general — or (6) some masculine noun just given in the text, though θάνατος (*thanatos*, "death") in v. 9 is the nearest masculine noun. If it is neuter, it may point to some neuter noun either in the immediate context — (7) *pathematos* ("suffering") also in v. 9 is the nearest neuter noun — or an assumed word, (8) αἷμα (*haima*, "blood"), (9) σπέρμα (*sperma*, "seed"), (10) γένος (*genos*, "race"), or (11) some other — or (12) it may be used absolutely as in John 10:30. See Ellingworth for discussion of these options. He says the majority of ancient and modern commentators and modern translations understand it as referring to God, i.e., "of one [that is, God]." Bartels says the phrase "points to the closest possible unity of believers with Jesus.[33] It is interesting that

---

[33]K.H. Bartels "One, once, only," in NIDNTT 2:716-725, p. 724.

Adam, the biological and sociological father of the whole human family, is not even named in Hebrews.

Jesus is the one who **makes men holy**, assisted by the Holy Spirit (Rom 15:16). BAGD defines the verb ἁγιάζω (*hagiazō*; NIV, "makes holy") to mean "to make holy, consecrate, sanctify." It is used of things and of people. Things are "made suitable for ritual purposes." Christians "are consecrated by baptism." BAGD then defines the adjective "holy," (ἅγιος, *hagios*) as "*dedicated to God, holy, sacred*, i.e., reserved for God and his service." In a similar sense a man's wife is "holy" to him, i.e., separated from all other women to be especially his. That separation does not make her better than others, but she has become special to him. Christ loved the church and gave himself up for her to "set her apart" for himself. He gives all husbands the same challenge to make their wives special (Eph 5:25-27).

Ordinarily the present tense means a continuous activity, as Westcott says it means here, "the continuous, personal application of Christ's work," suggesting a steady stream of conversions as Acts 2:47 reports. Turner prefers to understand it as a "*Gnomic Present* used in generalizations or proverbs."[34] Ellingworth examined the tenses of the word ἁγιάζω (*hagiazō*, "sanctify") in Hebrews. He says the timeless present tense participles here are used like nouns. By using an aorist tense in 10:29, Christ's blood, i.e., his sacrificial death, is seen as a past event. In 10:10 the perfect tense shows that his death procured continuing effects. In 9:13-14 *hagiazō* and *katharizō* ("cleanse, purify") are used synonymously with the second verb appearing as a future tense to indicate our eventual total cleansing. Like the word "saved," the verb "being sanctified" has a past finished aspect, a present continuous aspect and a future anticipated aspect.[35]

---

[34]Nigel Turner, *Syntax*, Volume III in James Moulton, *A Grammar of New Testament Greek* (Edinburgh: T. & T. Clark, 1963), p. 63. He lists Matt 7:17; John 7:52; 2 Cor 9:7 and James 1:13-15 as other examples of the "Gnomic Present."

[35]The Bible says Christians "were saved" at conversion (Rom 8:24), "are

A person becomes sanctified, from the divine perspective, by the Holy Spirit (Rom 15:16); from the human perspective, by one's faith in Christ upon turning from Satan to God (Acts 26:18). This separates a person from the former wicked life. It is parallel to being washed and justified (1 Cor 6:9-11). Those who are sanctified will receive an inheritance (Acts 20:32). Sanctification makes a person useful to the Master and prepared to do any good work (2 Tim 2:20-21; cf. Eph 2:10). It is so important, because without sanctification (NIV, "holiness") no one will see the Lord (12:14). Today anyone can turn to him and become sanctified. There will come a day when one's condition will be made permanent; the wicked will remain wicked and the holy will remain holy (Rev 22:11). Jesus was "set apart" by God and sent into the world as the Messiah (John 10:36-38). In a similar way he prayed that his disciples would be "sanctified" and sent into the world (John 17:16-19). In one fascinating passage, Christians are urged to "sanctify" Jesus, i.e., to set him apart into a special place in their hearts. This will make them ready to give an answer to everyone who asks the reason for their hope (1 Pet 3:15).

The book of Hebrews reports that the blood of animals in OT times was sprinkled on the people to sanctify them to become outwardly cleansed (9:13). By contrast in NT times the blood of Christ, poured out when he died, sanctifies people (10:10, 14, 29; 13:12; see 2:11). They are "made perfect forever" (10:14). Hebrews normally used the adjective "holy" to refer to the Holy Spirit (2:4; 3:7; 6:4; 9:8; 10:15). It is also used of Christians ("holy brothers" 3:1), sometimes without a noun, i.e., "saint" (6:10; 13:24). The neuter adjective "holy" is used either of the OT tabernacle (9:1, 2, 3, (8?), 24, 25; 13:11) or of the true tabernacle in heaven (8:2; 9:8, 12; 10:19. See 9:23-25).

The reason why Jesus is not ashamed to call them "brothers" is because Jesus and redeemed humans are joined in the same family. Evidence for his family pride is immediately

---

being saved" in the process of Christian living (1 Cor 1:18) and "will be saved" in the end (Matt 10:22).

presented from three OT verses. The NIV "**So** Jesus is not . . ."
lacks the fully worded clarity of the Greek connecting phrase
(διὰ ἣν αἰτίαν [*dia hēn aitian*], literally, "on account of which
reason" or "for which reason"). This is the only place in
Hebrews where the word *aitia* ("cause, reason") occurs. A similar word αἴτιος (*aitios*) appears in 5:9 in the phrase, "source
of eternal salvation" (KJV, "author of eternal salvation") without any other NT occurrence. BAGD notes that *aitia* in
Matthew 19:10 indicates a formal *case* or example in an argument, and functions as a legal technical term for a *formal
charge* or *accusation*, even a *reason for capital punishment*, (John
18:38; 19:4, 6), the Latin *causa capitalis*. Since it is a unique
phrase in Hebrews and carries these heavy connotations, it
may be better to express the idea more fully. Verse eleven was
linked to the previous verse with the simple, common word
gar ("for, because"). The NIV does not express that connection at all. The verses are tied together this way:

> (2:10) In bringing many sons to glory, it was fitting that God,
> for whom and through whom everything exists, should make
> the author of their salvation perfect through suffering.
> (2:11a) **[Because]** both the one who makes men holy and
> those who are made holy are of the same family.
> (2:11b) **[For this reason]** (NIV, "So") Jesus is not ashamed to
> call them brothers.

Jesus is **not ashamed** to call them brothers. Similarly, God
is not ashamed to be called the God of the patriarchs (11:16).
As the author of Hebrews often does, the longer form of the
verb is used (ἐπαισχύνομαι, *ep-aischynomai*, "to be ashamed")
where the shorter form would suffice (*aischynomai*, "to be
ashamed"). The longer form is used mostly by Paul and
Hebrews, whereas the shorter form is used by other NT
authors as well. The LXX uses the short form generously, but
the long form only three times. The intimacy of family bond-
ing removes all shame regarding other family members.
Hence, Jesus will not tolerate any shame of him. "If anyone is
ashamed of me and my words in this adulterous and sinful
generation, the Son of Man will be ashamed of him when he

comes in his Father's glory with the holy angels" (Mark 8:38; contrast 1 John 2:28). The counterpart of shame is confidence or faith, a major emphasis of the book of Hebrews. It is more striking for variety to say he is not ashamed of them, than to say that he trusts them.

2:12 He says, "I will declare your name to my brothers; in the presence of the congregation I will sing your praises."

Pointing to his disciples, Jesus had said, "Here are my mother and my brothers. For whoever does the will of my Father in heaven is my brother and sister and mother" (Matt 12:49-50; Mark 3:34-35). Three OT verses now follow in Hebrews to demonstrate Jesus' family solidarity with his people. Montifiore sees in these quotations three different proofs of family kinship: (1) Psalm 22:22, where Jesus calls them brothers; (2) Isaiah 8:17, where he shares with them the human attitude of faith in God; and (3) Isaiah 8:18, where he speaks of them as children of God.[36] Psalm 22 and Isaiah 53 are the two fullest OT descriptions of Jesus' experience on the cross. It is not surprising to hear the NT understanding words from those chapters as the words of Jesus.

2:13 And again, "I will put my trust in him." And again he says, "Here am I, and the children God has given me."

The verses from Isaiah 8 are more difficult for modern western students of the Bible to hear as the words of Jesus. Some think that Isaiah could predict nothing beyond human foresight. In this view, the author of Hebrews creatively put the words of the prophet in Jesus' mouth adapting them for his own purposes. In another view, the Holy Spirit inspired all Scriptures, Old Testament and New Testament. The Holy

---

[36]Jesus called God "my Father" (Matt 7:21; 10:32; etc.); but when speaking to his hearers or disciples he called him "your Father" (Matt 5:16, 45; 10:20; etc.). He never called God "our Father" including himself with them as equals. The only time he said "our Father" was when he taught the disciples to pray "Our Father" (Matt 6:9). He did not include himself in the word "our," for the model prayer continues, "Forgive us *our* debts." Clearly Jesus had no transgressions to need forgiving.

Spirit helped the writer of Hebrews know what application he intended when he first inspired Isaiah to write the words. What the Holy Spirit inspired Isaiah to write was designedly bigger than Isaiah's own circumstances. He expressed Jesus' own attitude about his unity with the family of believers. This would be like Caiaphas words which the Bible itself says reached beyond his own understanding,

> Then the chief priests and the Pharisees called a meeting of the Sanhedrin.
> "What are we accomplishing?" they asked. "Here is this man performing many miraculous signs. If we let him go on like this, everyone will believe in him, and then the Romans will come and take away both our place and our nation."
> Then one of them, named Caiaphas, who was high priest that year, spoke up, "You know nothing at all! You do not realize that it is better for you that one man die for the people than that the whole nation perish."
> He did not say this on his own, but as high priest that year he prophesied that Jesus would die for the Jewish nation, and not only for that nation but also for the scattered children of God, to bring them together and make them one.
>
> (John 11:47-52).

In the Isaiah context the words appear as the words of the prophet Isaiah. Isaiah did explain his family's role as "signs and symbols," "Here am I, and the children the LORD has given me. We are signs and symbols in Israel from the LORD Almighty, who dwells on Mount Zion" (Isa 8:18). Motyer thinks Isaiah included his disciples or even a whole remnant with his family as signs, but he pays no attention to the inspired use made of the verses in Hebrews.[37]

---

[37]J. Alec Motyer, *The Prophecy of Isaiah* (Downers Grove: InterVarsity Press, 1993), pp. 92-96. Alexander summarizes the three major interpretations of Isaiah 8:17-18: (1) Isaiah is the speaker and with their odd names he and his children are signs and wonders, "personified prophecies," to Israel; (2) the Messiah is the speaker and the children are his spiritual seed (as in Isa 53:10); or (3) Isaiah is the speaker, and with his children they are a type of Christ. On the basis of the quotation in Heb 2:13 he prefers the second

¹⁴Since the children have flesh and blood, he too shared in their humanity so that by his death he might destroy him who holds the power of death — that is, the devil — ¹⁵and free those who all their lives were held in slavery by their fear of death. ¹⁶For surely it is not angels he helps, but Abraham's descendants. ¹⁷For this reason he had to be made like his brothers in every way, in order that he might become a merciful and faithful high priest in service to God, and that he might make atonement for^a the sins of the people. ¹⁸Because he himself suffered when he was tempted, he is able to help those who are being tempted.

^a*17* Or *and that he might turn aside God's wrath, taking away*

2:14 Since the children have flesh and blood, he too shared in their humanity.

Once again the NIV omits the conjunction, "therefore," which ties this verse to the preceding as a conclusion from it. The phrase τὰ παιδία (*ta paidia*, "**the children**") is picked up from the last verse of the quotations. An additional step is now taken to show Jesus' full identity with humanity. People have "**flesh and blood.**" Jesus did, too. Actually the order of the words here is "blood and flesh" as in Ephesians 6:12, which NIV translates "flesh and blood." Three other NT instances of this pair of words all follow the normal English order (Matt 16:17; 1 Cor 15:50 and Gal 1:16). Even when discussed together, though not paired in the phrase, "flesh and blood," the word "flesh" normally is discussed first. See Deuteronomy 12:27; Psalm 50:13; Ezekiel 39:17-18; John 6:53-56; etc.

In the phrase "have flesh and blood" the word "have" looks innocent enough. Beneath it lies a perfect tense of

---

view. Then he concludes, "a double sense ought not to be assumed where a single one is perfectly consistent with the context, and sufficient to explain all apparent contradictions, as in this case." Joseph Alexander, *Commentary on the Prophecies of Isaiah*; two volumes complete and unabridged in one (Grand Rapids: Zondervan, 1953), I:192-193.

κοινωνέω (*koinōneō*, "to share, to have in common"). The perfect tense goes beyond the present tense by drawing attention to the *effects* or *consequences* of sharing flesh and blood, as well as to the deed itself. Being flesh and blood carried with it terrible consequences, for example, weakness, death, fear, dominance by Satan, and continued deterioration since Adam's fall away from God. The words κοινός (*koinos*, "common") and κοινωνία (*koinōnia*, "fellowship") are related to it. It was the common plight of man.

A different word expresses that Jesus "**shared**" (μετέχω, *metechō*, "to share, have a share") in their humanity. The word μέτοχος (*metochos*, "partner") is related to it. To extend this metaphor one could say Jesus did not simply possess flesh and blood in common with man; he became a business partner with them in managing it. This verb is put in an aorist tense,[38] since it is Jesus' whole sharing with humanity that is the point. It seems be too narrow to limit this to the incarnation, as Westcott does. That was the time when he joined humanity, but his participation extended far beyond his birth. By uniting with people in their predicament he made different consequences possible. He destroyed Satan, freed men from fear of death, and opened an avenue for continuous help in struggling against temptation.

The word *paraplesiōs* ("similarly;" NIV "**too**") is another word unique to the NT and the LXX. Its cognate *paraplesios* ("coming near, resembling") in Philippians 2:27 is also unique to the NT and the LXX. Their simpler companion *plesion* ("near, neighbor") is frequent in the NT as well as the LXX.

so that by his death he might destroy him who holds the power of death — that is, the devil —
Two purposes are given in explaining why Jesus joined humanity. He came: (1) to destroy the devil; and (2) to

---

[38]Westcott finds "a similar contrast of tenses" in 1 Cor 15:4; 1 John 1:1; Col 1:16; John 20:23, 29. He sees the difference between κοινωνέω and μετέχω in 1 Cor 10:17-21 and 2 Cor 6:14. Brooke Foss Westcott, p. 52.

remove man's fear of death. First, he came to **destroy the devil**.[39] God has allowed Satan astonishing freedom (Luke 4:6; 1 Cor 10:13). Satan rebelled at the beginning and has always appeared in opposition to God and his people. He drew a large number of other angels away from God. He lures people into sin (Gen 3:1-19; 6:1-7), for example, Peter (Matt 16:23), Judas (Luke 22:3; John 13:27), Elymas (Acts 13:10) and Ananias and Sapphira (Acts 5:1-11). He even tried to entice Jesus to sin (Matt 4:1-11; Luke 4:1-13). He hinders the gospel (Mark 4:15; Acts 26:18; 1 Thess 2:18) and spreads destruction (Matt 13:24-30, 36-43). He blinds the eyes of unbelievers (2 Cor 4:4; Eph 2:2; Col 1:13). His cunning ranges from fearsome lion-likeness (1 Pet 5:8) to beauty like an angel of light (2 Cor 11:14). He is the father of lies (John 8:44; Eph 6:11). His demise is sure (Matt 25:41; John 12:31; 16:11; Rom 16:20; Rev 20:1-15; 21:8). Satan probably did not understand what God was going to achieve through Jesus' death. None of the rulers of this age understood it or they would not have crucified Jesus (1 Cor 2:6-10). On the cross Jesus crushed the head of the serpent (Gen 3:15). As Jeremiah learned, good work is not entirely building things up. Some things must be torn down (Jer 1:9-10).

2:15 and free those who all their lives were held in slavery by their fear of death.

Second, Jesus **removed man's fear of death**. He has not

---

[39]The NIV follows the Greek text here, "him who holds the power of death — that is, the devil." Six times our author makes a further identification with the words τοῦτ' ἔστιν (*tout' estin,* "that is"), in 2:14; 7:5; 9:11; 10:20; 11:16 and 13:15. The NIV uses only a dash "—" in 11:16 and 13:15.

Biblical names for the devil reveal his character: Satan (Hebrew meaning "accuser"), Beelzebub (Baal-zebub, "Lord of flies;" perhaps a taunting twist on Baal-zebul, "Lord Baal"), Belial ("worthlessness," parallel to the word "death" in Ps 18:4; in NT sometimes spelled "Beliar"), Adversary, Deceiver, Dragon, Enemy, Evil one, Father of Lies, Murderer, Sinner, Tempter. See Charles Williams, "Satan," in *The International Standard Bible Encyclopaedia,* five volumes, edited by James Orr, et al (Grand Rapids: Eerdmans, 1939), IV:2693-2696.

removed death yet, but the fear of it. By dying himself and rising to life again, he not only broke Satan's grip on death, but demonstrated to man that death was overcome. Paul declared,

> Having canceled the written code, with its regulations, that was against us and that stood opposed to us; he took it away, nailing it to the cross. And having disarmed the powers and authorities, he made a public spectacle of them, triumphing over them by the cross (Col 2:14-15).

The famous chapter on the resurrection, 1 Corinthians 15, explains how Jesus' resurrection opened the way for man's resurrection (cf. Heb 10:20). That chapter concludes with the victory cry, "Where, O death, is your victory? Where, O Death, is your sting? . . . Thanks be to God! He gives us the victory through our Lord Jesus Christ" (vv. 55-57). God had already made his ultimate intention quite plain in Hosea 13:14, "I will ransom them from the power of the grave; I will redeem them from death." As a Christian, Paul's fear of death was gone. He said that because he was in Christ, death was better than living. "To live is Christ and to die is gain. . . . I am torn between the two: I desire to depart and be with Christ, which is better by far; but it is more necessary for you that I remain in the body" (Phil 1:21-24). Thus, when Christians thought of fellow-believers who had died, they were urged not "to grieve like the rest of men, who have no hope" (1 Thess 4:13).

2:16 For surely it is not angels he helps, but Abraham's descendants.

With the conjunction "**for**" the logic moves forward to reassert man's superiority over angels. Angels assist in Christ's redemptive deeds for man; they do not receive the benefit of those deeds as man does. Man is the focus of redemptive history. There is no hint in the Bible that angels ever were rescued from their sin like people are. Angels never die (Luke 20:34-38). A major part of Jesus' full identification with man was his death. A major part of Jesus' work as high priest revolved around his death. To redeem man he bypassed angels, descended beneath them (2:5-9) and became like man "in every way" (2:17). At the resurrection men will take on some of the traits that make angels different from man now (Matt 22:30). Had Jesus come to redeem angels, he could have taken on the nature of angels instead of the nature of man.

Jesus' work does not reach all of mankind, but only **"Abraham's descendants."** The phrase "Abraham's descendants" is literally "seed of Abraham." In Galatians 3:15-18 Paul made a big point about the "seed of Abraham" in Genesis 12:7; 13:15; etc. being singular, hence referring to Christ. In the very next paragraph Paul uses the singular "seed" to refer to the many people who became "seed of Abraham" by faith in Christ, "If you belong to Christ, then you are Abraham's seed, and heirs according to the promise" (Gal 3:29). Here in Hebrews the phrase is not quoting an OT passage, so the phrase is used of the many descendants of Abraham even though the word "seed" is singular. In the Christian era anyone who believes in Jesus becomes a "descendant of Abraham" by faith, not by flesh. Not everyone who was of the flesh line of Abraham was a "Jew," but only those whose hearts were given to God on God's terms (Rom 2:28-29).

The gospel is only potentially valuable for everyone. Although God loves all the world (John 3:16), only those who hear the gospel can believe it (Rom 10:17). The value of Christians' telling others about Jesus' work can hardly be overemphasized (2 Cor 5:17-20). God only redeems those who believe. Abraham "believed God, and it was credited to him as righteousness. Understand, then, that those who believe are children of Abraham" (Gal 3:6-7). Abraham "is the father of all who believe [both circumcised and uncircumcised]" (Rom 4:9-12). "If you belong to Christ, then you are Abraham's seed, and heirs according to the promise" (Gal 3:29). Paul quoted Isaiah 28:16 to show this idea, "Anyone who trusts in him will never be put to shame. For there is no difference between Jew and Gentile — the same Lord is Lord of all and richly blesses

all who call on him" (Rom 10:11-12). Both the old covenant
and the new covenant link believers to God with the faith of
Abraham. How the new covenant replaced the old covenant,
yet fulfilled promises recorded in the old covenant, is more
fully explained in chapters six and eight.

The word δήπου (dēpou, "**surely**") once again finds the
author preferring a long word where a shorter one would suffice. Other editors of the Greek NT differ, as Moulton and
Geden, who list dēpou here as two separate words, dē and pou.
Otherwise the NT uses dē ("indeed") but five times (plus a variant reading in Acts 6:3);[40] pou ("somewhere") but four; and
dēpou ("of course, surely") only here. BAGD says of the enclitic
pou, that after a negative it means "nowhere." Thayer thinks the
word "is used when something is affirmed in a slightly ironical
manner, as if with an affectation of uncertainty."[41] Perhaps our
author is saying, "I hardly think he helps angels!"

It is not angels he **helps**. The verb "helps" (ἐπιλαμβάνομαι,
epilambanomai) normally in the NT means "to take hold of,
catch." Ellingworth thinks the present tense points to Christ's
present activity on behalf of his people, arguing on the basis of
its being surrounded by aorist tenses about the incarnation
("shared," v. 14; see above) or the death of Christ and its effects
("might destroy," v. 14; "might free," v. 15). He took upon himself the nature of humans, not angels, to get hold of them and
bring them to glory. He became like his brothers in every way
(v. 17), except, of course, that he never sinned (4:15).

**2:17 For this reason he had to be made like his brothers in
every way, in order that he might become a merciful and
faithful high priest in service to God, and that he might
make atonement for the sins of the people.**

Jesus became like man "**in order that**" (ἵνα, hina, "that, in
order that") he might help man. Christians will be eager to

---

[40]The NIV only translates δή ("therefore") in 1 Cor 6:20. Elsewhere it is
not translated.

[41]Thayer thinks the word δή is shortened from ἤδη ("now, already") which
appears quite often in the NT though never in Hebrews.

know Jesus' goals. Hebrews has four such statements expressing
Jesus' goals (2:14, 17a; 10:9; 13:12). In 2:14 Jesus shared flesh
and blood with man *so that* by dying he might destroy Satan's
power and remove man's fear of death. In 2:17a his full identification with man is required *in order that* he might become a
merciful and faithful high priest and make atonement for man's
sins. In 10:9 he set aside the first covenant *[in order]* to establish
the second. In 13:12 he suffered outside the city gate *[in order]*
to make the people holy through his own blood.

What was his way of helping man? He became **like his
brothers in every way**. He became a merciful and faithful
high priest and in that role made atonement for the sins of
the people. Much is made of copies and shadows in Hebrews,
while this word "like" (ὁμοιόω, *homoioō*, "to be like") is otherwise avoided, since it would put the work of Jesus and others
on an equal footing. In one sense Jesus never did become
exactly like any other person in the human family. No one
else could live perfectly. No one else could remove other people's sins by dying for them. No one else had his kind of
access to the Father in heaven. No one else had the power to
burst death after being held by it. In struggling against sin,
Jesus was truly tempted and suffered because of it (2:18).

The phrase "in service to God" (τὰ πρὸς τὸν θεόν, *ta pros
ton theon*) is literally, "the things toward God" or following
BAGD "the things *with reference to* God." The exact phrase
appears in 5:1 where the NIV translates "in matters related to
God." Blass and Debrunner call this use of the accusative an
"accusative of respect and adverbial accusative."[42] They also
found this precise phrase in Romans 15:17. There Paul boasts
in Christ Jesus of "the things with reference to God." The NIV

---

[42]F. Blass, et al, *A Greek Grammar of the New Testament* (Chicago: The
University of Chicago Press, 1961), pp. 87-88. The article by itself, without a
noun, is often used in the NT accompanied by an adjective or prepositional
phrase. Some are evidently adverbial. For example, Acts 4:29 begins with
the phrase καὶ τὰ νῦν (*kai ta nun*), literally, "And the now things," or more
loosely, "And as far as current things are concerned . . ." The NIV simplifies
by translating, "Now . . ."

translates, "in my service to God." Much of the high priest's work was certainly liturgical, hence in "service" to God, that is, not terminolgy of a servant, but of a religious activity like a church "service." Ellingworth also found the phrase in Exodus 4:16; 18:19 and Deuteronomy 31:27. Josephus contrasted "the things with reference to God" with "the things with reference to men" (Josephus, *Antiquities*, IX:236 [IX.xi.2]).

The term **"high priest"** appears here for the first time in Hebrews (of Jesus in 2:17; 3:1; 4:14-15; 5:5, 10; 6:20; 7:26; 8:1; 9:11; and of Levitical high priests in 5:1; 7:27-28; 8:3; 9:7, 25; 13:11).[43] Here alone the descriptions **"merciful"** and **"faithful"** are attached to it. In 4:14 he is called "a great high priest." Jesus was faithful in that he successfully completed his mission of providing **atonement for the sins of the people** (v. 17). He was merciful in that he suffered so that he could stand alongside of other sufferers and help them (v. 18). His faithfulness will be immediately compared to Moses' faithfulness (3:1-6) and contrasted with the Israelites' unfaithfulness (3:7-19). He offers mercy to all who cry out to him in need (4:16). However, for those who turn against him, the severity of punishment is much greater than the severity of OT punishment (10:26-31; 2:1-4).

The verb "to make atonement" (ἱλάσκομαι, *hilaskomai*, "to propitiate, expiate") is a present tense, which Westcott explains as the one eternal act of Christ (10:12) here regarded in its continuous present application to men (5:1-2). The verb is again in the NT only in Luke 18:13; the noun *hilasmos* ("expiation, propitiation") only in 1 John 2:2 and 4:10; and the noun *hilastērion* ("that which propitiates, the lid on the ark of the covenant") only in Romans 3:25 and Hebrews 9:5. There are many theories explaining in greater detail how the atonement works. The Bible explains *that* the atonement works to

---

[43]The term "priest" (ἱερεύς, *iereus*) is used of Jesus (5:6; 7:3, 21; 8;4; 10:21 ["a great priest"]); of Melchizedek (7:1, 3), of both Jesus and Melchizedek in the phrase, "a priest in the order of Melchizedek" (5:6; 7:11, (15), 17, 21), and of Levitical priests (7:20, 23; 8:4; 9:6; 10:11).

save man, but does not detail fully just *how* it works. The idea of Jesus' procuring salvation for believers by dying for them is so central to Christianity that church history is full of attempts to flesh out this skeletal concept.

Morris has summarized these theories under six major headings.[44] (1) The subjective view or moral influence theory. Christ's death moves us to respond to the love of Christ. (2) The victory theory, also called the devil ransom theory, the classical theory, or the fishhook theory of the atonement. God offered Jesus as a ransom to free man. Satan agreed, but could not hold Christ in death. (3) The satisfaction theory. Sin was such an insult to the dignity of God that God must act to rectify it. Yet man did the sin, so man must pay for it. Hence, Jesus, being both God and man, was needed. (4) The penal substitution theory. Jesus took the sinners' place bearing the penalty of sin which we should have borne. (5) The sacrifice theory. Jesus died as a sacrifice for man's sin. (6) The government theory. As head of all government God passed a law that the soul that sins shall die. God did not want sinful man to die. Thus he accepted the death of Christ instead, while demonstrating the depth of sin and the lengths to which God would go to uphold the moral order of the universe.

One of the major concepts in Hebrews is **sin**. The book has much to say about its nature, its consequences and its removal through Christ. As a singular form, "sin" is seen as a debility of man. As a plural form, "sins" are the individual deeds of misbehavior, parallel to "wickednesses" (8:12) or "lawlessnesses" (10:17). Men are commonly careless (2:1-3), fearful (2:15) and hardened by sin (3:13). Ten verses mention "sin" (singular — three of these are of "sin offerings" — 10:6, 8; 13:11); sixteen mention "sins" (plural); one has both (9:28; cf. 10:17-18).

Singular "**sin**." The nature of sin is pleasurable (11:25), deceitful (3:12), easily entangling (12:1), thus requiring a

---

[44]Leon Morris, "Atonement, Theories of the," in *Evangelical Dictionary of Theology*, pp. 100-102.

struggle to be overcome (12:4). Jesus alone of all men was free from sin (4:15), set apart from sinners (7:26), though opposed by sinful men (12:3). Thus he was able to sacrifice himself to bear the sins of others (9:26, 28; 10:18, 26; cf. Isa 53). The OT system required repeated sin offerings (10:6, 8; 13:11). Jesus offered himself once for all as God's full and final sin offering forever for man's sin. When he returns at his second coming, it will not be to bear sin again, but to bring salvation (9:28).

Plural "**sins**." The OT sacrifices of bulls and goats could never remove sins (10:4, 11). These were instead an annual reminder of sins (5:1, 3; 7:27; 9:7; 10:3). By contrast the sacrifice of Jesus successfully removed sins once for all time (5:1; 7:27; 10:12). It is described as providing purification for sins (1:3), making atonement for sins (2:17), or dying as a ransom to set us free from sins (9:15). Hence, believers are no longer guilty (10:2). Because of Jesus' death and work as high priest, God forgives sins (10:18). He no longer remembers any sins of one who is in the new covenant which Jesus made available (8:12). However, if a person keeps on sinning, there is no other sacrifice for his sins (10:26).

The book of Hebrews does not discuss how sin (singular) began, as Romans 5:12-21 does, but how it has been brought to an end by Christ. It does not make lists of sins (plural) like Romans 1:29-31 or Galatians 5:19-21, but treats them as a collection of misdeeds or a blight on human character which Jesus removed by his death and high priestly ministrations. The behavioral emphasis of the book is thus not on a wide range of good deeds, but is instead on faith, i.e., trusting God and remaining faithful. The central sin of all is not believing in Jesus (John 16:8-11). Sometimes those who are faithful are rewarded in this life. All of the faithful will be amply rewarded in the next (Luke 18:29-30).

2:18 Because he himself suffered when he was tempted, he is able to help those who are being tempted.

Jesus' suffering came from temptation, as does our suffering. It made him able to help all of us who also suffer and are tempted. Knowing that he also suffered, we open ourselves to him. His suffering made him perfect, i.e., made him complete (τελειόω, *teleioō*, "to complete, bring to an end, bring to its goal") as the God-man who would bring us to glory (2:10). By his suffering he became the "source of eternal salvation" for all who obey him, the "high priest" in the new order, and the one who makes his people holy (5:8-10; 13:12). As he learned obedience in suffering (5:8; 13:11-13), we are to obey in the face of shame and suffering (5:8; 10:32-34; 12:1-12; 13:12-13). Our obedience despite suffering is encouraged by doctrine (5:9), example (11:8), and direct command (13:17). The statement that Jesus only suffered once, not many times, since the creation of the world, focuses on his death, his greatest suffering (9:25-28). It does not deny the reality of the many other occasions in his earthly life when his heart hurt (Matt 9:36; 23:37-39; Mark 10:20-22; John 6:67; etc.).

Jesus **suffered when he was tempted**. Was he tempted by his sufferings or did he suffer by being tempted? An aorist participle (here, "when he was tempted") normally precedes the time of the main verb (here, "suffered"). Thus, the temptation resulted in his suffering. Moses was tempted by pleasure (11:25). Jesus never succumbed, though tried in every way we are (4:15). Everyone else is overcome (Rom 3:23). The devil is called "the tempter" because he constantly tries to lead us away from God (Matt 6:13; Rev 3:10). Among his many lures (James 1:2) the Bible names probing questions (Matt 16:1; 19:3; 22:35), pleasure (Heb 11:25), deprivation of normal desires (1 Cor 7:5; 1 Tim 6:9; Heb 3:8-9; James 1:13-14), especially concerning wealth (1 Tim 6:9-10), and even helpfulness (Gal 6:1). Wrong desires lead to sin which brings death (James 1:15). Temptations can be useful. They can bring joy through growing (James 1:2-4), through proving our faith (1 Pet 1:6-7), and ultimately through winning the crown of life (James 1:12). God guards Christians against temptations that could overwhelm them. He provides a way of escape. "No temptation has seized you except what is com-

mon to man. And God is faithful; he will not let you be tempted beyond what you can bear. But when you are tempted, he
will also provide a way out so that you can stand up under it"
(1 Cor 10:13). It is certainly not man's place to tempt God
(Acts 15:10; Ps 78:18; Mal 3:13-15; Cf. Gal 2:14), nor Jesus
(1 Cor 10:9), nor the Holy Spirit (Acts 5:9). Ahaz knew it was
a big thing to tempt God, though he did it anyway (Isa 7:12).
The Israelites' temptation of God will become the center of
the extended discussion of Heb 3:7-4:11.

He is **able to help** those being tempted. He can save completely those who come to God through him (7:25). He offers
mercy and grace on a continual basis to help in time of need
(4:15). The word "help" is in Hebrews in three forms: a verb
(2:18, βοηθέω, *boētheō*, "to help, come to the aid of"), a noun
(4:16, βοήθεια, *boētheia*, "help"), and an adjective (13:6,
βοηθός, *boēthos*, "helpful, helper"). The Lord is a helper, able
to help those being tempted in their time of need. Hagner
says, "the writer cannot resist a brief pastoral note about the
practical benefit of having Jesus as our high priest."

HEBREWS 3

III. GOD OFFERS REST TO ALL WHO TRUST HIM (3:1-4:16)

A. JESUS IS SUPERIOR TO MOSES (3:1-6)

¹Therefore, holy brothers, who share in the heavenly calling, fix your thoughts on Jesus, the apostle and high priest whom we confess. ²He was faithful to the one who appointed him, just as Moses was faithful in all God's house. ³Jesus has been found worthy of greater honor than Moses, just as the builder of a house has greater honor than the house itself. ⁴For every house is built by someone, but God is the builder of everything. ⁵Moses was faithful as a servant in all God's house, testifying to what would be said in the future. ⁶But Christ is faithful as a son over God's house. And we are his house, if we hold on to our courage and the hope of which we boast.

Jesus has been shown to be superior to prophets (1:1-3), to angels (1:4-2:5), to men (2:6-18), to Satan (2:14-16), now to Moses (3:1-6). Actually, Jesus was not directly contrasted with men. He was seen as becoming fully a brother with them by entering flesh and blood. But he was the only man who fulfilled the exalted position God designed for man to hold (2:6-10), and their final salvation was dependent on his overcoming Satan and death, not on their achievement (2:14-18).

Chapters three and four show how God offers eternal "rest" to those who obey him. They may be divided into three major sections: 3:1-6 showing Jesus' superiority in faithfulness over Moses' faithfulness; 3:7-19 showing Israel's failure of faith which made them fall in the desert; and 4:1-13 showing the Sabbath-rest to which God brings his faithful people. The last three verses (4:14-16) are actually an introduction to the discussion of the priesthood of Christ which is presented in chapters five through seven. Israel's loss was not due to Moses' incompetence as though he was unfaithful. He was faithful in his role as servant. More significantly, Jesus also stands before us, faithful as a son. The two chapters are sprinkled with warnings. Even with trustworthy leaders, people may be lost because of their own unfaithfulness. Our author urges his readers not to copy Israel's unnecessary demise.

Like all other humans, Moses was not perfect; but his faithfulness, not his flaws of character, is the point of the author's argument here. Both Moses and Jesus were faithful to the one who appointed them. Jesus' position as son over God's house made him superior to Moses whose position was as a servant in God's house (3:5-6). Jesus is even superior to Moses, the grand head of all the Old Testament system.

3:1 Therefore, holy brothers, who share in the heavenly calling, fix your thoughts on Jesus, the apostle and high priest whom we confess.

No NT verses are unrelated to their contexts. There is some link between every verse of the NT and the verses before it and those after it. Sometimes an author prods his readers to notice this connection, like here. The whole second chapter concerning Jesus' faithfully carrying out of his rescue of man may highlight the need for our faithfully clinging to him so we can enter that eternal rest (chapter 3-4). Since this very word ὅθεν (*hothen*, "therefore") also begins 2:17 and 3:1, the writer probably thought of 2:17-18 as one unit of thought based on its preceding verses as though he presented 3:1ff. in one unit of thought based on 2:17-18. The previous paragraph about Jesus as the merciful high priest to this one about Jesus as the faithful high priest are both expansions of the phrase "merciful and faithful high priest" in 2:17. The writer reminds his readers of that connection with the word **"therefore."**

The causal connection of this word **"therefore"** (ὅθεν, *hothen*, "from where, from which, therefore," actually an adverb) is expressed by the NIV every time it occurs in Hebrews, except in 11:19 where the anemic "and" appears. It is translated in the NIV, "for this reason" (2:17); "therefore;" (3:1 and 7:25); or "hence" (8:3; 9:18; and 11:19). It normally moves the logic forward at the sentence level (2:17; 7:25; 8:3; 9:18; 11:19), although here it may be at the paragraph level. In 2:17-18 Jesus was just called a "faithful high priest" who is able to help those who are being "tempted."

Holy brothers, who share in the heavenly calling. He has stood with his readers ("we" in 1:1f.; 2:1, 3; see 4:1-3). Now for the first time he directly addresses them ("you").[1] **"Holy"** or "saint" (ἅγιος, *hagios*) is used of Christians elsewhere in Hebrews (6:10 and 13:24). This was one of Paul's common designations for his readers (Rom 1:7; 1 Cor 1:2; 2 Cor 1:1; Eph 1:1; Phil 1:1; Col 1:2). See also the verb form, we have been "made holy, sanctified" (2:11; 9:13; 10:10,14,29; 13:12). In Hebrews the Spirit of God is also called holy, i.e., the "Holy Spirit" (2:4; 3:1,7; 6:4; 9:8; 10:15). The plural form (lit., "holies") is used to designate the tabernacle sanctuary, i.e., the "Holy Place" (8:2; 9:1,2,3,8,12,24,25; 10:19; 13:11).

The readers are addressed as **"brothers"** again in 3:12; 10:19; and 13:22 and "beloved" in 6:9. The other four vocative forms, that is, nouns of direct address, in Hebrews are all in quotations from the LXX (1:8,10; 10:7; 12:5). In the first three Jesus is addressed as "God" and "LORD." In the last (12:5) the reader of Proverbs is addressed as "My son." The longest phrase of direct address is in 3:1, "holy brothers, who share in the heavenly calling." The phrase "holy brothers" occurs again in the NT only in a variant reading of 1 Thessa-

---

[1]Ellingworth finds this direct address ("you") in 7:4; 10:19-36; 12:3-8, 12-25a; 13:1-5, 7-9, 16f., 21a, and 22-25. Ellingworth, p. 197.

lonians 5:27. "Brothers" is the most common form of address in all NT epistles.[2]

Christianity is not designed to be lived alone. Hebrews states four things in which Christians **share**: in the heavenly calling (3:1); in Christ (3:14); in the Holy Spirit (6:4); and, with all people, in a father's discipline (12:8). Outside of Hebrews the NT only uses this noun in Luke 5:7 of fishing partners. Its cognate verb carries the broader idea of sharing. Christ shared humanity with us (2:14); but he "belonged to" (lit., "shared") a different tribe than priests, i.e., the tribe of Judah, not the tribe of Levi (7:13). Immature people "live on" (lit., "share") milk (5:13). All NT occurances of the verb μετέχω (metechō, "to share") outside of Hebrews are in

---

[2]Direct address in NT epistles is interesting. Sometimes "brothers" is personalized to "my brothers" (Rom 15:14; Phil 3:1; James 1:2; 2:1; etc.), even to "my beloved brothers" (1 Cor 15:58; James 1:16, 19; 2:5). Paul called the Thessalonians "brothers beloved by God [or the LORD] (1 Thess 1:4; 2 Thess 2:13). Compare Paul's endearing "my child" (2 Tim 2:1) or simply "child" (1 Tim 1:18). But he also wrote the invigorating "O man of God" (1 Tim 6:11). John is most famous for his tender "my little children" (1 John 2:1, 18, 28; 3:7, 18; 4:4; 5:21). It becomes part of his trilogy: "little children," "fathers," "young men" (2:12-14).

Sometimes individuals or groups are addressed by name: Corinthians (2 Cor 6:11), Galatians (Gal 3:1), Philippians (Phil 4:15), Timothy (1 Tim 1:18; 6:20); Kuria (2 John 5). See Paul's groups in Eph 5:22-6:9 and Col 3:18-4:1. John also has a group of groups in 1 John 2:12-14. Sometimes strong adjectives are used even in epistles: "O foolish Galatians" (Gal 3:1), "You foolish man" (James 2:20), "you adulterous people" (James 4:4), "you sinners" (James 4:8), "you double-minded" (James 4:8), and the distant "O man who . . ." (Rom 2:1, 3, where NIV has nothing in 2:1 and "you, a mere man" in 2:3). Phil 4:4 has the complimentary, "loyal yokefellow" (NIV, but NIV margin, "loyal Syzygus"). These may not differ greatly from conversational use, but they become much more visible and formal in writing.

The words of address help us see behind the scenes. Paul wrote "brothers" to the Corinthians twenty times in the first epistle, but only three times in the second. Though he was so sharp with the Galatians, he called them "brother" nine times. Per page the Thessalonian letters have the term "brothers" most frequently, nineteen times. Except for the ascriptions of praise to God in Revelation, Phil 4:1 has the largest collection of terms in one direct address, "my brothers, beloved and longed for, my joy and crown."

1 Corinthians 9-10. Plowmen and threshers share the crop (9:10), so Paul expects to share the fruit of his labor (9:12). People share in a meal (10:30). Christians are said to be all one loaf and to share the same loaf which is Christ (10:17). Since they share the table of the LORD, it is not possible to share the table of demons also (10:21).

Although the Christian **calling** is only mentioned here in Hebrews with the noun, its verbal counterpart, "to call" appears a half dozen times. The verb "to call" may mean either (1) to give a name to something perhaps indicating the meaning of the new role, or (2) to invite into a new role. The first idea is used when Jesus calls men "brothers" (2:11) and when God designates the time "today" (3:13). The second is used when Jesus was called into the high priesthood by God (5:4), when Abraham was summoned to go to some future inheritance (11:8), and when people are invited to walk with God (9:15). Only the last instance is a perfect tense,[3] which brings to the readers' attention both the finished initial call and the subsequent adventures and benefits that grow out of that response. It is this last sense of "call" which is used here.

The call is potentially for everyone, but it is effective only for those who respond (Acts 2:38-40). This was true of God's call to Abraham, Moses, Isaiah, Peter and Andrew, Paul, etc. It is a consistent concept of Scripture that God calls people to himself. He does not coerce them. He does not save them against their will. Whatever his plans for individuals, families or nations, he allows men to respond from their own choice. God is a gentleman. He simply calls; he does not coerce. See Isaiah 55:1-3. His occasional additional strong measures, for

---

[3]The perfect tense is used in 1 John for many of the verbs that describe the beginning act of becoming a Christian and the results which follow that act—knowing Jesus (2:4; see 3:6 and 5:20) or the Father (2:13,14); knowing love (3:16; 4:16; see 3:1); trusting God's love (4:16); loving God (4:10); being born of God (2:29; 3:9; 4:7; 5:1,18); having sins forgiven (2:12); passing out of death into life (3:14); winning the victory over the world (2:13; 4:4; 5:4) and the evil one (2:14); receiving the Holy Spirit (4:13); and having God's love perfected in us (2:5; 4:12,17-18).

example with Jonah, only serve to underline the general freedom which he allows. Many exhortations are found in Hebrews, clarifying the results of obedience and disobedience. The choice is left with men.

The Christian calling is a **heavenly** (ἐπουράνιος, *epouranios*) calling, an upward call leading to heaven (Phil 3:14).[4] Hebrews repeatedly contrasts what is physical, temporary and visible with what is spiritual, permanent and invisible.

One should examine other passages that describe this heavenward call of God in Christ (Matt 9:13; Rom 8:28-30; 9:22-26; 11:29; 1 Cor 1:9,26-31; 7:15,17-24; Gal 5:13; Eph 1:17-23; 4:1-6; Phil 3:12-15; Col 3:15; 1 Thess 2:10-12; 4:7-8; 2 Thess 1:11-12;2:13-16; 1 Tim 6:12; 2 Tim 1:8-10; 1 Pet 1:13-16; 2:9-10; 3:8-9; 5:10-11; 2 Pet 1:3-11). Of course there are many others which describe this call but do not use the word "call."

Fix your thoughts on Jesus. "You are what you think." "You become what you think about all day long." Non-Christians know the power of the mind to shape our future by focused thought. It is no surprise to find this kind of direction also in the Scripture. To help us achieve this focus there are four Gospels telling the story of Jesus' ministry on earth. No other events are repeated four times in the Bible in such detail. We would all be much better off if we spent more time thinking about Jesus.

No other person stands so tall. He is our model for living, for speech, conduct, purity, sympathy, prayer and selfless serving. He is our savior. Without his death we would die forever. With his death we can live forever. He is our high priest. No one else could enter God's presence for us to make atonement for us. No one else could intercede for us like Jesus. He is our forerunner. He made a way for us to follow that leads to glory.

---

[4]Ellingworth notes three ways of understanding the relation of the call and heaven: (1) from heaven (e.g., Peshitta, Bleek); (2) to heaven (e.g., Windisch, Montefiore); or (3) both (e.g., Bengel, Spicq, Braun, Attridge, Grasser).

Liddell and Scott defines the verb *katanoeo* ("fix your thoughts on") as "1. notice, observe carefully; 2. look at with reflection, . . . contemplate."[5] G. Harder says,

> A strengthened form of *noeo* is *katanoeo* (Hdt. Onwards), to direct one's mind and interest towards something, to notice and perceive it . . . Thus *katanoeo* can mean to observe, test, comprehend, understand, in the latter sense being almost synonymous with *syniemi*, to understand.[6]

Later he adds,

> Lk. 20:23 shows that *katanoein* includes what goes on behind the scenes. In the same way, Heb. 3:1 means that it is not the outward figure of Jesus that we should look to, but what he really is, as the emissary of God, as the real High Priest, and as the proper object of Christian faith.[7]

The verb occurs again in Hebrews in 10:24 where we are urged to "consider how we may spur one another on toward love and good deeds."

Apostle. Jesus chose twelve of his followers and called them "apostles" (Luke 6:13-16). Barnabas was also called an apostle (Acts 14:14), as were Paul (2 Cor 1:1) and Epaphroditus (Phil 2:25, NIV translates ἀπόστολος [*apostolos*] here as "messenger"). Paul was an apostle of Jesus. Barnabas and Epaphroditus should probably be called apostles of the church, perhaps "missionaries" says LS (p. 99). Jesus was an apostle "sent from God" (Matt 10:40; etc.). The verb ἀπο–στέλλω (*apostellō*, "I send") was used of many different people who were sent to do a specific task. It was used of Moses (Exod 3:10; 7:16; Num 16:28-29); but since this is not the point of the comparison in this paragraph, it is not mentioned.[8] The

---

[5]LS, p. 416.

[6]NIDNTT, 3:124.

[7]Ibid., 3:129.

[8]The Rabbis argued whether a priest was an agent (*sheliah*, the Hebrew equivalent of "apostle") of God or of the worshiper when he offered a sacrifice for someone. See Yoma 19a-b (Soncino, p. 83), Nedarim 35b (Soncino edition, p. 107) and Kiddushin 23b (Soncino edition, p. 113).

Father evidently has the role of principle planner and principle administrator. Jesus was sent out from him to do the specific task of redeeming mankind. As God's apostle, he was
commissioned with the task of setting up the system of
Christianity which we confess. He did the task well, though his
position, not his performance, is the focus of the paragraph.

The word "apostle" probably should not be understood
simply as one who has been sent, but as one who has been
both properly equipped and commissioned. Whatever preparation, training or authorization is necessary to carry out the
intended mission has been provided along with the "send-
off." See others who were "prepared and sent," (Acts 8:14;
10:20-21; 15:27; 19:22; 2 Cor 8:22-23; 12:16-18; Phil 2:19-23,
25, 28-30; 2 Tim 4:12). The rabbis said, "A man's messenger is
like the one who sent him" (M.Berakoth 5:5). The solemnity
of this remark may be seen in its context, "If he that says the
Tefillah[9] falls into error it is a bad omen for him; and if he was
the agent of the congregation it is a bad omen for them that
appointed him, because a man's agent is like to himself."

Besides apostle Jesus also filled the role of **high priest**.[10]
Hebrews will actually call him "priest" (ἱερεύς, *hiereus*) in
7:3,11,15,17; 8:4, "great priest" (ἱερεὺς μέγας, *hiereus megas*) in
4:14; 10:21 or "high priest" (ἀρχιερεύς, *archiereus*) in 2:17; 3:1;
4:15; 5:5,10; 6:20; 7:26; 8:1; 9:11,25. Other passages imply this
role for Jesus, but do not directly state it, as 13:11ff. There
are passages applying the LXX statements to Jesus (5:6; 7:21).
The main section in Hebrews that discusses his priesthood,
Hebrews 4:14-7:28, contrasts Jesus with priests in general, not
necessarily with the high priests. Hebrews 2 places Jesus
alongside humans as their brother, not as their ruler (2:17).

---

[9]*Tefillah* literally means simply "prayer," but it is the name given to the
prayer par excellence, i.e., the "Eighteen Benedictions," which were recited
three times a day.

[10]Montefiore reminds us that Philo even called Moses a high priest (*de
Vita Moys*. 2.3). Hugh Montefiore, *The Epistle to the Hebrews* (Peabody, MA:
Hendrickson, 1964, reprinted 1987), p. 71.

One could almost say, "chief among equals." The OT high priest was the leader of all priests and one of them. So it is fitting for Jesus the priest among a kingdom of priests to be called the high priest, as principal among them.

The sacrifice described in Hebrews 9 was that on the Day of Atonement in which the high priest had the predominant place. In that setting Jesus would be contrasted with the Jewish high priest. This usage naturally carried over to the other times when Jesus is referred to in the book of Hebrews.

Whom we confess. The Christian confession revolves around the mission of Jesus. The good news they told was about Jesus' coming to rescue man and his atoning work for us. Those who did not confess Jesus were no part of his people. Confession of Jesus is a necessary and natural part of belonging to him and to the Father (Matt 10:32-33; 1 John 2:22-23; 4:1-3). The hope we confess is based on Jesus' faithful work as high priest (4:14-16; 10:22-23). Confession of Jesus should not be confused with confession of sins. Sins should be confessed to God who promises to forgive his people who confess their sins to him (1 John 1:9). Confession of Jesus is the open acknowledgement before men of who Jesus is and what he has done for our redemption. It is the center of evangelism.

3:2 He was faithful to the one who appointed him, just as Moses was faithful in all God's house. 3:3 Jesus has been found worthy of greater honor than Moses, just as the builder of a house has greater honor than the house itself.

The measure of faithfulness could be best assessed by **the one who appointed him**. God said, "This is my Son, whom I love; with him I am well pleased" (Matt 3:17). When Jesus finished his work of providing purification for sins, God welcomed him to sit down at his right hand on his throne and promised to make all of Jesus' enemies a footstool for his feet (1:13). The honor given to Jesus is as much greater than the honor given to Moses as the honor given to a builder is greater than the house he built. Among all those whom Jesus redeemed, he also redeemed Moses by his death on the cross. Moses did not redeem Jesus.

Moses' exasperation at the people's grumbling led him to disobey God by striking the rock for water rather than speaking to it as God had commanded. This dishonored God enough in not trusting him totally, that God would not let Moses bring Israel into the promised land (Num 20:2-13, 24; 27:14; Deut 1:37; 3:23-28; 32:50-52; Ps 106:32-33). It is possible that God wanted this incident to provide some lesson for future generations as he did with the bronze snake (John 3:14-16 based on Num 21:4-9). They could just look at the snake and be healed. One could look in faith at Jesus on the cross and be healed. If Moses had obeyed, God might have said his people could just speak to him (the rock) and find God's provision for their need.

The point of the author here about Moses is his predominant faithfulness, however, not his occasional failure. "Moses was faithful in all God's house" (v.2). This very faithfulness of Moses is specifically stated by God when Miriam and Aaron challenged Moses' preeminent position,

> Listen to my words: "When a prophet of the LORD is among you, I reveal myself to him in visions, I speak to him in dreams. But this is not true of my servant Moses; he is faithful in all my house. With him I speak face to face, clearly and not in riddles; he sees the form of the LORD. Why then were you not afraid to speak against my servant Moses? (Num 12:6-8).

3:4 For every house is built by someone, but God is the builder of everything.

Design logically presupposes a designer. Many Christian and non-Christian philosophers alike hold the idea of design to be the most significant concept in understanding the ultimate origin of our universe. Hebrews says it simply, "Every house is built by someone." The statement is made here as another reason why Jesus is worthy of greater honor than Moses. His high status is no arbitrary accident of a blind universe.

The builder of all things is God. The word "builder" (participle from the Greek verb, κατασκευάζω, *kataskeuazō*) may be defined as "to make ready, prepare; to build, construct, create; to furnish."[11] Thiele cites classical examples of preparing various things: meals, a room, festal routes, a ship, preparing for battle, even formal teaching on various subjects.[12] The LXX uses it also to describe the work of creation. Hebrews has about half of the NT uses. People prepared the tabernacle (9:2,6), and Noah prepared an ark (11:7, as 1 Pet 3:20). John the Baptist prepared a people (Luke 1:17) and a way (Matt 11:10 and parallels) for Jesus.

The word "God" does not have an article, thereby stressing the essence more than the identity of God. Westcott calls it "the character of God as God."[13] Since Jesus is seen as the builder of the house, he is functioning at the level where God functions. He was called "God" in 1:8-9 by applying Psalm 95 to him. He was virtually called God in 2:5-9 where he returned to a God-level position above the angels after being beneath them for a little while during his mission on earth. Moses did not function at this level. Jesus' status as the unique Son of God further supports this idea.

Moses appears several times in the book of Hebrews. His parents hid him for three months at his birth because of their faith (11:23). Moses exercised this same faithfulness as a servant in all God's house (3:2, 5). When mature, he chose the Jews and their Messiah rather than the pleasures of the Egyptian palace (11:24-26). He led Israel out of Egypt (3:16; 11:27, 29), at which time he kept the Passover and its sprinkling of blood (11:28). Though full of fear at Mt. Sinai (12:21), he received and "proclaimed every commandment of the law to all the people" (9:19) including guidelines about priests (7:14) and punishment (10:28). Under his direction the tabernacle was built exactly like the pattern God showed

---

[11]BAGD, p.418.

[12]F. Thiele, "*kataskeuazō*," in NIDNTT, 3:118-120.

[13]Westcott, p. 77.

him (8:5). He inaugurated the covenant agreement by sprinkling blood on the scroll, all the people, the tabernacle and everything in it (9:19-21).

In Revelation 15:3 those who were victorious over the beast sing "the song of **Moses** the servant of God and the song of the Lamb." Moses is mentioned more times than Abraham in the NT.[14]

Moses wrote more pages of the Bible than anyone else. Moses gave the law as well as the plans for the tabernacle and its service which were perpetuated and embellished in the temple worship. Moses inaugurated the priesthood of Aaron. Moses delivered the people of God from Egyptian bondage, implementing the severe plagues on Egypt, leading in the miraculous crossing of the Red Sea and guiding them safely in the desert for forty years. Moses divided up the promised land as an inheritance and set up Joshua to bring them victoriously into it. Only Moses had spoken to God face to face (Deut 34:10; see also Exod 33:11 and Num 12:6-8). It is not strange that Lauterbach can describe the Jew's supreme admiration for Moses this way,

> Of all Biblical personages Moses has been chosen most frequently as the subject of later legends; and his life has been recounted in full detail in the poetic haggadah. As liberator, lawgiver, and leader of a people which was transformed by him from an unorganized horde into a nation, he occupies a more important place in popular legend than the Patriarchs and all the other national heroes.[15]

The Mishnah says, "none in Israel is greater than he [Moses]. . . . Whom have we greater than Moses? (M.Sotah 1:9).

---

[14]Paul Ellingworth has found that Abraham is mentioned 72 times in the NT, 10 times in Hebrews (2:16; 6:13; 7:1, 2, 4, 5, 6, 9; 11:8, 17); Moses 79 times in the NT, 11 times in Hebrews (3:2, 3, 5, 16; 7:14; 8:5; 9:19; 10:28; 11:23, 24; 12:21). *The Epistle to the Hebrews*, p. 194.

[15]J.Z. Lauterbach, "Moses," in *The Jewish Encyclopedia*, 9:44-57, p.46.

3:5 Moses was faithful as a servant in all God's house, testifying to what would be said in the future.

The NIV in verse five sounds like Moses was doing the testifying. The fact that Moses was faithful as a servant was what became a testimony (lit., "into a testimony") of things to be spoken later. Moses did prophesy about these things, but that is not the point of this passage. The form λαληθησομένων (*lalēthēsomenōn*; NIV, "what would be said in the future") is the only future passive participle in the NT.

3:6 But Christ is faithful as a son over God's house. And we are his house, if we hold on to our courage and the hope of which we boast.

Moses was virtually unparalleled as a servant of God, but he was still merely that — a servant. In striking contrast, Jesus "is" (not was) faithful as "a son" (not a servant). Moreover, while Moses served "in" God's house, Jesus is "over" God's house. The superiority of Jesus over Moses could not be more clearly shown. Better than the prophets (1:1-2), better than the angels (1:4-13), better even than Moses, only Jesus is given the name "son."

A similar thought to the expression "we are his house" is found in 1 Timothy 3:15 and 1 Peter 4:17. Compare the OT phrase "house of Israel." The image of a spiritual building is found in 1 Corinthians 3:10-12; Ephesians 2:19-22 and 1 Peter 2:4-8. It is a beautiful parallel expressing our mutual interdependence. Although the words οἶκος (*oikos*) and οἰκία (*oikia*), both translated "house," are quite interchangeable, only *oikos* appears in Hebrews (3:2-6; 8:8,10; 10:21; 11:7). It is used of both God's house and man's house. Montefiore explains that

> In the author's day the 'extended family', with its large variety of age and its ramifications of relationship, offered a closer analogy to the Church of God than the present smaller unit of the Western family, usually comprising only parents and children.[16]

---

[16]Montefiore, p.74.

Eager to emphasize the certainty of God's promises, many have been blind to any conditions God attached to them, as though fulfilling God's conditions would constitute some kind of "work" by which one earned the right to receive those promises.

We are his, **if we hold on.** The Christian's position as part of the house of God is conditional. He must remain faithful. The conditionality is emphasized even more by the use of a special emphatic word ἐάνπερ (*eanper*, "**if**"), which appears only here, 3:14, and 6:3 in the whole NT. Thayer says of the enclitic particle -*per*, which is here appended to the ordinary word *ean* ("if,") that "the idea of the word to which it is annexed must be taken in its fullest extent."[17]

How can one avoid the conditions which God places on his promises? "*If* you forgive . . . when they sin against you, your heavenly Father will also forgive you" (Matt 6:14, emphasis added, also below). "*If* you have faith, . . . you can say to this mountain . . . and it will move" (Matt 17:20-21). "*If* you remain in me and my words remain in you, ask whatever . . . and it will be given you" (John 15:7). Can one dismiss forgiveness or faith or remaining in Jesus as mere verbiage and not real conditions? May his commands be ignored and one still expect to receive his promises? How could Noah expect to be saved from the coming flood if he did not obey God's command to build an ark? (Gen 6:14ff.). How could Abraham expect God to fulfill his promise if he would not leave his homeland? (Gen 12:1-4). How would the hearers at Pentecost expect to receive forgiveness of sins and the gift of the Holy Spirit if they did not fulfill the conditions Peter laid before them? (Acts 2:38). "He who stands firm to the end will be saved" (Matt 10:22). Is there some other way to be saved by which the condition Jesus stated may be ignored?

---

[17]Thayer, p. 500. He adds, "In the N. T. it is affixed to the pron. ὅς and to sundry particles, see διόπερ, ἐάνπερ, εἴπερ, ἐπείπερ, ἐπειδήπερ, ἥπερ, καθάπερ, καίπερ, ὅσπερ, ὥσπερ." Of these Hebrews uses ἐάνπερ (3:14; 6:3); καθάπερ (4:2); καίπερ (5:8; 7:5; 12:17); and ὥσπερ (4:10; 7:27; 9:25). I also found καθώσπερ in 5:4.

Let the author of Hebrews speak. Can a person be saved who "drifts away," ignoring the great salvation Jesus has brought? (2:1-4). Will God's rest be acquired by those who "turn away" and do not "hold firmly till the end?" What if we make no attempt to "encourage one another daily"? (3:13-14). He said we should "make every effort to enter that rest" or we would "fall" (4:11). Can one please God who will not "leave the elementary teachings . . . and go on to maturity?" (6:1). We say instead, "Let the word of Christ dwell in you richly" (Col 3:16). "If you do these things, you will never fall" (1 Pet 1:10).

The general meaning of of κατέχω (katechō, "**to hold on to**") is clear enough. Interesting pictures emerge if one applies the nautical imagery of this word from Acts 27:40, "to steer toward;" or the legal imagery of "taking possession of property" from Matthew 21:38. **Courage** and **hope** become major parts of good Christian living. It takes courage to approach God initially (10:19) and repeatedly (4:16). His gracious offer fills us with hope (6:18) for help when we come to him. If our hope can be sure, we can be sure (6:11-12; 10:23; 11:1). Ours is a much better hope than anyone has had before us (7:19). "The hope of which we boast" could be literally translated, "the pride of hope" (τὸ καύχημα τῆς ἐλπίδος, to kauchēma tēs elpidos) or as BAGD suggests, "that for which we are proud to hope." Encouragement and hope are provided by fellow Christians (here), by the LORD (2 Thess 2:16) and by the Scripture (Rom 15:4).

B. PSALM 95:7-11 (3:7-11)

[7]**So, as the Holy Spirit says:**
"Today, if you hear his voice,
[8]**do not harden your hearts**
as you did in the rebellion,
during the time of testing in the desert,
[9]**where your fathers tested and tried me**

and for forty years saw what I did.
[10]That is why I was angry with that generation,
and I said, 'Their hearts are always going astray,
and they have not known my ways.'
[11]So I declared on oath in my anger,
'They shall never enter my rest.'"[a]

[a]*11* Psalm 95:7-11

3:7 So, as the Holy Spirit says: "Today, if you hear his voice,

The lengthy passage from Psalm 95:7-11 is quoted to expand on the idea of 3:6 that we must hold on to our courage and hope in order to remain a part of the house of God. It is only those who remain faithful to the end who will find themselves in heaven sharing the eternal "rest" with God when all of earth history is over. Israel failed to remain faithful. Consequently, they lost this rest. The shepherd-heart of our author does not want his Christian brothers to suffer the same loss.

There are two parts of Psalm 95, an invitation to worship (1-7a) and a warning against disobedience (7b-11). God should be worshipped because he is "the great God" controlling all nature, and he is "our God" making us "the people of his pasture." The rest of the Psalm warns us not to lose that privilege (Ps 95:7b-11). This latter portion urges the necessity of faithfulness, and thus is very appropriate to cite in a section arguing the need for faithfulness.

3:8 do not harden your hearts as you did in the rebellion, during the time of testing in the desert,

This discussion about the incidents at Massah and Meribah illustrate how the OT can help us. Only a few weeks after Israel had been delivered from the Egyptian army at the Red Sea, they begin to grumble at God's provisions. Moses named the place Massah and Meribah, Hebrew names meaning "Testing" and "Quarreling" (Num 17:7). A similar grumbling against God occured near Kadesh as the nation approached

Canaan. In this incident Moses became exasperated with the people and struck the rock instead of speaking to it as God directed. He was punished by being denied entrance to the land (Num 20:1-13, 24). Moses referred to this grumbling in his speeches in Deuteronomy (6:16; 9:22; 33:8). God reminded Moses of this infraction when he was preparing to die (Deut 32:48-52). The problem made such an impression that it is mentioned repeatedly in Psalms (Ps 81:7; 95:8; 106:32-33). By the time of Ezekiel the northern location had become a place-name, Meribah Kadesh, used in marking the boundaries of the land (Ezek 47:19; 48:28). The author of Hebrews chose to use the record in the ninety-fifth Psalm.

The LXX differs from the MT in two significant points. Instead of using the Hebrew names, Meribah and Massah, it translates them respectively as παραπικρασμός (*parapikrasmos*, "Provocation") and πειρασμός (*peirasmos*, "Testing").[18] Secondly, it ascribes the Psalm to David in its title. In a somewhat similar fashion the apostles and Christians, when praying about the first opposition to the fledgling church, ascribed the second Psalm to the **Holy Spirit** through David (Acts 4:25-26). The Hebrew text had left it anonymous. Like those praying believers, the author of Hebrews attributes the text ultimately to the Holy Spirit. Compare Hebrews 9:8 and 10:15 where the Holy Spirit is stated to be the ultimate author in producing Bible texts.[19] Sharing in the Holy Spirit (6:4)

---

[18]Brenton's edition of the LXX prefers the reading *pikrasmos* ("Irritation"), while noting that *peirasmos* "is the reading of several editions." Launcelot Lee Brenton, *The Septuagint Version of the Old Testament with an English translation* (London: Samuel Bagster and Sons Limited, n.d.), p. 756. Rahlfs' edition of the LXX has no notation of this variant reading. Alfred Rahlfs, editor, *Septuaginta*, eighth edition, two volumes (Wurttembergische Bibelanstalt Stuttgart, 1935), II:104.

[19]The Jewish leaders were very much aware of the difference between the OT literature, Genesis through Malachi, and the Apocryphal literature of the intertestamental period. "Our Rabbis taught: Since the death of the last prophets, Haggai, Zechariah and Malachi, the Holy Spirit [of prophetic inspiration] departed from Israel; yet they were still able to avail themselves of the *Bath-kol*" (Sanhedrin 11a, Soncino edition, p. 46). Blau defines "bath

and insulting the Spirit of grace (10:29) may therefore refer either to the indwelling presence of the Holy Spirit who enters at the time of conversion or to the Bible which the Holy Spirit has graciously provided for our guidance.

3:9 where your fathers tested and tried me and for forty years saw what I did. 3:10 That is why I was angry with that generation, and I said, 'Their hearts are always going astray, and they have not known my ways.'

The NT text differs from the LXX in one further point. First, notice the LXX ambiguity. The LXX put the phrase "forty years" between the statements about (1) the fathers who disbelieved though "seeing my works" and (2) God's "being angry with them." Thus it is left unclear which thing lasted for forty years. The Hebrew text of the Psalm positions the phrase in the same place with the same ambiguity. The editors of both the MT and the LXX punctuate the text to indicate that God's wrath lasted for forty years.

3:11 So I declared on oath in my anger, 'They shall never enter my rest.'"

God expressed his anger with the solemnity of an oath statement, "I declared on oath in my anger, 'They shall never enter my rest.'" This is consistent with the forty years' time during which all of the disbelieving generation died, except Joshua and Caleb (Num 14:26-35). On the other hand, Amos 5:25-27, which Stephen quoted in Acts 7:42-43, sounds like the unfaithfulness of Israel lasted for forty years in the wilderness. This matches the OT picture of Israel's behavior during the desert wandering. The author of Hebrews adds the word διό (*dio*, "therefore") after the phrase "forty years," thus making the forty years describe the Jews' misbehavior, not God's wrath.

---

kol" as "A heavenly or divine voice which proclaims God's will or judgment, His deeds and His commandments to individuals or to a number of persons, to rulers, communities, and even to whole nations." Ludwig Blau, "*Bat kol*" in *The Jewish Encyclopedia*; 2:588-592, p. 588.

Three major concepts are drawn from the Psalm: an idea called "today," the "hardening" of hearts, and God's "rest." These concepts are rather intertwined in the section (3:12-4:11), although God's rest comes into focus in chapter four. In the same way that the exhortation of 2:1-4 followed immediately after a long collection of OT verses quoted (1:5-13), so the exhortation of 3:12ff. follows immediately after the long OT quotation of 3:7-11.

C. HOLD FIRM TO THE END (3:12-15)

[12]See to it, brothers, that none of you has a sinful, unbelieving heart that turns away from the living God. [13]But encourage one another daily, as long as it is called Today, so that none of you may be hardened by sin's deceitfulness. [14]We have come to share in Christ if we hold firmly till the end the confidence we had at first. [15]As has just been said:
"Today, if you hear his voice,
do not harden your hearts
as you did in the rebellion."[a]

[a]15 Psalm 95:7,8

Unbelief can spring up in the most unexpected places. Who would have thought that those who personally witnessed the ten plagues on Egypt, the crossing of the Red Sea and the awesome year of events at Mt. Sinai would ever turn away from God with sinful, unbelieving, hard hearts? But they did. The book of Hebrews repeatedly urges its Christian readers not to walk down the same unbelieving path. They are "**brothers**" now. He wants them to remain brothers. He calls them brothers in 3:1, 12; 10:19 and 13:22; as Jesus had called them brothers (2:11-12; see 2:17). Compare 13:1 and 23.

As repentance turns toward the living God, unbelief turns away from him (Compare Acts 3:19; 9:35; 11:21; 20:21; 26:18-20 and 1 Thess 1:19 with Rom 3:12; Gal 4:9; 1 Tim 5:15 and Heb 12:25). Unbelief is a basic sin (John 16:8-9). It is always expressed in self-willed distrust of others. Such a person is unyielding to another's wishes or judgments. All that matters is one's own opinion. This not only damages relations with God. Relations with others degenerate into this same self-centered independence. That is why the alternative to this kind of heart is interdependence (3:13). Christians are not designed to live by themselves. Henry warns us that if we allow ourselves to distrust God, we will soon desert him. When we distrust others, we will readily desert them, too.

Since the designation of God as **"the living God"** was introduced in the scene at Sinai, it has an ominous overtone (Deut 5:26). "It is a dreadful thing to fall into the hands of the living God" (Heb 10:31). It was the expression used in oath statements in court (Matt 26:63). To live for him takes away this fear and lets us serve him gladly (9:14; 12:22; 1 John 4:18). It is a good designation, for God is full of life and all life comes from him (John 5:21; 10:10).

3:13 But encourage one another daily, as long as it is called Today, so that none of you may be hardened by sin's deceitfulness.

Daily we must **encourage one another**. The present tense indicates repetition.[20] If encouragement is only once a month, it will not help carry burdens. If encouragement is only once a week in the general assembly of believers, it will not meet the daily needs of living. The beginning church spent time together daily (Acts 2:46). Besides daily food (Matt 6:11; Acts 6:1; Titus 3:14; James 2:15) there were daily struggles of cross-bearing (Luke 9:23; 1 Cor 15:31; 2 Cor 11:28) and need for daily renewal (2 Cor 4:16) when daily facing the unregenerate world (1 Thess 4:12; 2 Pet 2:8). The work of evangelism was

---

[20]Ellingworth points out that the Greek phrase for "daily" (καθ' ἑκάστην ἡμέραν, *kath' hekastēn hēmeran*) is stronger than the more common phrase for "daily" (*kath' hēmeran*) which is used in 7:27 and 10:11 of the temple liturgy and in Acts for daily Christian activities, i.e., meeting in the temple, eating, teaching, preaching, distribution of funds, study of scriptures, and discussion (Acts 2:46f.; 5:42; 17:11, 17; 19:9; cf. 6:1). Ellingworth, p. 223.

done daily (Acts 2:47; 5:42; 16:5; 17:17; 19:9). One of the great weaknesses of the church today may be this general lack of *daily interdependence* with its accompanying openness in joy and sorrow, in sins and victories.

Westcott reported Bengel's insight that the Greek text (παρακαλεῖτε ἑαυτούς, *parakaleite heautous*) properly says, "Encourage *yourselves*" rather than, "Encourage *one another.*" This "suggests the close unity of the Christian body."[21]

The statement, "As long as it is called Today,"[22] does not sound like the invitation will always exist. One day the end will come when Jesus returns to bring the long-awaited salvation (9:28). Tomorrow may be too late. Since the statement is from the Psalms, the time called "Today" existed in the time of the Psalm writer. Thus the invitation to enter his rest was open previous to the Christian era. Israel's failure did not close heaven forever to wayward mankind.

Muscles become stiff from lack of use, coldness, disease or age. Hearts become hard in the same ways. Here it is attributed to **sin's deceitfulness**. This could say Satan's deceitfulness, for his work is behind all sin. He is the father of lies. Much of his approach is bluffing and empty deception (John 8:44). He wants us to believe that he is far more knowledgeable and powerful than he is. He will flee if resisted (James 4:7). Dods traces the psychological order of hardening thus, "sin, a deceived mind, a hardened heart, unbelief, apostasy."[23]

On the other hand, part of the danger of sin is that we treat it so lightly that we do not take adequate precautions to prevent its terrible work. Wealth also is deceitful, promising what it does not deliver and raising false hopes of its power to satisfy (Matt 13:22). Moses saw through this deception of sin, and he chose to leave all the privileges of the palace of Egypt to escape from it (11:24-26). Adam and Eve did not see

---

[21]Westcott, p. 84.

[22]By using the neuter article (τό, *to*) before the adverb, "today," the Greek construction presents the word "today" here as a one word quotation from the Psalm, rather than simply a part of an ordinary sentence. See BD §267.

[23]Dods, IV:276.

through it and they brought huge evil on the world instead of
the improvement they anticipated (Gen 3). As faith comes by
hearing the message of God and obeying it, so hardening
comes by hearing and not obeying (Rom 10:17; John 15:22-
25).

Pharaoh hardened his own heart early in the plagues (8:15,
32; 9:34). God hardened Pharaoh's heart later when Pharaoh
did not have the strength to keep resisting as he wanted to do
(9:12; 10:1, 20, 27; 11:10). If one persists in an evil direction,
eventually God may help him go farther down that path than
he could go on his own strength. See 2 Thessalonians 2:11.

3:14 We have come to share in Christ if we hold firmly till the end the confidence we had at first.

We have come to share in Christ (lit., "For we have
become partners of Christ"). The noun μέτοχος (*metochos*,
"partner, partaker") is primarily a term found in Hebrews
(1:9; 3:1, 14; 6:4; 12:8). It is only outside of Hebrews in Luke
5:7 of partners in a fishing business. The cognate verb μετέχω
(*metechō*, "to share, have a share") is used in Hebrews of Jesus'
sharing flesh and blood with us (2:17), of infants using milk
(5:13), and of Jesus' not being a part of the tribe of Levi
(7:13). It is outside of Hebrews only in 1 Corinthians 9:10, 22;
10:17, 21 and 30.

The perfect tense of the verb "become" (NIV "**have come
to**") indicates a decisive time when this partnership became a
reality and brings the results of that relationship before us as
well.[24] This dramatic event and new status is given as the reason to beware and to encourage one another. The NIV omits
the connecting word γάρ (*gar*, "because"). The word "partners"
(NIV "share") is a bit ambiguous here. It would mean either
(1) Christ as an equal partner with Christians, or (2) human
partners with one another who both belong to Christ. The first
could be argued from Jesus' brotherhood with man, which has
just been developed in chapter two. He generously shares his

---

[24]At conversion we became *metochoi* ("partners") of the Holy Spirit (6:4).

throne with Christians (Matt 25:21; Rev 3:21). The second could be argued from Jesus' position as high priest and sacrifice as well as author and finisher of our salvation. Davidson remarks that "The idea of a mystical union with Christ is not prominent, if at all found, in the Epistle; he is the Captain, Forerunner, High Priest, Brother, but always distinct. With this understanding, however, partakers *of* (xiii.10) is more probable than partakers *with* Christ (ii.10)."[25] This is about as near as Hebrews comes to the frequent Pauline phrase "in Christ."

The very strong word for "**if**" (*eanper*, discussed above in 3:6) indicates a very real danger of not remaining faithful till the end. A good beginning does not guarantee a good finish. As the king of Israel said, "One who puts on his armor should not boast like one who takes it off" (1 Kgs 20:11). The Hebrew readers have had a good beginning like the church at Ephesus (Heb 10:32-39; Rev 2:4-5). Now they need to finish well.

3:15 As has just been said: "Today, if you hear his voice, do not harden your hearts as you did in the rebellion."

The requirements in the Psalm are applied directly to Christian readers. With this approach the OT is much more of a direct guide for Christians, than simply a record of God's past dealings with his people. In a sense the new covenant is complete in itself. In another sense, the new covenant expresses a continuing record with the old of God's dealings with man. It is a further step in his revelation to man. Hence, the OT should hold much material useful to make today's Christian life count for God. Paul must have been referring to the OT when he made the following statements:

> Everything that was written in the past was written to teach us, so that through endurance and the encouragement of the Scriptures we might have hope (Rom 15:4).
> Do your best to present yourself to God as one approved, a workman who does not need to be ashamed and who correctly

---

[25]A.B. Davidson, *The Epistle to the Hebrews* (Edinburgh: T. & T. Clark, n.d., [Seventeenth thousand,1950]), p. 90.

handles the word of truth (2 Tim 2:15).

The holy Scriptures . . . are able to make you wise for salvation through faith in Christ Jesus. All Scripture is God-breathed and is useful for teaching, rebuking, correcting and training in righteousness, so that the man of God may be thoroughly equipped for every good work (2 Tim 3:15-17).

D. UNBELIEVING ISRAELITES FELL IN THE DESERT
(3:16-19)

[16]**Who were they who heard and rebelled? Were they not all those Moses led out of Egypt?** [17]**And with whom was he angry for forty years? Was it not with those who sinned, whose bodies fell in the desert?** [18]**And to whom did God swear that they would never enter his rest if not to those who disobeyed[a]?** [19]**So we see that they were not able to enter, because of their unbelief.**

[a]*18 Or disbelieved*

With a series of questions the author highlights various facets of the unfaithfulness and fall of those who died in the forty years of desert wandering. What was their sin? "They heard and rebelled." "They sinned." "They disobeyed." What were the terrible consequences of their sin? God "was angry for forty years." Their "bodies fell in the desert." Worst of all, God "swore that they would never enter his rest." Meyer remarks on the dreariness of chapter three, "How dreary those incessant funerals! How monotonous the perpetual sounds of Oriental grief moaning through the camp! What wonder that Psalm 90 [the only Psalm ascribed to Moses], written among such scenes, is so inexpressibly sad!"[26]

These were the very people whom Moses led out of Egypt. These were the people who witnessed the plagues and the

---

[26]F.B. Meyer, *The Way into the Holiest: Expositions of the Epistle to the Hebrews* (Fort Washington, PA: Christian Literature Crusade, 1982), p. 47.

cloud of fire, the manna and the quail, the very people who heard God's voice at Sinai. Westcott makes the horrible observation that, "The Old Testament is in fact a record of successive judgments of Israel out of which a few only were saved."[27] Davidson reminds us that "Israel's defection was universal, and that it happened when the memory of their deliverance from Egypt was fresh."[28]

---

[27]Westcott, p. 79.
[28]A.B. Davidson, p.90.

HEBREWS 4

E. A SABBATH REST FOR THE PEOPLE OF GOD (4:1-5)

[1]Therefore, since the promise of entering his rest still stands, let us be careful that none of you be found to have fallen short of it. [2]For we also have had the gospel preached to us, just as they did; but the message they heard was of no value to them, because those who heard did not combine it with faith.[a] [3]Now we who have believed enter that rest, just as God has said,

"So I declared on oath in my anger,
'They shall never enter my rest.'"[b]

And yet his work has been finished since the creation of the world. [4]For somewhere he has spoken about the seventh day in these words: "And on the seventh day God rested from all his work."[c] [5]And again in the passage above he says, "They shall never enter my rest."

[a]2 Many manuscripts *because they did not share in the faith of those who obeyed*   [b]3 Psalm 95:11; also in verse 5   [c]4 Gen. 2:2

4:1. Therefore, since the promise of entering his rest still stands,

A second major idea is drawn from Psalm 95. God still offers his eternal rest to believers. That idea will be expanded beginning at 4:3. The first two verses may be better understood as the conclusion of chapter three than the beginning of chapter four. In view of the bad experience of the people of Israel, it is very important to be careful that we do not also fall short of this rest. Compare Romans 3:23. If our perseverance should *"fall short"* (ὑστερέω, *hystereō*) like the wine at the

wedding feast in Cana, the party could be ruined (John 2:3).
If our faith runs out like the prodigal son's money, we may
find ourselves very impoverished (Luke 13:14). It is easy for
this deficiency to come on us unnoticed, like the rich young
ruler's lack of freedom from his wealth (Matt 19:20). There is
some encouragement in Jesus' parable of the wedding feast.
When those who were first invited refused to come, the king
did not abort the banquet, but sent out a broader invitation
so that someone would attend his festivities (Matt 22:1-10).
Evidently in heaven God wants to have close to him people
made in his own image.

**let us be careful that none of you be found to have fallen
short of it.**

This is the only place where the NIV translates the verb "to
fear" (φοβέω, *phobeō*) as to "**be careful.**" Elsewhere it translates indicating fear, even terror, and sometimes reverence.
The word and its cognates are used in Hebrews in 2:15; 4:1;
10:27, 31; 11:23, 27; 12:21; 13:6. The phrase, "Be careful," is a
little weak for this verb. Fear is a powerful motive. It is not
wrong to be motivated by fear, especially with so much at
stake. Jesus taught fear as a motive (Matt 10:28; Luke 12:4-5).
It should not be the only motive. Neither should love be the
only motivating force. Ideally every feeling of man should be
stimulated to give a balanced, holistic response of all we are
to whatever God wants us to be.

**4:2 For we also have had the gospel preached to us, just as
they did; but the message they heard was of no value to
them, because those who heard did not combine it with
faith.**

The Israelites **had the gospel preached** to them in the
sense of receiving good news. The verb εὐαγγελίζω (*euangelizō*,
"to bring good news, proclaim") and its noun εὐαγγέλιον
(euangelion, "the good news brought, gospel") are general
words about any good news. They came to be used in a special
sense by Christians to mean the central story about Jesus'

death, burial and resurrection and the subsequent blessings which are offered through those events. Of course, this information about Jesus was not available to people in OT times. The general offer from God was the same, i.e., if his people would be faithful, they could be with him forever in his eternal rest. In this sense, **"we also have had the gospel preached to us, just as they did."** The ultimate offer is the same. The faith is the same. Only the specific deeds by which God asked us to express that faith are different. Compare Galatians 3:8, "The Scripture foresaw that God would justify the Gentiles by faith, and announced the gospel in advance [προευαγγελίζομαι, *proeuangelizomai*, "to proclaim good news in advance"] to Abraham: 'All nations will be blessed through you.'" By using the word "gospel" in Hebrews 4:2 rather than the more general "good news," the NIV has invited misunderstanding. It is curious that the word *euangelion* ("gospel") itself is not used in the book of Hebrews.

The grammatical construction needs to be noted. A perfect tense calls attention to a finished deed plus the new condition resulting from that deed. A perfect periphrastic has a perfect tense participle and some form of the verb, "to be." Thus it goes beyond a perfect tense, by drawing attention to both the finished deed and the result and then emphasizing the result. Thus the special focus is on the end result: we have been evangelized — we have the good news! The similar statement in Hebrews 10:10, "we have been made holy," likewise puts emphasis on the holiness which is the resulting state.

Israel's problem was that they did not **combine** the message with faith. The verb συγκεράννυμι (*synkerannymi*, "to combine, blend") in its only other NT occurrence is used of God's putting the parts of the body together into a harmonious whole (1 Cor 12:24). From this Paul argues that there should be no division in the church. Liddell and Scott suggests that the word was used in classical circles of forming close friendships. Moulton and Milligan reports a medical receipt which has the instructions appended, "Give to drink with raisin wine and honey and pine-cones mixed." A *kerameus* is a potter; *keramos* the potter's clay or pottery; and *keramion*, an earthenware vessel or pot. From this group of words we get the English word "ceramic." The family of words indicates a very thorough mixing.

The point of the statement in Hebrews is that there must be more than casual response to God's message. Faith must be closely bonded with the message in thorough, minute detail. There is no place here to pick and choose which part of the Bible we want and which we will discard. For the gospel to have value, it must have faith mixed all through it. It must be trusted in all its parts. This does not mean that we will not examine the messsage in great detail. The Christians in Berea were commended for examining the Scriptures to see if what Paul said was true (Acts 17:11-12). This undergirded their faith with knowledge. It did not replace it. Westcott says, "The people fell away when the divine voice was still sounding in their ears."[1]

Hedinger had an interesting illustration of the value of faith in hearing the message.

> Food if it is to nourish must go into the blood, and lay itself upon the body. And if the word is to profit it must be transformed through faith, like the juice of food, into the spirit, mind, and will of the man, that the whole man may become as the word is and requires, that is, holy, righteous, pure, and good. Hearing alone profits as little as an undigested food in a bad stomach."[2]

4:3 Now we who have believed enter that rest, just as God has said, "So I declared on oath in my anger, 'They shall never enter my rest.'" And yet his work has been finished since the creation of the world.

In the next several verses the author will explain more about the God's "rest" (4:3-11). The NIV "now" with which

---

[1]Westcott, p. 80.

[2]Davidson reports this illustration from Tholuck, who in turn had copied it from Hedinger's New Testament (1704). A. B. Davidson, p. 91.

verse three begins is too casual. The Greek word *gar* ("because," NIV "now") gives verse three as the reason underlying the previous statement that the gospel is of no value unless mixed with faith. Believers have done this and are on the way toward God's rest. The phrase **"we who have believed"** is an aorist tense. By a decisive act of belief these became followers of Christ. They are now **entering**[3] (present tense of continuing action) the "rest" which God withheld from the unbelieving Israelites. The entrance has begun, but it is not viewed as completed until they have remained faithful to the very end (3:14; 4:1). The people of Israel were also in the process of entering the promised land when their sin cut them down. Faith was the issue in the Psalm also, which is quoted again.

4:4 For somewhere he has spoken about the seventh day in these words: "And on the seventh day God rested from all his work."

The text cites Genesis 2:2 to explain that God created the world in six days and rested on the seventh day. In the phrase **"the seventh day,"** the NIV adds the word "day" which is assumed. Turner says that "In dates in the papyri the word ἡμέρα ["day"] is almost always omitted."[4] Ellingworth is very perceptive in noting what this passage of Hebrews does *not* contain in its use of Genesis 2:2. Unlike Philo there is no speculation on the nature of the "rest." Unlike later Jewish and Christian thinking there is no expectation of a thousand years of rest before the end. There is no trace of allegory, even as much as in 2 Peter 3:8. There is no hint that God is now inactive. There is no intermeshing with the Christ event to which the author will not return till 4:14.[5]

---

[3]A variant reading gives a present subjunctive form, which makes the statement, "We are entering" into an exhortation, "Let us enter."

[4]Turner, Moulton, p. 17.

[5]Ellingworth, pp. 248-249.

4:5 And again in the passage above he says, "They shall never enter my rest."

In the incident recorded in Numbers 13-14 God prohibited Israel from entering Canaan. This evidently means that they could not enter heaven either. Later, in the time of David,[6] God explained that he had sworn that those unfaithful Israelites would never enter his rest.

F. A SABBATH-REST REMAINS (4:6-11)

[6]**It still remains that some will enter that rest, and those who formerly had the gospel preached to them did not go in, because of their disobedience. [7]Therefore God again set a certain day, calling it Today, when a long time later he spoke through David, as was said before:**

"Today, if you hear his voice,

do not harden your hearts."[a]

[8]**For if Joshua had given them rest, God would not have spoken later about another day. [9]There remains, then, a Sabbath-rest for the people of God; [10]for anyone who enters God's rest also rests from his own work, just as God did from his. [11]Let us, therefore, make every effort to enter that rest, so that no one will fall by following their example of disobedience.**

[a]7 Psalm 95:7,8

4:6 It still remains that some will enter that rest, and those who formerly had the gospel preached to them did not go in, because of their disobedience.

Yet the same Psalm said that if the Psalm hearers did not

---

[6]This is the only place in Hebrews where the human author of a Scripture is named. Ordinarily the idea is the only important consideration in an Old Testament quotation. Thus the Holy Spirit (3:7; 10:15) or God the Father (1:1, 5, 6, 13; 3:18; 4:3, 7-8; 5:5; 7:21; 8:8; see 6:13; 13:5) are usually considered to be the authors of OT verses. Here, however, the date of the passage is important, to show that it falls chronologically after the time of the entrance into Canaan. So David is named as the author.

harden their hearts, there was still an opportunity to enter God's rest. From the time of Joshua to the time of David, the doorway remained open to those who did not disobey God.

4:7 Therefore God again set a certain day, calling it Today, when a long time later he spoke through David, as was said before: "Today, if you hear his voice, do not harden your hearts."

Verse seven concludes that God set a certain "day" called "Today" in which he would allow people into his rest. Thus there remains a "rest" for the people of God. Dods refers to "the grand passage on God's Rest in Philo, De Cherubim, c. Xxvi., and also Barnabas xv."[7]

4:8 For if Joshua had given them rest, God would not have spoken later about another day.

The Greek name Ἰησοῦς (*Iēsous*) is the same spelling for **Joshua** and for Jesus. Ellingworth presents three ways of understanding the name here. It may point to: (1) the historical Joshua; (2) Jesus Christ, not Joshua; or (3) the historical Joshua, but with some kind of play on the word thus alluding to Jesus as well. The LXX used the Greek name *Iēsous* for the several different Hebrew spellings of the name Joshua: יְהוֹשֻׁעַ, יְהוֹשֻׁעַ (*yehoshua'*), יֵשׁוּעַ (*yeshua'*), etc.[8] The point of the passage is that if the Israelites upon entering Canaan under the leadership of Joshua had entered the "rest" God spoke about, then he would not have spoken later in David's day about another day of rest. This later statement shows that there still remains a "rest," even a "Sabbath-rest," for the people of God. God's blessings are not spiritual alone; he gives physical blessings also.

The fact that Israel's entrance into Canaan was not the same as entrance into God's eternal rest may be established

---

[7]Dods, p. 281.
[8]Henry Redpath, *Supplement* to Edwin Hatch and Henry Redpath, *A Concordance to the Septuagint*, two volumes including Supplement (Graz, Austria: Akademische Druck- U. Verlagsanstalt, 1954), (II) Supplement, page 84.

along other lines. There are numerous OT passages which predict that God would regather his people and bring them back to the land. Many of these passages use terminology that cannot describe a literal return to the physical land on the east end of the Mediterranean Sea. For example, see Isaiah 10:20-23; Ezekiel 20:34-38; 37:21-25.

4:9 There remains, then, a Sabbath-rest for the people of God;

The "rest" is a σαββατισμός (sabbatismos, "**Sabbath-rest**"). This is the only place in the OT or NT where this word occurs. Its cognate verb, σαββατίζω (sabbatizō, "to observe the Sabbath") appears in the LXX only a very few times; both the people and the land are said to rest. Elsewhere the word κατάπαυσις (katapausis, "rest") has been used (3:11, 18; 4:1, 3 [twice], 5, 10 and 11) and its verb καταπαύω (katapauō, "to rest") three times (4:4, 8, 10).[9] Moulton and Milligan logically suggest that the author coined the word.[10] Lampe shows that the unusual word was picked up by the church fathers. Westcott reminds us that "The Jewish teachers dwelt much upon the symbolical meaning of the Sabbath as prefiguring 'the world to come.'"[11]

Some groups today want to observe a seventh day of rest as a "Sabbath." The Sabbath was part of the old covenant. It is not in the new covenant. Like many things in the OT it point-

---

[9]LS appears to understand the noun κατάπαυσις and the verb καταπαύω more of a place of rest or residence, in contrast to the pair of similar words, the noun ἀνάπαυσις ("rest") and the verb ἀναπαύω ("to rest"), more of ceasing from bodily activity. Deut 12:9 and Ps 131:14 support the former definition, while Rev 4:8 and 14:13 support the latter. Ruth 3:1 argues against this distinction. Jesus' famous invitation in Matt 11:28 could be understood either way.

[10]Ellingworth says sabbatismos occurs here for the first time in any Greek literature, citing Moffatt, Spicq and Lane for who agree. Ellingworth, p. 255.

[11]Westcott, p. 98. For further information about the Jewish ideas about the Sabbath prefiguring the world to come see the standard reference works. There is an anthology on the practice, art and theology of the Sabbath by Abraham Millgram, Sabbath: The Day of Delight (Philadelphia: The Jewish Publication Society of America, 5712-1952).

ed forward to the ultimate reality in Christ, in this instance the "Sabbath-rest" in heaven. The book of Hebrews shows that Jesus has brought the promised new covenant which replaces the old (8:1-13 and Jer 31:31-34). A covenant or will is an adequate entity in itself. A second will is executed according to what it says, not according to what any previous wills had said. There are no items carried over from previous wills unless these items are also spelled out in the new will. So it is with the new covenant which Jesus brought. Whatever the OT said was binding then; whatever the NT says is binding today. The NT has dropped many things that were in the old. Animal sacrifices are gone. The tabernacle and temple are gone. A special physical land is gone. Priests are gone, as a separate class of people. There is no hint that somehow some things are still binding from the OT. God has canceled the OT as a covenant, i.e., the written code, nailing it to the cross of Christ. The Sabbath day is specifically named, along with foods and festivals and New Moon celebrations, as one of those things which has no value today (Col 2:13-17). These things are understood as mere "shadows" of the reality which is found in Christ. The "rest" promised in Hebrews four is the eternal rest with God when the labors of this life are finished.

4:10 for anyone who enters God's rest also rests from his own work, just as God did from his.

There is an obvious connection with the seventh day rest which God required in the ten commandments. When God spoke the ten commandments at Mt. Sinai, he explained that he was basing the people's six days of work and the seventh day of rest on his own activity in creation (Exod 20:8-11). This is also the pattern for the eternal rest. First the work, then the rest. Thus, "**anyone who enters God's rest also rests from his own work just as God did from his**" (4:10). The section has made clear that there is work now. Effort must be exerted in remaining faithful and helping others to remain faithful.

Indeed, that is the focus of the very next verse, "**Let us, therefore, make every effort to enter that rest.**" The only alternative is to **"fall"**[12] by **disobedience**. The fall of the Jewish people by their rejection of Jesus is much more fully expanded in Romans 9-11. Those chapters describe "the great transition," as God turns from special treatment of the physical nation of Jews as his people under the old covenant to special treatment of the spiritual nation of Christians as his people under the new covenant. Those chapters conclude the doctrinal section of Romans (chapters 1-8) and prepare for the practical section (chapters 12-16).

4:11 Let us, therefore, make every effort to enter that rest, so that no one will fall by following their example of disobedience.

God's people must "make every effort" to enter God's rest. The word σπουδάζω (*spoudazō*, "to hurry, make every effort") and its family of words is used in the NT most of the time where someone is traveling or urged to travel. Terminology of travel is appropriate here for those "entering" that rest.

The readers are warned that they must not follow the **example** (ὑπόδειγμα, *hypodeigma*) of disobedience of the early Jews. Note these other uses of the same word. The tabernacle sanctuary was a "copy" (*hypodeigma*) and shadow of what is in heaven (8:5). These "copies" of the heavenly things had to be purified with animal sacrifices (9:23). Here as in 2 Peter 2:6 the word is used as an example of something bad. The NT elsewhere used it of good examples (John 13:15 and James 5:10). The rest of the NT uses this word of good examples to follow (John 13:15; James 5:10 and 2 Pet 2:6). The related words δεῖγμα (*deigma*, "example," in Jude 7) and δειγματιζω (*deigmatizō*, "to expose to public disgrace," in Matt 1:19 and Col 2:15) carry a bad connotation; while the frequently used word δείκνυμι (*deiknymi*, "to show, explain") does not.

---

[12]After listing Christian things to do Peter says, "Therefore, my brothers, be all the more eager to make your calling and election sure. For if you do these things, you will never fall" (2 Pet 1:10).

The NIV embellishes this verse a bit in trying to smooth it out. The NIV "fall by following" is in the Greek a single word "fall"; i.e., "so that no one might fall in that example of disobedience." The readers' problem is to avoid falling. The text has introduced an example of others before who fell. Thus the NIV adds the words "by following" as though the readers' fall would be by following the earlier fall of Israel.

G. THE MESSAGE FROM GOD DOES ITS PART
TO SAVE US (4:12-13)

[12]**For the word of God is living and active. Sharper than any double-edged sword, it penetrates even to dividing soul and spirit, joints and marrow; it judges the thoughts and attitudes of the heart. [13]Nothing in all creation is hidden from God's sight. Everything is uncovered and laid bare before the eyes of him to whom we must give account.**

4:12 For the word of God is living and active.
The word "**therefore**" (*gar*) connects 4:12-13 to the previous statements, as the following section on Jesus as our high priest is linked to these with the word οὖν (*oun*, "therefore;" see 4:14). **The word of God** is given as a powerful aid in entering God's rest. It helps us to become faithful and to remain faithful "holding firmly till the end." Paul wrote,

> Therefore, my dear friends, as you have always obeyed — not only in my presence, but now much more in my absence — continue to work out your salvation with fear and trembling, for it is God who works in you to will and to act according to his good purpose (Phil 2:12-13).

Tobin has demonstrated that the Greek word λόγος (*logos*, "word") "has a wide variety of meanings and is common to all periods of Greek literature, both prose and verse."[13] In gener-

---

[13]Thomas H. Tobin, "Logos," IV:348-356 in *The Anchor Bible Dictionary*, six volumes, edited by David Freedman, et al (New York: Doubleday, 1992),

al, the NT uses this wide variety. He says:

> It can mean a statement (Luke 20:20), an assertion (Matt
> 15:12), a command (Luke 4:36), a report or story (Matt 28:15),
> a proverb or saying (John 4:37), an oracle or prophecy (John
> 2:22), a speech (Matt 15:12), or the matter under discussion
> (Mark 9:10; John 14:24). . . . It can be used of *written* words and
> speeches, as well as of the separate books of a larger work (Acts
> 1:1; Heb 5:11). . . . also . . . to mean "ground" (Acts 10:29) or
> "reason" (Acts 18:14) for something. . . . In many cases the
> "word of God" is simply the Christian message, the gospel.[14]

The "word of God," has been understood in this context to
mean (1) Jesus; (2) the Bible; or (3) the message from God.
Jesus is called the "the word" in John 1:1 and "the word of
God" in Revelation 19:13. "The word of God" is a fitting designation for the collection of sacred Scriptures. But the NT
writings were not yet fully collected when Hebrews was written. Furthermore, the *logos* was just mentioned in 4:2 as something that was heard. In 13:7 the readers are urged to
"Remember your leaders, who spoke the word of God to
you." The message from God has been in the writer's mind
from the opening verse (1:1-2; 5, 6, 8, 10, 13; 2:1-2, 6; 3:1, 7,
16, 18). Hence, the third view appears more fitting. The word
logos appears again in 4:13 in the sense of a settlement of an
account. Compare Matthew 18:23 and 25:19.

The Holy Spirit surely works on people's hearts previous
to their knowing the gospel (John 16:7-11). Just as surely he
who gave us the Bible will work effectively in believing minds
that are filled with thoughts from the Bible. One who does
not read the Bible is no better off than one who cannot read
the Bible. Perhaps he is no better off than one who will not
read the Bible. It hardly demonstrates faith in God to ignore
the tools he has given us to guide us.

The message of this book is **living and active**. This is no

---

IV:348. See also H.D. McDonald, "Word, Word of God, Word of the Lord,"
in *The Evangelical Dictionary of Theology*, pp. 1185-1188.
     [14]Tonin, ibid., IV:351.

dead, dry, dusty curio. It is **living** (Deut 32:47; Ps 19:7ff.; Isa 55:11) like the living God (3:12; etc.), like the living Son who intercedes for us (7:8, 25). The word stands prominantly at the beginning of the sentence. Moulton and Milligan found the word "active" (ἐνεργής, *energēs*) used of a mill that was in "working" order, of "wrought" iron, and of "tilled" land. Lampe found it used in the church fathers to describe an "active" life and a "fervent" prayer.

Sharper than any double-edged sword, it penetrates even to dividing soul and spirit, joints and marrow; it judges the thoughts and attitudes of the heart.
The word of God is "**sharper** than any double-edged sword." Dods says the phrase "sharper than" "is a more forcible comparative than the genitive [by itself]." Then he points to Luke 16:8 and 2 Cor 12:13.[15] The sword was the most widely used weapon of the ancient and medieval worlds. The two-edged sword is a common simile for sharpness (Prov 5:4; Rev 1:16; etc.). Gordon says,

> "The sword . . . is the most frequently mentioned weapon in the Bible. The earliest swords in the ancient world were usually straight, double-edged and more akin to daggers, being used for stabbing . . . [In the last half of the 2nd millennium BC] the longer-bladed sword began to be used widely. . . . In both Testaments the sword is frequently used, by metonymy, for war, or as a symbol for the word of God."[16]

The sword was primarily used for **penetrating** and cutting. Here the focus is on penetration. Beginning with psychological terms, "soul and spirit," the text moves to physiological terms, "joints and marrow." One would expect the reverse order. Finally, the description proceeds to the most secret part of man, "the thoughts and attitudes of the heart." This is

---

[15]Dods, p. 281.
[16]R.P. Gordon, "Armour and Weapons," in *The New Bible Dictionary*, second edition, edited by J.D. Douglas, et al; (Wheaton: Tyndale House Publishers, Inc., 1982), p. 84.

so thorough that nothing is hidden from God's sight.

The sword was a feared weapon, often used in threats (Exod 5:3, 21; 15:9; etc.). Perhaps the power of words made the sword an apt image of the tongue. "Reckless words pierce like a sword, but the tongue of the wise brings healing" (Prov 12:18). Jesus is often pictured with a sword coming out of his mouth (Isa 49:2; Rev 1:16; 2:16; 19:15, 21). No one ever spoke with as much power as Jesus.

The phrase, "soul and spirit" is not designed to be a full psychological analysis of man any more than "body, soul and spirit" has that purpose in 1 Thessalonians 5:23. They seem to be simply a way of designating the whole of a person. "Soul" and "spirit" are put in parallel lines as synonyms in Job 7:11 and Isaiah 26:9. The point here is to show that nothing is beyond the penetrating power of the word of God. A sword not only penetrates joints, where bones join, but into the center of the bones, into the **marrow** itself. So powerful is God's word. It penetrates the inmost parts of a person. Those who heard Peter's message about Jesus on the day of Pentecost "were cut to the heart" and cried out "What shall we do?" (Acts 2:37). The jailer at Philippi found the same deep probing of the message (Acts 16:30).[17]

In its irresistable penetration the word **judges** as well. It lays bare the **thoughts and attitudes of the heart**. See Luke 2:35; John 3:19-21; 1 Corinthians 14:22-25. When we read other literature, we are in control. When we read the Bible, it is in control. It lets us see things in ourselves that are otherwise hidden from our own eyes. The Bible pronounces sentence on secret thoughts. We know it knows, and we know it is right in what it discloses. This is exactly what we would expect from literature which God generated. "God knows the thoughts of man" (Ps 94:11). See also Proverbs 15:26. Jesus

---

[17]Psalm 119 discusses the law of God in all 176 verses. It focuses on the guiding, nurturing helpfulness of the words of God, and does not address this probing, penetrating power. On the contrary, this paragraph in Hebrews does just the opposite by noting the penetration rather than the guidance of the word of God.

knew what people were thinking when he was with them even when they did not tell him (Matt 9:4; 12:25; Luke 9:46-48; John 2:23-25). There are no private thoughts and feelings. God knows them all. Dods says,

> The word of God coming to men in the offer of good of the highest kind tests their real desires and inmost intentions. When fellowship with God is made possible through His gracious offer, the inmost heart of man is sifted; and it is infallibly discovered and determined whether he truly loves the good and seeks it, or shrinks from accepting it as his eternal heritage.[18]

The **heart** represents the center of one's personal and moral life. "Above all else, guard your heart, for it is the well-spring of life" (Prov 4:23). In the new covenant God writes his laws directly on the heart (8:10; 10:16). At the end of this chapter the author encourages believers to approach God confidently in prayer, but in this approach the heart must be true or genuine (10:22). "Blessed are the pure in heart, for they shall see God" (Matt 5:8). Such hearts are continually being strengthened by God's grace (13:9). The warning not to harden the heart was repeatedly quoted in Hebrews 3-4 (3:8, 15; 4:7). Their hearts were inclined to go astray from God (3:10; Matt 13:15; 15:8; Mark 3:5). The readers, too, are warned against having a sinful, unbelieving heart that turned away from God (3:12).

4:13 Nothing in all creation is hidden from God's sight. Everything is uncovered and laid bare before the eyes of him to whom we must give account.

Nothing in all creation is hidden from God's sight. This is consistent with his having created all things. It is not consistent with the idea which some scholars hold that God is simply a creation of man's fertile imagination. Both words, "thoughts" (ἐνθύμησις, *enthymēsis*) and "attitudes" (ἔννοια, *ennoia*), have the preposition "in" (ἐν, *en*) prefixed to them.

---

[18]Dods, p. 28.

Perhaps this is to emphasize that these are the deepest, most inward, feelings and musings of a person. Even these are open before God. "He reveals deep and hidden things; he knows what lies in darkness, and light dwells with him" (Dan 2:22). "Therefore judge nothing before the appointed time; wait till the Lord comes. He will bring to light what is hidden in darkness and will expose the motives of men's hearts. At that time each will receive his praise from God" (1 Cor 4:5). One of the deceptions of man is his belief that he can keep his private thoughts concealed from God.

Everything is uncovered and laid bare before him. The word "**uncovered**" (γυμνός, *gymnos*), could be translated "naked, bare, uncovered, without an outer garment." The Greeks exercised and performed many gymnastic sports with no clothes at all so as to remove all hindrance. A lightly armed soldier was also considered "naked." In this context it is clear that no one should think he can conceal anything from God.

The verb τραχηλίζω (*trachēlizō*, "**laid bare**"), here a perfect participle, occurs nowhere else in the NT or LXX. Liddell and Scott explains that it means either "to take by the throat," or "to bend back the victim's neck, hence to expose to view, lay bare." The noun to which it is related is clearly τράχηλος (*trachēlos*, "the throat, neck") which occurs several times in the NT. This second word is an even bolder picture of man's helplessness in the hands of God. It is as though he either has us by the throat like a wrestler or has our neck bent back ready to slay us as an animal sacrifice. Men may prance a little now in insolent arrogance, but there will be none of that in the judgment day.

H. JESUS, THE GREAT HIGH PRIEST (4:14-16)

[14]Therefore, since we have a great high priest who has gone through the heavens,[a] Jesus the Son of God, let us hold firmly to the faith we profess. [15]For we do not have a high priest who is unable to sympathize with our weaknesses, but

we have one who has been tempted in every way, just as we are — yet was without sin. ¹⁶Let us then approach the throne of grace with confidence, so that we may receive mercy and find grace to help us in our time of need.

ᵃ*14 Or gone into heaven*

There are three major sources of power in Christianity that are evident here. The powerful book is seen in 4:12-13; the powerful Lord in 4:14-15; and the powerful privilege of prayer in 4:16. The three sections are linked with the conjunction *oun* (NIV, "then") beginning 4:14 and 16.

4:14 Therefore, since we have a great high priest who has gone through the heavens, Jesus the Son of God, let us hold firmly to the faith we profess.

This verse moves into the heart of the book. Jesus is seen as the Christians' **high priest**. He was already presented as high priest in 2:17-3:1, "that he might make atonement for the sins of the people." From here to the end of chapter seven various aspect of Jesus' priesthood are explained.

The structure of the sentence gathers several traits of Jesus together as a basis for the exhortation to hold firmly to the faith. He is a "great high priest" (ἀρχιερεὺς μέγας, *archiereus megas*). This unusual tautology, joining "great" with "high priest," occurs again in 1 Maccabees 13:42 of Simon Maccabee. Jesus will be called a "great priest" in 10:21. Just how great is seen in the further list of traits.

First, he **has gone through the heavens**. His work of atoning was not done on earth. His work was done beyond the heavens. He went into the very presence of God. "He went through the greater and more perfect tabernacle that is not man-made, that is to say, not a part of this creation" (9:11). The Jewish high priest went through the earthly tabernacle to get to the inmost room to carry out his mission on the Day of Atonement (9:1-14; Lev 16:1-34). His work was only a shadow and copy of what Jesus did (8:3-6; 10:1-5). Jesus "went through" something to do his work. The perfect tense shows not only the deed of passing through, but also the new status or results from that achievement. An aorist tense would have presented the deed without drawing attention to the results of that deed. Jesus not only crossed the gulf between God and man; he has bridged the gulf to God's presence. No OT high priest obtained this result.

Since the structure of heaven is far out on the edge of our comprehension, it may be more prudent to be cautious and reserved in handling specialized terminology about it. Gaster indicates some of the wide ranging imagery used to describe the heavens as a metal strip, as a curtain, as a garment, with windows, storehouses, stages and pillars.[19] To this one might add its armies, its gates and doors, its foundations, its bottles, etc.[20] Paul was caught up "to the third heaven" (2 Cor 12:2). Extrabiblical sources have embellished biblical sketches far beyond biblical data.[21] It is very crude to think that Jesus journeyed like a space traveller through a series of physical "heavens" to get to God's presence. Yet this highly physical picture seems to be very appealing to scholars who draw up various

---

[19]T.H. Gaster, "Heaven," in *IDB*; 2:551-552.

[20]See Eliezer Katz, editor, *A Topical Concordance of the Old Testament* (Jerusalem, "Kiryat-Sefer" Ltd., 1992), pp. 238, 439, 635, 891.

[21]For Rabbinic ideas of heaven see "God and the Universe," chapter II in A. Cohen's, *Everyman's Talmud*, pp. 27-58. The Rabbis found seven biblical names for the heavens and the corresponding seven strata of the earth expressed in seven biblical names for the earth. The world was founded on the Eben Shetiyyah, i.e., the "Foundation Stone" on which the ark of the covenant had rested; hence, this was the center of the earth (Yoma 54b in *The Babylonian Talmud*, edited by I. Epstein; London: Soncino Press, *Seder Mo'ed*, III,257). See also Chagigah 12a-13a, 14b in The Babylonian Talmud, Seder Mo'ed, IV,66-81, 90-91, especially note #10 on page 90. Robert Oden reports that "Von Rad, Eliade, and others . . . claim that historiographical, functional, and soteriological concerns dominate in the religion of Israel as speculative, cosmological concerns dominate elsewhere, for example in ancient Egypt, Mesopotamia, or India." Oden objects to this view, asserting that "the ancient Jewish community which based its beliefs and rituals upon the Hebrew Bible clearly saw cosmogony as basic to its religion." See Robert Oden "Cosmogony, Cosmology," pp. I:1162-1171, in *The Anchor Bible Dictionary*, I:1163. *The Jewish Encyclopedia* has its main discussion of the seven heavens under the article, "Angelology," by Kaufmann Kohler, I:583-597.

physical sketches of the "ancient" ideas of the heavens. How could the Holy Spirit say anything at all about the heavens without appearing too physical in whatever description he gave? If we scarcely understand earthly things, how far short do we come in grasping heavenly things? Somewhere we cross over beyond stark bare literalism into figurative language.

Second, he is **Jesus**. It has been argued that the name "Jesus" refers to his humanity, while the name "Christ" refers to his deity. If that is the case, then both his humanity and deity are shown here. As high priest he is the God-man, the only person in existence who has this duality in himself. It is difficult to support this distinction on the basis of the data in the book of Hebrews. "Jesus" appears ten times (2:9; 3:1; 4:14; 6:20; 7:22; 10:19; 12:2, 24; 13:12, 20).[22] "Christ" appears nine times (3:6, 14; 5:5; 6:1; 9:11, 14, 24, 28; 11:26). "Jesus" and "Christ" appear together three times (10:10; 13:8, 21). The NIV sometimes adds the names "Jesus" or "Christ" when the Greek text simply said "he."[23] The same idea is often associated with each designation. There is "the blood of Jesus" (10:19) and "the blood of Christ" (9:14). Both "Jesus" (4:14; 6:20) and "Christ" enter the sanctuary (9:24). Both "Jesus" (8:6; 12:24) and "Christ" (9:15) are seen as mediator of the new covenant. It was certainly a divine, not a human, person who was made a little lower than the angels. But he is called "Jesus" (2:9). The differentiation does not seem to hold in the book of Hebrews.

It might be argued from the data in the book of Hebrews that the name "Jesus" is used when the idea of salvation from sins is being discussed (all uses of the name "Jesus," but 13:20). This would be appropriate, since the name "Jesus" points to his saving us from our sins (Matt 1:21). The name "Christ" is sometimes used when our service is in mind (3:6, 14; perhaps 9:14. See 11:26). The word "Christ" means

---

[22]The name "Jesus" ('Ιησοῦς, *Iēsous*) occurs in 4:8, but probably means Joshua, not Jesus Christ.

[23]The NIV adds the name "Jesus" sometimes when the Greek text has "he:" 2:11; 3:3; 5:7; 7:24; 8:6. It adds the name "Christ" in 9:15, 26; 10:5.

anointed or inaugurated for some role or mission. Hence it may suggest the mission of serving God.

Third, he is **the Son of God**. The idea of Jesus as "Son" dominated the first two chapters. The message of God through the Son supersedes all that was said before through the prophets (1:1-2). The Son dominates all of redemptive history (1:2-4). The Son is vastly superior to angels (1:4-14). Infractions against the new covenant which he brought are far more dangerous than infractions against the old covenant which angels brought (2:1-4). The role of mankind at the head of all creation is only fully met in Jesus, the supreme "Son of man" (2:5-10). He became a brother with the sons God brings to glory (2:11-13) and broke Satan's power over them (2:14-18). The Son's faithfulness was greater than a servant's faithfulness (3:1-6). At 3:7 the idea of sonship falls out of view. Jesus will be called "Son" only a few more times (5:5, 8; 7:28), but "Son of God" in horror at his being scorned by those who once believed (6:6 and 10:29). Once Melchizedek will be compared to "the Son of God" (7:3).

4:15 For we do not have a high priest who is unable to sympathize with our weaknesses, but we have one who has been tempted in every way, just as we are — yet was without sin.

Fourth, he is perfect. Although **tempted in every way** we are tempted, he **was without sin**. In 2:17 he was called a "merciful and faithful high priest." His faithfulness has already been established (3:1-6). His mercy will now be expanded beyond the statement of 2:18, "Because he himself suffered when he was tempted, he is able to help those who are being tempted." He not only was tempted, he was tempted in every way, just as we are. Yet he remained without sin. His sinlessness is repeated in 7:26 and 9:14. It is hard for us to imagine how powerful temptation can become, for we collapse before it reaches its peak. He did not. Dods makes the observation that if Jesus would have sinned, "he would have had a thousandfold better excuse than ever man had."[24]

---

[24]Dods, p. 284.

Fifth, he is **able to sympathize** with our weaknesses. This is presented in a negative way. He was **not** a high priest who is **unable to sympathize with our weaknesses**. It might be supposed that a high priest so grand that he could enter God's presence was so superior to us that he could not understand our lowly struggles on earth. The word συμπαθέω (*sympatheō*, "to sympathize") appears in the NT again only in Hebrews 10:34. The Hebrew readers would certainly identify with this idea. In their early days as Christians they were mistreated and stood side by side with others who were abused. They had even "sympathized" with people in prison (10:32-36; see also 13:3).

Perhaps the deep force of this word is best seen in its uncompounded form, "to suffer." *Paschō* is "to suffer;" *sympatheō*, "to suffer with, or sympathize." Westcott says "It expresses not simply the compassion of one who regards suffering from without, but the feeling of one who enters into the suffering and makes it his own."[25] Suffering is widely discussed in the NT. Usually it is the suffering of Jesus which is addressed, although he suffered for the benefit of mankind. In Hebrews suffering is always the suffering of Christ (2:8-10; 5:8; 9:26; 13:12) with the one exception noted above (10:32-34).

He sympathizes with our **weaknesses** (ἀσθένεια, *astheneia*), not with our deliberate hard-hearted sinfulness. H.G. Link says that in classical usage the word is applied to any kind of weakness, primarily to bodily weakness, especially sickness, but also to the frailty of women, of human nature, even of economic weakness, rarely also of moral weakness.[26] The NT does use the idea of moral weakness. One of the beautiful realities of Christianity is that Jesus took our "infirmities" onto himself (Matt 8:17). When Paul was struggling, God reassured him that, "My strength is made perfect in [human] weakness" (2 Cor 12:9; see 13:9). The case of Israel's behavior in the desert was not weakness, but hardened, long-term

---

[25]Westcott, p. 106.
[26]NIDNTT, 3:993-996.

disobedient rebellion. Weakness of faith is one thing (Rom 14:1; 15:1; 1 Cor 8:9-12). Lack of faith is quite another. Weakness grieves God; hardness angers him. He will help the weak. He will expel the disobedient. To one he offers mercy and grace (4:16; 11:34; Rom 8:26). To the other he promises harsh judgment (3:11, 18; 12:10:31).

4:16 Let us then approach the throne of grace with confidence, so that we may receive mercy and find grace to help us in our time of need.

Based on Jesus' function as our high priest, Christians are encouraged in general to **"hold firmly to the faith we profess"** (v. 14), and specifically to **"approach the throne of grace with confidence."** Again in 6:18 it is left to us to "take **hold** of" what God has offered us. Because Jesus has gone into God's presence, Christians can come with **confidence** into his presence. Later, this will be called "a new and living way opened for us" which we can confidently enter (10:19-22). Paul explained that in Christ and through faith in Christ "we may approach God with freedom and confidence" (Eph 3:12) To all who ask he gives generously without finding fault (James 1:5). John went even farther when he said, "This is the confidence we have in approaching God: that if we ask anything according to his will, he hears us. And if we know that he hears us—whatever we ask—we know that we have what we asked of him" (1 John 5:14-15). The privilege of prayer was designed to be used.

Meyer cites William Law's words, "Reason always follows the state of the heart." Then he adds his own observation on why an exhortation to prayer follows the report of Israel's unfaithfulness,

> More scepticism may be traced to a neglected prayer closet than to the arguments of infidels or the halls of secularists. First, men depart from God; then they deny Him. And, therefore, for the most part, unbelief will not yield to clever sermons on the evidences, but to home thrusts that pierce the

points of the harness to the soul within. . . . The hardest hearts were soft once, and the softest may get hard.[27]

It is Jesus' person and performance that makes our salvation secure, not our own. People know this intuitively as John explained in 1 John 3:20-23. There are two possible centers of attention for Christians. When we focus on ourselves, our hearts condemn us. We know we are imperfect and not worthy of heaven. But God sees the bigger picture. "He knows everything." When we focus on Jesus, our hearts do not condemn us. We know he is perfect in every way. Hence, "we have confidence before God." We pray with "confidence" (παρρησία, *parrēsia* in Heb 4:16 and 1 John 3:21). Our prayers are answered, because we keep doing (Greek present tense verbs) his commands and the things that please him.

Moulton and Milligan found the word **"help"** (βοήθεια, *boētheia*, "help, rescue") and its verb βοηθέω (*boētheō*, "to help") "perpetually recurring at the end of petitions" in papyrus material. Jesus is able to help (2:18). Now we see him offering to help (4:16). Verb and noun forms of this word abound in the LXX, but not in the NT. A quote from Psalm 118:6-7 is the only other place they appear in Hebrews, "The Lord is my helper; I will not be afraid" (13:6). The idea of "help" presupposes that we are trying to overcome the weaknesses and cannot do so on our own. It does not suggest that we passively come to God pleading that he do for us what we refuse to allow him to do through us.

Prayer is designed in part **"to help us in our time of need."** If καιρός (*kairos*, "time, favorable time") "characterizes a critical situation, one which demands a decision,"[28] as Hahn puts it, then *eu-kairos* ("favorable opportunity"), is a wonderful opportunity. Its family of words is used in this sense in the NT, although these words do not occur again in Hebrews. The "time of need" may imply that we are even less able than

---

[27]F.B. Meyer, pp. 51-52.
[28]H.C. Hahn, "Time: *kairos*," in NIDNTT, 3:833-839, p. 833.

normal to pray right, think right or even have the inclination right which would lead us to pray. We may be in trouble, but he understands the clumsy cry of our heart, and gives the necessary help.

In our finest moments needs are not seen as crushing burdens to be stoically borne, but opportunities to link with God in bringing his mercy and grace to bear in human situations. This is true whether the need is one's own personal need or a need of others. The Savior made the vessels brim with the best wine only when Cana's own supply ran short. This gives a whole new dimension to the idea of praying continually (1 Thess 5:17).

Nor are these needs said to be primarily "physical needs" of health. The larger the needs which we can see, the greater the urgency for our diligent praying about those needs. This ministry of praying for others exercises one of the finest privileges of the Christian priesthood. Jesus' work as high priest was not simply to change us into his people, but to use us as his people to meet the needs of others by our alert requests in prayer. There is one critical limitation. God leaves the initiative to us. He will help us when we approach him. He does not promise to drag us into some prayer endeavor which we have not willingly chosen. How happy are the growing believers whose eyes see ever larger needs, whose prayers direct the power of God to meet those needs and whose hands reach out with divine mercy and grace. Needs become especially acute when they rise from being tempted. Jesus may have been able to overcome all temptation, but the rest of us are not. We need one another's alertness and assistance. With this offer of mercy and grace we are better able to restore those who are caught in a sin (Gal 6:1-2). Grace is given as needs arise. It is not stored up beforehand.

H.H. Esser says words about **grace** are about things which "produce well-being."[29] Though Jesus came in the first place by the grace (χάρις, *charis*) of God (2:9), one could easily miss his grace (12:15), or insult the Spirit of grace (10:29). The

---

[29]H.H. Esser, "Grace," in NIDNTT, 2:115-124.

heart is strengthened by grace (13:9) so we can serve God acceptably (12:28). The NIV of 12:28 says "let us be thankful, and so worship God acceptably." Literally, one might say, "Let us have grace, through which we might serve God acceptably." BAGD translates 12:28 like the NIV.[30]

Mercy (ἔλεός, *eleos*), on the other hand, has to do with compassion or pity, the opposite of envy. Esser compares three similar words: *eleos* of the feeling of pity, οἰκτιρμός (*oiktirmos*) of the exclamation of pity, and σπλάγχνα (*splangchna*) of the inward parts where pity is felt.[31] The first is only here in Hebrews, though Jesus is a "merciful" and faithful high priest in 2:17. The second is only in 10:28 in Hebrews, of people who rejected the law of Moses, who thus died without "mercy." The third is quite often in the NT, but never in Hebrews. From his throne God hears our prayers, feels pity toward us and extends his good will toward us by sending the help we need. It is peculiar that grace and mercy are never again put together in the NT except in introductory greetings, "Grace, mercy and peace . . ." (1 Tim 1:2; 2 Tim 1:2; Titus 1:4 in variant reading; 2 John 3).

[30]The word is so widely used that BAGD (pp. 877-878) offers five definitions: (1) *graciousness, attractiveness*; (2) *gracious care* or *help, goodwill*; (3) *practical application of goodwill, benefaction*; (4) exceptional effects produced by divine grace; and (5) *thanks, gratitude.*

[31]H.H. Esser, "Mercy, Compassion," in NIDNTT, 2:593-601, p. 593.

HEBREWS 5

IV. JESUS IS SUPERIOR TO THE PRIESTHOOD OF THE OLD COVENANT AND A PRIEST FOREVER BY GOD'S OATH (5:1–7:28)

A. REQUIREMENTS OF THE HIGH PRIEST (5:1-4)

[1]Every high priest is selected from among men and is appointed to represent them in matters related to God, to offer gifts and sacrifices for sins [2]He is able to deal gently with those who are ignorant and are going astray, since he himself is subject to weakness. [3]This is why he has to offer sacrifices for his own sins, as well as for the sins of the people.

[4]No one takes this honor upon himself; he must be called by God, just as Aaron was.

Though the discussion of the new covenant in chapter eight is probably the centerpiece of the letter, the theme to which chapters five through seven are devoted is of no small significance for it represents the unique contribution of Hebrews to New Testament christology. In chapter five, our writer continues to develop the theme first introduced in 2:17-3:1 and resumed in the last section of chapter four (4:14-16) — that of Jesus' ministry as the great high priest of the Christian. The chapter break, then, does not represent a major transition. This occurred in v. 14 where the word **Therefore** does not so much draw a conclusion from what precedes it but (along with the present adverbial participle (ἔχοντες, *echontes*, **since we have**) anticipates and provides a

reason for[1] the following exhortation, **let us hold firmly**
(κρατῶμεν, *kratōmen*, a hortatory subjunctive). Though it is
not translated in the NIV, there is a connective in 5:1 — (*gar*,
"for"). Its use here, however, is not so much argumentative as
explanatory[2] as the writer now describes in more detail (5:1-
10) how Jesus fulfills the requirements of the high priestly
office and is thus able to meet the central needs to be
addressed by every high priest. In vv. 1-4, we see these
requirements and needs described.

**5:1 Every high priest is selected from among men and is
appointed to represent them in matters related to God, to
offer gifts and sacrifices for sins.**

Our writer begins by describing what is required of **every
high priest.** Jesus is thus to be measured by those requirements specified in the Mosaic law for the Aaronic priesthood
— by the authority of Scripture rather than by popular opinion or mere human precedent. The term employed here is
the same one previously applied to Jesus (ἀρχιερεύς,
archiereus, 2:17, 3:1, 4:14, 15). Outside of the Gospels and
Acts, where it is used both in reference to "chief priests"
(when in the plural) or the "high priest" (when in the singular), it occurs only in Hebrews. The prefix (ἀρχ–) adds the
concept of rank or degree to the root word (ἱερεύς, *hiereus*)
which in the New Testament is simply translated "priest."[3]
That Jesus is to be considered *the high* priest is clear from the
approaching parallel with the Day of Atonement (cf. Heb 9,
Lev 16) and reference to Jesus as "great priest" (ἱερέα μέγαν,
hierea megan, a title used of the high priest in the LXX, Lev
21:10, Num 35:25) in 10:21.

---

[1]The syntax of the Greek text here is the same as that described by
Chamberlain as an "elliptical condition" (the protasis implied by the participle). This is probably a first-class conditional sentence (employing a subjunctive in the apodosis) which assumes the condition to be true.

[2]Westcott, p. 118.

[3]William Chamberlain, *An Exegetical Garmmar of the Greek New Testament*
(Grand Rapids: Baker, 1941. Reprinted 1979), p. 16.

Verses 1-3 are devoted to the first requirement — that the high priest be selected **from among men** (ἐξ ἀνθρώπων, *ex anthrōpōn*). This probably has Exodus 28:1 as its background, where God commanded that Aaron and his sons be brought "from among the sons of Israel" (NASB; ἐκ τῶν υἱῶν Ἰσραηλ, *ek tōn huiōn Israēl*, LXX). Both the participle (which the NIV renders "is selected") and the main verb (καθίσταται, *kathistatai*, "is appointed") are in the passive voice, which indicates that another party is doing the choosing and appointing. The same verb (a form of καθίστημι, *kathistēmi*) appears in 7:28 when the writer notes that "the law appoints men in their weakness as high priests" but the case can be made that the more immediate context of 5:4 is probably in mind here ("he must be called by God"). Both forms are also in the present tense — the customary tense form for broad, general statements, as Lenski points out.[4]

The word rendered **selected** (λαμβανόμενος, *lambanomenos*, present tense participle) is capable of a stronger translation such as "taken" (KJV, NASB). At times, it is even used in a violent sense — such as when the tenants "seized" the servants and "took" the son and killed him in Jesus' parable of the vineyard (Matt 21:35, 39) or when Pilate "took" Jesus and had him flogged (John 19:1). However, the notion of being "selected" or "chosen" (RSV) out of a larger number (such as when God "takes" a people for himself from the Gentiles, Acts 15:14) probably fits the context better (since the verb is followed by a genitive case of source or origin). This same word is used in the LXX of Numbers 8:6 where the Lord commands Moses to "take" the Levites.[5]

---

[4]R.C.H. Lenski, *The Interpretation of the Epistle to the Hebrews and the Epistle of James* (Minneapolis: Augsburg, 1966), p. 156. Though this material may be explanatory, it is possible, then, to see an incipient argument here. Anticipating the conclusion about the superiority of Christ's high priesthood, this is not only the beginnings of a lesser to greater argument (human imperfection to divine perfection) but a classification argument (what is true of the class is true of the member) both framed within an appeal to the authority of Scripture. The fact that the description of requirements is selective is suggestive along these lines as well.

[5]Ellingworth, p. 273.

The verb **is appointed** (καθίσταται [*kathistatai*] — a compound form of ἵστημι [*histēmi*], "to stand, set or put something in a place") can also be translated "ordain"[6] and is used of governors (Acts 7:10), rulers or judges (Acts 7:27, 35), and elders (Titus 1:5) in the NT. The appointed duty of the high priest toward men is **to represent them in matters related to God.** If the two clauses of the sentence are taken together, then, we see him as being "from men for men."[7] The structure of the Greek text brings this idea out more clearly for the words of the text appear in the following order: "from men selected, for men appointed."

As a representative of men[8] to God the purpose of his ministry is **to offer gifts and sacrifices for sins.** The Greek forms here (ἵνα προσφέρῃ, *hina prospherē*, "to offer") stress that the presenting of the offerings is the express purpose for which the high priest has been selected and appointed. This is the first of no less than twenty-one uses of this word (*prospherō*) in Hebrews. The frequency takes on additional significance when we consider that it occurs nowhere else in the NT outside of the Gospels and Acts. It is customarily used of the offering of gifts at the altar of the temple (as in Matt 5:23, 24; 8:4; etc.) and is the same word which will be used in 9:14 when we read that Christ "offered himself."

There is considerable variation and overlap in the terms used for gifts and sacrifices in the Hebrew MT, the Greek LXX and Rabbinic literature.[9] In 8:3, both of these terms are used again (δῶρα, *dōra*, "gifts" and θυσίας, *thysias*, "sacrifices") but in 8:4 only "gift" (*dōra*) is used with no apparent difference in meaning, suggesting that the two terms are probably

---

[6]As in KJV; see BAGD, p. 390.

[7]Crouch, p. 139.

[8]Though this is the only time when the NT uses ἄνθρωπος (usually a more generic term than the words λαός, "people" and ἔθνος, "nation") in reference to the work of the high priest, there is probably little significance to the choice of the word here since the writer uses laov(in the same manner in verse 3.

[9]Ellingworth, p. 274.

synonymous and both are offered for sin.[10] In light of what the writer will have to say in chapter nine, the reference in mind here is probably to the gifts and sacrifices to be offered on the Day of Atonement (Lev 18).

5:2 He is able to deal gently

Though the NIV begins a new sentence here, the Greek text is a continuation of the sentence which began in the previous verse. The phrase **is able** actually translates a present tense adverbial participle. This means that the circumstance indicated by the participle — the ability **to deal gently** — coincides both with the condition of being "selected from among men" (also a present participle) and the appointment to represent men (v. 1). The condition is a requirement for the appointment because the ability is a requirement for the role.

The word translated "deal gently" (μετριοπαθεῖν, *metrio-pathein*; KJV "have compassion") occurs only here in the NT and not at all in the LXX. It is a compound word joining forms of *metrios* (moderate) and *pathos* (passion, affection)[11] and is used in the sense of "moderation" in secular Greek literature.[12] It could be taken as a stylistic variation and synonymous with terms συμπαθῆσαι (*sympathēsai*, "sympathize," 4:15) and ἔπαθεν (*epathen*, "suffer," 5:8) in the sense of having "some fellow-feeling for," as Ellingworth suggests.[13] This fits the context but the idea of "moderating one's anger" — achieving a mean between "indifference and sentimental indulgence" — fits the context as well and seems more consistent with its use

---

[10]An alternative view is that of Westcott who suggests that there is sometimes a distinction between δῶρα (meal offering) and θυσίας (blood offering) and thus the phrase "for sins" applies only to θυσίας. As Westcott himself points out, however, δῶρα can also be used to describe offerings of all kinds (blood or not, as in 11:4) (p. 119).

[11]BAGD, p. 515, 603.

[12]Moulton and Milligan cite a passage from *Aristeae ad Philocratem Epistula* (p. 406) and Zodhiates alludes to Plutarch (p. 975). Ellingworth suggests that it can denote "a happy mean between two extremes," citing passages from the Peripatetics, Philo and Josephus among others.

[13]Ellingworth, p. 275.

elsewhere as noted by Kistemaker[14] and Lane.[15] The high priest, then, neither winks at the sins of his people nor deals with them harshly.

with those who are ignorant and are going astray

These arc attributive present tense participles (τοῖς ἀγνο–οῦσιν καὶ πλανωμένοις, *tois agnoousin kai plan ōmenois*) which suggests that the writer probably has general life patterns in mind. In the NT, ἀγνοέω (*agnoe ō*) can be used of either a lack of knowledge or awareness, as when Paul announces his attention to proclaim to the Athenians something "unknown" to them (Acts 17:23) or when he informs the Galatians how he was at one time "personally unknown" (KJV, "unknown by face") to the churches of Judea (Gal 1:22). Or it can refer to a lack of understanding or recognition, as when Mark and Luke note that Jesus' disciples failed to understand the meaning of his teaching that he would be killed and raised (Mark 9:32, Luke 9:45) or when Luke later notes that the rulers of Jerusalem did not recognize Jesus as the Messiah (Acts 13:27).

In some instances, it refers specifically to an ignorance that leads one to error or sin, as when Paul rebukes the one who "ignores" (NASB, "does not recognize") the fact that what he was writing was the Lord's command (1 Cor 14:38) or when Peter writes that men "blaspheme in matters they do not understand" (2 Pet 2:12). In such cases, it is clear from the context that the word refers to a lack of understanding or recognition rather than a lack of knowledge or awareness. The choice of this particular word, then, suggests that the writer probably has in mind the "unintentional sin" referred to in Leviticus 4. This fits well in Hebrews 5 where atonement for sin is such an important part of the context (vv. 1, 3; 7:27; 9:7, 12, 14, 26, 28).

---

[14]Simon Kistemaker, *Exposition of the Epistle to the Hebrews*. New Testament Commentary (Grand Rapids: Baker, 1984), p. 132.

[15]William Lane, *Hebrews 1-8*. Word Biblical Commentary, Vol. 47A. Edited by David A. Hubbard, John D.W. Watts, and Ralph P. Martin (Dallas: Word Books, 1991), p. 108.

Πλανάω (*planaō*) can mean "to lead astray," "cause to wander," "mislead" or "deceive."[16] This is the same word Jesus uses of the sheep who "wanders away" in Matthew 18:12 (cf. also 1 Pet 2:25) and our writer will use the word again in 11:38 to describe how the prophets "wandered" in deserts, mountains, caves and holes in the ground. In a more figurative sense, however, it can mean to "deceive" or "seduce" a person into an error of judgment (Matt 24:4ff; John 7:12, 47; Gal 6:7; Rev 12:9; etc.) which often directly results in sinful behavior (1 Cor 6:9, 15:33; Titus 3:3; Rev 2:20). This is the same word used in 3:10 when our writer quoted Psalm 95:10 to describe how the *hearts* of the Israelites were "always going astray."

The NIV translation in 5:2 — "going astray" — doesn't really do justice to the passive form of the participle which could be translated "are led astray," suggesting the idea of victimization. The fact that, in the Greek text, one article is used for both participles suggests that they both describe the same group of people and that either (1) the ignorance/misunderstanding is thus a result of having been led astray (although no specific agent is named) or (2) taken together the terms cover both unintentional sins (which stem from misunderstanding) and intentional sins (which stem from the kind of rebellious heart described in 3:7-11). The fact that one who "sinned defiantly" was to be "cut off from his people" (Num 15:30) — even as God was sentencing the rebellious Israelites to die in the wilderness — poses a problem for the second possibility, however.

since he himself is subject to weakness.

This phrase explains *why* the human high priest is able to deal gently with such people. The conjunction ἐπεὶ (*epei*) appears frequently in the letter (4:6; 5:2, 11; 6:13; 9:17, 26; 10:2; 11:11) and can be used of either time ("as," "when," "after that") or of ground or motive ("since" or "inasmuch as")[17] as it is here.

---

[16]BAGD, p. 665.
[17]BAGD, p. 284.

Περίκειται (*perikeitai*, "is subject to") is used only five times in the NT but the other instances suggest some interesting imagery. In Mark 9:42 and Luke 17:2, Jesus uses the word in reference to the millstone "tied around" the neck of the one who should wish to be thrown into the sea. Paul uses the word while under arrest in Rome when he says "I am *bound* with this chain" (Acts 28:20). Our writer uses the word again in 12:1 when he reminds us that we are "surrounded" by a great cloud of witnesses. This is how the human high priest experiences weakness — it is like a stone about his neck, a chain that binds him, a crowd that surrounds him.

'Ασθένειαν (*astheneian*) is usually used in reference to a person who is physically weak or ill. It is used in the Gospels to describe those who were healed by Jesus (Matt 8:17 cf. Isaiah 53:4; Luke 5:15; 8:2; 13:11, 12; John 5:5; 11:4) or Paul (Acts 28:9), Timothy's stomach problems (1 Tim 5:23), etc. In Matthew 25, Jesus uses *asthenēs* when referring to those who are "sick" or in prison (vv. 39, 43, 44) and Peter uses it when exhorting husbands to treat their wives "with respect as weaker vessels" (1 Pet 3:7). Although our writer seems to use the term in this sense in 11:34, it is unlikely that he is so using it either here or in 7:28 when he again refers to the human high priests as "weak." Used figuratively, either *astheneia* or *asthenēs* can mean a kind of ineffectiveness (1 Cor 2:3; 15:43; 2 Cor 12:9; etc.), as when Jesus describes his "weak" flesh when struggling in Gesthemane or when Paul uses it in reference to the "weak" things of the world (1 Cor 1:27) or a "weak" conscience (1 Cor 8:7, 10). Thinking along these lines, Ellingworth suggests that, in this context, we consider it "the intellectual and moral weakness which leads to failure to do God's will."[18] It is in this sense that the human high priest is one with his fellow man, able to both identify and empathize with his plight.

5:3 This is why he has to offer sacrifices for his own sins, as well as for the sins of his people.

This verse completes the long and complex Greek sen-

---

[18]Ellingworth, p. 268.

tence which began in v. 1. A more form-literal translation of v. 1 might be "and because of it (NASB)." The "it," specifically, is the "weakness" mentioned in v. 2 (*astheneian*, with which the Greek pronoun agrees in gender and number).

The verb here is ὀφείλει (*opheilei*), which can simply be translated "should" (Luke 17:10; John 13:14; Acts 17:29; 1 Cor 7:3 etc.) or "ought" (Rom 15:1; 1 Cor 7:36; 9:10; etc.) but includes the sense of "owing a debt." It is used of financial debts (by Jesus in his parables about the unforgiving servant — Matt 18:28, 30, 34 — and the shrewd manager — Luke 16:5, 7; by Paul when he exhorts us to "let no debt remain outstanding" — Rom. 13:7, 8; also Phlm 18, 19) but also by Jesus in the model prayer in reference to the debt of sin (Matt 6:12, ὀφειλ-ήματα [*opheilēmata*] and ὀφειλέταις [*opheiletais*]; Luke 11:4 joins ὀφείλοντι [*opheilonti*] and ἁμαρτίας [*hamartias*], the same word translated "sin" here in Heb 5:1; cf. Luke 13:4). In other words, the verb **has to** here probably denotes a strong sense of obligation to pay a debt incurred by sin. Because the human high priest shares in the weakness and sin of his fellow man, he is obligated to offer sacrifices for himself as well as for others. This obligation is described in Leviticus 4:3-12 and 16:6-17 (for himself first on the Day of Atonement).

The word **offer** (*prospherei*) translates a form of the same verb used in v. 1. Here, however, the Greek text contains no object and our translators supply "sacrifices" on the basis of v. 1. It seems appropriate that the same object is implied but if "gifts and sacrifices" (v. 1) are to be taken together as ὑπὲρ ἁμαρτιῶν (*hyper hamartiōn*, "for sins"), then probably both are in mind here as well when the writer uses a similar phrase with the same meaning — περὶ ἁμαρτιῶν (*peri hamartiōn*, "for sins"). Crouch suggests that since both the verb ("has") and the infinitive ("to offer") are in the present tense, the obligation to offer such gifts and sacrifices is continual just as the debt created by repeated sin and weakness.[19]

---

[19]Owen Crouch, *God Has Spoken: Expository Preaching and Teaching – Hebrews* (Joplin, MO: College Press, 1983. Reprinted 1990), p. 140.

5:4 No one takes this honor upon himself; he must be called by God, just as Aaron was.

The first three verses of the chapter have described the first requirement of a high priest — that he be selected from among men. In verse four, we are introduced to the second requirement — that he be called by God. In his unique role, then, the high priest both represents men to God and God to men.

Our writer employs antithesis here. That is, he first states the truth negatively and then positively. On one hand, **no one** takes this honor upon himself. This statement seems emphatic when contrasted to the reference to "every high priest" in v. 1. The NIV now uses **takes** to render the same verb which it previously rendered "selected" in v. 1 (*lambanei*). This is in keeping with stronger translation possible for the word and here the stronger translation is probably to be preferred when we consider the likely background of this statement. Bruce notes several cases, between 174 BC and AD 67, of men being appointed to the office who were neither descended from Aaron nor called by God.[20] Our writer, however, has demonstrated no inclination to compare Jesus to specific human priests but rather measures him against selected requirements from Scripture. It is more probable that, if anything, the writer may have had in mind the examples of what happened to Korah (Num 16), Saul (1 Sam 13) and Uzziah (2 Chr 26) when they presumed to take priestly duties upon themselves.

Serving as high priest is described as an **honor**. Though this is a unique use of τιμὴν (*timēn*) in the NT, it is clear from the present context that our writer is referring to the sense of honor or respect attached to serving in the role of high priest. It is also possible that he is anticipating the use of the term ἐδόξαζεν (*edoxazen*, "glorify") when describing the appointing of Christ in v. 5 since in chapter two both the terms δόξῃ (*doxē*, "glory") and τιμῇ (*timē*, "honor") have been used

---

[20]Bruce, p. 92, *n*19.

together to describe the "crowning" of the Son who is greater than the angels (2:7, 9). Elsewhere in the NT the term is usually used to convey a sense of financial worth or value (Matt 26:6, 9; Acts 4:34; 5:2, 3; 7:16; 19:19; figuratively of Christ's death in 1 Cor 6:30 and 7:23; possibly in 1 Tim 5:17) or in the broad sense of respect, though an object is specified[21] — father and mother (Matt 15:4, 6; 19:19; Eph. 6:2), Jesus as Son and his Father (John 5:23), widows (1 Tim 5:3), the king (1 Pet 2:17), a wife (1 Pet 3:7), and possibly elders (1 Tim 5:17). Although the NT nowhere else uses the noun by itself for an office, Josephus uses it in this same way of the high-priestly office[22] as does Philo.[23] Like vessels which are made "noble" because they are set aside for "noble" purposes (Rom 9:21; 2 Tim 2:20-21), so is the high priest.

The conjunction **but** marks the turn to the truth stated positively. On the other hand, **he must be called by God.** Our writer here resorts to a stylistic device known as "zeugma" — the omission of a verb in a parallel clause. The point here is more than technical. The style of the Greek text in both verses 4 and 5 is an important part of the way our writer draws parallels and contrasts between Jesus and human priests typified by Aaron. Hence we will see this device again soon and its import will become clearer when we consider verse 5. In this instance, ἀλλά (*alla*, "but") is not followed by a main indicative verb but a present passive participle (lit., "being called"). The continuation of the idea of being "selected" or "taken" (*lambanō*) is the main thought and the present participle is probably modal (i.e., explaining how the selection takes place — "he is selected by being called by God"). Καλούμενος (*kaloumenos*, "called") can be taken to mean "to urgently invite someone to accept responsibilities for a particular task"[24] in the same sense that God, in the OT, called his servants and his people.

---

[21]Instances cited included uses of the verb form τιμάω as well as the noun τιμή.

[22]Josephus, *Ant.* 12:42, 157, cf. BAGD, p. 818.

[23]Compare Ellingworth, p. 280.

[24]LN, p. 424.

Just before our writer turns from what is true of "every priest" to what is true of Christ, he alludes to the specific example of Aaron, the inaugural high priest from whose line of descent succeeding high priests were to come. Exodus 28 describes the call he received directly from God. Aaron did not volunteer but was chosen by God. Later, when Korah and other Levites rose up to oppose Moses and Aaron, God reaffirmed his choice of Aaron and destroyed those who attempted to take the role for themselves (Num 16).

B. JESUS FULFILLS THE REQUIREMENTS AND
OFFERS ETERNAL SALVATION (5:5-10)

⁵So Christ also did not take upon himself the glory of becoming a high priest. But God said to him,
"You are my Son;
today I have become your Father.[a]"[b]
⁶And he says in another place,
"You are a priest forever,
in the order of Melchizedek."[c]
⁷During the days of Jesus' life on earth, he offered up prayers and petitions with loud cries and tears to the one who could save him from death, and he was heard because of his reverent submission. ⁸Although he was a son, he learned obedience from what he suffered ⁹and, once made perfect, he became the source of eternal salvation for all who obey him ¹⁰and was designated by God to be high priest in the order of Melchizedek.

[a]5 Or *have begotten you*   [b]5 Psalm 2:7   [c]6 Psalm 110:4

Now that the requirements for "every high priest" have been described, Jesus will be measured against these criteria in order to show why he is the "*great* high priest" of the Christian (4:14). Shifts in the verb forms from present tenses

(vv. 1-4)[25] to past (aorist) tenses (vv. 5-10) signify the transition from the general, broad descriptions of what is required of every high priest to the specific, historical descriptions of what Jesus experienced — just as a syllogism proceeds from its major premise of a general truth about a class to its minor premise about the truth of a particular case. We will see here not only the fact that Jesus was so appointed (from among men and by God) but also what Jesus endured on the way to that appointment and what that appointment has achieved for us.

5:5 So Christ also did not take upon himself the glory of becoming a high priest. But God said to him, "You are my Son; today I have become your Father."

The final phrase of verse 4 and the initial phrase of verse 5 create a "pivot" around which this transition turns and together serve as just one example of the many parallelisms which help to draw the evaluative comparison. The order of the text illustrates more clearly how this "pivot" functions:

. . . just as also Aaron.

So also Christ . . .

This is the same basic form of comparison made on a smaller scale in verse three (NIV, "as well as for"; literally, "just as . . . "so also" [καθὼς περὶ . . . οὕτως, *kathōs peri . . . houtōs*]) but now it forms the pivotal comparison of this section of the letter.

Other parallelisms assist in drawing the comparison. If we observe the style of the Greek text closely and note the recurring use of the "zeugma" as described in v. 4 above, we can see in v. 5 an antithesis which parallels that of v. 4:

not to himself one takes . . . but . . . being called by God
Christ not himself was glorifying . . . but . . . the one who said

---

[25]The verb "was" (NIV) does not actually appear in the Greek text of v. 4 which literally reads, "just as also Aaron." Translators supply the implied verb in order to render the verse in acceptable, readable English prose.

When it is observed that both verses employ zeugma in the second half of the antithesis, the parallels stand out quite clearly. Just as no one took the honor to himself, so Christ did not glorify himself ("honor" and "glory" are now seen as serving parallel functions in these sentences).[26] Both antitheses turn on the same conjunction (ἀλλα, *alla*). The one who "said" (though not specified in v. 5) is clearly the same one who "called" (God). The progression from "selecting" (λαμβάνει, *lambanei*) to "glorifying" (ἐδόξαζεν, *edoxazen*) would appear to be more than a coincidence. When God appointed his Son, he did so in a much more glorious way than when he ever appointed any human priest. The combination of "honor" and "glory" recalls the coronation imagery of 2:7-9 (Ps 8).

The argument proceeds, then, not only from major premise to minor premise (class to member) but from lesser to greater. Not only does Jesus' greater glory become clear but his greater humility. Though the glory he received was far greater, it was still pronounced *upon* him. He did not grasp it or "take" it unto himself.

The last time our writer referred to "Christ," he referred to him as "Jesus the Son of God" (4:14). We noted there how some have suggested that the name "Jesus" refers to his humanity while the name "Christ" refers to his divinity but also that the distinction does not seem to hold in Hebrews. Just as the letter describes his "blood" (9:14; 10:19), his entry into the sanctuary (4:14; 6:20; 9:24), and his role as mediator of the new covenant (8:6; 9:15; 12:24) so does it describe his role as high priest in both terms (Jesus and Christ). It is more probable that our writer chooses to refer to him as "the Christ" (the definite article appears in the Greek text) because he is in the process of citing two Messianic passages from the Psalms.

Whether "Jesus" or "Christ," he is now also clearly seen to be "Son of God" in either case since our writer returns again

---

[26]The καθώσπερ καὶ ᾽Ααρών . . . Οὕτως καὶ ὁ Χριστὸς parallel creates a slight chiasmus here (οὐχ ἑαυτῷ τις - ὁ Χριστος οὐχ ἑαυτὸν).

to Psalm 2:7 ("You are my Son"), first cited in 1:5 to demonstrate his superiority to the angels. The same pronouncement demonstrates the superiority of his divine call to be our high priest.

5:6 And he says in another place, "You are a priest forever, in the order of Melchizedek."

Our writer offers not one witness but two[27] to back his claim about Jesus' appointment. Though he has used Psalm 2:7 previously, he now uses it in a different connection, pairing it with Psalm 110:4 (Ps 110:1 was introduced in 1:13). Just as he has appealed to Scripture to establish the requirements, so he also appeals to Scripture to demonstrate that Jesus not only measures up to these criteria but surpasses them as a great high priest with no equal. The pairing of Psalm 2:7 and Psalm 110:4 also ties the notions of Sonship and Priesthood together, just as they were in 4:14.[28] This can be said of no one but Jesus Christ. No one else can be both Son and Priest in as great a way as he.

This is the first reference in the letter to "the order of Melchizedek." However, this phrase does not seem to be as important in this verse as is the reference to the priesthood since the quote is introduced as evidence that the Christ did not try to take the priesthood for himself. That the phrase is repeated in v. 10, however, suggests that it will become important — as, in fact, it becomes the next major theme of the letter (6:20), following the lengthy excursus which begins in 5:11. This same phrase ("order of Melchizedek") will be found in

---

[27]It is possible, though not certain, that this could be an attempt to provide the minimum of two witnesses required by the OT law (Deut 19:15 cf. Matt 18:16).

[28]This connection was probably hinted at as early as 1:3 where the "Son" is said to have "provided purification of sins." Lane suggests that these are the "primary models for the writer's christology" and notes how, though no other Christian writer of the period drew attention to Psalm 110:4, there are more references to this passage than to any other biblical text and it was subsequently cited often as proof of Jesus' everlasting priesthood (p. 118).

5:10; 6:20; 7:11; and 7:17 (Ps 110:4 again cited). Chapter seven will be completely devoted to explaining what is merely anticipated here — the significance of Melchizedek's priesthood for understanding the high priestly ministry of Jesus.

What the Psalmist and subsequently our writer mean by the "order" of Melchizedek (κατὰ τὴν τάξιν, *kata tēn taxin*) deserves some explanation. Although the NIV here retains the choice of the KJV, NASB, and RSV, it may still not be the best possible rendering. It is, admittedly, the same word used in reference to the "division" of priests in which Zechariah served (Luke 1:8) and seems to be used of Melchizedek in the same manner in which it is used of Aaron in 7:11. But there is no biblical or historical evidence to suggest any continuation of such a "class" or "order" of priesthood beyond the life of Melchizedek himself, unless our writer has Jesus in mind as the unique successor after a gap of many centuries. Nor can this be taken as a reference to any kind of order within the existing Levitical priesthood for Melchizedek served both before and outside of that covenant. The word is used on only two other occasions in the NT, when Paul describes an "orderly" way of conducting affairs (1 Cor 14:40; Col 2:5).

There is suggestive evidence from other sources, however. Bauer suggests "nature, quality, manner" as possible translations based upon usage in secular literature[29] and Moulton and Milligan suggest "character" or "quality" based upon similar references, including 2 Maccabees 9:18.[30] Hence, others have suggested such translations as "according to the nature of"[31] or "of the same kind."[32] This makes sense of the variation in 7:15 when our writer refers to another priest "like Melchizedek" (κατὰ τὴν ὁμοιότητα, *kata tēn homoiotēta*).

---

[29]BAGD, p. 804.

[30]MM, p. 625.

[31]Ellingworth, who also offers "after the manner of" as suggested by the Jewish Publication Society, pp. 283-284.

[32]Leon Morris, *The Expositor's Bible Commentary*, Vol. 12. Edited by Frank E. Gaebelein (Grand Rapids: Zondervan, 1981), p. 49.

In the end, we should observe that the main thrust of the comparison seems to be more important to our writer than is a strict succession of order or any comparison of personal characteristics between Melchizedek and Jesus — the fact that both are priests "forever." Although Melchizedek is called a priest "forever" (εἰς τὸν αἰῶνα, *eis ton aiōna*) this description is also applied to the Levitical priests in the OT (Exod 29:9, *eis ton aiōna*, LXX; 1 Chr 15:2, ἕως αἰῶνος, *heōs aiōnos*, LXX). But our writer has something different in mind. He is priest "forever" (εἰς τὸ διηνεκές, *eis to diēnekes*, "continually, for all time") in that he is "without a genealogy . . . without beginning of days or end of life" (7:3). The point of the comparison is to see how Jesus becomes "another priest like Melchizedek . . . one who has become a priest not on the basis of a regulation as to his ancestry but on the basis of the power of an indestructible life" (7:15-16). The "forever" dimension is the ultimate point of the comparison (cf. also 7:28). If the comparison to Aaron should, perhaps, cause a reader to object to Jesus as high priest because he lacked the required ancestry, he will soon be reminded that there are better reasons to accept him as an even greater high priest.

5:7 During the days of Jesus' life on earth, he offered up prayers and petitions with loud cries and tears to the one who could save him from death, and he was heard because of his reverent submission.

Now that our writer has appealed to the authority of Scripture in order to demonstrate that Jesus the Son and Messiah has been appointed by God to be a priest, our writer turns our attention to the earthly life of Jesus to demonstrate his identification with the experiences of men. The order is chiastic: (1) the high priest must be chosen from among men (vv. 1-3), (2) the high priest must be called by God (v. 4), (3) Jesus was called by God to be priest (vv. 5-6), and (4) Jesus was a full participant in our human struggles. In these next two verses, we will read about what Jesus went through in order to sympathize with our weakness (4:15), why Jesus is able to deal gently with us (5:2), and so is able to represent us in matters related to God (5:1).

The phrase "the days of Jesus' life on earth" (NIV) somewhat softens the impact of the Greek phrase which calls our attention more directly to the physical nature of his incarnation – literally, "the days of his flesh" (σαρκὸς, *sarkos*). Though this is the same word which figures so prominently in Paul's discussion of our "sinful nature" in Romans 7-8, where he opposes living "according to the sinful nature" (NIV; KJV, "flesh") and living "according to the Spirit" (Rom 8:4), it is otherwise used simply in reference to the body, i.e., "the material that covers the bones of a human or animal body" or of our "human descent."[33] This is probably the extent of the term's meaning here but the context certainly suggests that even if Jesus (the "antitype" of Adam, Rom 5:14ff.) never sinned, he experienced every temptation experienced by those of "sinful nature" (4:15).

The rest of this verse is probably a description of Gethsemane. In the Gospels, we often find Jesus in prayer but here the phrase "with loud cries and tears" suggests a particularly intense period of prayer and the aorist tense of the main verb (ἔμαθεν [*emathen*], which does not occur until v. 8) suggests that our writer has in mind a particular event rather than a general custom (for which an imperfect tense would probably be used). At Gethsemane we know that he "began to be sorrowful and troubled" (Matt 26:37; "deeply distressed," Mark 14:33), that he "was overwhelmed with sorrow to the point of death" (Matt 26:38; Mark 14:34), that his "body" (σάρξ, *sarx*, i.e., "flesh") was "weak" (*asthenēs*) (Matt 26:41; Mark 14:38), that he was "in anguish" and "prayed earnestly" while "his sweat was like drops of blood falling to the ground" (Luke 22:44). We read here that he prayed "to the one who could save him from death," and it was in Gethsemane when he prayed in death's shadow, the cross looming before him.

---

[33]BAGD, pp. 743-744.

Here we encounter a problem for the text tells us that "he was heard." Did Jesus pray, asking to be spared from death on a cross? This seems to be what we read in the synoptics when Jesus prays, "My Father, if it is possible, may this cup be taken from me" (Matt 26:39 cf. Mark 14:36, Luke 22:42). If so, it is not easy to explain how God "heard" or answered him. Εἰσ–ακούω (*eisakouō*) can be translated "obey"[34] and is the same word used when Zechariah (Luke 1:13) and Cornelius (Acts 10:31) are told that their prayers have been "heard" (answered) and when Jesus' refers to the answers which pagans expect for their prayers (Matt 6:7).

Two explanations are possible. One is that God's answer is seen in the "angel from heaven" who "appeared to him and strengthened him" (Luke 22:43). Perhaps Jesus' agony over the cross was so great that it threatened to crush him even in the garden. Another is that, while the angel represents God's immediate response, God's ultimate answer was not to "rescue" (σῴζω, *sōzō*) Jesus from the cross but from death through the resurrection. After all, it is because of his resurrection that he is able to serve as priest *forever* (Heb 7:16, 28). A form of *sōzō* is used similarly of Jesus' raising of Jairus' dead daughter (Luke 9:50).

In whichever sense Jesus was heard, it was "because of his reverent submission" (εὐλαβείας, *eulabeias*). NASB renders the word "piety," while RSV translates it as "godly fear."[35] If the reference here is to Gethsemane, then this alternative is clearly to be preferred for even as Jesus prayed there we remember well what he said to his Father: "Yet not as I will, but as you will" (Matt 26:39; cf. Mark 14:36; Luke 22:42).

5:8 Although he was a son, he learned obedience from what he suffered

For a better understanding of this statement, it is important to note that we have here the completion of a sentence which actually began in v. 7. The main verb is ἔμαθεν

---

[34]BAGD, p. 232, cf. 1 Cor 14:21.
[35]In keeping with Bauer, see BAGD, p. 321.

(*emathen*, "learned"). The two forms in v. 7 are aorist adverbial participles (he "offered up," προσενέγκας [*prosenengkas*] and "was heard," εἰσακουσθεὶς [*eisakoustheis*]) which means that they have an antecedent time relationship to the main verb. This is not to imply that Jesus was not obedient throughout his life. However, the "obedience" described here in v. 8 is not merely that of Jesus' entire obedient life but refers in particular to that degree of submissive obedience which the cross demanded and which Jesus could only experience and practice through the events of Gethsemane and Golgotha. The point is that *even in the midst of this kind of suffering* Jesus continued to obey.

Keeping in mind that the two verses are part of the same sentence sheds possible light on another potentially problematic dimension of this verse. The concessive conditional phrase "Although he was a son" may, in a way, be troublesome for it seems to suggest that Jesus learned obedience *in spite of* his Sonship (rather than because of it or through it, more natural thoughts for us). The concessive force of the phrase, however, comes not from the participle (ὢν, *ōn*, "being" a son) but from the conjunction which introduces it (καίπερ, *kaiper*). The present tense of the participle merely signifies a simultaneous time relationship with some other event (i.e., the state of being a son persisted while some other event(s) took place).

The question we should ask here is, "which event?" The four major translations (NIV, NASB, RSV, KJV) each begin a new sentence here, conveying the impression that *kaiper* ("although") looks *forward*. However, in every other place where this conjunction is used in the NT — including both other occurrences in Hebrews (Phil 3:4; Heb 7:5; 12:17; and 2 Pet 1:12) — it looks *backward*, connecting the phrase to follow with what *precedes* it. That being the case, then, we have good reason to understand the phrase "although he was a son" as referring to what has already been described in v. 7. The idea is not that he "learned" in spite of being a son but that, even though he was God's Son, he endured "days of the flesh" along with the temptations and sufferings that accompany them. Though God's Son, he has earned the right to represent us (5:1) and is still able to sympathize with our weaknesses (4:15).

5:9 and, once made perfect, he became the source of eternal salvation for all who obey him 5:10 and was designated by God to be high priest in the order of Melchizedek.
The long, complicated sentence which began in v. 7 can be seen as completed by the end of v. 8[36] and the focus now shifts. The Scriptures have testified to the fact of Jesus' call by God to be our high priest (vv. 5-6). Our writer has described what Jesus went through "in the flesh" to qualify him for that role (vv. 7-8). In verses 9-10 he will describe the results of what Jesus endured. There are three.

First, he was **made perfect**. τελειωθεὶς (*teleiōtheis*, from τελειόω [*teleioō*], cf. also τελέω [*teleō*], τέλος [*telos*] and τέλειος [*teleios*]) conveys the ideas of "finishing," "fulfilling" or "making complete." It can convey the idea of perfection in a righteous (or moral) sense[37] as it seems to later in the letter when our writer notes that the law could not do this for a person (7:19) nor could the gifts and sacrifices offered by the human priests (9:9) but that only the one sacrifice offered by Jesus could (10:14). It is probably best to understand all of these as references to our "justification" (being put right in our position with God) rather than to our "sanctification" (achieving perfect righteousness in the condition of our lives). But since Jesus had no need to be justified or "put right" with God (because he had never sinned), this cannot be the meaning here.

The word is also used in reference to the "fulfilling" of predictive prophecy (John 19:28), the completion of a task (John 4:34; 17:4; Acts 20:24) or a period of time (Luke 2:43),

---

[36]The editors of the Nestle-Aland Greek New Testament (27th edition) do not mark this with a period but καὶ begins a new thought in v. 9 which supplies its own main verb (ἐγένετο).

[37]LN, p. 747.

and of reaching a full age or adulthood (1 Cor 14:20; Heb 5:14). It is the same word Paul uses in the sense of spiritual "maturity" or "completeness" (which is being like Christ — Eph 4:13; 1 Cor 13:10). Here, it seems best to take the notion of "completeness" or "fullness" in relationship to the sufferings just described. Having "finished" his suffering — completed it to the fullest extent possible, a painful death on the cross — and having completely and fully identified with our temptations (in *every* way, 4:15) and our total life experience in the flesh, suffering yet also obeying, he can now identify with man to the fullest extent. It is just as our writer said in 2:10 — the one who is the author of salvation is the one made "perfect through suffering."

The second result is that he has been **designated by God to be high priest**. We list this second because, even though this does not follow the formal order of the text, it follows the time sequence indicated by the Greek forms. Both "made perfect" and "was designated" are aorist passive adverbial participles which modify the main verb "became" (ἐγένετο, *egeneto*). The main verb is in the past (aorist) tense as well, suggesting that at a particular point of time in the past Jesus became the source of our salvation. The other events, however, precede this point in time ("once" suggests this for the first participle) and an argument could even be made that the relationship is causal.

The word translated "designated" (προσαγορευθεὶς, *prosagoreutheis*) is used in the LXX and in secular literature of a "friendly and peaceful greeting," the "calling of someone by name," and of the "giving of a name to someone . . . especially as an expression of friendship or honour."[38] Here, however, it should probably not be taken in a sense much different that the words previously used to describe Jesus' appointment (λαμβάνω, *lambanō*, "selected" and καλέω [*kaleō*], "called") by God (τοῦ θεοῦ, *tou theou*, cf. v. 4) although it could suggest, as Ellingworth argues, that it is the title of high priest which is

---

[38]Ellingworth, p. 296.

given to Jesus (as a result of his suffering and exaltation) while the high priesthood is itself eternal.[39] In some places the word for "high priest" (ἀρχιερεύς, *archiereus*) is used in connection with Melchizedek (5:10; 6:20) while in other places the word "priest" (ἱερεύς, *hiereus*) is used (5:5; 7:1, 11, 17, 21), although, strictly speaking, it is Christ who is called the "high priest" (after the order of Melchizedek). On the phrase "after the order of Melchizedek," see 5:6.

The final and ultimate result of what Jesus endured is that **he became the source of eternal salvation for all who obey him**. The word rendered "source" (NIV, NASB, RSV; "author," KJV) is αἴτιος (*aitios*) and is used only here in Scripture. The related *aition* occurs but seldom but conveys the idea, as can *aitios*, of "cause." It is used three times in Luke's account of Pilate's report that he found no "basis" or "grounds" for the charges against Jesus (23:4, 14, 22) and otherwise occurs only in Acts 19:40 when the city clerk at Ephesus dismissed the crowd because their was no "reason" for the commotion. Either "cause" or "source" is an acceptable translation because either word attributes the originating cause of our salvation to Jesus.

Since these verses (9-10) use aorist participles to describe what preceded Jesus' becoming the source of our salvation, it might be argued that both contribute to its cause and its source — that is both the suffering through which he as made perfect (the cross) as well as his ongoing ministry as our great high priest. The NT describes our salvation (σωτηρίας, *sōtērias*) as, at the same time, a past, present, and future event. It is a completed act in the sense that we were/have been justified or put right with God. Jesus accomplished this at the cross and becomes an accomplished fact for us when we enter the new covenant through our faith and its attendant manifestations (Rom 3:21-26; 5:1-11; 8:1-4). It is an ongoing act in the sense that we are being/in the process of being made holy and righteous in the actual condition of our lives

---

[39]Ibid.

(sometimes referred to as "sanctification"). This is a result of our renewal and recreation in Christ as a result of the work of his Spirit in our lives (2 Cor 2:15; 1 Cor 1:18; Phil 2:12-13; 1 Pet 2:2; 2 Cor 3:18). Our writer actually refers to both of these dimensions of our salvation at the same time in 10:14 ("he has made perfect forever those who are being made holy"). But there is also a sense in which we will be saved when someday we attain to that for which we wait and hope for — that salvation "that is ready to be revealed in the last time" (1 Pet 1:5, 9 cf. also Rom 8:22-26; 1 Thess 5:18; Rom 13:11) — all that we anticipate that heaven and eternity will hold for us (what some call our "glorification" or "consummation").

When considered this way, it is clear that Jesus has everything to do with our salvation in all three senses. His cross makes our justification possible. His Spirit makes our sanctification actual. His promised return will make our consummation final. As we live between what he has done for us and what he will do for us, we continue to be saved by what he now does for us. Herein lies the significance not only of the regenerating ministry of his Spirit but the need for his priesthood. Through his cross — the one and only sacrifice necessary — he has already purchased the forgiveness of our sins. Through his mediation — he continues to deal gently with us in our weakness and represents us to God the Father that we might be seen in him while we grow to become more like him.

Finally, we note that, though this salvation is available to anyone, it is not effectual for everyone. He is the source of eternal salvation for "all who obey him." It is appropriate and no coincidence that our writer uses the same word to describe here what is required of us as he has previously used to describe what Jesus "learned" from his suffering (ὑπακού–ουσιν [hypakouousin], cf. ὑπακοήν [hypakoēn] in v. 8). As obedience was required of Jesus that he might become our savior and great high priest, so it is required of those who would be saved by his sacrifice and mediation. The point is not that our obedience earns the salvation but that it is the only response of which faith is capable (Eph 2:8-9; cf. James 2:14, 17-18, 22, 24).

C. [EXCURSUS: RESPONDING TO GOD, 5:11-6:12]

1. Still Infants (5:11-14)

[11]We have much to say about this, but it is hard to explain because you are slow to learn. [12]In fact, though by this time you ought to be teachers, you need someone to teach you the elementary truths of God's word all over again. You need milk, not solid food! [13]Anyone who lives on milk, being still an infant, is not acquainted with the teaching about righteousness. [14]But solid food is for the mature, who by constant use have trained themselves to distinguish good from evil.

These verses form an interruption to the main flow of thought concerning the high priesthood of Jesus which dominates Hebrews 5-7. Jesus was quite fully introduced as high priest in 4:14-16 and shown to fully represent man (5:1-3) and God (5:4-6). He won this status through submissive suffering. Once perfected he could offer eternal salvation to all who obey him (5:7-10).

At this point the author of Hebrews breaks away in frustration. He suggests that his readers are so slow to learn that they need someone to rehearse elementary truths all over again, though they should be able to do the teaching themselves. Half a dozen "elementary teachings" are listed in 6:1-2. By contrast, mature people would be acquainted with "the teaching about righteousness" (5:13) and could "distinguish good from evil" (5:14).

The many links between 5:1-10 and 6:13-chapter 7 suggest that the author returns to discuss further the ideas about Psalm 110:4 which he interrupted: (a) quotations of Psalm

110:4 in Hebrews 5:6; 7;17, 21; (b) Melchizedek — only in chapter 5-7 (5:6, 10; 6:20; 7:1, 11, 15, 17); (c) specifically "the order of Melchizedek" (5:6, 10; 6:20; 7:11, 17); (d) priests; (e) especially high priest; (f) man (ἄνθρωπος, *anthrōpos*; 5:1 [twice]; 6:16; 7:8 represent four of the ten times this word occurs in Hebrews) and (g) Melchizedek is mentioned at the point of departure (5:10) and reappears in 6:20-chapter 7.

This section shows how we must respond to God. It is necessary to grow (5:11-14). Six subjects form a foundation for beginning this response (6:1-3). There is a deep danger in ending one's response to God (6:4-6). Two illustrations show good and bad responses (6:7-8). Finally, readers are encouraged to be diligent to the very end (6:9-12).

5:11 We have much to say about this, but it is hard to explain because you are slow to learn.

The phrase **much to say** must be a relative phrase for 13:22 calls this whole writing "only a short letter." It does not take very many heavy, new ideas to make a lesson "much." The ideas in Hebrews chapter 7ff. about Melchizedek, about the changing priesthood, law, and covenant, and about Jesus' heavenly offering replacing the tabernacle offerings have been "much" for subsequent generations of Christians to ponder.

The difficulty of explanation is not due to the advanced complexity of the subject matter, but to the dullness of the readers who are "slow to learn" (νωθροὶ . . . ταῖς ἀκοαῖς, *nōthroi . . . tais akoais*). The context here suggests mental or moral slothfulness (slow "of hearing"), for they evidently could have become teachers, but did not. Instead, they remained unskilled, needing others to teach them, and basic truths at that. They were like infants who feed on milk, not yet on solid food. In 6:12, the word "slow" (*nōthroi*) will be contrasted with those who operate "through faith and long-suffering." This suggests a meaning like "distrusting and easily discouraged." *Nōthroi* appears only in these two places in the NT.

It gets worse. "You *are* slow to learn" would be better expressed, "You *have become* slow to learn." γεγόνατε (*gegonate*) is a perfect tense form of γίνομαι (*ginomai*), not a form of εἰμί (*eimi*, to be). The simple phrase, "You are (slow)," sounds like a perpetual trait. The longer form, "You have become (slow)," indicates that the readers had not always been slow, dull or slothful, but had become that way by their inattention to teachings that had been available to them. The plural ἀκοαῖς (*akoais*, "hearings")[40] undergirds this disgraceful assessment. One should immediately read 6:9-12 and 10:32-36, where the readers are commended for their fine traits, in order to avoid a totally bleak picture of the first readers.

5:12 In fact, though by this time you ought to be teachers, you need someone to teach you the elementary truths of God's word all over again. You need milk, not solid food!

After a reasonable amount of time a Christian ought to become a teacher. It is the natural outcome of growth in Christ. It is the means by which the ever-expanding church reaches out with the gospel. It is the plan of the great commission. "Therefore go and make disciples of all nations [a teaching process], baptizing them in the name of the Father and of the Son and of the Holy Spirit, and teaching them to obey everything I have commanded you [a teaching process]. And surely I am with you always, to the very end of the age" (Matt 28:19-20).

Before long believers were assembling daily in one another's homes and in the temple to talk about Jesus and "the Way." They gathered with hungry ears for they had "devoted themselves to the apostles' teaching and to the fellowship, to the breaking of bread and to prayer" (Acts 2:42). Soon they "filled Jerusalem with their teaching." Within a short time

---

[40]Bauer defines ἀκοή as (1) that by which one hears: a. "faculty of hearing;" b. "act of hearing, listening;" c. "organ of hearing, the ear;" (2) that which is heard: a. "fame, report;" b. "account, preaching" (BAGD, pp. 30-31). "Slow to learn" is literally "slow to the hearings," i.e., "slow to respond to the [numerous] reports or teaching sessions."

severe persecution drove them from the sacred city, but ordinary Christians "preached the word wherever they went"
(Acts 8:4).

"Preached" in our culture sounds like the activity of a pro-
fessionally trained clergy. Here Acts does not use the formal
word "preach" (κηρύσσω, *kēryssō*), but the informal word "tell
good news" (εὐαγγελίζω, *euangelizō*). How does the good
news spread about a young couple expecting their first child?
How does the good news spread about a super sale at a
department store? How does the good news spread about
someone's recovering from a death-threatening illness? Then,
we may ask, who would be willing to spread the good news
about forgiveness and salvation and new life available through
the death of Jesus, the Messiah? That is the very significant
question which arises from this whole section (5:11-6:12). The
first readers were clearly failing to respond as they should.

The last phrase of v. 12 and verses 13-14 ("You need milk,
not solid food!") paint a picture for our minds that would be
humorous if it were not sad. The first readers were apparently much like the "fat babies" about which one contemporary
Christian performing artist sings. Their poor spiritual tum-
mies — they can't take too much. In the words that follow, we
read about the risk which attends the "fat baby" syndrome, its
alternative and the means by which we can grow out of it.

**5:13 Anyone who lives on milk, being still an infant, is not
acquainted with the teaching about righteousness. 5:14 But
solid food is for the mature, who by constant use have
trained themselves to distinguish good from evil.**

The risk which attends **being still an infant** is that we are
not acquainted with the teaching about righteousness.
Whether the infant diet results in this malnourishment or
whether being underfed keeps one an infant is not clear from
the grammar here (e.g., does a lack of acquaintance with the
word of righteousness result in one not growing or does a
refusal to grow lead to the lack of acquaintance?). But the cor-
relation is sufficiently clear and verses 11-12 suggest that a

lack of opportunity for such teaching or nourishment was definitely not the problem. In either case, so long as one is an infant, one is not acquainted with "the teaching (λόγου, *logou*) about righteousness[41] (δικαιοσύνης, *dikaiosynēs*)." This is in contrast to the "elementary truths" mentioned in v. 12 and which will be listed in 6:1-2. It probably looks forward to the ability to "distinguish (διάκρισιν, *diakrisin*) good from evil" in v. 14. We have already described in what sense salvation involves not only being "put right" with God (the justification accomplished at the cross) but "becoming right" in the way we live our lives (the obedience which it prompts from us and into which we grow, cf. 5:9). Not only does such a person find himself at a loss for moral and ethical direction but is possibly at risk of losing his salvation.

The alternative is to seek a growth that enables us to become **mature**. Τελείων (*teleiōn*) is the same word used in v. 9 to describe how Jesus was "once made perfect."[42] Just as his obedience calls for ours (ὑπακούω, *hypakouō*, 5:8 cf. 5:9), so his "perfection" becomes the standard by which we measure our "maturity" (cf. Eph 4:13 where Paul also uses the same word to describe our "maturity" which is measured by the degree to which we attain "to the whole measure of the fullness of Christ," cf. also 1 Cor 13:10). If it is a fact that we are to measure ourselves by the "whole measure" of his "fullness," this may well include the practice of reverent submission and obedience in the midst of our suffering, just as it did for Jesus, although the model of righteous living that his

---

[41]The word "righteousness" (δικαιοσύνη) appears again as chapter 7 begins although it is only found in Hebrews six times (1:9; 5:13; 7:2; 11:7, 33; 12:11). The root of δικαιοσύνη (δικ–) appears seven times in four other words: "righteous" (δίκαιος in 10:38; 11:4 and 12:23); "regulations" (δικαιώματα in 9:1, 10); "wickedness" (ἀδικίαις, 8:12); and "unjust" (ἄδικος, 6:10). "Good" and "evil" appear even less frequently in Hebrews, never again together. "Good" (καλός) is in 5:14; 6:5; 10:24; 13:9, 18. Its adverbial form, "honorably" (καλῶς) occurs in 13:18. "Evil" (κακός) is only found here in 5:14. Twice it is part of the compound verb "mistreated" (κακουχέομαι), in 11:27 and 13:3.

[42]Only here does Hebrews use this word of a person other than Christ.

example provides is probably more prominent in a context concerned about "the word of righteousness" and the ability "to distinguish between good and evil." The alternative to perpetual infancy (or perhaps death from malnutrition) is growth toward a maturity in which we become more like Jesus, finding in him the moral direction we need and the strength to follow it even in the most difficult of circumstances.

We also read here of the means by which that growth is achieved — **solid food,** that is, the constant use of and training in the practice of distinguishing between good and evil. The Greek text here includes the words for both the process (γυμνάζω, *gymnazō*) and the product (ἕξις, *hexis*). Although *gymnazō* (NIV, "trained," KJV "exercised") was the word used to describe the training of the Greek athletes (who trained naked, cf. *gymnos* in 4:13; cf. English "gymnasium"), the word is never used in this literal sense in the NT but is used to provide an image which helps to understand both the benefits of God's discipline (12:11) and the need to put effort into our spiritual growth (1 Tim 4:7). The tense of the word here is perfect, suggesting that such a person has trained for some time with abiding results. *Hexis* (NIV "constant use," NASB and RSV "practice") here probably refers to the characteristic state which results from the process.[43] Having been trained (γεγυμνασμένα, *gegymnasmena*) for some time, their "faculties" (RSV, τὰ αἰσθητήρια, *ta aisthētēria*) are "practiced" (*hexin*).[44]

The purpose (πρὸς, *pros*)[45] of this practice and training is to "distinguish" (*diakrisin* as in 1 Cor 12:10) between good and

---

[43]Ellingworth, p. 309. He also notes that this word is used in the apocrypha (Sirach: Prologue, 11) of a "skill acquired through the study of Scriptures."

[44]An alternative translation of this verse might read: "But solid food is for the mature who, because of practice, have faculties which have been trained for distinguishing between good and evil."

[45]Bauer suggests that the preposition is used for purpose here but acknowledges that πρός can also be used of result (p. 710). The context actually permits either sense here.

evil. This is a possible allusion to Numbers 14:23 in the LXX (which describes the children of the wilderness generation who "do not know good nor evil") or to Deuteronomy 1:39 (which refers to the same "children who do not yet know good from bad"). Ellingworth notes that this is a rare term but when used elsewhere it involves practical action (Rom 7:21; 12:21; 16:19; 1 Pet 3:11=Ps 34:15; 3 John 11). In other words, the hard work that we invest in nourishing ourselves on the teaching about the word of righteousness pays off in the practical moral and ethical guidance that we need for daily life.

HEBREWS 6

2. On to Maturity (6:1-3)

¹Therefore let us leave the elementary teachings about Christ and go on to maturity, not laying again the foundation of repentance from acts that lead to death,ᵃ and of faith in God, ²instruction about baptisms, the laying on of hands, the resurrection of the dead, and eternal judgment. ³And God permitting, we will do so.

ᵃ*1* Or *from useless rituals*

Therefore continues and draws to a conclusion the thoughts of the previous section. In 5:11 the author announced that he had much to say which was "hard to explain," in 5:12-14 he expressed concern over his readers' lack of maturity which stemmed from an inadequate spiritual appetite and he now concludes that a command is in order. He shifts to less judgmental first person plural statements which suggest identification with his readers, perhaps to offer hope and/or to soften the sting of the harsh rebuke just delivered. Whereas Paul, in a similar situation, judged that he must continue to give the Corinthians milk (1 Cor 3:2) for they were still not ready for solid food, our writer here assesses his readers differently. Ready to progress to solid food, they are challenged to move ahead. To remain on their pabulum diet is unnecessary and would be counterproductive to their spiritual health.

In these three verses, our writer identifies six **elementary teachings about Christ**. As we assess our own spiritual growth, we should want to know what these elementary teachings are and what we are expected, at some point in our growth, to do with them. The author of Hebrews first deals with the latter question.

6:1 Therefore, let us leave the elementary teachings about Christ and go on to maturity, not laying again the foundation . . .

The command here is to **go on to maturity** (φερώμεθα, *pherōmetha*, a hortatory subjunctive, serves as the main verb of the sentence). However, before we can do this, something else must happen first, as expressed by the aorist adverbial participle (ἄφεντες, *aphentes*). We must first **leave** the elementary teachings. This does not mean that we are to abandon them, to forget them or to consider them irrelevant, although ἀφίημι (*aphiēmi*) can convey this meaning.[1] Lane suggests the idea of "leave standing" or "let remain" which seems more in keeping with the only other use of the verb in this letter (2:8).[2] They are, after all, the **foundation**. The point is not that we cease to need them. If the foundation of a house is permitted to crumble, the integrity of the entire structure is threatened.[3] As Alexander Maclaren once said, "Growth in the knowledge of Jesus Christ is not a growing away from the earliest lessons, or a leaving them behind, but a growing up to and into them."[4]

---

[1] It is the same word used in the Gospels when Jesus tells the Pharisees that they have "let go" of the commandments of God (Mark 2:8). Paul uses the word to refer to "divorce" (1 Cor 7:11). In Revelation 2:4, the angel accuses the church of Ephesus of having " forsaken" its first love.

[2] It is also used similarly elsewhere in the NT, such as when we read that the disciples "left" their nets, their boat and their father to follow Jesus (Matt 4:20, 22 and Mark 1:18, 20), when Jesus refers to stones "left" one on another (Matt 24:2), when the Jewish leaders were afraid to "leave" Jesus "going on" the way he was (John 11:48), or when Jesus promised to "leave" his peace with his disciples (John 14:27).

[3] Though used figuratively here, θεμέλιον was also used literally of the foundation of a house or building (Luke 6:48, 49; 14:29; Acts 16:26).

[4] Alexander Maclaren, "Growth," *Twenty Centuries of Great Preaching: An Encyclopedia of Preaching*, Vol. 5. Edited by Clyde E. Fant and William E. Pinson (Waco: Word, 1971), p. 28.

Once the foundation of a house has been laid, however, it
need not be laid **again**. It is time to proceed with the rest of
the house — to continue to build *on top of* the foundation. It is
time to **go on to maturity**. Φερώμεθα (*pherōmetha*, "go on") is
in the present tense which suggests that we are to *continually*
put forth an effort to grow. We are either moving forward or
backward in our spiritual growth. If we are not making every
effort to move forward, then we are probably sliding backward.[5] This form can be read as either a passive or middle
voice verb. Some take it as passive and suggest that we see
here an acknowledgment of the activity of God or a "personal
surrender to God's active influence."[6] However, reading this
as a middle ("actively exerting oneself to make progress"[7])
seems a better fit for a context in which the writer is entreat-
ing his too passive readers to accept more responsibility for
their spiritual growth (see notes to 5:12-14). Though some
object to the translation of τελειότητα (*teleiotēta*) as "maturity,"[8] this exact word is so seldom used in the NT (and

[5]Bruce suggests that φερώμεθα is used "of swift and energetic movement"
(p. 110). There is some precedent for this in the NT (the "violent" wind in
Acts 2:2) but it does not seem likely in many contexts.

[6]See Westcott (p. 143) and Lane (p. 140) who suggest the rendering "let
us be carried forward [by God]." Ellingworth (p. 312) and Morris (p. 54)
concur. This is not theologically unacceptable if we understand Scripture to
teach that our salvation (especially in its present tense of sanctification) is a
cooperative work between the Holy Spirit working within us (2 Cor 3:18)
and our own dedicated effort (Phil 2:12-13; 1 Pet 2:2). Neither is our justification a unilateral transaction either on God's part (a view necessitated by
such doctrines as total depravity, unconditional election, spiritual illumination, limited atonement, irresistible grace and perseverance of the saints) or
on our part (a legalistic work-salvation) but a result of the new covenant
relationship described here in Hebrews — a covenant in which God has
acted first through Christ to secure the possibility of our salvation but into
which we must enter via faith and its attendant manifestations so that we
might appropriate that salvation for ourselves.

[7]So Kistemaker, pp. 152,157.

[8]Lane suggests (1) that the word describes a goal rather than the process,
(2) that translating it as "maturity" implies a state achieved gradually by successive steps of development rather than as an accomplishment of God
through Jesus Christ whereas it (3) describes a result of the action of God

nowhere else in Hebrews) that a firm distinction between this and related forms seems tenuous. It is probably best to read it in much the same way that we have read *teleiōn* ("the mature") in 5:14 and in contrast to νάπιος (*napios*, "infant," 5:13) since 6:1 represents the conclusion of that argument. However, the author's ongoing concern that his readers "not drift away" (2:1), not turn away from God as Israel did in the wilderness but "hold firmly till the end" (3:7-15), not fall short of "the promise of entering his rest" (4:1), "through faith and patience inherit what has been promised" (6:12), "hold unswervingly to the hope" (10:23), "persevere so that" they would "receive what he has promised" (10:36) and "run with perseverance the race marked out" for them (12:1) is also an important part of the larger context and so the final realization of their hope and God's promise is probably not far from view here.

of repentance from acts that lead to death, and of faith in God,

These "elementary teachings about Christ"[9] are probably those described as "the elementary truths of God's word" in 5:12. When, in 5:12, the writer stated that his readers needed

---

rather than a gradual transformation of character (pp. 131-132). Such conclusions, however, seem to be unduly influenced by his decision to read φερώμεθα as passive and to take the term to describe our immediate justification as a result of our position in Christ rather than our progressive sanctification. We have argued that the latter idea is a better fit for the immediate context.

[9]The genitive case here ("of the Christ") could be taken as either subjective or objective. If taken as subjective, it would probably imply that the writer has in mind some words spoken by Christ on these matters. If taken as objective, it would probably mean that he is simply referring to foundational doctrinal instruction (cf. "the principles of the doctrine of Christ," KJV) of the early church. Since the latter would certainly have been apostolic and patterned on the teaching of Christ anyway, it may make little difference how it is taken. Some see here a reference to instruction based on an existing catechesis (Bruce suggests one influenced by *Didache* and *The Epistle of Barnabas*, p. 113). This is possible but not a necessary conclusion.

to be taught them all over again, he was probably employing hyperbole since his ultimate point was that they had already spent too much time on them and should have moved beyond the foundations.

The conjunctions in the Greek text divide the six "elementary teachings" into three pairs:[10] (1) repentance and faith, (2) baptisms and laying on of hands, and (3) resurrection and judgment.[11] Some of these anticipate dimensions of the high priestly christology which will be developed in subsequent chapters (the "much more" — 5:14 — which the author will have to say when he completes his excursus and returns to his main argument in 6:12). Here, though, we should ask in what sense they are foundational.

It is appropriate that repentance and faith should be paired together given the integral connection attributed to

---

[10]This actually depends upon whether, in 6:2, the genitive διδαχῆς (*didachēs*) is retained or whether the variant of the accusative (διδαχήν) is read here. Some commentators have opted for the accusative, believing that the construction is less awkward if διδαχήν is taken with μετανοίας (*metanoias*) as an object of καταβαλλόμενοι (*kataballomenoi*; Kistemaker, p. 153; Bruce, p. 110; Lane, p. 132). As a result, they suggest that the first two items alone (repentance and faith) are "foundational" whereas the subsequent four items are "instructions." Although there is some early support for the accusative, the textual support for the genitive is, on the whole, stronger. Plausible accounts for the rise of either variant have been made. Elsewhere in the NT, there is no theological justification for considering the final four items as of secondary significance.

[11]Bruce suggests that "practically every item could have its place in a fairly orthodox Jewish community" and, quoting Nairne, that all belonged to the creed of a Pharisaic Jew (p. 112). There is little need to resist this claim since, as he points out, the Christian faith incorporated many existing Jewish beliefs and practices. Our writer's treatment of faith in Hebrews chapter 11 even suggests an essential continuity between the old and new covenants — in both, it is by faith that we are commended as righteous (11:4 cf. Rom 1:17). Throughout the letter, the covenants are not discontinuous. Though the first is "obsolete" (8:13) it is because the new covenant is merely "superior" (8:6), the "reality" for which the old was a "shadow" (10:1). But just as Christ's perfect sacrifice has made the continuation of the old sacrifices unnecessary (9:12-14; 10:10-14) so even those practices which are continued have taken on a new significance when reframed within the Christian faith.

them throughout the NT.[12] Regardless of whether our writer
was acquainted with the book of Acts, it is difficult to imagine
that he would not have been familiar with the pattern of conversion described there, in which repentance is described as
the natural and expected consequence of faith (Acts 2:38;
3:19). **Repentance** (*metanoia*) means "a change of mind"
which includes a feeling of "remorse" for our sins but also
encompasses a commitment to a "turning about" in our lifestyle.[13] One might thus say that repentance is a change of attitude toward sin which leads to a desire to change our behavior accordingly. The **acts that lead to death** (lit., "dead
works") are probably the sins which carry death as their consequence (as in Romans 6:23). Our writer uses this same
phrase again in 9:14 (the only other time it appears in the
NT) where it makes more sense if read as referring not, as
some suggest,[14] to the Levitical regulations themselves but to
those sins and the consequent guilt which created the need
for the cleansing sacrifice (in 9:9 the gifts and sacrifices of the
old covenant, in 9:14 the cross). Repentance, however, is
foundational to the Christian life not only in that it represents
an initial turn from sin and toward God but also in that it
describes the whole life change which is to forever follow.

Hebrews is renowned for its teaching about **faith** (πίστις,
pistis, "to believe to the extent of complete trust and
reliance"[15]). The word appears twenty-five times in chapter
eleven alone.[16] It appeared earlier in 4:2,3 where we caught a
glimpse of its foundational significance — the gospel preached

---

[12]The intimate relationship between faith and repentance should caution
us against overreacting to the reversal of the expected order here. It is true
that Scott, Campbell and other early leaders in the Stone-Campbell movement purposely place faith before repentance in describing the conversion
process. Yet their ultimate point — and the thrust of NT teaching — is that
they are so closely bound together that we are mistaken if we unduly separate them.

[13]BAGD, p. 512.

[14]As does Lane, p. 140.

[15]LN, p. 376.

[16]Counting forms of both πίστις and πιστεύω.

to us is of no value to us unless we respond in faith. Faith is foundational to life in the new covenant in that it encompasses our belief that the gospel preached to us is true, our trust in Christ's sacrificial death for our justification in God's sight, and our willingness to continue to trust in God's promises and will for our lives so that we always strive to obey him in all things (Matt 28:20). Apart from the response of faith, we may hear and understand the gospel but it makes no difference either in terms of our forgiveness or our manner of living (cf. Heb 11:4, "without faith it is impossible to please God").

6:2 instruction about baptisms, the laying on of hands,

Two features of this verse tend to obscure our understanding of the second pair of "elementary teachings." First, our writer uses a plural noun — "baptisms." Several possible explanations have been proposed:

1. Jewish ceremonial washings or purification ceremonies practiced at Qumran rather than Christian baptism (cf. RSV, "instruction about ablutions").[17]
2. Purification rites which may have been practiced by early Christians in addition to Christian baptism.[18]
3. The distinction between Christian baptism and other baptisms or purification rituals (including John's baptism and/or Jewish ceremonies, Qumran rituals, pagan rites, the Jewish rite of baptizing proselytes).[19]
4. Triple immersion in the name of the Father, Son and Holy Spirit.[20]

---

[17]So Bruce (p. 116), Morris (p. 53), Attridge (p. 164), and Kistemaker (following Beasley-Murray in the *New International Dictionary of New Testament Theology*, p. 155; cf. NIDNTT, 1:149).

[18]Both Bruce and Attridge refer to a practice described by Hippolytus in *Apostolic Tradition* (3rd century) of baptism on Sunday following a ritual bath for the removal of impurities on the preceding Thursday (Bruce, p. 116; Attridge, p. 164).

[19]So Ellingworth (p. 315) and Thompson (p. 84).

[20]So Tertullian (c.200) as mentioned by Kistemaker (p. 154) and Ellingworth (p. 315).

5. Separate baptisms of water, blood, fire and the Holy Spirit.[21]

6. The baptism of several candidates at once.[22]

Although there are references to (2), (4) and (5) in the writings of the church fathers (3rd-4th centuries), there is simply no NT warrant for such practices. The chief argument for (1) is drawn from the fact that our writer uses not the word βάπτισμα (*baptisma*, the usual word for "baptism" in the NT) but βαπτισμός (*baptismos*, which is clearly used in Mark 7:14 and Hebrews 9:10 in reference to Jewish ceremonial washings). However, this is thin proof to justify the conclusion since (a) the rarity of the term in the NT does not justify pressing a firm distinction between the two terms,[23] (b) Hebrews 9:10 speaks negatively of the "various washings" in mind there whereas 6:2 describes them as foundational Christian doctrine, and (c) it is difficult to see how instructions about ceremonial washings could be part of "the elementary teachings about Christ" since, as our writer will go on to point out, they are superseded within the new covenant. There is little reason, then, to conclude that our writer has anything other than Christian baptism in mind since either (3) or (6) offer possible explanations for the plural. The most plausible alternative may be (3) since it is clear that the early church found it necessary for many years to distinguish between different baptisms (Acts 19:3-6) and questions about the distinction between this new Christian rite and the old covenant practices would have been natural for the audience of this epistle.

A second obscure feature in this verse is the reference to "the laying on of hands." The nature and purpose of the

---

[21]So Augustine as noted by Kistemaker (p. 154) and Ellingworth (p. 315).

[22]Kistemaker (p. 154) and Ellingworth (p. 315).

[23]A probable fourth occurrence of βαπτισμός is in Colossians 2:12 where βαπτισμῷ (rather than βαπτίσματι) has significant textual support. Metzger suggests that it be preferred because copyists were more likely to alter βαπτίσματι than vice versa (p. 623). If this reading is adopted, Paul uses βαπτισμός in reference to Christian baptism.

practice are not described for us here and its significance varies throughout the NT. In the Gospels, it is frequently mentioned as part of Jesus' healing activity and his blessing of children. Elsewhere, it is sometimes associated with setting people apart for service (Acts 6:6; 13:3; 1 Tim 4:14; 5:22; 2 Tim 1:6). In Acts, it is associated with receiving the gift of the Holy Spirit (8:17; 9:17; 19:6; and possibly the meaning of Paul's reference to "gift" in 1 Tim 4:14; 2 Tim 1:6). Here it may be best to understand its significance as having some connection to the gift of the Holy Spirit since (1) in the Acts accounts baptism, as here, is also a part of the context and (2) taken together, the reference to faith, repentance, baptism and the gift of the Holy Spirit make perfect sense as "elementary teachings" in light of the clear pattern of conversion modeled in the NT (cf. Acts 2:38).[24]

the resurrection of the dead, and eternal judgment.

Whereas the first pair of elementary teachings has to do with our initial response to the gospel and the second with the commencement of our new covenant relationship with God which grows out of it, the third pair looks forward to a final, eschatological consummation of that relationship. The doctrines of resurrection and judgment are logically related (cf. 9:27). Though neither are unique to Christianity (both can be found in the OT[25] and the Pharisees believed in the resurrection of the dead[26]), both events find new significance in Christ (cf. Col 1:18; Rom 6:5; 1 Cor 15:20ff; Matt 5:31ff; John 5:22, 27; Acts 17:31).

Since the "resurrection" is described in general terms ("of the dead") it is probably best taken as referring to a resurrection of both the righteous and the wicked (as described in John 5:28-29; cf. Heb 12:23 where God is described as the

---

[24]However, it is not impossible to read this as a commissioning to service since all who are baptized into Christ are called to ministry and service.

[25]Isa 26:19; Dan 12:2; Mark 12:26 cf. Exod 3:6.

[26]Luke gives this as a distinguishing characteristic of the Pharisees in Acts 23:8.

judge of "all men"). Κρίμα (*krima*, "judgment") and its deriva-
tives can be used specifically in the sense of "punishment,"
"damnation," "condemnation" or the act of judging a person
as guilty and thus liable to punishment.[27] But it can also be
used generally of a mere "decision" or "evaluation" apart
from any positive or negative connotation.[28] It is used both
ways in Hebrews (negatively in 10:27, 30; 13:4 — generally in
4:12; 9:27; 12:23) but if our writer has in mind a judgment of
both the righteous and the wicked then the latter is clearly
demanded by the context.

'Αἰῶνος (*aiōnos*, "eternal") reminds us that this judgment is
final and permanent. Christians look forward to an eternity in
the presence of their beloved Savior and heavenly Father
while those outside of Christ can expect nothing but condemnation. This was probably an important reminder to readers
who lived in a day when people widely doubted the account-
ability promised by resurrection and judgment — just as the
Athenians sneered at the notion (Acts 17:32) and the Sadducees rejected it (Matt 23:31; cf. Mark 12:18; Luke 20:35; Acts
4:2; 23:6). For the same reason, it is probably a timely
reminder for Christians today as well.

6:3 And God permitting, we will do so.

This brief verse accomplishes several purposes at once.
First, it summarizes the thrust of 6:1-3 since the phrase "we
will do so" (lit., "and this we will do"[29]) looks back to the command in v. 1 ("go on to maturity"). In addition to looking
back, it also serves as a transition to the section beginning
with v. 4 (NASB, RSV, KJV all translate the Greek connective,
"for," omitted in the NIV). It also anticipates the subject

---

[27]Matt 23:33; Mark 14:64; John 7:51; Rom 5:16; 1 Cor 11:32; 2 Cor 3:9;
James 5:12; 2 Pet 2:3.

[28]Luke 23:24; John 7:24; Rom 11:33; 1 Cor 2:2; 7:37; 10:15; Acts 4:19;
15:19.

[29]Καὶ τοῦτο is the object. Here the neuter singular pronoun, as it often
does, refers not to any particular word in the context but to the entire preceding idea in general.

matter of vv. 4-8 since the phrase "God permitting" not only confesses a dependence upon God for attaining maturity (as all of our lives are subject to God's permissive will, James 4:15) but implies that the final outcome is not yet certain.[30] Finally, the repetition of the first person plural (as in v. 1) suggests that both writer and reader (as all Christians) are somewhere in the process of attaining maturity. None have yet arrived. But all look forward to attaining it unless, rather than growing, we instead fall away. This possibility is contemplated in the verses that follow.

3. Those Who Fall Away (6:4-8)

[4]**It is impossible for those who have once been enlightened, who have tasted the heavenly gift, who have shared in the Holy Spirit, [5]who have tasted the goodness of the word of God and the powers of the coming age, [6]if they fall away, to be brought back to repentance, because[a] to their loss they are crucifying the Son of God all over again and subjecting him to public disgrace.**

[7]**Land that drinks in the rain often falling on it and that produces a crop useful to those for whom it is farmed receives the blessing of God. [8]But land that produces thorns and thistles is worthless and is in danger of being cursed. In the end it will be burned.**

[a]6 Or *repentance while*

These are troublesome verses in at least two senses. First, the apparent suggestion that some who fall away from Christ are so beyond repentance that their recovery is impossible may seem to us harsh, pessimistic and unfeeling. Second, they

---

[30]This is reinforced by the tense of the Greek verbs. ἐπιτρέπῃ (*epitrepē*, "permit") is a present tense which could also be translated "if God continues to permit" or "so long as God permits." The future tense (ποιήσομεν, *poiēsomen*) looks forward to the potential completion of the act.

have been the occasion for centuries of theological controversy — is it possible for one who has been truly converted to lose his or her salvation? How we read these verses in relation to the first concern is likely to influence our understanding of God's compassion and/or our judgments regarding others. How we read them in relation to the second affects our view of the essential nature of the New Covenant which our writer is soon to describe. It is of the utmost importance, then, that in considering these verses we restrict our observations to what is clearly and expressly stated in the text and refrain from ungrounded speculation. Taken as a whole, four significant truths are expressed in these verses.

(1) It is possible to "fall away." This seems quite clear from v. 6 which expressly states this possibility ("if they fall away"). παραπίπτω (*parapiptō*) occurs only here in the NT[31] but related forms (*piptō* and *ekpiptō*) appear in several places, including three times in Hebrews. The word is most often used in a literal sense — of a person falling down to the ground to worship, pray, beg, or in fear (cf. Matt 2:11; 4:9; 17:6; 18:26; Luke 5:12; John 11:32; etc., often this way in Revelation); of a house or tower falling down (Matt 7:25, 27; Luke 11:17; 13:4; etc.); of a sparrow to the ground (Matt 10:29); a seed to the ground (Matt 13:4ff; John 12:24; etc.); crumbs from a table (Matt 15:27; Luke 16:26), and other examples. However, it is also used figuratively — of the potential "dropping out" of the Law (Luke 16:17); of dying (Luke 21:24); or of a lot that has been cast (Acts 1:26). Our writer has used *piptō* to describe the death of the Israelites in the wilderness (3:17) and will use it to describe the fall of the walls of Jericho (11:30) but clearly neither sense is appropriate here.

In 4:11, however, our writer used *piptō* when he set before his readers the promise of rest (4:1) but knew that it would be possible for them to "fall" and not enter into it because of

---

[31]Lane makes an interesting observation, noting, "In Hebrews the characteristic terms for sin that display contempt for God are compounds of παρα–, many of which occur nowhere else in the NT" (p. 142).

their disobedience (4:6, 11). Paul used the word similarly when he described the "stumbling" of Israel (though, in that case, their "fall" was not "beyond recovery," Rom 11:11) and contrasted the "sternness of God to those who fell" and the "kindness" to those who "continue" (Rom 11:22). After yet another warning from Israel's history, he commanded the Corinthians to "stand firm" and "don't fall" (1 Cor 10:12) and, when the Galatians were in danger of returning to legalistic bondage, he commanded them to "stand firm" and declared that those who were trying to be justified by the law had "fallen away from grace" (Gal 5:1, 4).[32]

The word, then, can also refer to a type of disobedience which removes people from the divine covenant and its promises. Lane notes that, in the LXX, *parapiptō* has reference to "the expression of a total attitude reflecting deliberate and calculated renunciation of God" and that the aorist tense in this verse "indicates a decisive moment of commitment to apostasy."[33] Moulton and Milligan note that the word was used in some early papyri to describe "breaking terms of a contract, rendering it invalid"[34] and so Louw and Nida suggest that the term means "to abandon a former relationship or association."[35] To understand it so here is clearly in keeping with our author's continuing concern about a possible "turning away" (Heb 3:12; 12:25) on the part of his hearers.

Here, then, is an important truth. It is possible, once in a covenant relationship with God, to remove ourselves from that covenant relationship by our own deliberate choice.

(2) Their prior Christian condition is described as fact. Three features of these verses suggest that the author considered them to have, in fact, been Christians. The first is the ἅπαξ . . . πάλιν construction (*hapax . . . palin*, literally, "once . . . again," although NIV incorporates this idea into its transla-

---

[32]However, Louw and Nida suggest that Galatians 5:4 could also be translated "you no longer experience God's grace" (p. 808).

[33]Lane, p. 142; cf. RSV.

[34]MM, pp. 488-489; also in *The Oxyrhynchus Papyri*, Vol. I, 95:34 (AD 129).

[35]LN, p. 449.

tion of v. 6 as "brought back" rather than "brought again"). This suggests that the writer considered them to have, at a time in the past, attained a certain position in their relationship with God, to have lost it, and to be in need of it again. The "falling away" has, then, effected a real change in that relationship.

Second, their former conditions are described with aorist tenses which lack the dimension of present consequences carried by the perfect tense but nevertheless convey the idea of past, historic reality. In fact, when the NIV renders v. 6 "if they fall away," it breaks the parallelism of the Greek text in which the subjects are described by five consecutive aorist participles. The final participle could just as well be translated like each of the previous four — "and who have fallen away." Each of the previous four descriptions, then, as much as the last, could be described as "decisive moments."

Finally, the descriptive phrases employed in vv. 4-5 suggest the fact of their prior Christian condition. First, they had **once been enlightened**. Our writer uses this same word (φωτίζω, *phōtizō*)[36] in 10:32 when he encourages his readers to "remember those earlier days after you had received the light," a phrase which parallels "after we have received the knowledge of the truth" in 10:26. The word should probably be taken, then, as referring to "instruction"[37] or an "intellectual illumination that removes ignorance through . . . the preaching of the gospel."[38] Paul similarly uses a form of the word in 2 Corinthians 4:4, 6 when he refers to "the light of the gospel of

---

[36]The KJV renders it "illuminated," a term which many associate with a unilateral operation, performed by the Holy Spirit, which grants revelation or understanding irrespective of the will or any condition in the individual chosen by God to receive it and which is necessitated by the depraved condition of fallen man. There is little evidence to compel such an understanding of this term, however, apart from *a priori* theological commitments. The reading suggested in the comments on this verse fits equally well with the context of any NT passage which might be so construed.

[37]Ellingworth, p. 320.

[38]Lane, p. 141.

the glory of Christ" and "the light of the knowledge of the glory of God" which were preached to his readers.[39]

They had also once **tasted the heavenly gift** and **shared in the Holy Spirit**. Here we see, as in 2:9, a figurative use of γεύομαι (*geuomai*, lit., "taste"[40]) in the sense of "experience."[41] The reference to "heavenly gift" and "Holy Spirit" are probably synonymous — in Acts, δωρέα (*dōrea*, "gift") is used exclusively of *the* gift which is the Holy Spirit.[42] Μέτοχος (*metochos*) has already been used by our writer to describe the "companions" above which the Son has been set (1:9), the "partnership" which holy brothers share in their heavenly calling (3:1), and the fact that so long as Christians hold firm they continue to "share" in Christ.[43] He will again use it in 12:8 when distinguishing between true and illegitimate sons (the former are "partakers" in God's discipline). Here, then, the term seems to suggest the "partnership," "fellowship" or "companionship" into which each person enters who has experienced or received the Holy Spirit. The fact of their Christian condition

---

[39]Some, including Bruce, see in this word a reference to baptism which is mentioned in 6:2. As he (p. 120) and others point out, there is second century evidence for a use of this word in such connections (Syriac Peshitta, Justin Martyr) but the connections he suggests with NT passages seem tenuous and Lane is probably correct to point out that "prior to the middle of the second century there is no clear evidence that φωτίζειν means "to baptize" (p. 141).

[40]Used of wine (Matt 27:34, cf. John 2:9) and food (Luke 14:24; Acts 10:10; 20:11; 23:14) or in an undefined sense (Col 2:21).

[41]Used of our experience of death (Matt 16:28; Mark 9:1 and Luke 9:27; John 8:52; just as in Heb 2:9) and of the Lord's goodness (1 Pet 2:3).

[42]Acts 2:38; 8:20; 10:45; 11:17. Paul uses the word in a broader sense to refer to God's grace toward those in Christ (2 Cor 9:14-15) or some particular manifestation of it (the "grace" of preaching to the Gentiles, Eph 3:7; that grace manifested in the apportioning of gifts to equip God's people for service and maturity, Eph 4:7; the gift of righteousness which leads to life as opposed to the trespasses which lead to death, Rom 5:15). Taken either way, the term still clearly describes a definite and true Christian experience.

[43]Similarly, Luke uses it to describe the fishing "partnership" of Peter, James, and John while Paul uses μετοχή to describe the inability of light to have "fellowship" with darkness when discouraging believers from marrying unbelievers (2 Cor 6:14).

is thus confirmed not only by their individual experience of the Spirit's presence in their lives but also by the reality of the fellowship which they had thus come to share with like others.

Finally, they had also **tasted the goodness of the word of God and the powers of the coming age**. This is now the third time our writer has paired "word" and "power" to describe God's word. We read earlier that it is by "his powerful word" that the Son sustains all things (1:3). But here the pair seems to echo 2:1-4 where we read that the salvation first announced by the Lord was later testified to by "signs, wonders and various miracles [δύναμις, *dynamis*, "powerful act"] and gifts of the Holy Spirit." As 6:1-2 resembles the pattern of conversion described in Acts, so this verse appears to reflect an important dimension of God's confirmation of his gospel for *dynamis* is regularly used there to describe the display of the Spirit's power which often accompanied the preaching of the word.[44] If so, then these final descriptions flow out of the first two and join them together (instruction of the word and experience of the Holy Spirit), further confirming the fact of the Christian condition described here.

(3) Those who fall away cannot be restored so long as they persist in their flagrant and public rejection of Christ. The subject of ἀνακαινίζω (*anakainizō*, in this context, "to cause to change to a previous, preferable state"[45]) is not identified and could be either God (the convicting ministry of his Spirit), other Christians seeking to "restore"(RSV) their fallen brother or sister, or both. Regardless of the agent and in spite of persistency in the effort (the writer shifts from past oriented aorist tense forms to the present, continual, tense here), the word **impossible** (v. 4) makes it clear that in their present condition

---

[44]Acts 1:9 (cf. 2:4, 16-17); 2:22; 3:12; 4:7, 22 (cf. 4:31); 6:8; 8:13 (cf. 8:10); 10:38; 19:11.

[45]So Louw and Nida (p. 157) who point out that in other contexts forms of the word can mean "to cause something to become new and different, with the implication of becoming superior" (cf. 2 Cor 4:16 and Col 3:10 where ἀνακαινόω appears and Rom 12:2 and Titus 3:5 where ἀνακαίνωσις is used). Ἀνακαινίζω appears only here in the NT.

they will not respond. It is important that we consider the nature of that condition and precisely what is described as impossible.

What is their condition? The last part of v. 6 describes the degree to which their lives have actually turned in the opposite direction — **they are crucifying the Son of God all over again and subjecting him to public disgrace**. Just how they do so is not specified. Perhaps upon their rejection of the Christ they once embraced they have come to engage in active and public opposition to his gospel, perhaps their return to an open lifestyle of sin and immorality cause the gospel to be disgraced or both. Regardless, the outcome is the same. It is clear, in a public sense for all to see and know, that they no longer regard Jesus as the Savior crucified for their sins. Their rejection is so extreme that it is as if they were nailing him to the cross all over again. There is nothing in these verses to suggest that the atonement which Jesus accomplished at the cross does not apply to the future sins of those who remain within their covenant relationship with God, repentant and grateful for the sacrifice made by their Savior. Those described here refuse to repent and have decided to reject him. This resembles closely the description of a clear and final rejection of Christ described by Peter (2 Pet 2:20-22).

However, lest we adopt too extreme a posture in regard to those whom we deem to have so "fallen away," we should also consider what is precisely said to be "impossible." It is neither their forgiveness or salvation which is said to be impossible but their own decision, in their present condition, to repent. The NIV offers an interpretive rendering of the Greek syntax which, unfortunately, creates confusion. The word **because** (v. 6) does not represent the presence of such a conjunction in the Greek text but a decision on the part of the translators to interpret the relationship between two adverbial participles ("crucifying" and "exposing to public ridicule") and the main verb of the sentence ("it is impossible") as one of cause. However, the participles are in the present tense form which indicates a coordinate time relationship between these activities and the impossibility of their repentance (whereas the aorist tense is more commonly used for actions that precede the verb).[46] In other words, we could read the text as saying, "*so long as* they are crucifying and subjecting," which would admit the ultimate possibility of restoration should such a person ever decide to stop these activities and repent.

(4) *God will be faithful in his response.* The phrase **to their loss** (v. 6) indicates the results for those who so fall away and refuse to repent. Having removed themselves from their covenant relationship with God, it is reasonable to assume that they lose claim to the covenant promises. They can only expect to receive from God what they otherwise would have, had they rejected the gospel to begin with and remained outside of that covenant relationship — his rejection and condemnation. As our writer put it in 2:3, "how shall we escape if we ignore such a great salvation?" These four verses, then, seem to represent our writer's worst fears for his readers.

Yet we must also understand that such an end represents God's faithful response in terms of the gospel presented to us in the NT. It is nothing else, more or less. After describing the covenant in more detail, our writer will stress that "he who promised is faithful" (10:23) but at the same time remind us that "if we deliberately keep on sinning after we have received the knowledge of the truth, no sacrifice for sins is left, but only a fearful expectation of judgment and of raging fire that will consume the enemies of God" (10:26-27). God is a God of grace but also of justice (6:10) and such rejection is part of the faithful response which he has promised. Paul echoes the same thought in Romans when, after noting that Israel had not fallen beyond recovery (11:11), he went on to warn them, "Consider therefore the kindness and sternness

---

[46]According to MHT, the Greek participle "had originally no temporal function . . . but eventually, the aorist participle came to denote a time which was past in relationship to the main verb, and the present participle time which was contemporaneous" (MHT, Vol. III, p. 79). Exceptions to the case can be found but this is the general rule in Greek syntax.

of God: sternness to those who fell, but kindness to you, provided that you continue in his kindness. Otherwise, you also will be cut off" (11:22).

The analogy in verses 7-8 serves as an illustration of this truth. Soil and vineyard imagery were prominent both in the ministry of Jesus[47] and the preaching of Isaiah[48] and our writer could easily have either or both in mind. God sends his rain on all[49] just as his word is preached to all (Matt 13:1ff), and the end result is determined by what grows out of the soil. God has acted once and for all (cf. 10:12) to make our salvation possible. He now responds to us based upon how we respond to him. The curse may, at present, be regarded as a mere "danger" but "in the end" (eschatologically) such land can only expect to be "burned" (see 10:27 where God's judgment is described as a "raging fire" and 12:29, "God is a consuming fire").

At the outset of this section, it was suggested that how we read these verses affects our understanding of God's compassion, our judgments regarding others, and our view of the essential nature of the New Covenant. How this is so can now be seen more clearly. First, we see here the bilateral nature of the New Covenant. The blessings of this covenant are not unilaterally and unconditionally bestowed in either a universal or partial sense. Our response to what God has done in Christ (faith, repentance and baptism) is foundational in the creation of this covenant relationship and continuing in the

---

[47]In his parable of the soils (Matt 13:1ff, Mark 4:1ff and Luke 8:4ff) and the parable of the tenants (Matt 21:33ff, Mark 12:1ff and Luke 20:9ff). Earlier, Jesus had cursed the fig tree which bore no fruit (Matt 21:18ff, Mark 11:12ff) as an object lesson which prefigured the judgment described in the parable of the tenants. Jesus also used tree and fruit imagery in his sermon on the mount to explain how to recognize false teachers ("by their fruit you will recognize them," 7:20).

[48]In Isaiah 5, the prophet's Song of the Vineyard, Israel is compared to a vineyard which was destroyed after it yielded only bad fruit when its creator looked for a crop of good grapes.

[49]One might compare Matt 5:45, although Jesus there seems to be speaking literally while our writer is here speaking analogically.

commitment (expressed by these) to Christ's Lordship is an essential condition for continuing that relationship. It is possible to be in fact and truth a Christian who possesses a real covenant relationship with God and then to decisively abandon that relationship. The choice is ours and in no way adds to or detracts from his compassion for us. It is God's desire that all people everywhere would repent (Acts 17:30) but it remains for us to do so of our own free will.

These verses are also suggestive as to how we see ourselves and others. Many want to know, "have I committed apostasy and am I therefore beyond the grasp of God's grace?" The answer suggested here is that the only people beyond the grasp of God's grace are those who wish to be. Anyone who is willing to repent — probably anyone who cares enough to ask the question — can be restored to his or her relationship to God on that condition. As to whether others around us are in such an "apostate" condition is a decision that should be left to God since any decision to repent places a person outside of the class described here and we can never be sure whether or not a person will someday make that decision. Our most appropriate response is to never give up in our efforts to restore them and allow God to make, "in the end," the decision about their eternal fate.

4. Confident of Better Things (6:9-12)

[9]Even though we speak like this, dear friends, we are confident of better things in your case — things that accompany salvation. [10]God is not unjust; he will not forget your work and the love you have shown him as you have helped his people and continue to help them. [11]We want each of you to show this same diligence to the very end, in order to make your hope sure. [12]We do not want you to become lazy, but to imitate those who through faith and patience inherit what has been promised.

Following his harshest words yet, our writer offers a vote of confidence and a word of comfort. Warning and encouragement are offered together as motivation. He addresses them as **dear friends** although the word (ἀγαπητός, *agapētos*, "object of one's affection, one who is loved"[50]) is capable of a stronger translation, such as "beloved." This is the only place in Hebrews where our writer so addresses his readers, his most tender expression following his harshest words of warning. The first person plural (**we**) may be a collective reference to writer and readers as in 6:1 but since the readers are addressed directly and in the second person (**your case**) it is more probable that it here refers to the writer and his associates (cf. 5:11; 13:18).

Πείθω (*peithō*, "are confident") includes the idea of persuasion (cf. KJV, "are persuaded" and 1 Cor 2:4 where Paul refers to *peithos*, "persuasive words") but often, as here, brings into focus the trust, confidence or sureness that results from it. Our writer will use it again in 13:18, "we are *sure* that we have a clear conscience." The contrast in tenses is worth noting as well. Whereas "we speak" clearly communicates the idea of the present tense of the Greek verb, "we are confident" seems to reflect the same tense when, in fact, the verb is in the perfect tense form which usually describes an action which began or occurred in the past but carries results into the present (lit., "we have been confident"). The writer may be "speaking" now but his confidence in them is nothing new but continues into the present.

The word for **better** occurs more times in Hebrews than in the entire rest of the NT and is a significant word in our writer's purpose, although its true significance lies ahead (chapters 7-11, where old and new covenants are compared). Here, what is better is the **salvation** which he expects for his readers, rather than the loss referred to in v. 6 or the judgment described in v. 8 — the eternal salvation of which Jesus is the source for all who obey him (5:9).

---

[50]LN, p. 294.

Two reasons are given for his confidence. The first is the character of God: **God is not unjust** (ἄδικος, *adikos*). In other contexts, *adikos* and its related forms[51] usually receive a stronger translation such as "unrighteous(ness)," "iniquity," "evil (doer)", or "wicked(ness)." In v. 8, our writer used *adokimos* to describe "worthless" thistles and *adikia* will appear in 8:12 in reference to the "wickedness" which God, through the prophet Jeremiah, promised to forgive. However, the verb can also mean "to hurt or to harm, with the implication of doing something wrong or undeserved"[52] (cf. Matt 20:13; Luke 10:19; Acts 25:20) and Peter uses *adikia* to describe the pain of "unjust" suffering which Christian slaves are exhorted to endure. The closest parallel in the NT to what we read here is in Romans 3:5 where Paul poses the rhetorical question of whether God would be "unjust" to bring his wrath upon us in light of our unrighteousness. Here, the point is not that we can be so righteous as to deserve salvation as our "just" reward but that God will be "just" and faithful in relationship to his covenant promises and the lives of the readers give evidence that they continue in that relationship with him.

Thus follows the second reason for the writer's confidence: the evidence of salvation which he sees in their lives. As in so many places in Scripture, **work** and **love** are joined together. Paul wrote of a "labor prompted by love" (1 Thess 1:3) and John encouraged Christians to "not love with words or tongue but with actions and in truth" (1 John 3:18). Our writer will join these same terms[53] in 10:24 when he exhorts his readers to "spur one another on toward love and good deeds."

As elsewhere, it seems clear that the work is the outward evidence or proof of the love which, in this case, is **shown** in the **help** given to God's people. Ἐνδείκνυμι (*endeiknymi*)

---

[51]The adjective ἄδικος, ον is used here. Related forms include the noun ἄδικος, ου (m), ἀδικία, ἀδίκως, ἀδόκιμος, ἀδικέω.

[52]LN, p. 231.

[53]Ἀγάπη and ἔργον appear together both in 6:10 and 10:24.

means "show" or "cause to be made known" in the sense of proof, evidence, verification or indication.[54] For example, it is the same word Paul uses in 2 Corinthians 8:24 when he urges his readers to "show (*endeiknymi*) proof (ἔνδειξις, *endeixis*)" of their love "so that the churches can see it" (lit., "in the presence of the churches") by participating in the collection for the Christians in Jerusalem. The word for "help" (διακονέω, *diakoneō*)[55] is usually translated "serve" or "minister." Examples of their service to others are offered later in the letter. In 10:33-34, we read that they "stood side by side" with those who were insulted and persecuted, even when it meant receiving the same treatment themselves. In 13:1-3, we read that they expressed their love by entertaining strangers and remembering those in prison.

Much of this resembles what Jesus described in his saying about the sheep and the goats (Matt 25:31ff). Here, their love is "shown **him**,"[56] just as in 13:2 some people "entertained angels without knowing it" and in Matthew 25 the one who serves "one of the least of these brothers of mine" serves Jesus himself. Ministering to God's people manifests a love for God himself and serves as observable evidence that we belong to him.

6:11 We want each of you to show this same diligence to the end, in order to make your hope sure.

His confidence, however, does not keep our writer from worrying about the possibility that his readers might give up. Thus he now turns from the past and the present to the

---

[54]LN, p. 341.

[55]The repetition moves from past actions (aorist tense) to present actions (present actions) and probably anticipates the reference to the future in v. 11 when ἐνδείκνυμι ("show") is repeated, completing the chiasm ("show . . . serve . . . serve . . . show").

[56]Literally, "to his name." Morris notes that "'Name' in antiquity summed up all that the person was" (p. 57) but others suggest that the phrase simply means "for his sake" (cf. Ellingworth, p. 331 and Lane, p. 133). In either case, it is clear that deeds directed toward others reflect a love directed toward God.

future. He wants his readers to "keep on showing" (an accept-able translation of the present tense form) the evidence of their love for God "to the end." This latter phrase hearkens back to the eschatological reference in v. 8 (hence the NIV, "to the *very* end"). Ἐπιθυμέω (*epithymeō*, "want") occurs only here in Hebrews but as elsewhere in the NT it communicates a very strong desire.[57] It is used in the Gospels to describe sex-ual "lust" (Matt 5:28), the "longing" of the prophets and right-eous men to hear the teachings of the Messiah (Matt 13:17; cf. 1 Pet 1:12), the "longing" of the prodigal son to eat with the pigs (Luke 15:16) and of Lazarus to eat what fell from the rich man's table (Luke 16:21). It is also used to describe "covetous-ness" (Acts 20:33; cf. Paul's use of the term in connection with the tenth commandment, Rom 7:7; 13:9; James 4:2).

Not only does he want them to keep showing the evidence of their love for God but to do so with "this same diligence." In some contexts, this word (σπουδή, *spoudē*) includes the idea of haste, quickness, hurriedness or eagerness (Mark 6:25; Luke 1:39; Phil 2:28; possibly Luke 7:4 and Titus 3:13). But here the word functions as an opposite to the word "lazy" in v. 12 (νωθρός [*nōthros*], translated "slow" in 5:11) and so prob-ably carries the sense of "working hard" or "not letting up."

The goal of this diligence is to make their hope sure (lit., "the full assurance of hope," NASB). Πληροφορία (*plērophoria*, "assurance") and its cognates include the notion of "com-pleteness" or "fullness" — whether it be "to tell fully" or "relate fully the content of a message," to "fully accomplish one's task" or "be completely successful," to be "fully persuad-ed," or to "be completely certain of the truth of something."[58] Ἐλπίς (*elpis*, "hope") can refer to the act of expecting but in Hebrews tends to mean the thing expected/hoped for (here, probably the "promises" referred to in v. 12).[59] The true

---

[57]This is also consistent with the observations made by MM based upon early papyri (p. 239).

[58]Louw and Nida, pp. 161, 371, 411, 655.

[59]So Ellingworth, p. 332.

significance of these terms is seen in their relationship to πίστις (*pistis*, "faith," v. 12). In 10:22, our writer refers to the "full assurance [πληροφορία, *plērophoria*] of faith" and in 11:1 he will write that "faith is being sure [ὑπόστασις, *hypostasis*, "substance"] of what we hope for [ἐλπίζω, *elpizō*]." The concepts of faith, hope, and assurance are interrelated — "hope" describing what we look forward to, "faith" the trust or belief that we will in fact receive what we expect, and "assurance" the present experience of certainty which grows out of faith. The diligence with which we continue to serve is an ongoing sign that we have lost none of these.

6:12 We do not want you to become lazy, but to imitate those who through faith and patience inherit what has been promised.

The Greek text actually continues the sentence which began in v. 11 — literally, "in order that you might not become," indicating the desired result. It is first described negatively and then positively. Νωθρός (*nōthros*, "lazy") is repeated from 5:11 (where the author charged his listeners with being "slow to learn"), framing the excursus and relating the intervening discussion to his initial concern. He hopes, then, that the rebuke of 5:11-14, the exhortation of 6:1-3, the warning of 6:4-8 and the encouragement of 6:9-12 will motivate his readers to get on with their spiritual growth, for therein lies the secret to endurance and perseverance.

If they do so, they can become "imitators." Our writer will use the same word in 13:7 when exhorting his readers to imitate the faith of their church leaders but here the word anticipates, immediately, the reference to Abraham in vv. 13-15 and, eventually, "the ancients" of chapter 11 where their faith will be more fully defined and illustrated. Faith and patience (μακροθυμία [*makrothymia*], cf. 6:15) are the qualities demanded in the interim wait for "what has been promised." They are natural counterparts, for the period of waiting which requires patience is usually the strongest test of our trust.

D. GOD'S OATH MAKES HIS PURPOSE SURE (6:13-20)

[13]When God made his promise to Abraham, since there was no one greater for him to swear by, he swore by himself, [14]saying, "I will surely bless you and give you many descendants."[a] [15]And so after waiting patiently, Abraham received what was promised.

[16]Men swear by someone greater than themselves, and the oath confirms what is said and puts an end to all argument. [17]Because God wanted to make the unchanging nature of his purpose very clear to the heirs of what was promised, he confirmed it with an oath. [18]God did this so that, by two unchangeable things in which it is impossible for God to lie, we who have fled to take hold of the hope offered to us may be greatly encouraged. [19]We have this hope as an anchor for the soul, firm and secure. It enters the inner sanctuary behind the curtain, [20]where Jesus, who went before us, has entered on our behalf. He has become a high priest forever, in the order of Melchizedek.

[a]14 Gen. 22:17

In the Greek text, the conjunction *gar* ("for") directly connects these verses to v. 12. Though moving away from his parenthetical address, our writer will make a gradual transition back to his main argument. This transition will be complete by v. 20 when he returns to the theme mentioned in 5:10, just before he broke off to address his readers slowness of learning (5:11). The example of Abraham, then, appears to serve two purposes: (1) to illustrate the relationship between faith, patience and hope (cf. vv. 12, 15, 18-19) and (2) to prepare for the argument about the greatness of Melchizedek (7:4, 6, 7).

Abraham is a key figure in Hebrews, being mentioned no less than ten times,[60] and his significance in NT theology is

---

[60]2:16; 6:13; 7:1, 2, 4, 5, 6, 9; 11:8, 17.

twofold:[61] (1) God's promise to him frames the purpose and method of the plan of redemption, announcing the gospel and (2) his faith in that promise models the way of righteousness which is revealed in the gospel (Rom 1:17). In the Greek text, our author places Abraham's name in the initial position for emphasis, presumably to take advantage of the *ethos* provided by his example, although its persuasiveness for his readers was probably due more to his status as the patriarch of Israel.[62]

The thrust of these verses, however, is what God did when he took the initiative to act toward Abraham, and the grammar of the sentence makes it clear that he performed two acts at the same time. He made a "promise" (present adverbial participle) and he "swore" or took an oath (main verb). For now, our writer only adds that when God swore, he "swore by himself." So God himself stated (Gen 22:16) when repeating his promise to Abraham and so Moses had remembered when interceding with God on behalf of the Israelites (Exod 32:13). The reason given for God so swearing was that he was simply too great to be confined to the human custom of swearing by someone greater than themselves (v. 16). God's oath and promise, then, are what Abraham had to place his faith in and their significance will be discussed in vv. 17-18.

Our writer cites a portion of Genesis 22:17 as it is found in the LXX, with the exception of substituting "you" for "your seed." Whatever the reason, it makes no difference in the sense of the passage. The first record of this promise is in Genesis 12:1-9 and it is repeated in 13:14-17; 15:5; 17:2, 19; 26:3 (to Isaac); and 28:14 (to Jacob). 22:17, however, is the only statement of the promise to Abraham which includes the reference to the oath.

---

[61]See Acts 3:25; 7:17; Romans 4:13; Galatians 3:8, 14, 16, 18 as well as Hebrews 11 regarding this twofold significance of the model of Abraham.

[62]Since they had yet to benefit by the clear teaching of chapter 11 and we cannot be certain to what extent (if any) the readers would have been familiar with the teachings in Romans and Galatians.

6:15 And so after waiting patiently, Abraham received what was promised.

Our writer now turns from God's promise and oath to Abraham's response, which models exactly what is required of the readers (cf. v. 12). *Makrothymeō* means "to demonstrate patience despite difficulties" or "in the face of provocation or misfortune"[63] and hence the usual translation in the KJV is "suffer long." Abraham was already 75 years old when God first made his promise to him (Gen 12:4) and waited another 25 years before Isaac was finally born (21:5). His fathering of Ishmael by Hagar at Sarah's behest (Gen 16) illustrated how trying the wait was. The citation of Genesis 22:17 in v. 14 would probably have reminded the readers of how God tested Abraham by commanding him to sacrifice the promised son (Gen 22:1-19). And yet Abraham's obedience in this case illustrated the extent to which he had grown in his faith and ability to "wait patiently" on the promises of God.

As a result ("after waiting patiently" translates an aorist adverbial participle which could be easily read as causal in this context), Abraham "received what was promised." How this was so might be difficult for some of us to imagine. He had been promised a great nation, a multitude and yet when he died he had but the one son of the promise and two grandsons (Gen 25:7, 26).[64] Yet Abraham clearly considered this a wondrous miracle (Gen 17:17; 18:11-12; 21:7) as did our writer (Heb 11:11) and so it is possible that the reference here is simply to the birth of Isaac. Or perhaps it was simply that through Isaac's birth Abraham saw "the things promised" and "welcomed them from a distance," receiving the promise in this sense, while the "descendants as numerous as the stars" represented another sense in which our writer later says he "did not receive the things promised" (11:11-13). The point for the readers is the same: to receive what God has

---

[63]LN, p. 307.

[64]In addition to Ishmael by Hagar and six children by Keturah and their descendants (Gen 25:2-4).

promised as Abraham did, they must also wait patiently as Abraham did.

6:16 Men swear by someone greater than themselves, and the oath confirms what is said and puts an end to all argument.

As he continues to illustrate for his readers the importance of faith and patience in making their hope sure, the writer now shifts his attention back to God again, turning from Abraham's faith to God's faithfulness. This verse introduces the first part of an argument from lesser to greater (from what men do to what God does) but also anticipates one of the forthcoming arguments about the superiority of Christ's priesthood (7:20ff).

The present tense form of "swear" clearly suggests customary action here. In ancient cultures, the seriousness of taking an oath was suggested by the fact that many viewed them as dangerous since breaking them was often associated with a curse ("one who is quick to take an oath, will be quick to meet his death"[65]). Yet they served the important purpose of enhancing the credibility of claims not readily accessible to empirical confirmation by adding the threat of curse or hope of blessing, placing the promise under the agency and judgment of the gods or king.[66] Some oaths were considered binding upon subsequent generations as well.[67] Similarities in

---

[65]So Fensham illustrates from ancient Egyptian sources ("Oath," *International Standard Bible Encyclopedia*, G. Bromiley, ed., Vol. III, p. 572.

[66]So Gregory, "Oath," *Zondervan Pictorial Encyclopedia of the Bible*, Vol. IV, p. 476. Ellingworth distinguishes between the "promises" as referring to the entire series of promises made in Gen 12-17 as a unity and the "oath" as a climactic swearing by God following the offering of Isaac. Pressing the distinction in this manner is probably unnecessary in light of the function and purpose of the oath described here.

[67]According to Fensham (p. 573), this was at least true both of the Hittites and the Hebrews. In the Old Testament, Israel took Joseph's bones with them when they left Egypt to fulfill an oath made over 400 years before (Exod 13:19 cf. Gen 50:25-26) and David made amends to the Gibeonites for Saul's breaking of an oath taken by Israel in the days of Joshua (2 Sam. 21:2, 7; Josh 9).

terminology between oaths in the Old Testament and those of other ancient cultures suggest that they served the same basic functions for Israel. The third and ninth commandments (Exod 20:7, 16), even if not limited to this, clearly applied to the sanctity of oaths within the covenant community. Jesus' command in Matthew 5:33-37 indicates that the Jews of his day did not take oaths as seriously as they should have.[68]

This same purpose of the oath is clearly indicated by our writer here. It "confirms what is said" and "puts an end to all argument." The RSV is more form-literal here: "in all their disputes an oath is final for confirmation." 'Αντιλογία (antilogia, "argument") literally means "to speak (legō) against (anti)"[69] and in classical Greek rhetorics served as a technical forensic term.[70] Εἰς βεβαίωσιν (eis bebaiōsin, "for confirmation") was also a technical legal term used "to denote legally guaranteed security" whether of a lease, a title to property, a sale or delivery, etc.[71] Adding an oath to a promise was

---

[68]The significance accorded the oath in Hebrew culture was paralleled in Greco-Roman culture as well. As Lane points out (p. 151), Cicero indicated that in Roman forensics an oath was considered final confirmation (Topica, 20.77).

[69]Kistemaker, p. 178.

[70]For example, Aristotle uses the word to describe the "conflict of opinion" (Freese) or "two sides of a question" (Kennedy) to which deliberative rhetoric is addressed (Rhetoric, 1414b3) and the "contradiction" to which an appeal to ethos makes one vulnerable (Rhetoric, 1418b25). It is also reported to have been the title of a text on rhetoric by the early sophist Protagoras (Diogenes Laertius 3.37) whose treatment of rhetoric centered on the notion of dissoi logoi — "two-fold discourses," or the belief that there are two contrary accounts (logoi) concerning everything, one of which is stronger at a given time (Schiappa, "Protagoras," Encyclopedia of Rhetoric and Composition: Communication from Ancient Times to the Information Age, Theresa Enos, ed., (New York: Garland Pub., 1996). Lane describes the prominence of technical legal language in the passage and notes that "the distinctive character of the vocabulary finds ample illustration in the LXX and in contracts preserved among the papyri" (p. 149; cf. MM, pp. 48, 448, 457).

[71]So MM define the phrase from many examples in the papyri, supporting the theory of Diessman and suggesting (1) that the LXX adopted it as legal phraseology in Lev 25:23 and (2) that this forensic flavor is still notable in Phil 1:7 and Heb 6:6 (pp. 107-108).

considered sufficient evidence to "cause someone to be firm or established in belief"[72] and ended the need for doubt or debate.

6:17 Because God wanted to make the unchanging nature of his purpose very clear to the heirs of what was promised, he confirmed it with an oath.

Verses 17-20 describe the second half, or conclusion, of the lesser to greater argument. In this verse, we read *why* God chose to confirm his promise with an oath[73] — he "wanted to make the unchanging nature of his purpose very clear." "Want" (βούλομαι, *boulomai*) includes the idea of intent and deliberateness, as suggested by the use of the word "purpose" to translate the cognate noun (βουλή, *boulē*) later in the same sentence. "Make clear" (ἐπιδείκνυμι, *epideiknymi*) continues the forensic terminology in this section. It could be translated "prove" as it is elsewhere, when in Acts 18:28 we read that Apollos proved "in public debate" that Jesus was the Christ. A cognate (*apodeiknymi*) is used in Acts 25:7 where we read that the Jews were unable to "prove" their charges against Paul in court.[74] What God wanted to prove was "the unchanging nature of his purpose." Ἀμετάθετος (*ametathetos*, "unchange-ableness") appears only here and in v. 18 in the NT but Moulton and Milligan point out that in the papyri, "the word was used as a technical term in connexion with wills" (p. 26) — i.e., they were fixed at death (cf. 9:16, 17).

---

[72]LN, p. 377.

[73]The Greek text actually continues the sentence begun in v. 16, appending v. 17 with an initial prepositional phrase (ἐν ᾧ). Crouch (p. 168) and Westcott (p. 160) both suggest that the phrase refers back to the general idea of man's customs of oath taking and its use in finalizing disputes (e.g., "wherein"). Ellingworth (p. 340-341), Lane (p. 148), Moule (*Idiom Book*, p. 131-132) and Blass, Debrunner and Funk (#219), however, all take it as causal and this is consistent with the apparent meaning of the same struc-ture in Hebrews 2:18.

[74]According to MM, the papyri also attest to this usage of the word, using it to describe "clearing" oneself in court, "verifying" the condition of land, or "proving" a charge in the presence of witnesses (p. 237).

God wanted to make this clear to "the heirs of what was promised." Inheritance terminology is frequent in Hebrews (1:2, 4, 14; 6:12, 17; 9:15; 11:7, 8; 12:17). Here it is a carryover from v. 12. It fits well into the forensic/legal terminology but its significance here seems to be theological as well. The thrust of the immediate context is that the readers were the heirs of the same promises made to Abraham (6:12, 15, 17) and this is not a unique idea in the NT (cf. Gal 3:7-9, 16-20; Acts 3:25). The use of the present tense form (which could be translated, "because God *always wants*") suggests a continuing purpose expressed through an oath binding throughout subsequent generations (see comments on v. 16 above). Thus the promises which God confirmed to Abraham (and by extension even to Christians today), not only encompass God's dealings with Israel and the coming of the Christ as the promised blessing (Acts 3:25) but also the eschatological hope of the Christian (Heb 1:14; 9:15).

6:18 God did this so that, by two unchangeable things in which it is impossible for God to lie, we who have fled to take hold of the hope offered to us may be greatly encouraged.

This verse describes the result God had in mind (the Greek text actually begins this verse with "so that,"[75] continuing the sentence which has extended through vv. 16-17). God wants for us to be "greatly encouraged." Παράκλῃσις (*paraklēsis*) "may mean either 'encouragement,' 'exhortation,' or both."[76] Our writer will use the word again in 12:5 to describe the "word of encouragement" offered by Scripture to help us in our struggle with sin and in 13:22 when closing the letter, appealing to readers to bear with "his word of exhortation," that is, his "short letter."[77] Paul similarly uses the word in con-

---

[75]Ἵνα used with the subjunctive (ἔχωμεν).

[76]Ellingworth, p. 343.

[77]The idea of "comfort" is prominent in the use of the word elsewhere in the NT (παράκλητος, for example, is used as a title for the Holy Spirit in John 14-16) but this sense does not seem to fit either (1) any of the contexts in which the word is used in Hebrews or (2) the purpose of the letter in light of the situation of its recipients.

nection with hope (Rom 15:4; 2 Cor 1:5-7; 2 Thess 2:16). What is unique about the present verse is the strength added to the expression (ἰσχυρὰν παράκλησιν, *ischyran paraklēsin*, literally, "we have a *strong encouragement*"). God not only wants for us to be perfectly clear about his purpose for us (to inherit the promises, v. 17) but for us to be continually[78] confident while we wait patiently for its completion.

This encouragement is intended for those "who have fled to take hold of the hope offered." Καταφεύγω (*katapheugō*) is used only here and in Acts 14:6, where we read that Paul and Barnabas fled to Lystra and Derbe to escape stoning in Iconium. *Pheugō* is more common in the NT and usually retains this idea of "fleeing for safety" or "becoming safe by taking a refuge" (as elsewhere in Hebrews, 11:34 of the prophets who "escaped the edge of the sword" and 12:25 of the inability of those who refuse Jesus to "escape" punishment) although the prepositional prefix probably adds a greater degree of intensity.[79] Here the word describes the haste and intensity with which we take hold of our hope. God's encouragement is meant to sustain us in the faith required to wait patiently for what he has promised us, "in order to make our hope sure" (6:11).

It is through[80] "two unchangeable things" that God so encourages us. As his purpose is unchanging (ἀμετάθετον, *ametatheton*) so are these things (*ametathetōn*) by which he encourages us about that purpose. They are, it seems quite clear from the context, the promise and the oath added to it.[81] In these, "it is impossible for God to lie." This truth is well attested to throughout Scripture (Num 23:19; 1 Sam

---

[78]The probable significance of the present tense subjunctive, ἔχωμεν.

[79]Louw and Nida, pp. 190, 240.

[80]Διά with the genitive for agency.

[81]Ellingworth sees in the reference to δύο πραγμάτων ἀμεταθέτων ("two unchanging things") an appeal to the two witnesses required by the law (Deut 17:6). For support, he appeals to the author's repeated use of two or more texts (1:5-13; 5:5f; 10:30) and the attention given to this same requirement later (Heb 10:28). This is possible, but it is not demanded by anything in this text or its immediate context.

15:29; Titus 1:2). The case presented for remaining diligent to the end, and so inheriting the hope promised through faith and patience, is not merely forensic but an ethical one (in the sense of *ethos*, character). In the end, we trust in the word of God (both the promise and the oath to add strength to the pledge) because we trust the person of God.

6:19 We have this hope as an anchor for the soul, firm and secure.

As our writer draws his appeal to a conclusion, he moves to the present and returns to the use of the first person plural as in 6:1 (as a collective reference to author and readers, rather than as in 6:9 where "we" is used opposite "you"). In these last two verses of the chapter, two images[82] are employed to illustrate what hope does for those who, in faith, wait patiently to inherit what has been promised.

The first of these images is that of the anchor. As an anchor steadies and holds a ship in place, so hope does for our lives.[83] It makes us "firm and secure."[84] Βέβαιος (*bebaios*, "firm") is a cognate of the same word used in v. 16 to describe how an oath "puts an end" (lit., acts as "final confirmation") to argument. Here, it is our lives which are "tied down" or "established" in a sure and certain manner. As such, they are also made "secure" (ἀσφαλής, *asphalēs*, "safe and hence free from danger"[85]). Life can be as stormy as a rough sea.[86] Those

---

[82]In the Greek text, vv. 19-20 actually continue a long, complex sentence which began in v. 16. Two subordinate clauses describe the word ἐλπίδος ("hope"): (1) ἣν ὡς ἄγκυραν ἔχομεν . . . and (2) εἰσερχομένην . . . .

[83]Ψυχή, (*psychē*) "soul," can also mean "life" in the broader sense (BAGD, p. 893; LN, p. 262) and the latter makes more sense in this context since our writer focuses on the present rather than contemplating the future of some disembodied spiritual state.

[84]Morris also points out that the two words are a standard expression in Greek ethics (p. 61). To what extent our writer may have this background in mind is difficult to say.

[85]LN, p. 239.

[86]Kistemaker reminds us that "the Hebrews of Old Testament times and the Jews of the first century had a dislike for the sea" (p. 176). Perhaps this is

who possess this hope for the future, however, have the spiritual resources to survive the dangers of the present.

It enters the inner sanctuary behind the curtain, 6:20 where Jesus, who went before us, has entered on our behalf.

The second image has to do with the service performed by the high priest on the Day of Atonement (Lev 16). The outer part of the sanctuary of the tabernacle (and later the temple) consisted of the Holy Place (which held the table of showbread, the golden lampstand, and the golden altar of incense; Heb 9:2). The altar of incense stood on the west side of the Holy Place in front of a veil which separated it from the inner (and smallest) part of the sanctuary — the Most Holy Place, which held the ark of the covenant (containing the ten commandments, the gold jar of manna, and Aaron's staff; Heb 9:3-4) and where God himself was declared to dwell (between the cherubim on the mercy seat, which rested on the ark; Heb 9:5). The high priest alone was to enter this inner sanctuary once a year to offer sacrifices to atone for "all the sins of the Israelites" (Lev 16:33-34; Heb 9:7). Our writer will make more extensive use of this imagery in chapter 9.

How does our "hope" enter this sanctuary?[87] Our writer follows this statement by returning to his discussion to the high priestly ministry of Jesus which he began back at the end of chapter four and continued into chapter five. Because "we have such a high priest who has gone through the heavens," we, too, can "approach the throne of grace with confidence" (4:14, 16). Jesus is the one who has "entered on our behalf" and, because of his sacrifice, we have a hope which extends far beyond anything in this world but also into the next,

---

because the Israelites seldom occupied coastlines and thus had little contact with the sea (Paterson, "Sea," *Zondervan Pictorial Encyclopedia of the Bible*, Vol. 5, p. 316). If so, the danger and fear with which they regarded the sea may have served to the readers as a picturesque reminder of the perils of not making their hope sure, described earlier in the chapter (6:4-8, 11).

[87]See Ellingworth (p. 345) on "hope" (ἐλπίς) rather than "anchor" (ἄγκυρα) as the subject of "enter" (εἰσέρχομαι).

bringing us into the presence of God himself.[88] It is this anticipation which "anchors" our lives even now.

He has become a high priest forever, in the order of Melchizedek.

Our writer employs this last image not only to illustrate the promise which hope holds for his readers but to complete his return to the main line of discussion — the high priestly ministry of Jesus. When he left off, he had just noted that Jesus was "designated by God to be a high priest in the order of Melchizedek" (5:6, 10). Here he repeats the statement and will proceed to discuss its significance in chapter seven.

---

[88]Though it is true that Christians experience the presence of God in the present through the indwelling presence of the Holy Spirit (1 Cor 6:19), our writer has here been discussing the hope which consists of the promises for which we patiently wait in faith. As a result, the immediate context here seems to suggest that the reference in v. 20 is to a future (perhaps even eschatological, depending upon one's view of the intermediate state) experience, although we certainly begin this experience in the present as a result of the justification which Jesus accomplished for us at the cross.

HEBREWS 7

E. MELCHIZEDEK LIKE THE SON OF GOD (7:1-3)

Having returned to the subject, our writer will now complete his description of the priestly ministry of Jesus. His climactic discussion of the nature of the new covenant in chapter 8 will tie together the preceding discussion about Jesus' priesthood (chapters 5-7) and the subsequent discussion about Jesus' sacrifice (chapters 9-10) as integral components of the covenant, both of which demonstrate its superiority to "that first covenant" (8:7). The present chapter builds on what was introduced in chapters five and six to provide the doctrinal substance of this unique dimension of New Testament Christology.

Others have referred to the awkwardness of introducing the figure of Melchizedek into the line of argument, suggesting that it is an unnecessary complication of the contrast between the old and new priesthoods.[1] We could argue, however, that quite the opposite is true, for the figure of Melchizedek plays an essential role in the argument of our writer. The messianic application[2] of Psalm 110:4 (5:6; 6:20; 7:17, 21) serves as important textual grounding for the legitimacy and superiority of Jesus' ministry as high priest. 7:13-16 suggest the need to defend the legitimacy of viewing Jesus as the messianic high priest in light of his ancestry and "the

---

[1]So Ellingworth (p. 351).

[2]Jesus' exchange with the Pharisees (Matt 22:41-46; Mark 12:35-37; Luke 20:41-44) suggests not only that he took this Psalm as messianic but that such an understanding was widespread enough to be shared by the Jewish leadership of his day.

order of Melchizedek" provides a transcendent standard to which our writer appeals. Further, our author sees even greater significance in the specific parallels which introduce the issues of resurrection and oath. Hence, Melchizedek plays a key role in our writer's argument, offering scriptural grounds both for (1) the legitimacy of viewing Jesus as messianic high priest and (2) the two key themes which demonstrate the superiority of his "permanent priesthood" (7:24).

These first three verses identify several key characteristics in which "this Melchizedek" (v. 1) is "like the Son of God" (v. 3). The foundational similarity is that "he remains a priest forever." In the Greek text, these three verses represent a single, complex sentence in which "remains" (v. 3) serves as the main verb and "Melchizedek" is qualified by several descriptive phrases organized around a series of participles. Each of these characteristics introduces a theme which will be elaborated upon at some later point in the chapter[3] and collectively they progress from historical description (v. 1) to messianic interpretation (v. 2) to that specific parallel which forms the heart of the chapter (v. 3).

¹This Melchizedek was king of Salem and priest of God Most High. He met Abraham returning from the defeat of the kings and blessed him, ²and Abraham gave him a tenth of everything. First, his name means "king of righteousness"; then also, "king of Salem" means "king of peace." ³Without father or mother, without genealogy, without beginning of days or end of life, like the Son of God he remains a priest forever.

---

[3]Ellingworth notes the chiastic structure of the first ten verses: meeting (1a), blessing (1b), tithe (2) and tithe (4b), blessing (6b), meeting (10b) (p. 350). This serves as a nice description of the first ten verses which function as a unit, framed by the *inclusio* "met Abraham" (vv. 1, 10), yet the parallels suggested in vv. 2b-3 are germane to the discussion in vv. 11ff as well.

7:1 This Melchizedek was king of Salem and priest of God Most High.

Having alluded again to Psalm 110:4, our writer turns to the account in Genesis 14:17-20 to suggest more specific parallels between Melchizedek and Jesus.[4] These passages, together with the middle chapters of Hebrews, represent the only references to Melchizedek in Scripture.[5] According to the Genesis narrative, Abraham recognized Melchizedek as serving the same God as he by (1) giving him a "tenth of everything" (14:20) and (2) referring to the Lord by the same title ("God Most High," 14:22).[6]

His status as both king and priest was not unique in antiquity.[7] As to their possible significance here, we can observe that (1) elements of both kingship and priesthood are present in Psalm 110:1-4 (v. 1 having already been cited in 1:12),

---

[4]Verses one and two consist predominantly of phrases drawn directly from the LXX. Lane suggests that our writer here employs a common rabbinic principle of interpretation known as *gezarah shawah* (p. 158). Laid down by Hillel early in the first century (Trotter, p. 190), this principle assumes that "if two separate passages of Scripture contain the same word, the verbal analogy provides sufficient reason for explaining one text in light of the other" (Lane, p. 159).

[5]Lane identifies several other literary traditions pertaining to Melchizedek which were contemporaneous with Hebrews (pp. 160-162). Among the pseudepigrapha of the OT (Ethiopic MSS of *Jubilees*) and the fragments of Qumran (1QapGen 22:13-17 and 11qmelch) is evidence that he was a significant figure in the apocalyptic tradition of first-century Judaism (pp. 160-161). For Philo he is a symbol of the "right principle" in an individual (p. 161). The targumim identify him as Shem, Noah's son and suggest that, at the meeting with Abraham recorded in Genesis 14, the priesthood was transferred, making the Levitical priesthood its legitimate heir (p. 162). There is also some Gnostic speculation about Melchizedek in fragments from Nag Hammadi (p. 162).

[6]Waltke also points out that the understanding of God as creator of matter (as Melchizedek professed, Gen 14:20) was foreign to the polytheistic religions of the Ancient Near East and that Abraham, in contrast to the offering made to Melchizedek, refused a gift from the king of Sodom, thus refusing public affiliation with him ("Melchizedek," *Zondervan Pictorial Encyclopedia of the Bible*, Vol. 4, pp. 177-178).

[7]Morris notes that it was not uncommon for one individual to combine both roles (p. 63).

(2) v. 14 of the present chapter reminds readers that Jesus descended from the tribe of Judah, as any successor to the royal line of David would have been, and (3) Jesus is described as both priest and king within the broad scope of NT Christology. In the verses that follow, however, our writer shows little interest in expounding upon the significance of the dual role, choosing to focus on Jesus' ministry as high priest. Even in v. 2 he is less concerned with the office of king than with the messianic significance of "righteousness" and "peace" (see notes below). Probably, then, the title occurs here simply because it is extracted from the Genesis passage.

Salem is probably a shortened form of Jerusalem (cf. Ps 76:2), although its exact identification has been debated.[8] This was c.1000 years prior to David's conquest of the city (2 Sam 5:6-10). Our writer, however, is more interested in its typological significance than in its historical identity (v. 2).

He met Abraham returning from the defeat of the kings and blessed him,

When the kings of Sodom and Gomorrah rebelled against their subjection to the king of Elam, Lot was seized and carried away during the battle in the Valley of Siddim (Gen 14:1-12). Abraham (then Abram) learned of this and led his own trained men in attack of the captors, rescuing Lot along with the others and their possessions (Gen 14:13-16). Upon Abraham's return, he was met by the king of Sodom and by Melchizedek, although there is no previous reference to indicate that Melchizedek was involved in the conflict (Gen 14:17-18). Melchizedek brought out bread and wine, pronounced a blessing upon Abraham, and received from him "a tenth of everything" (Gen 14:19-20). Our writer glosses over some of

---

[8]Morris points out that the LXX of Gen 33:18 identifies it with Shechem (p. 62) and Lane refers to the support for this theory offered by Kirkland (p. 164). Westcott notes that in the time of Jerome it was identified as a Salem "near Scythopolis" (p. 170) or the Salim referred to in John 3:23 (as noted by Ellingworth, p. 355). Josephus associated it with Jerusalem (*Jewish Wars* 6.438 and *Antiquities* 1.180).

these details in order to foreground his similarities with Jesus. He will return to the act of "blessing" in vv. 6-7.

7:2 and Abraham gave him a tenth of everything.

Genesis 14:20 is the first reference to the tithe in the Bible, indicating that it existed as a practice even before it was commanded in the Law given through Moses. In Egyptian, Syrian, and Babylonian cultures of antiquity, tithes were both political (taxes imposed by rulers) and religious (presented as offerings) and could consist of produce, property or the spoils of war.[9] In Abraham's case, it is clear from the Genesis narrative that his gift was intended to honor and praise God as his provider and protector since, apart from the tithe offered to the priest, his share in the spoils was refused (Gen 14:22-24).

The word here translated "gave" (μερίζω, *merizō*) is not the same word employed in v. 4 (δίδωμι, *didōmi*) and is supplied by the author rather than the text of the LXX (which employs *didōmi*). It often includes the idea of "division" (μερίσμος, *merismos* is used in 4:12 to describe the division between soul and spirit wrought by the word of God) or "distribution" (of the gifts of the Holy Spirit in 2:4). It is the same word which, outside of Hebrews, is used to describe the sharing of possessions within the early church (Acts 2:45, *diamerizō*), the distribution of the two fish among the more than 5,000 people miraculously fed by Jesus (Mark 6:41), and in Jesus' description of a kingdom or house against itself (Matt 12:25-26; Mark 3:24-26). Although "to give a part of"[10] is probably the best translation in relationship to the tithe, Ellingworth is thus probably correct in suggesting that the word is more specific than *didōmi* and "heightens the idea of sharing a tenth."[11]

---

[9]C.L. Feinberg, "Tithe," *Zondervan Pictorial Encyclopedia of the Bible*, Vol. 5, p. 757.

[10]LN, p. 568.

[11]Ellingworth, p. 356.

First, his name means "king of righteousness"; then also, "king of Salem" means "king of peace."

The significance accorded to name changes and to etymological interpretations of names throughout the OT[12] suggests the possible import of a name to Jewish readers. Guthrie suggests that "names denoted the nature as well as the identity of the person."[13] Here our writer engages in a combination of etymological and "typological exegesis"[14] to describe the Messianic significance of the "type" or pattern to be found in the person and priesthood of Melchizedek.

The name "Melchizedek" is composed of the Hebrew word for king (*melek*)[15] to which is added a pronoun suffix (*melki*, "my king") and the word for righteous or righteousness (*zedek*).[16] A literal etymology, then, is "my king is righteous" but our writer offers an interpretive rendering, "king *of* righteousness." The word for Salem (*shalem*) is a cognate of the Hebrew word for "completeness, soundness, welfare, [or] peace" (*shalom*).[17] Morris observes that the Greek word which

---

[12]Bietenhard, NIDNTT, 2:649.

[13]Guthrie, p. 156.

[14]So Bruce (p. 135) describes the author's hermeneutic. "Typology" is "a method of Biblical exegesis or interpretation in which persons, places or things of the OT are interpreted as being foreshadows or prototypes, of persons, events or things in the NT" (Richard Soulen, *Handbook of Biblical Criticism.* 2nd ed. Atlanta: John Knox Press, 1976, 1981, p. 206). The OT reference serves as an historical pattern which anticipates a more ultimate, subsequent or transcendent reality. Hence, our writer often refers to these as "copies" or "shadows" (8:5; 10:1). As such, the shadow or copy draws its significance from the "reality" rather than vice versa, which may be why our writer (v. 3) will point out that Melchizedek is like the Son of God (vs. the Son of God is like Melchizedek). Yet, his exegesis here is not strictly typological for it proceeds out of the etymological significance of the names. Although the exact nature of etymology is subject to some debate, here our writer analyzes these names by breaking them down into their component parts (Soulen, p. 65). Both Philo and Josephus offer similar interpretations of Melchizedek's name and titles yet there are key differences as well and it is uncertain whether their work would have been known to our writer.

[15]BDB (מֶלֶךְ), p. 572.

[16]BDB, (צֶדֶק), p. 841.

[17]BDB, (שָׁלוֹם), p. 1022.

our writer employs here (εἰρήνη, *eirēnē*) conveys a negative idea ("absence of war") but that in both the NT and in the LXX (where it regularly translates *shalom*) it picks up the notion of "positive blessing."[18] Both righteousness and peace were part of the Jewish expectation for the Messianic kingdom (Isa 9:6-7) and in the NT it is clear that Jesus is both our righteousness (Rom 3:21-2; 2 Cor 5:21) and our peace (Eph 2:14-18; Col 1:19-20). Although our writer does not elaborated upon these specific themes, they are certainly the purpose of the sacrifice presented by Jesus the high priest (7:27; 9:14, 17-28).

7:3 Without father or mother, without genealogy, without beginning of days or end of life, like the Son of God he remains a priest forever.

A priest's genealogy was of great significance because of the commandments of the law (which limited the high priesthood to descendants of Aaron — Exod 28-29 — and the priesthood to the Levites — Num 3, 8, cf. Heb 7:11) and the precedent of history (when, following the exile, those who could not produce their family records were excluded from the priesthood, Neh 7:64). Because Jesus was not of priestly lineage according to the law (7:14), this dimension of the Melchizedek "type" is important for establishing a pattern which transcends those legal requirements and demonstrates Jesus to be "another priest like Melchizedek" (7:11, 15). That our writer probably has the question of genealogy in mind is suggested by his use of the word ἀγενεαλόγητος (*agenealogētos*, "without genealogy"). Whereas ἀπάτωρ (*apatōr*, "without father") and ἀμήτωρ (*amētōr*, "without mother") were commonly used for children whose parents had died or were unknown,[19] there is no other evidence of any use of this word in Greek literature.[20] Moulton and Milligan note that it is "a

---

[18]Morris, p. 63.
[19]BAGD, p. 46, 82.
[20]BAGD, p. 8.

good sample of a class of words which any author might coin for a special purpose."[21]

Our writer refers here not to historical facts about Melchizedek but to what Scripture fails to record about him, employing an argument from silence which, Bruce notes, played "an important part in rabbinical interpretation of scripture."[22] As with the etymology employed in v. 2, the method is employed to offer a typological interpretation which anticipates the resurrection of Jesus — "like the Son of God he remains a priest forever." The use of a passive form in the Greek (possibly "being compared to"[23]) may reflect the fact that Jesus is the point of comparison, rather than Melchizedek. In other words, we recognize the ways in which Melchizedek's priesthood foreshadowed that of Jesus only after we see the realities in Jesus himself.

Jesus is first introduced to us as God's "Son" in the second verse of the letter and our writer's first use of the title "Son of God" is when he introduced his discussion of our "great high priest" (4:14), although a title which alludes to his divine identity could be part of the focus on his eternal nature both here and later in the chapter (7:16-17, 21, 23-24). His ability to serve as a permanent priest as a result of his resurrection becomes the main point of the comparison with Melchizedek ("forever" is the repeated element — 5:6; 6:10; 7:17, 21, 24) and, together with the sufficiency of his sacrifice, will serve as the main proof of the superiority of his priesthood.

F. MELCHIZEDEK GREATER THAN ABRAHAM (7:4-10)

⁴Just think how great he was: Even the patriarch Abraham gave him a tenth of the plunder! ⁵Now the law

---

[21]MM, p. 3.

[22]Specifically, for the exegetical purposes of the rabbis, nothing was to be regarded as having existed before it was first mentioned in Scripture (Bruce, p. 136).

[23]LN, p. 618.

requires the descendants of Levi who become priests to collect a tenth from the people — that is, their brothers — even
though their brothers are descended from Abraham. [6]This
man, however, did not trace his descent from Levi, yet he
collected a tenth from Abraham and blessed him who had
the promises. [7]And without doubt the lesser person is
blessed by the greater. [8]In the one case, the tenth is collected by men who die; but in the other case, by him who is
declared to be living. [9]One might even say that Levi, who
collects the tenth, paid the tenth through Abraham,
[10]because when Melchizedek met Abraham, Levi was still in
the body of his ancestor.

**7:4 Just think how great he was: Even the patriarch Abraham
gave him a tenth of the plunder!**

Although the NIV translates "how great he was," the
Greek syntax is more naturally read as present tense, parallel
to μένει (*menei*) in v. 4.[24] For the sake of the parallel with
Christ, neither the priesthood nor the greatness of the priest
are confined by time. Although the verb **think** could be
taken as either indicative or imperative, the context probably
justifies Lane's suggestion that it is an "oratorical imperative"
by which the main theme of the section "is announced
homiletically."[25] Here we find the main claim in the argument of vv. 4-10: the surpassing greatness of Melchizedek.
The initial phase consists of a lesser to greater argument
which proceeds from Abraham to Melchizedek. Eventually,
Abraham will be treated as a representative figure of the
entire Levitical priesthood in order to demonstrate the surpassing greatness of Melchizedek's priesthood as well. The
two main "proofs" of Melchizedek's greatness are the tithe
(which Abraham gave to Melchizedek) and the blessing
(which Melchizedek gave to Abraham).[26]

---

[24]The ellipse of ἐστιν is usually to be supplied as present indicative
(Moulton, Howard and Turner, Vol. III, p. 295).

[25]Lane, p. 167.

[26]Bruce discusses the problems which this comparison caused for Jewish

The force of the argument, then, depends upon "how great" Abraham was in the eyes of the readers. Just how great he was is suggested by the syntax of the sentence. Although English syntax forces us to render "the patriarch Abraham" or "Abraham the patriarch," Greek syntax permits a separation of the name from the title. The actual order of words is as follows:[27]

to whom – also – a tenth – Abraham – gave –
of the plunder – the patriarch

It is worth noting which terms occupy the prominent positions. The word "tenth" occupies the initial place, frequently a position which foregrounds the primary focus of the sentence – as, in fact, the tenth serves as the dominant subject of vv. 4-10. The other position of emphasis is the final position which our author, by choice rather than necessity, gives to the title "the patriarch." The title itself is rare in the NT, occurring elsewhere only in Acts 2:29 (of David) and 7:8 (of the twelve sons of Jacob). By choice of both term and syntax our author seems to be using the linguistic alternatives available to give the strongest possible presence to the *ethos* of Abraham, the great father of the nation of Israel. Jesus' confrontations with Jewish leaders suggest the great significance they attached to being "children of Abraham" (Matt 3:9; John 8:33ff). When Jesus suggested his own superiority to Abraham, their response was "Who do you think you are?" (John 8:53). Yet this is exactly the point which the author of Hebrews is about to make.

Ἀκροθίνιον (*akrothinion*, "plunder") occurs only here in the NT. A literal etymology suggests "top of the heap" (ἄκρος, "highest" and θίς, θίνος, "heap"),[28] hence the suggestion "first

---

exegetes. Some identified Melchizedek with Shem and found no offense in the respect paid by Abraham to a venerable ancestor. Others engaged in "remarkable exegesis" of the Genesis narrative to suggest that Melchizedek's priesthood was superseded by a priesthood given to Abraham (pp. 139-140 n. 26).

[27]This sentence, ᾧ καὶ δεκάτην Ἀβραὰμ ἔδωκεν, represents the vocabulary of the LXX but does not reproduce the actual syntax of the phrase.

[28]So Kistemaker, p. 191.

fruits"[29] or "best part"[30] of the booty. Our author, however, does not seem as concerned with what Abraham gave or why but with the simple fact that he gave the tenth.[31]

7:5 Now the law requires the descendants of Levi who become priests to collect a tenth from the people — that is, their brothers — even though their brothers are descended from Abraham.

This verse serves two purposes. First, it introduces the descendants of Levi, extending the argument from Abraham to the Levitical priesthood and anticipating the shift in focus which will begin in v. 11. Second, it adds a further measure of the greatness of Melchizedek — the authority by which the tenth is collected.

The "descendants of Levi"[32] are described, at the same time, as one in nature with their fellow descendants of Abraham and yet exalted in stature. Their identity with their fellow descendants is stressed by the progression from "people" to "brothers." Since all Israelites were descended from Abraham, the Levites possessed no inherent superiority. The collected tithes "even though"[33] — concessive condition — they were from "the loins of Abraham" (KJV), a more literal translation which the NIV replaces with a second instance of the word "brothers."[34]

---

[29]BAGD, p. 33.

[30]LN, p. 58.

[31]Bruce notes a lack of evidence that the practice, in the Greek city states, of giving a tenth of the spoils of war to a deity was ever observed in Israel. In fact, the laws of the Israelite *herem* (Deut 20:16-18; Josh 6:21, 24) demanded that all of their spoil be devoted to God (p. 140).

[32]The genitive here is probably an instance of what Chamberlain calls the "Hebraistic genitive," which functions primarily as a genitive of definition or quality and which is common in the LXX (p. 30; see also Moulton, Howard and Turner, Vol. II, p. 440).

[33]Now the second case of καίπερ with the participle, following the main verb. See also notes on 5:8.

[34]Ellingworth suggests that there is "increasing emphasis" in the progression from τὸν λαόν to τοὺς ἀδελφοὺς to ἐξεληλυθότας ἐκ τῆς ὀσφύος Ἀβραάμ.

Their authority for collecting tithes is derived. The NIV simply renders "the law requires" which fails to indicate the presence of both the words ἐντολή (*entolē*, "commandment") and νόμος (*nomos*, "law") in the text. One might render the phrase: they "have the commandment to collect tithes from the people according to the law." *Entolē* is never used in the letter apart from *nomos* which itself appears no less than fourteen times in the letter.[35] Whereas *nomos* appears to refer primarily to the whole law of Moses (as in 9:19 and 10:28), *entolē* seems to refer to a specific commandment[36] — in this case the commandment found in Numbers 18:21, 24. Though like their brothers in their descent from Abraham, the Levites were authorized by the law of Moses to receive the tithe from their brothers.

7:6 This man, however, did not trace his descent from Levi, yet he collected a tenth from Abraham and blessed him who had the promises. 7:7 And without doubt the lesser person is blessed by the greater.

This verse completes the contrast anticipated in v. 5[37] yet the participle γενεαλογούμενος (*genealogoumenos*, "trace descent") echos the adjective ἀγενεαλόγητος (*agenealogētos*, "without genealogy) in v. 3 as well. The point of the first part of this verse is that Melchizedek lacked the authorization to receive a tithe which the Levites derived from the law of Moses. The questions as to whence Melchizedek derived his authority and/or whether his authority was derived in its nature are left

---

[35]Ἐντολή also appears in 7:16, 18 and 9:19. νόμος also appears in 7:12, 16, 19, 28; 8:4, 10; and 9:19.

[36]Contrary to the pattern of the LXX, in which the word is usually plural, the author of Hebrews uses the word exclusively in the singular and never with the definite article.

[37]Καὶ οἱ μὲν (v. 5) . . . ὁ δὲ μὴ (v. 6) . . .. The contrast is heightened by a shift from the present tenses in v. 5 (which describe the perpetual authority of the command from generation to generation) to perfect tenses in v. 6 (δεδεκάτων and εὐλόγηκεν which describe historical events with consequences in the present).

unanswered at this point. But the fact that he received it from Abraham suggests that it was possible to have such authority apart from the Law of Moses.

The other sign of Melchizedek's greatness is the blessing he bestowed upon Abraham when he said,

"Blessed be Abram by God Most High,
    Creator of heaven and earth.
And blessed be God Most High,
    who delivered your enemies into your hand"
                                            (Gen 14:19-20).

Our writer draws the conclusion for his readers: the facts that (1) Abraham gave tithes to Melchizedek and (2) Abraham received a blessing from Melchizedek suggest that even the great patriarch recognized the surpassing greatness of the one who was priest of God Most High. This is true even though Abraham already "had the promises" before he encountered Melchizedek (see notes on 6:12, 13, 15, 17).

Our author returns to the forensic terminology of 6:16 (χωρὶς δὲ πάσης ἀντιλογίας [chōris de pasēs antilogias], "without doubt" or "without any argument") to express his conclusion with a high degree of certainty.[38] The word translated "greater" here, however, is not the same word translated "great" in v. 4. Here our writer employs κρείττων (kreittōn), elsewhere translated "better" or "superior," a word which he uses no less than twelve times in this letter.[39] It was used in 1:4 to describe the Son's superiority to the angels and will be the key word used to describe the myriad ways in which the new covenant is superior to the old (see 7:19, 22; 8:6; 9:23; 11:40). Melchizedek's superiority to Abraham and the Levites

---

[38]Lane notes that the phrase was commonly used in the papyri to stress the certainty of a statement (drawing upon Moulton and Milligan, p. 48) although Ellingworth notes that the use of χωρὶς rather than ἄνευ (as in the example cited by Moulton and Milligan) adds even greater strength to the expression (p. 366).

[39]It occurs a total of only six times in the rest of the NT (1 Cor 7:9; 11:17; 12:31; Phil 1:23; 1 Pet 3:17; 2 Pet 2:21).

sets the stage for our writer's description of the superiority of the Son's priesthood and covenant.[40]

7:8 In the one case, the tenth is collected by men who die; but in the other case, by him who is declared to be living.

Here our author employs the same construction used to create the contrast of vv. 6-7[41] to point out the key difference between Melchizedek and the Levites. We learn two important truths about his qualification to receive the tithe: (1) it is based on life rather than law and (2) it is inherent rather than derived.

The key contrast here is between life and death. The phrase "men who die" renders a present tense adjectival participle which could easily be translated "men who are dying" or "men who are in the process of dying" (or even "mortal men," NASB). Even as they serve in their priestly office, the mortal Levites are dying. But in the "other case," the priest lives (also a present tense). From the permanence of his life his greatness is derived and by virtue of the fact that "he remains a priest forever" (7:3) he is worthy to receive the tithe.

The description of Melchizedek here anticipates the greater point about Jesus "who has become a priest not on the basis of a regulation as to his ancestry but on the basis of the power of an indestructible life" (7:16) and who therefore "has a permanent priesthood" (7:24), superior to that of other priests. In neither case is it necessary for the law to authorize their priesthood. Their own permanence of life exalts them. Yet the life is not without a witness (μαρτυρέω, *martyreō*, "declare" or "bear witness"). This is the same term used regularly in Acts to describe the "witness" or firsthand "testimony" which the apostles bore to the resurrection of Jesus (1:8; 2:32;

---

[40]The style of 7:4-7 is suggestive of its emphasis. Synonymous epistrophe is employed to give presence to ὁ πατριάρχης (v. 4), 'Αβραάμ (v. 5) and 'Αβραάμ (v. 6a) although v. 6 employs a chiasmus — δεδεκάτωκεν 'Αβραάμ καὶ τὸν ἔχοντα τὰς ἐπαγγελίας εὐλόγηκεν — ending with εὐλόγηκεν just as v. 7 ends with εὐλογεῖται.

[41]Μὲν . . . δε.

3:15; 4:33; 20:21, 24). Yet, if the occurrences of the term in chapter 11 are taken as references to Scripture,[42] then the author of Hebrews almost always uses the word in reference to Scripture[43] and in the immediate context the allusion would appear to be to Psalm 110:4 which is introduced with the same word (*martyreō*, "it is declared").

7:9 One might even say that Levi, who collects the tenth, paid the tenth through Abraham, 7:10 because when Melchizedek met Abraham, Levi was still in the body of his ancestor.

These last verses complete the transition from Abraham to Levi and the comparative worth of the Levitical priesthood will figure prominently into the remainder of the chapter. The argument is extended from Abraham to the Levites via the genealogical connection through which Abraham is treated as a representative figure of his future ancestors.[44] The point is that if Melchizedek is greater than Abraham, then he is also greater than the Levites.

There is some disagreement as to whether this verse represents an additional "afterthought"[45] or the actual climax of the writer's argument.[46] Since the comparison between the

---

[42]See 11:2, 4, 5, 39 (NIV translates "commends"). Directly, the term in chapter 11 seems to refer to the response of God to the faith of those mentioned. Here the term probably carries more the idea of "speak well of" or "approve of" since the notion of "reputation" is also part of the semantic range of this term and its cognates (LN, p. 418) and 11:4 suggests that God is, at least in some sense, the agent. And yet it is clearly the case that the "witnesses" (12:1) in the chapter are drawn from OT Scripture and that it was through the accounts preserved in OT Scripture that the commendations were brought to the readers of Hebrews.

[43]3:5; 7:8, 17; 10:15, 28; 11:2, 4, 5, 39; 12:1.

[44]Bruce notes that, in biblical thought, an ancestor was regarded as containing within himself all of his descendents (see Gen 25:23; Mal 1:2; Rom 9:11ff. regarding Jacob and Esau as well as Rom 5:12 regarding Adam) (p. 142).

[45]The term used by Bruce who suggests rendering ὡς ἔπος εἰπεῖν as "so to say" (p. 142).

[46]Bauer suggests "to use just the right word" (BAGD, p. 305) and Hering opts for "to give the real point" (p. 59).

priesthood of Jesus and that of the Levites is the core of the rest of the chapter, treating these verses as a mere after-though seems to understate their significance. Yet vv. 7-8 would seem to best express the climactic point of the section. Westcott's suggestion that the opening phrase (translated "one might even say") "serves to introduce a statement which may startle a reader, and which requires to be guarded from misinterpretation" thus seems more appropriate to the context.[47] Though the point is not anticlimactic, our writer never-theless attaches a lesser degree of certainty to it than he did to the conclusion advanced in v. 7, introduced by the phrase "without doubt" in v. 7. Our writer draws this portion of his discussion to a close by framing it with an *inclusio* ("met Abraham" as in 7:1 and "Melchizedek" is the last word in the Greek sentence whereas "This Melchizedek" opens 7:1).

G. JESUS IS HIGH PRIEST BASED ON HIS RESURREC-TION WHICH INTRODUCES A BETTER HOPE (7:11-19)

[11]If perfection could have been attained through the Levitical priesthood (for on the basis of it the law was given to the people), why was there still need for another priest to come — one in the order of Melchizedek, not in the order of Aaron? [12]For when there is a change of the priesthood, there must also be a change of the law. [13]He of whom these things are said belonged to a different tribe, and no one from that tribe has ever served at the altar. [14]For it is clear that our Lord descended from Judah, and in regard to that tribe Moses said nothing about priests. [15]And what we have said is even more clear if another priest like Melchizedek appears, [16]one who has become a priest not on the basis of a regulation as to his ancestry but on the basis of the power of an indestructible life. [17]For it is declared:

---

[47]So Ellingworth who suggests rendering the phrase "almost, practically" as "qualifying a too absolute expression" (p. 368).

> "You are a priest forever,
> in the order of Melchizedek."[a]

[18]The former regulation is set aside because it was weak and useless [19](for the law made nothing perfect), and a better hope is introduced, by which we draw near to God.

[a]*17,21* Psalm 110:4

This section introduces the running theme of the remainder of the chapter — "perfection." Just as vv. 1-10 are set apart by *inclusio* ("met Abraham," v. 1 and v. 10) so are vv. 11-19 which open with the question as to whether "perfection" could have been attained through the Levitical priesthood (v. 11) and close with the affirmation that the Son "has been made perfect forever" (v. 28). Similarly, a reference to the inability of the law to make anything "perfect" frames the first phase of the discussion.

Our writer begins the present section by turning his attention to the Levitical priesthood but before he is finished he will introduce Jesus into the fuller discussion of Melchizedek for the first time (v. 14, the first reference to him since 6:20). The climax of the section is the "better hope" which is introduced by his priesthood (v. 19). In subsequent sections, we will read of the "better covenant" guaranteed by the oath (vv. 20-22) as well as those aspects of the priesthood of Christ which enable it to accomplish what the Levitical priesthood could not — the permanency of his priesthood (vv. 23-25) and the sufficiency of his sacrifice (vv. 26-28).

7:11 If perfection could have been attained through the Levitical priesthood (for on the basis of it the law was given to the people), why was there still need for another priest to come — one in the order of Melchizedek, not in the order of Aaron?

To begin his demonstration of the superiority of Christ's priesthood, our writer introduces a sign argument: the fact that the Scriptures confer a priestly identity upon the Messiah is a sign that the perfection of believers demanded more than the Levitical priesthood could accomplish and that this priesthood was never intended by God to exhaust the priestly functions.[48] The argument is cast in a first class conditional sentence.[49] The protasis ("if" clause) assumes the condition to be true (for the sake of argument, apart from its objective truth or falsity) and the apodosis (the second part) expresses the conclusion. It is common for the apodosis to take the form of a rhetorical question (i.e., one which presents the conclusion by suggesting its own answer) as it does here (cf. Matt 12:27).

The "perfection" of Christ, believers and the interconnection between the two "perfections" comprise one of the central themes of the letter (2:10; 5:9; 6:1; 7:11, 19, 28; 9:9; 10:1, 14; 11:40; 12:2, 23) and are an integral aspect of its theology of salvation (including the vocation of Christ as Savior and Priest as well as the salvation of believers as it consists of their justification, sanctification and glorification).[50] Given the variety of objects and dimensions associated with the theme of perfection, the significance of each reference must be carefully considered in its own immediate context as well as within the broader context of the letter.

To this point in the letter, we have learned that Christ's suffering made him "perfect" as the author of our salvation (2:10), as both the source of our salvation and our high priest (5:9-10). The context of chapter 5 was suggestive as to at least

---

[48]Bruce discusses Jewish expectation of a new age of restoration in which a worthy priest would come who would be what the Aaronic priest was to be ideally. Yet even this priest was expected to be of the tribe of Levi (p. 144).

[49]Chamberlain, p. 195.

[50]Paul Blowers suggests that the "perfection" of Christ described in Hebrews is primarily in his vocation as Savior and High Priest, that the "perfection" of Christians (at different times) incorporates three dimensions (the perfecting and cleansing of conscience, the perfection of sanctification, and the consummation of glorification), and that it is the full scope of Christ's own perfection (embracing his incarnation, suffering, cross and exaltation) which provides for believers an access to each of the dimensions of their own perfection ("Patterns of Perfection in Hebrews," unpublished paper presented to a Fellowship of Professors at Johnson Bible College, Sept. 21, 1990).

one dimension of how Christ's suffering "perfected" him for his role as our priest — he is able to "sympathize with our weaknesses" (4:15) and thus able to "deal gently with those who are ignorant and going astray" (5:2) — although the cross, which made him "perfect" as our Savior, was probably not far from view (see notes on 5:9-10). 5:14 and 6:1 introduced us to the "perfection" of believers — in these contexts, the "present" dimension of their salvation, the ongoing process of their sanctification or growth toward "maturity" (as the NIV translates cognates of the same Greek word; see comments on 5:14).

It is probably the "perfection" of believers which our writer has in mind in the present verse — and the inability of the Levitical priesthood to attain it (in any of its dimensions) — since the purpose of the sacrificial system which that priesthood oversaw was to deal with the sins of the people.[51] The rest of the chapter progresses from the perfection of believers (here and v. 18), to the perfection of Christ and the connection between the two (vv. 24-28). In the intervening argument, the two ways in which Jesus "has been made perfect" (v. 28) — his death and resurrection — serve as the two proofs of the superiority of his priesthood.

Another important issue introduced in this verse is the connection between the priesthood and the law. The Greek grammar is not clear about the relationship and this has given rise to competing views about two aspects of this verse. First, there is ambiguity as to the antecedent of the pronoun ("on the basis of *it*"). Technically, Greek syntax would permit either "perfection" or "Levitical priesthood" as the antecedent. The latter would seem the better choice since (1) it is difficult to make sense of "perfection" as the genitive case object of the preposition which precedes the

---

[51]Although it is possible to suggest that the "perfection" here referred to could also extend to the priesthood itself since (1) the object of the perfection is not unambiguously stated in the text and (2) the priests themselves could not be "perfect" for their vocation as Christ is (7:23, 27).

pronoun[52] and (2) the context seems to favor the connection between law and priesthood (v. 12, see also v. 5, 28).[53]

Second, the meaning of the preposition ἐπί (*epi*) followed by the genitive is still difficult to construe with precision in this context ("on the basis of," NIV and NASB;[54] "under," KJV, RSV, and NRSV). The verb in this case (νενομοθέτηται, *nenomothetētai*, "receive law(s)[55]") is rare in the NT[56] but Lane notes that it occurs elsewhere[57] with *epi* followed by the genitive in a manner which supports the rendering "in the case of" or "concerning." This also seems more natural in a context which stresses that the law authorized the priesthood rather than vice versa (v. 5, v. 28). Either way, what seems most important to our author is that what is true of one is also true of the other (cf. v. 11 and v. 19) and what affects the one affects the other as well (v. 12).

Aaron was last mentioned in 5:4. Here our writer mentions him again, perhaps because it is more appropriate to connect his name (rather than that of Levi) with the "order" (τάξις, *taxis*). Outside of this verse, this term is used only in relation to Melchizedek and it may well be that our writer has in mind 5:4-6 when his first appeal to Psalm 110:4 was introduced by the comparison of Christ to Aaron. The Son, after all, is not merely another priest but "high priest" (4:14; 5:10; 7:26-28).

7:12 For when there is a change of the priesthood, there must also be a change of the law. 7:13 He of whom these

---

[52]None of the relationships suggested by ἐπί with the genitive lend themselves to taking "perfection" as its object. Variants which replace the genitive with dative or accusative lack any significant textual support.

[53]Conversely, one could argue that v. 19 posits a close relationship between law and perfection but the proximity of v. 12 is difficult to ignore.

[54]After Bauer (p. 286) and Blass, Debrunner, Funk (p. 123).

[55]BAGD, p. 542.

[56]Only here and in Hebrews 8:6.

[57]Philo, *On the Special Laws*, 1.235 and 2.35 are cited as examples (Lane, p. 174).

things are said belonged to a different tribe, and no one from that tribe has ever served at the altar. 7:14 For it is clear that our Lord descended from Judah, and in regard to that tribe Moses said nothing about priests.

The sign argument for the need of another priesthood, coupled with the parenthetical acknowledgment of the legal basis for the Levitical priesthood, permits our writer to address directly an issue anticipated in vv. 5-8: the relationship between the law of Moses and the priesthood after the order of Melchizedek. It would have been natural and quite probable for Jewish readers to question our writer's claim that Jesus was a priest on the basis of his known ancestry. This verse and Revelation 5:5 are the only verses outside of the Gospels to confirm the royal lineage of Jesus, but the fact that they do suggests that it was well known within early Christian communities. Our writer was confident that it was "clear" (the προ– in προδῆλος (*prodēlos*) is intensive,[58] hence "perfectly clear," NASB) to his readers.

Our author draws upon two established premises to resolve this issue. The first is the close tie between the Levitical priesthood and the law which authorized it. The second is what is known to be true about Jesus.

Verses 5 and 11 have both argued the close relationship between the Mosaic law and the Levitical priesthood, and now our writer advances a conclusion: they are so closely bound together that a change in one demands a change in the other. The law authorized that priesthood (v. 5) and the bulk of its regulations pertained to its function (v. 12). Any significant change in either the law or priesthood would necessitate (ἀνάγκη, *anangkē*, from ἀναγκάζω, *anangkazō*, "to compel, to force"[59]) corresponding changes in the other. Μετατίθημι (*metatithēmi*, "change") can literally mean "transfer" or "convey to another place"[60] and this would seem to

---

[58]MM, p. 538.

[59]LN, p. 476.

[60]In the papyri, there is an instance of its use to refer to the removal of stairs from a house during repairs and in several cases it is used of the mili-

support a reading similar to that of ἀθέτησις (*athetēsis*, "set aside) in v. 18. However, this literal sense of the term depends upon a spatial context clearly lacking here and the relationship between νόμος (*nomos*, v. 12) and ἐντολή (*entolē*, v. 10) (see comments on 7:5) could easily justify a distinction between *metatithēmi* (v. 12) and *athetēsis* (v. 18) as well. Hence, the idea is probably not that law and priesthood are "removed" but that they have changed from one state to another.[61]

The second working premise of our writer consists of what is known to be true **about Jesus.** Each of these three verses is introduced by an explanatory γάρ (*gar*, "for," omitted from v. 13 in the NIV) and in each case the progression in thought is from a known truth about Jesus to some consequence pertaining to the law.

The syntax of v. 12 is that of the elliptical condition.[62] The "when" phrase translates a present tense participle which describes the set of circumstances or conditions which prompt the subsequent action.[63] Since the law authorized (v. 5) and instructed (v. 11) the priesthood, we would expect a change in the law to affect a change in the priesthood. Instead, we read the reverse. Similarly, vv. 13-14 each proceed from what is known about **"the one of whom these** things **are spoken" (he "belonged** to a different tribe") and "our Lord" (he "descended from Judah") to their obvious import in view of the law ("no one from that tribe has ever served at the altar . . . in regard to that tribe Moses said nothing about priests").

---

tary transfer of soldiers to new villages or companies (MM, p. 405). Acts 7:16 employs the word in this sense to describe the removal of the bodies of Jacob and his sons to graves in Hebron. In Hebrews, it appears in 11:5 (twice, along with μετάθεσις as here) to describe the "taking" of Enoch and in 12:27 of the eschatological "removal" of created things.

[61]So LN, p. 155.

[62]Chamberlain, pp. 199-200.

[63]Though an aorist participle here would suggest antecedent action and perhaps expressly attribute a causal relationship between the participle and the verb, there is probably little difference in the sense here.

What is true about our Lord determines what can be said to be true of the law — not vice versa. As subsequent verses make clear, his greatness so transcends that of the Levitical priests that the old legal requirements are no longer relevant.

7:15 And what we have said is even more clear if another priest like Melchizedek appears,

"What we have said" includes the main line of argument introduced in v. 11 and now further proof is offered to make the case "even more clear."[64] Not only does Scripture anticipate "another priest" (vv. 11, 15) but he has, in fact, appeared. Again our author uses ἀνίστημι (*anistēmi*, "appears"), the same word translated "to come" in v. 11, indicating that what was predicted has now come to pass.

This priest is "like Melchizedek" (lit., "in the likeness of," the same syntax **rendered** "in the order of" in v. 11).[65] Although cognates of ὁμοιότης (*homoiotēs*, "likeness") are frequent in the parabolic language of the Gospels and the typological exegesis of our author is reminiscent of similitude, he has not shown any inclination to employ the word in this sense.[66] It is perhaps best taken as a stylistic variation[67] which means no more than "in the same way as."[68]

7:16 one who has become a priest not on the basis of a regulation as to his ancestry but on the basis of the power of an

---

[64]Whereas πρόδηλον ("clear") is used in v. 14, the word here is κατάδηλον, which appears only here in the NT and conveys the sense of "quite clear" or "certain,' (MM, p. 325). The statement here is stronger than that in v. 14.

[65]Κατὰ τὴν ὁμοιότητα parallels κατὰ τὴν τάξιν in v. 11.

[66]In the NT, ὁμοιότης appears only in Hebrews 4:15 and 7:15. Ὁμοίως will appear in 9:21. No figurative or symbolic dimensions appear to be intended in these contexts.

[67]So Ellingworth (p. 378). Our author has used κατὰ τὴν τάξιν in 6:20 and 7:11 (twice) and will be forced to use it again in v. 17 when quoting Psalm 110:4.

[68]This exact phrase occurs nowhere else in the NT although it occurs in the papyri in this "weakened sense, according to Moulton and Milligan (pp. 448-449).

indestructible life. 7:17 For it is declared: "You are a priest forever, in the order of Melchizedek."

Yet the key similarity between Jesus and Melchizedek is by no means insignificant for it is the ultimate proof that he has appeared as the Messianic High Priest. In v. 8 we learned that Melchizedek's right to receive the tithe (and thus to serve as priest) was based on life rather than law and was inherent rather than derived (see comments there). Here we see that the same is true of Jesus' qualifications to serve as our great high priest. It is on the basis of "the power of an indestructible life" rather than "a regulation as to his ancestry" (lit., "law of a fleshly commandment"). Our writer employs rare terms and structures his sentence in a manner that heightens the contrast:

not according to — law   — of — commandment — fleshly
but according to — power — of — life   — indestructible

Aside from this verse, the form σάρκινος (*sarkinos*) is rare in the NT.[69] A variant in v. 16 substitutes the more common σαρκικός (*sarkikos*) but the textual evidence strongly favors *sarkinos*; and ἀκαταλύτου (*akatalytou*) does not appear elsewhere in the NT. Yet both are employed here in an epistrophic style which foregrounds their presence. Just as the mortal priests are already in the process of dying (see comments on v. 8) as they serve, so the law which authorizes and regulates their priesthood partakes of that same temporary, fleshly existence which is doomed to pass away. Jesus, on the other hand, has been raised to a life which cannot be destroyed and is thus "endless."[70]

It is this "forever" dimension of his high priesthood to which Psalm 110:4 bears "witness" (μαρτυρέω, *martyreō*, translated "declare" both here and in v. 8) as in 5:6 (as a result of

---

[69]Rom 7:14; 1 Cor 3:1; 2 Cor 3:3 and possibly 2 Cor 1:12. Σάρξ, of course, is quite common in the NT but this adjective form is rare. Moulton and Milligan distinguish between σάρξ, ("flesh"), σαρκικός (nature and character of σάρξ) and σάρκινος (made or composed of σάρξ, as in the case of "leather ropes," p. 569).

[70]BAGD, p. 30.

which he is the source of "eternal" salvation), 6:20 and 7:3. By virtue of his resurrection, Jesus is clearly proven to be the Messianic High Priest by a standard which transcends the Mosaic covenant, outlasts its law and is derived from no authority external to its own.

7:18 The former regulation is set aside because it was weak and useless 7:19 (for the law made nothing perfect), and a better hope is introduced, by which we draw near to God.

The dawning of the Messianic High Priesthood has significant and specific consequences for the believer, some of which are described here as our "better hope." When the topic of "hope" has arisen previously in the epistle (3:6; 6:11, 18), our writer has focused on its benefits for and demands upon the believers' life in the present. Here, however, he describes qualities of the hope itself (for ἐλπίς [elpis] in Hebrews see comments on 6:11).

First, it is a "better" hope. κρείττονος (kreittonos, "better") is a key word in the letter. It first appeared in 1:4 when the Son was contrasted with angels, later in 6:9 to express our author's confidence in his readers and then in 7:7 to distinguish the greater stature of the one who pronounces blessing upon another (thus of Melchizedek in relation to Abraham). Here, however, is the first in a significant series of comparisons designed to demonstrate the superiority of the new covenant (cf. 7:22; 8:6; 9:23; 11:40; 12:24).[71]

In this case, the hope introduced by Christ's eternal priesthood is better than that regulation which has been "set aside." Ἀθέτησις (athetēsis, "annulment"[72]) probably carries a legal force in this context as suggested by its use in technical legal

---

[71]The word also appears in 10:34 to describe the "better and lasting "possessions" of believers in contrast to their property which had been confiscated. In 11:16 and 35 it does not refer directly to the new covenant but anticipates the reference in 11:40 which brings the new covenant into view as the climax of "what we hope for" (11:1).

[72]BAGD, p. 21.

formula in the papyri.[73] It has been set aside because it is
"weak" (or "ineffective," see comments in 5:2 on *asthenēs*) and
"useless" in bringing about that for which believers hope.
There is little difference between the meaning of the two
terms but the anaphora[74] (αὐτῆς ασθενὲς καὶ ἀνωφελές, *autēs
asthenes kai anōpheles*) creates a strong presence for the idea.
We hope to be "perfect" and to "draw near to God." Neither
the law nor the Levitical priesthood could accomplish our
perfection — past, present, or future (see comments on v. 11)
— nor consequently secure our ability to draw near to God
himself (which requires the removal of our sins as 10:1-4 will
explain in more detail) since it is by (or "through") this hope
that we do so.

This reference to the running theme of the chapter ("perfection," v. 11) also marks a transition to the second of the two
main proofs for the superiority of Christ's priesthood (resurrection and oath) which will subsequently be brought together to
explain how his perfection makes ours possible as well (v. 28).

H. JESUS IS HIGH PRIEST BASED ON GOD'S OATH WHICH PRODUCES A BETTER COVENANT (7:20-22)

[20]**And it was not without an oath! Others became priests
without any oath, [21]but he became a priest with an oath
when God said to him:**

"The Lord has sworn and will not change his mind:

'You are a priest forever.'"[a]

[22]**Because of this oath, Jesus has become the guarantee of a
better covenant.**

[a]*17,21* **Psalm 110:4**

---

[73]MM, p. 12. 'Αθετέω is similarly used in 10:28 and this dimension of
ἀθέτησις is probably not totally absent from 9:26 which is best taken as a
description of the believer's justification.

[74]Anaphora (repetition of beginnings) is primarily a rhetorical device for
the ear. We should keep in mind that the epistle was probably heard before
it was read.

Our author now returns to a theme introduced earlier (6:13-18) and also drawn from Psalm 110:4 (7:21) for a second major proof of the superiority of Christ's priesthood: the oath which God swore. Like the first proof, this one also has a significant consequence for the believer: a "better covenant."

The syntax of these verses suggests that they represent a single unit of thought. Verse 20 is introduced by καθ' ὅσον (*kath' hoson,* "to the degree that") which is completed by the phrase κατὰ τοσοῦτο (*kata tosouto,* "to the same degree") in verse 22.[75] Hence, the conclusion is announced in v. 22 ("Jesus has become the guarantee of a better covenant") and the grounds offered in v. 20a ("it was not without an oath" that he became priest). The parenthesis of 20b-21 provides the specific data.

7:20 And it was not without an oath!

Ellingworth suggests that the double negative is equivalent to a strong positive statement such as the one in the NEB: "How great a difference it makes that an oath was sworn!"[76] In the NT, ὀρκωμοσία (*horkōmosia,* "oath") appears only in this chapter and is a compound of the usual word for "oath" (ὅρκος, *horkos*) and the verb for "swear" (ὄμνυμι, *omnymi*)[77] — used separately in 6:16 — suggesting that the term foregrounds the act of taking the oath rather than the oath itself.[78] *Horkos* is a cognate of ἕκος (*hekos,* "fence"[79]) from which it probably draws its meaning ("something that shuts you in").[80]

6:13-18 form the background to this statement and have informed us of the significance of the oath (see comments on 6:16). Adding an oath to a promise was considered additional confirmation, sufficient evidence to establish someone in

---

[75]BAGD, p. 586.
[76]Ellingworth, p. 383.
[77]Kistemaker, p. 204.
[78]So Ellingworth (p. 383) and Westcott (p. 188).
[79]LS, p. 690.
[80]MM, p. 458.

their belief, ending the need for doubt or debate. God did it to confirm his promise to Abraham and now we learn that he has done the same in appointing Jesus as priest.

Others became priests without any oath,

What is true of Jesus was never the case for the others. They did not take the honor upon themselves but were called and appointed by God (5:1, 4). In this, Jesus was like them (5:5). But their call and appointment did not include an oath. The oath demonstrates the uniqueness and superiority of Jesus' priesthood.

7:21 but he became a priest with an oath when God said to him: "The Lord has sworn and will not change his mind: 'You are a priest forever.'"

Our writer returns to Psalm 110:4 for scriptural evidence of the oath. It has been cited previously in 5:6 and 7:17, and alluded to in 5:10; 6:20; 7:3, 11 and 15. But the use here is unique. The key phrase which occurs in all three citations — "You are a priest forever" — is retained but the phrase which follows — "in the order of Melchizedek" — is omitted while the preceding phrase — "The Lord has sworn and will not change his mind" — is now included. The focus is no longer on Christ's similarity to Melchizedek but on the oath of God, a dimension of his priesthood which is unique even in relation to Melchizedek. Both similarities and uniqueness have now been drawn from this messianic psalm.

Omnymi ("sworn") was part of the compound word translated "oath" in vv. 20-21 (*horkōmosia*, see comments on v. 20) and is the direct link between the psalm and our author's conclusion. Because he has sworn, we can know that the Lord will never "change his mind." *Metamelomai* often carries the force of "regret,"[81] but the context here (and in Psalm 110) justifies the rendering of the NIV which follows Bauer's recommendation.[82] The focus is on the permanency

---

[81]Bauer (BAGD, p. 511) and many examples in the papyri (MM, p. 403).
[82]Bauer, p. 511.

of Christ's priesthood (v. 24) and the certainty we can attach
to it.

7:22 Because of this oath, Jesus has become the guarantee of a better covenant.

The NIV renders "because" to suggest the concluding
force of *kata tosouto* which completes *kath' hoson* in v. 20 (see
comments on v. 20). The argument has progressed to its climax. Not only does the oath demonstrate the uniqueness and
superiority of Christ's priesthood, it also demonstrates the
superiority of the "covenant" of which he is the "guarantee."

This is but the first of 17 instances of διαθήκη (*diathēkē*,
"covenant") in the letter,[83] and it will become the climactic
theme of the letter in chapters 8 and 9 where we find 12 of its
17 occurrences. The full discussion of "superior" (*kreittonos*,
the same word translated "better" in this verse) will begin in
8:6 but the remainder of chapter 7 provides an approach to
this summit.

Ἔγγυος (*engyos*, "guarantee") occurs only here in the NT
and only three times in the LXX but was otherwise common
in legal and other documents of the period in connection
with down payments on debts and purchases or even a prisoner's bail or a bride's dowry. Moulton and Milligan point
out that it was probably derived from an old word for "hand"
(i.e., "what is put in hand").[84] Jesus himself, as the high priest
appointed by God's oath, is our guarantee that the new
covenant is better than the old. Verses 23-28 will explain in
what ways this is true.

---

[83]It also appears in 8:6, 8, 9 (twice), 10; 9:4 (twice), 15 (twice), 16, 17, 20; 10:16, 29; 12:24; 13:20.

[84]MM, p. 179.

I. JESUS' RESURRECTION CREATES A PERMANENT PRIESTHOOD (7:23-25)

²³Now there have been many of those priests, since death prevented them from continuing in office; ²⁴but because Jesus lives forever, he has a permanent priesthood. ²⁵Therefore he is able to save completely^a those who come to God through him, because he always lives to intercede for them.

ª25 Or forever

The next two sections (vv. 23-25, vv. 26-28) explain how the priesthood of Jesus accomplishes what the Levitical priesthood could not (v. 11) — the perfection of believers. The key to our salvific perfection is the perfection of Jesus in his priestly vocation ("perfect" in v. 28 completes the *inclusio*). Each of these sections (1) connects a kerygmatic event in the incarnate life of Christ to (2) his perfection for his ministry as high priest and (3) a consequence of his perfection which enables ours.

7:23 Now there have been many of those priests, since death prevented them from continuing in office; 7:24 but because Jesus lives forever, he has a permanent priesthood.

This first section proceeds from Jesus' resurrection. The structural contrast here is identical to that in vv. 20-21 (οἱ μεν . . . ὁ δε . . . [*hoi men . . . ho de . . .*], i.e., many to one) but the thematic contrast is more significant. The "death" of those many priests anticipates the statement that Jesus "always lives" in v. 25. Another parallel which heightens the contrast is more explicit in the Greek text. Death prevented those priests from "continuing in office" (the compound verb παραμένω, *parameno*, "remain with"[85]) whereas Christ "lives" (the simple form of the same verb, μένω, "remain"). Although "forever"

---

[85]BAGD, p. 620.

sometimes translates a stylistic variation (as in 7:3, εἰς τὸ διηνεκές, *eis to diēnekes*), here our author repeats the exact
phrase in Psalm 110:4 (εἰς τὸ αἰῶνα, *eis to aiōna*), perhaps to
reinforce the connection to the passage just cited.

Jesus' resurrection makes him perfect for his priestly vocation because it makes his priesthood "permanent."
'Απαράβατος (*aparabatos*) occurs only here in the NT and conveys the sense of "unchangeable."[86] Both legal and literary
use outside of the NT suggest "inviolable"[87] which reflects the
term's etymology (ἀ, "not" + παρά, "beyond" + βαίνω [*bainō*],
"go, walk"[88]). Because Jesus lives forever, there is no change
in the office and no successor will ever step into his role.

**7:25 Therefore he is able to save completely those who come
to God through him, because he always lives to intercede for
them.**

"Therefore" identifies the consequence for believers. Jesus
is thus able to "save completely." Σῴζω (*sōzō*, "save, rescue"[89])
is the common term for salvation in the NT. Our author uses
it occasionally[90] and employs "perfection" terminology to
articulate his theology of salvation (see comments on 5:9-10,
13-14 and 7:11; 6:1-8 contextualizes one dimension of our
perfection — sanctification — in the covenant nature of salvation). Here the phrase rendered "completely" (εἰς τὸ παντε-
λές, *eis to panteles*) does not represent the exact same terminology but in the context of the *inclusio* (v. 11, 19, 28) suggests the connection. Jesus is able to secure for us the perfection of which our salvation consists.

One means of this salvation is Jesus' intercessory ministry
as high priest which pertains to the present, continuing
dimension of our salvation. During this time when we "grow
up in" our salvation (1 Pet 2:2; cf. also Phil 2:12) — i.e., grow

---

[86]Both Louw and Nida (p. 156) and Bauer (BAGD, p. 80).

[87]MM, p. 53.

[88]Kistemaker, p. 205.

[89]BAGD, p. 768.

[90]Σῴζω only here and in 5:7; σωτηρία in 1:14; 2:3, 10; 5:9; 6:9; 9:28; 11:7.

to become sinless in the actual state of our lives after having received a sinless standing in the sight of God (Heb 10:14) — we still need a priest who can mediate our continuing relationship with God, one who can not only identify with our weaknesses and deal with us gently (see 4:14; 5:1-2) but who can also appeal to God on our behalf and enable us to receive the mercy and grace necessary for remaining in God's presence (4:15). Because Jesus "always lives" (πάντοτε [*pantote*] with the present tense ζῶν [*zōn*] strongly expresses the curative sense), he is always able to "intercede" for us. Ἐντυγχάνω (*entyngchanō*) was common in legal contexts for the "appeal" one might make to an authority or on behalf of a client[91] and it is so used in the NT (Acts 25:24). Paul uses this same word in Romans 8:34 to describe how the risen Jesus, who is now at the right hand of God, intercedes for us. As a result, no one can condemn us and nothing can separate us from his love.[92]

J. JESUS' DEATH PROVIDES THE PERFECT SACRIFICE (7:26-28)

[26]**Such a high priest meets our need — one who is holy, blameless, pure, set apart from sinners, exalted above the heavens. [27]Unlike the other high priests, he does not need to offer sacrifices day after day, first for his own sins, and then for the sins of the people. He sacrificed for their sins once for all when he offered himself. [28]For the law appoints as high priests men who are weak; but the oath, which came after the law, appointed the Son, who has been made perfect forever.**

In these last verses of the chapter, the author turns from the resurrection to the cross to describe the second way in

---

[91]MM, p. 219.

[92]In 1 Timothy 2:4-5, Paul describes Christ as our "mediator" (μεσίτης) but there the reference is to our justification — the past or accomplished dimension of our salvation — and the ransom which Jesus paid at the cross.

which the Son "has been made perfect forever" in his vocation as priest. As with the resurrection discussed in vv. 23-25,
he again describes how this event has made Jesus a perfect
priest and the consequence for believers.

**7:26 Such a high priest meets our need — one who is holy,
blameless, pure, set apart from sinners, exalted above the
heavens.**

That Jesus can meet our need is the climactic conclusion
not only of this chapter but of the entire section on his priestly ministry (extending as far back as 4:14). In fact, it is quite
possible that our author had these next verses in view when
he first introduced the themes of suffering, perfection and
priesthood in chapter 2, for the wording here mirrors that in
2:10 (ἔπρεπεν, *eprepen*, translated "is fitting" in 2:10 but
"meets our need" here).

To present Jesus as the perfect sacrifice, our writer first
reminds us of his sinless life. Under the Mosaic covenant it
had been required that sin and guilt offerings be "without
defect" (Lev 1:3, 10; 4:3, 23, 28, 32; and 5:15, 18; 22:17-25
specify those defects which made a sacrifice unacceptable).

The five descriptors in this verse progress from Jesus' character (three adjectives) to his station following his ascension
in which he serves as our high priest (two participles). There
is little to distinguish between the meanings of the three
adjectives but their cumulative sense is clear: what other
priests were only by ritual, Jesus was by nature ("without sin,"
4:15). The two participles suggest a different idea, however.
The passive use of χωρίζω (*chōrizō*, "separate") followed by
ἀπὸ (*apo*, "from") suggests separation of location.[93] Morris
notes that the Levitical high priest was required to leave
home for a period of seven days prior to the Day of Atonement in order to avoid ritual defilement. However, Jesus
maintained his purity while among us and was not "separated
from sinners" until his ascension, following his sacrifice and

---

[93]Lane, p. 192.

resurrection. As a result, he is "exalted above the heavens" where he is now able to intercede for us with our heavenly Father (Rom 8:34).

7:27 Unlike the other high priests, he does not need to offer sacrifices day after day, first for his own sins, and then for the sins of the people. He sacrificed for their sins once for all when he offered himself.

The first part of this verse continues the sentence which began in v. 26, adding a sixth descriptor which (1) is a consequence of Jesus' sinlessness and (2) explains why he is able to enter the presence of God ("exalted above the heavens") on our behalf. In 5:3, we were reminded that other priests had to offer sacrifices for their own sins as well as for those of the people (for themselves first on the Day of Atonement, that they might enter the presence of God purified, to then offer sacrifice for the people; Leviticus 16).

This, then, is ultimately why Jesus is a "fitting" high priest: he needs not a sacrifice *for* himself but alone was able to offer a sacrifice *of* himself. The deaths of the other high priests prevented them from continuing in office. His death executed his office and his resurrection enabled him to continue to serve as our intercessor. Their need to sacrifice both for themselves and for the people arose "day after day." His sacrifice was "once for all" for both the priest and the sacrifice were perfectly without defect. They offered sacrifices for themselves and for others. He offered a sacrifice *of* himself for others. Because of what he did not need, he could provide what we do.

Θυσίας (*thysias*, "sacrifice") appeared first in 5:1 but will now become a key point of comparison between the old and new covenants in chapters 8-10 and occurs more often in Hebrews than in the entire rest of the NT. On its use in the letter, see comments on 5:1.

7:28 For the law appoints as high priests men who are weak; but the oath, which came after the law, appointed the Son,

who has been made perfect forever.

The parallelism in this verse sums up the entire chapter around pairs of opposite terms. The law appoints *men* who are *weak,* whereas the *oath* appoints the *Son* who has been *made perfect.* The initial positions are occupied by that which appointed each priesthood (the law, 7:5, 11; God's oath, 7:20-22), the middle positions by those appointed (men who are dying, 7:8; the Son who lives forever, 7:16, 24), and the final positions by their fitness for the task (weak, 5:2; perfect, cf. the blamelessness of Jesus in 7:26 with the comments on ἀσθενής [*asthenēs*] in 5:2).

This verse actually ends with the word "perfect," framing an inclusio with v. 11 which begins with the same term. What the Levitical priesthood could not attain for us, Jesus does because he is the perfect high priest. His death was a perfect sacrifice which "once for all" provided for our atonement. His endless life enables him to intercede for us forever. He is thus able to "save completely" (v. 25). A summary of how his perfection leads to ours, according to vv. 23-28, might be as follows:

Event	Perfect Priest	Perfected Believers
resurrection	→ permanent priesthood	→ continuing intercessor
cross	→ perfect sacrifice	→ once for all forgiveness

HEBREWS 8

V. THE NEW COVENANT BROUGHT BY JESUS OUR HIGH PRIEST IS SUPERIOR TO THE OLD COVENANT (8:1-13)

We have now reached a very important junction in the letter. The heart of the document consists of two main ideas under the unifying head of the new covenant. Jesus is our high priest (chapters 5-7) as well as our sacrifice (chapters 9-10). These two dimensions of Jesus' ministry define the new covenant (chapter 8). Chapter 8 expounds Jeremiah 31:31-34 in much the same manner that chapters 5-7 expound Psalm 110:4. Verse 6 represents the summit of the document.

A. OUR HIGH PRIEST REIGNS AND SERVES IN THE TRUE TABERNACLE, PREFIGURED BY OLD TESTAMENT SHADOWS (8:1-5)

[1]The point of what we are saying is this: We do have such a high priest, who sat down at the right hand of the throne of the Majesty in heaven, [2]and who serves in the sanctuary, the true tabernacle set up by the Lord, not by man.

[3]Every high priest is appointed to offer both gifts and sacrifices, and so it was necessary for this one also to have something to offer. [4]If he were on earth, he would not be a priest, for there are already men who offer the gifts prescribed by the law. [5]They serve at a sanctuary that is a copy and shadow of what is in heaven. This is why Moses was warned when he was about to build the tabernacle: "See to it

**that you make everything according to the pattern shown
you on the mountain."ᵃ**

ᵃ5 Exodus 25:40

**8:1 The point of what we are saying is this: We do have such
a high priest, who sat down at the right hand of the throne
of the Majesty in heaven,**

The whole discussion about our high priest is brought into
focus just prior to our writer's discussion of the new covenant.
Bauer defines κεφάλαιον (*kephalaion*, "point" or "sum") as
"main thing, main point, summary, synopsis (limited to the
main points)" and translates this first phrase, "the main point
in what has been said [is this]."[1] The main point: that "such a
high priest" who "meets our need" (7:26) has, in fact, not only
come but has now taken his place at the right hand of God
and serves in the heavenly sanctuary on our behalf.

These two features of his priesthood preview the remainder of this section which uses them to introduce his description of the new covenant. The first of these features describes
when Jesus became our high priest (when he "sat down at the
right hand") and the second, *what* he does as our high priest
(he "serves in the sanctuary"). Both describe *where* he serves
("in heaven," "the true tabernacle set up by the Lord, not
man").

Royal imagery ("throne," "Majesty") recalls the parallel to
Melchizedek who was both king and priest (7:1). Jesus, similarly, is both king and priest. The one who rules the universe
also serves his "brothers" (2:11). This entire phrase recalls 1:3
and suggests that the "sum" thus takes in the entire scope of
the letter. The comments on that verse suggested that "the
Majesty" is a substitute for the name of God and that New
Testament references to Jesus sitting at the right hand of God
tend to emphasize his power and authority.

---

[1]BAGD, p. 429.

8:2 and who serves in the sanctuary, the true tabernacle set up by the Lord, not by man.

Though much has and will yet be made of the role of the priest in both covenants, this is the first direct reference to the "tabernacle." What is meant by "true" tabernacle (ἀλη-θινός, *alēthinos*, "real" vs. "apparent"[2]) will be explained further in verse 5 and in detail in chapter 9. Yet another dimension of the readers' beloved heritage is introduced to demonstrate the greatness of their Savior and his covenant.

8:3 Every high priest is appointed to offer both gifts and sacrifices, and so it was necessary for this one also to have something to offer.

The reference to "every high priest" being "appointed to offer gifts and sacrifices" is precisely the statement first made in 5:1. There, however, our writer was more concerned about what it meant for the priest to be "from among men" and thus "able to deal gently" with them. He referred to the "weakness" of the priest and thus to his need to offer a sacrifice for his own sins (5:2,3). Without commenting further upon the significance of the sacrifice, our author then turned his attention to (1) the necessity for a priest to be appointed by God and the scriptural proof of Jesus' appointment (5:4-10), (2) a digression to challenge his readers to grow spiritually (5:11-6:12), and (3) a return to the parallel with Melchizedek and subsequent significance of the oath and resurrection (6:13-7:25). Only at the end of chapter 7 has he returned to the significance of the sacrifice, completing the contrast between every other priest who needed to offer sacrifices for their own sins and Jesus who did not (7:26-28). Once placed in the larger context of tabernacle ritual and the new covenant promised through Jeremiah, Jesus' sacrifice will be presented as the ultimate proof of the superiority of the "new order" (9:10) and the defining event of the "new covenant" (9:15), themes which will be explained and applied throughout chapters 9 and 10.

---

[2]Bruce, p. 163, n. 17.

It is, of course, our sin which made it necessary for Jesus to offer his sacrifice, just as sin created the need for the gifts and sacrifices presented under the old covenant. However, the language here (ὅθεν, *hothen*, "so" or "therefore") suggests that our writer is referring to the necessity created by his classification argument (what is true of "every" priest must also be true of the "one" if, in fact, he is a priest).

8:4 If he were on earth, he would not be a priest, for there are already men who offer the gifts prescribed by the law.

This next verse, however, suggests that although Jesus was like other priests in that he offered a "gift,"[3] his ministry is yet different from theirs. "If he were on earth," he would have been a priest as they were. But we know that he sits at the right hand of God's throne in heaven. It was not during his incarnation but following his ascension that he began to serve in the sanctuary of the "true" tabernacle.

The present tense verbs here and in verse 5 ("there are already men who offer . . .They serve . . .") may suggest that our author writes before the destruction of the temple in AD 70. However, it is also possible that here, as in 5:1ff., the present tense is used as a customary way of making broad, general statements which serve as argumentative premises, (1) since the references are to the tabernacle, a "type" which would still provide the exegetical foundation for the argument apart from the fate of the temple and (2) as unlikely as it may have been for the author to overlook its destruction altogether.

8:5 They serve at a sanctuary that is a copy and shadow of what is in heaven. This is why Moses was warned when he was about to build the tabernacle: "See to it that you make everything according to the pattern shown you on the mountain."

Here is a key difference between the service of Jesus and that of the priests on earth. He serves at a "true" (or "real," cf.

---

[3]There is no clear distinction between the terms "gift" and "sacrifice" in Hebrews, the Old Testament, or rabbinic literature. See comments on 5:1.

verses 1-2) sanctuary "set up by the Lord" while they serve at one set up "by man" (v. 2) which is merely "a copy and a shadow of what is in heaven."

Ὑποδείγμα (hypodeigma, "copy") is sometimes translated "example" (in John 13:15 of that which Jesus set when washing the feet of his disciples, in James 5:10 when he mentions the "example" of the prophets in the face of suffering, and in 2 Peter 2:6 of the "example" which God made of Sodom and Gomorrah), even in Hebrews (4:11, of disobedience, by the Israelites in the wilderness). The rendering "copy" (or "imitation"[4]) seems a better fit for the context here, as well as in 9:23 (again in reference to the tabernacle but also to everything used in its ceremonies, 9:21-22). Σκία (skia, "shadow") can be used in a literal sense (as in Acts 5:15, of Peter's shadow which fell on those whom he passed, and as in Mark 4:32 of the "shade" provided by the branches of a tree). There is, of course, some transference in the figurative sense. Paul uses the term to refer to the legalistic rituals which are a "shadow" of things to come as opposed to the "reality" (σῶμα, sōma, "body") found in Christ (Col 2:17). In 10:1, our writer similarly points out that the law is a "shadow" of the good things that are coming, not the "realities" (εἴκων, eikōn, "image") themselves. Some see here the influence of Philo and his Platonic ideas but, in the context, it seems more likely that these terms merely serve as an apt metaphor to describe our writer's typological exegesis (since the two terms are here used opposite "pattern," τύπος [typos], which appears later in the verse).

As proof that the tabernacle and its rituals are to be so interpreted, our writer offers the warning given to Moses in Exodus 25:40 (LXX). The fact that Moses was warned to make *everything* according to the pattern — which had been provided by God himself — is offered as a sign that God intentionally designed the tabernacle and its rituals to imitate what he knew Jesus would someday do. The word "everything" is not

---

[4]BAGD, p. 844.

present in the text of the LXX but is added by our writer, presumably to suggest his point in appealing to the verse. *Typos* ("pattern") means "form, figure, pattern, model" but is sometimes specifically used of the "*types* given by God as an indication of the future, in the form of persons or things."[5] The details of the pattern will be developed in chapter 9.

B. OUR HIGH PRIEST IS MEDIATOR OF THE NEW COVENANT, PROMISED THROUGH THE PROPHET JEREMIAH (8:6-13)

[6]But the ministry Jesus has received is as superior to theirs as the covenant of which he is mediator is superior to the old one, and it is founded on better promises.
[7]For if there had been nothing wrong with that first covenant, no place would have been sought for another.
[8]But God found fault with the people and said[a]:
"The time is coming, declares the Lord,
when I will make a new covenant
with the house of Israel
and with the house of Judah.
[9]It will not be like the covenant
I made with their forefathers
when I took them by the hand
to lead them out of Egypt,
because they did not remain faithful to my covenant,
and I turned away from them,
declares the Lord.
[10]This is the covenant I will make with the house of Israel
after that time, declares the Lord.
I will put my laws in their minds
and write them on their hearts.
I will be their God,
and they will be my people.

---

[5]BAGD, p. 830.

[11]No longer will a man teach his neighbor,
or a man his brother, saying, 'Know the Lord,'
because they will all know me,
from the least of them to the greatest.
[12]For I will forgive their wickedness
and will remember their sins no more."[b]
[13]By calling this covenant "new," he has made the first
one obsolete; and what is obsolete and aging will soon disappear.

[a]8 Some manuscripts may be translated *fault and said to the people.*
[b]12 Jer. 31:31-34

**8:6 But the ministry Jesus has received is as superior to
theirs as the covenant of which he is mediator is superior to
the old one, and it is founded on better promises.**

It is no exaggeration to suggest that this verse is the centerpiece of the letter. "Ministry" translates the feminine form
(λειτουργία, *leitourgia*, "service, ministry") of the masculine
noun translated "serves" in v. 2 (λειτουργός, *leitourgos*, "servant, minister"; lit., "who is a servant" in 8:2). Now that the
superiority of Jesus' priesthood has been discussed in spatial
(where) and temporal (when) senses, our writer points us to
the inherent superiority of his service (what).

As in 1:4, the term "superior" translates two different
Greek terms (first διαφορώτερος, *diaphorōteros*, "greater," then
κρείττων, *kreittōn*, "better"). There is little to distinguish
between the significance of the terms (hence the NIV rendering) yet this is a good example of accumulating comparative
terms[6] for emphasis and to establish a coordinate relationship
between the greatness of two different things (in 1:4, the Son
and his name; here, his ministry and his covenant). This is
another in the series of "better" comparisons made throughout the letter (see comments on 1:4).

Διαθήκη (*diathēkē*) is clearly a key term in chapter 8-10, as
well as within the scheme of the document as a whole. Bauer

---

[6]So Ellingworth, p. 104.

suggests that, in the New Testament, the term represents "the declaration of one person's will, not the result of an agreement between two parties, like a compact or contract."[7] In other words, as in the case of a testament or a will (9:16), the one who creates the will or covenant sets the conditions and they are absolute, not subject to negotiation with another party. The following chart summarizes significant occurrences of the word in Hebrews as well as the important themes in its various contexts:[8]

Key Occurrences of διαθήκη in Hebrews		
The Covenant is . . .	• better	• 7:22; 8:6
	• founded on better promises	• 8:16
	• new	
	• (καίνη)	• 8:8 (Jer 31:31); 8:13 (implied); 9:15
	• (νέας)	• 12:24
	• not like that made with their forefathers	• 8:9 (Jer 31:32)
	• prophesied for "that time"	• 8:10; 10:16 (Jer 31:33)
	• like a "will," in force at the death of the one who made it	• 9:16, 17
	• put into effect with the blood of Christ	• 9:20; 10:29; 13:20
	• eternal	• 13:20
Jesus is . . .	• guarantee	• 7:22
	• mediator	• 8:6; 9:15; 12:24
	• the one who made it [and whose death put it into effect]	• 9:17
Those who are called . . .	• receive the promised eternal inheritance	• 9:15
	• are set free from sin	• 10:29

---

[7]BAGD, p. 183.

[8]In addition to the "key" occurrences listed here, the term appears in 9:4 when our writer refers to the "ark" and the "tables" of the old covenant and in 9:18 of that "first" covenant (also put into effect with blood).

the one who treats the blood of the covenant as an unholy thing	• deserves severe punishment	• 9:15

Each dimension of the covenant will be commented upon in due course, but taken together we see that Hebrews presents a well-rounded description of the nature of the new covenant which God offers to believers.

Two key features of the new and superior covenant are mentioned in the present verse. First, Jesus is our "mediator." In Hebrews, μεσίτης (*mesitēs*) is used only of Jesus' role in the new covenant (also in 9:15 and 12:24) in the same manner that Paul uses it of him in 1 Timothy 2:5. According to Bauer, it describes "one who mediates between two parties to remove a disagreement or reach a common goal."[9] In the papyri, the word was commonly used of the "arbiter" in legal and business transactions, including those in which someone may serve as "surety" for a debt.[10] Bruce offers the rendering "go-between"[11] but the references to his death ("ransom" in 9:15 and 1 Tim 2:5; "blood" in 12:24) are so prominent in New Testament contexts that Ellingworth appears to be correct in observing that Christ's mediation is unilateral,[12] i.e., it runs in one direction — from God to us. In no way, however, does this verse diminish the intercessory dimension of Christ's ministry described elsewhere (7:25; Rom 8:24).

Second, this covenant is "founded on better promises." In 7:22 we learned that God's oath made Jesus the guarantee of a better covenant but comments on chapter six noted that the oath was added to "what was promised" as confirmation. What, then, are the "promises"?

---

[9]BAGD, p. 506.
[10]MM, p. 399; cf. 7:22.
[11]Bruce, p. 167.
[12]BAGD, p. 410.

In Hebrews, ἐπαγγελία (*epangelia*) is always associated with the promises God made to Abraham — the promised land and the rest it offers — and with the final salvation of believers which that land and rest typify. 4:1 spoke of "the promise of entering his rest" which the Israelites failed to receive because, as a result of their rebellion, the promised land was refused to them. Yet that promise "still stands" (4:1), there remains another "Sabbath-rest for the people of God" (4:9), and the readers are exhorted to "make every effort to enter that rest" (4:11). 6:12, 15, 17 and 7:6 referred to "what was promised" to Abraham who, in one sense "received" it (6:15), although we later read that, while he would "receive as his inheritance" the "promised land" (11:8, 9), neither he, Isaac nor Jacob received "the things promised" but only "saw them from a distance," "admitted that they were aliens and strangers on earth" and longed "for a better country — a heavenly one" (11:13). Similarly, though in one sense the heroes of faith mentioned in 11:32 "gained what was promised" (11:33, they "conquered kingdoms"), yet none received "what had been promised" (11:39) for "God planned something better for us so that only together with us would they be made perfect (τελειόω, *teleioō*)" (11:40).

It is probably more than a coincidence that in 11:40 our writer would use that term which is so prominent in his own theology of salvation (see comments on 7:11). When we consider (1) the use of *epangelia* to describe the promises to Abraham, (2) the typological significance accorded to those promises, (3) the reference to our "promised eternal inheritance" in 9:15 (cf. 11:8-9), and (4) the contextual evidence (10:37-39) that the phrase "what he has promised" in 10:36 is a reference to the eschatological salvation of all believers, our writer's "theology of promise" becomes clear. What was first promised to Abraham in an earthly sense is also promised in an eternal and heavenly sense to all who belong to the community of faith — including believers today as well as the men and women of faith who lived under the old covenant. The promise is sure and together we will be "made perfect" so that we can receive our eternal inheritance — heaven and its rest, prepared for us by God (11:16)

8:7 For if there had been nothing wrong with that first covenant, no place would have been sought for another. 8:8 But God found fault with the people and said:

The sign argument in verse 7 follows the pattern of that offered in 7:11. The protasis ("if" clause) assumes the condition to be true (for the sake of argument, apart from its objective truth or falsity) and the apodosis (second clause) suggests the conclusion. Again, the argument is one of counter-condition in relation to what was predicted by the prophet (v. 8ff.). The fact that another, "new" covenant was prophesied is a sign that God did see a place for another covenant and thus that something was wrong with the "first" covenant. Why else would God plan and predict another?

The significance of this verse extends beyond its argumentative function in the letter, however. There are those today who would suggest that the "new" covenant was not much more than an afterthought in the purpose of God, a "Plan B" which followed the failure of "Plan A," a provisional measure made necessary by the temporary failure of Israel for whom God will still fulfill his promises in an earthly and literal sense following a heavenly rapture of the new covenant community. What our writer seems to suggest here is that the new covenant was, all along, a part of God's purpose for "that time" which was coming (8:8, 10), a time when the first covenant would become "obsolete" and "disappear" (see v. 13 below).

It is true that God "found fault with the people" and this is precisely what was "wrong with that first covenant" (8:7). Dealing only with "external regulations applying until the time of the new order" (9:10) rather than with internal realities (8:10), neither its law (7:18-19) nor its priesthood (7:11) could make people perfect.

"The time is coming, declares the Lord, when I will make a new covenant with the house of Israel and with the house of

Judah. 8:9 It will not be like the covenant I made with their forefathers when I took them by the hand to lead them out of Egypt, because they did not remain faithful to my covenant, and I turned away from them, declares the Lord.

Our writer cites Jeremiah 31:31-34 in its entirety[13] to demonstrate that God had included in his plan a place for another covenant (8:7), one which would be "new" and "not like" the covenant which he "made with their forefathers." Ἡμέρα (*hēmera*) is often translated "day" but in the plural refers to a longer period of time,[14] possibly "the time of a decisive event,"[15] but clearly a time which has now come in the view of our author. The prophecy cited not only announces the coming of the new covenant but describes it. The features prophesied for it are worth noting.

8:10 This is the covenant I will make with the house of Israel after that time, declares the Lord. I will put my laws in their minds and write them on their hearts. I will be their God, and they will be my people.

(1) The new covenant creates internal realities in the minds and hearts of believers, not just external regulations. The laws of that old covenant were written on tablets of stone (24:12; 34:1) but now God says he will put his laws in the minds and hearts of his people. We are no longer subject to the guardianship or trusteeship of that law for God has now sent the Spirit of his Son into our hearts to make us sons and heirs (Gal 4:2-7). The regulations of the law could moderate our outward behaviors (without making us righteous, Gal 3:21, cf. Heb 7:19), but the ministry of the Spirit which is part of the new covenant transforms us into his likeness (2 Cor 3:7-8, 18). In the new covenant, we are not simply told how to live a righteous life; in Christ we are new creations (2 Cor 5:17) who grow to be righteous through the sanctifying work of his Spirit.

---

[13]The LXX is cited with a few minor variations.

[14]"Time of life or activity," BAGD, p. 347.

[15]Ellingworth, p. 416.

(2) The new covenant restores fellowship between God and his people. "I will be their God, and they will be my people," said the Lord through his prophet Jeremiah. He had said the same through his prophet Ezekiel when he promised to put a new spirit in his people, to "remove from them their heart of stone and give them a heart of flesh" (11:19-20). The real change of heart and mind created by the ministry of the Spirit in the new covenant makes possible that restoration of our fellowship with God which is the entire purpose of his plan of redemption. God had desired nothing less with Israel under that old covenant (Exod 19:15f.) but the inability of its rituals and regulations to effect real change in them was manifest in their failure to "remain faithful," a failure which forced God to turn away from them (v. 9). This happened as God knew it would but his ultimate plan was for a new and different covenant which could restore that fellowship through the perfection of those who would draw near to him (7:19; 10:1ff.).

8:11 No longer will a man teach his neighbor, or a man his brother, saying, 'Know the Lord,' because they will all know me, from the least of them to the greatest.

(3) The new covenant offers knowledge of God to all. As the restoration of fellowship with God grows out of the real spiritual regeneration of his people, so their personal knowledge of him grows out of the restoration of fellowship. Verse 11 should not be taken to suggest that there will be no need for teaching within the new covenant community but that there will be no need for that teaching which leads people to "know" the Lord. The new covenant promises a personal relationship with God to all who enter it. The universality of the promise is conveyed by the progression from the more general term "neighbor" (πολίτης, *politēs*, "fellow-citizen, fellow-townsman"[16]) to the more intimate term "brother" and by the inclusive phrase, "from the least of them to the greatest." That our author would pen this letter demonstrates his belief

---

[16]BAGD, p. 686.

in the need for teaching within the new covenant community. Nevertheless, there is no spiritual "elite" within that community upon whom the rest are dependent for their personal knowledge of and relationship with God.

8:12 For I will forgive their wickedness and will remember their sins no more."

(4) The new covenant promises complete and final forgiveness for believers. Whereas relationship grows out of restoration and restoration out of re-creation, the "for" which introduces verse 12 renders a conjunction that suggests the underlying cause of all the above. The complete experience of features (1) - (3) is, of course, eschatological. In the meantime, we continue to have opportunity to teach those outside of the covenant community to "know the Lord," continue to experience the limits which our imperfections place upon our ability to draw near to God, and continue to struggle to become more like him. During this interim which ends only with our final, eschatological perfection, however, God has provided for our justification through that sacrifice which Jesus has made of his own life. As a result, we can even now begin to experience the first and growing fruits of that salvation provided by the new covenant. For his sacrifice not only satisfied the law's demands but has changed the way God views believers.

8:13 By calling this covenant "new," he has made the first one obsolete; and what is obsolete and aging will soon disappear.

From the literal sense of the word "new" in Jeremiah 31:31, our writer draws a chain of inferences to characterize the "first" covenant. By contrast, it is first "obsolete," then "obsolete and aging" and soon it will "disappear." Now that the "new order" has arrived, it is no longer needed and its regulations no longer apply (9:10). God himself has cancelled it (παλαιόω, *palaioō*, for which Moulton and Milligan suggest "abrogate" when used intransitively). If his readers were considering a return to that first covenant,[17] they would now have no reason to do so. This is one of the occasions in the letter when a reference to the destruction of the temple would certainly have strengthened our writer's argument, if it had already taken place. However, the argument does not depend upon this, for the temple had been destroyed before without the disappearance of the covenant or the law.

---

[17]MM, p. 475.

HEBREWS 9

VI. JESUS' SACRIFICE OF HIMSELF IS SUPERIOR TO THE SACRIFICES OF THE OLD COVENANT AND SETS US FREE FROM SIN (9:1–10:39)

The new covenant, which is superior to the old covenant, stands at the center of Hebrews (ch. 8). Its two main features, according to Hebrews, are its superior high priest (chs. 5–7) and its superior sacrifice (chs. 9–10). The sacrifice of the new covenant is discussed in three stages. First, the old covenant system at the tabernacle is presented as a background picture to help explain what Jesus did in the new covenant (9:1-10). Second, the effectiveness of the blood of Christ is described in detail (9:11-28). Finally, the sacrifice of Christ is exhibited as being made once, but effective for all time (10:1-18). The "therefore" of 10:19 introduces a section of exhortation based on this three staged discussion of Christ's sacrifice.

The central Old Testament quotation for this section is found in 10:5-7 and is taken from Psalm 40:6-8. Most sections of Hebrews place the major Old Testament quotation at the beginning of the section. Only the discussion of the covenant in chapter 8 and this discussion of the sacrifice in chapters 9-10 place the Old Testament quotation near the end.

A. THE TABERNACLE AND ITS TOOLS (9:1-5)

¹Now the first covenant had regulations for worship and also an earthly sanctuary. ²A tabernacle was set up. In its first room were the lampstand, the table and the consecrated bread; this was called the Holy Place. ³Behind the second

curtain was a room called the Most Holy Place, ⁴which had
the golden altar of incense and the gold-covered ark of the
covenant. This ark contained the gold jar of manna, Aaron's
staff that had budded, and the stone tablets of the covenant.
⁵Above the ark were the cherubim of the Glory, overshadowing the atonement cover.ᵃ But we cannot discuss these things
in detail now.

ᵃ5 Traditionally *the mercy seat*

9:1 Now the first covenant had regulations for worship and also an earthly sanctuary.

Our author explains that "the first covenant[1] had regulations for worship and also an earthly sanctuary." He discusses
them in the reverse order, beginning with the tabernacle and
its tools (vv. 1-5), and then proceeding to the central ceremony and its meaning (vv. 6-10). The Greek text ties this section
closely to chapter eight by using the conjunction οὖν (*oun*,
"therefore"). The NIV does not translate this word in six of its
thirteen appearances in Hebrews.[2] This is in keeping with
Bauer's suggestion that "at times it may be left untranslated."[3]
The KJV may be more satisfactory on this point by translating
the word each time it is used.

9:2 A tabernacle was set up. In its first room were the lamp-stand, the table and the consecrated bread; this was called the Holy Place.

In a table below we will describe the major utensils of worship in the tabernacle. The plans and construction of the
tabernacle and its furnishings are recorded in Exodus 25-40.
Hebrews only lists the lampstand and the table with its bread
in "the Holy Place" and the altar of incense and the ark in
"the Most Holy Place." Detailed descriptions of other items

---

[1]In verse one, the word "covenant" appears only in a few late manuscripts.
The NIV supplies it to avoid ambiguity as it does in 8:13.
[2]It is translated in 4:1, 11, 14, 16; 9:23; 10:19; and 13:15. It is not translated in 2:14; 4:6; 7:11; 8:4; 9:1; or 10:35.
[3]BAGD, p. 592.

can be found in Exodus: the upright boards for the sides of the tabernacle and the various curtains covering it; the court-yard with its altar of burnt offering, its wash basin and the numerous posts and curtains surrounding it; oil; incense; and priests' clothing. To carry on the worship as described in the Old Testament would have required many other items not named. There would have been facilities for cooking, dining and sleeping inside the courtyard; storage compartments for wood, incense, salt, wine and water; storage for knives, hooks, basins and carts. These items were all holy and whatever touched them became holy (Exod 30:22-29).

Before our author describes the main ceremony of "the Day of Atonement" (*Yom Kippur*) and its unique entrance into the Most Holy Place, he reviews the layout and furniture of the tabernacle for his readers. The tabernacle had two rooms.[4] The first room was "called the Holy Place" and housed the lampstand, the table and the consecrated bread. They are presented as three separate items, although the bread was placed on the table.

The "lampstand" was on the south side, opposite the table (Exod 26:35). It was solid gold (Exod 25:31; 37:22-23). The table and the altar of incense were completely overlaid with gold (Exod 25:24; 20:3). The lampstand was made of one talent of gold, i.e., about 65 pounds.[5] God wanted the best for his worship. It must have been an impressive sight. Since only a small amount of light would penetrate the thick coverings and the cracks around the edges of the curtains, the seven lamps of the lampstand provided the primary source of light. Its lamps were "tended continually" (Lev 24:4). In the days of Rehoboam the ten lampstands of Solomon's temple were lit every evening (2 Chr 13:11). A solid gold lampstand with oil supplied contin-uously from two trees formed one of Zechariah's night visions

---

[4]Josephus describes the tabernacle and its furnishings in *Antiquities 3.102-150*.

[5]D.J. Wiseman, "Weights and Measures," *The New Bible Dictionary*, 2nd ed., ed. by J.D. Douglas (Leicester, England: InterVarsity Press, 1982), pp. 1245-1249.

(Zech 4) to show that God's plans would not be achieved by might or power "but by my Spirit."

The "table" was on the north side opposite the lampstand. When the tabernacle was erected, this table was put in it first, then the lampstand, and then the altar of incense (Exod 40:4, 22-27). On this table, twelve fresh loaves of "consecrated bread" were placed each Sabbath, one for each of the twelve tribes of Israel. The priests were to eat the old bread "in a holy place' (Exod 25:30; Lev 24:5-9). It was left on the table even when the people were on the move at God's direction (Num 4:7). This table was evidently used for nothing but holding these loaves. It came to be called "the table for setting out the consecrated bread" (2 Chr 29:18). It is not difficult to see a connection between this weekly replenishing of bread and the weekly observance of the Lord's Supper in the early church (Luke 22:14-20; 1 Cor 11:23-34; Acts 2:42; 20:7).

These items were housed in "the Holy Place." The terms for various places in the tabernacle are a bit confusing. The whole tabernacle is called the "earthly sanctuary" (τό ἅγιον κοσμικόν, *to hagion kosmikon*) in 9:1 and "the first tent" (τῆς πρώτης σκηνῆς, *tēs prōtēs skēnēs*) in 9:8. "First" (in v. 8) contrasts the old and new covenants just as "first" and "second" do in 10:9. Konig says,

> This sanctuary of YHWH (Ex. xxv.8) was in the nature of things called the "dwelling" par excellence (*ha-mishkan*) and the "tent" par excellence (*ha-ohel*); but its most frequent designation is *ohel mo'ed* (*ib.* xxvii.21 *et seq.*). This term means "tent of mutual appointment," that is "place of meeting [of God with Moses and his successors]" (*ib.*xxv.22).[6]

The two components of the tent of worship are called "the outer room" (9:6, *tēn prōtēn skēnēn*, lit., "the first tent") and "the inner room" (9:7, τὴν δευτέραν, *tēn deuteran*, lit., "the second [tent]"). With curtains rather than wooden doors,

---

[6]Eduard Konig, "Tabernacle." *The Jewish Encyclopedia.* ed. by Isadore Singer, 11:656.

each of the two parts of the tent would look like a separate tent (see 9:3, 6). The outer room was also called "the Holy Place" (ἅγια, *hagia*, in 9:2).[7]

9:3 Behind the second curtain was a room called the Most Holy Place,

The inner room ("the second [tent]," 9:7) was "behind the second veil" (9:3). It was also known as "the Holy of Holies" (ἅγια ἅγιων, *hagia hagiōn*), i.e., "the Most Holy Place" (9:3).[8] In 9:8 the designation is shortened to "the holies" (τῶν ἁγίων) in the phrase "the way of holies" (τὴν τῶν ἁγίων ὁδὸν, *tēn tōn hagiōn hodon*, NIV "the way into the Most Holy Place").[9] Its counterpart, which Jesus entered in heaven, is designated in 9:12 as "the Most Holy Place" (*ta hagia*).

A summary look at the layout of the tabernacle might be as follows:

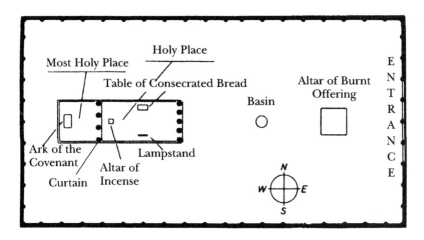

[7]Variant readings in this verse call it τὰ ἅγια ("the holies") or even ἅγια ἅγιων ("holy of holies,", i.e., "the Most Holy Place"), a phrase usually reserved for the inner room.

[8]Variant readings use the article (τὰ ἅγια τῶν ἁγίων or ἅγια τῶν ἁγίων, "the holy of holies").

[9]Τῶν ἁγίων can be read as masculine, feminine or neuter. Thus Elling-worth reminds us that the Syriac version understood this phrase in 9:8 as masculine, meaning "Christians." So it reads "the way of Christians."

9:4 which had the golden altar of incense and the gold-covered ark of the covenant. This ark contained the gold jar of manna, Aaron's staff that had budded, and the stone tablets of the covenant. 9:5 Above the ark were the cherubim of the Glory, overshadowing the atonement cover. But we cannot discuss these things in detail now.

Two items of furniture are associated with the inner room: the altar of incense and the ark of the covenant. The ark of the covenant was located within the Most Holy Place and behind the curtain. The altar was placed in front of the curtain that was before the ark (Exod 30:6). Both glistened with their golden overlay. Bauer suggests that θυμιατήριαν (*thymiatērian*) refers to "a place or vessel for the burning of incense . . . a censer" although he suggests the translation "altar of incense" for 9:4.[10] In the LXX, both 2 Chronicles 26:29 and Ezekiel 8:11 use the word of a censer held in someone's hand. However, the ordinary word for censer in the LXX was πυρεῖον (*pyreion*), a word which does not appear in the New Testament, and which may be understood as a firepot of some sort (Lev 10:1; 16:12; Num 16:6, 17-18; etc.). Liddell and Scott suggest "firesticks" for the plural form or "an earthen pan for coals" for the singular.[11] Gooding and Wiseman explain:

> Its form was usually . . . a bowl mounted on a pedestal . . . Small stone incense altars with concave bowls on legs are commonly found, or depicted in ancient art . . . Some censers were portable and made of bronze . . . or gold . . . and used for carrying a few burning coals.[12]

In giving the original plan for this altar, Exodus 30:1-10 used a different word (LXX θυσιαστήριον θυμιάματος, *thysiastērion thymiamatos*, "an altar of incense"). Later, when it was constructed, the LXX says that Bezalel "made the copper altar (τὸ θυσιαστήριον τὸ χαλκοῦν, *to thysiastērion to chalkoun*) out

---

[10]BAGD, p. 365.

[11]LS, p. 1556.

[12]D.W. Gooding and D.J. Wiseman, "Censer." *The New Bible Dictionary*, 2nd ed., ed. by J.D. Douglas, p. 181.

of the copper censers (τῶν πυρείων τῶν χάλκων, *tōn pyreiōn tōn chalkōn*), which belonged to the men who rebelled with the assembly of Core" (Exod 38:22).

Three items were in the "ark of the covenant": the jar of manna, Aaron's rod and the stone tablets which contained the ten commandments. The lid with its cherubim rested on top.

The NIV says the ark "contained" (ἐν ᾗ, *en hē*, lit., "in which were") the jar, the rod and the tablets. Numbers 17:10 says that Aaron's rod was put "in front of the [ark of the] Testimony." The ark was about 4.5×2.25×2.25 feet in size (Exod 25:10). Was Aaron's rod, including its budded branches, short enough to fit inside the ark, or did it simply lay in front of it? The Old Testament also reports that Aaron put the jar of manna "in front of the Testimony" (Exod 16:34), whereas Hebrews locates it "in" the ark. Both Deuteronomy 10:5 and Hebrews 9:4 indicate that the tablets of stone were "in" the ark but Deuteronomy 31:26 says they were "beside the ark of the covenant." When Solomon placed the ark in the newly completed temple, the Scripture reports that "there was nothing in the ark except the two stone tablets that Moses had placed in it at Horeb" (1 Kgs 8:9).

The phrase *en hē* ("in which") is used in 9:2 to describe the outer room "in which" were the lampstand, the table and the bread (the NIV reads, "In its first room were"). The altar of incense is not named among these items, but is listed among those in the inner room. What might the word "in" imply? Bauer defines ἐν (*en*, "in") with a range of meanings that point to close relationship as well as physical location.[13] Thus Aaron's rod may be "in" the ark in the sense that it has a close relationship to the ark, though not physically located inside of it. Likewise, the altar of incense may be "in" the inner room by being associated with it, while not being actually "in" its physical space. This seems to make sense even though the inner room is described in 9:3 as "behind the curtain." Accompanying his article on the tabernacle in the *Jewish Encyclopedia*, Konig has printed the title page from a Hebrew

---

[13]BAGD, pp. 258-261.

book by Yom-Tob Zahalon, *She'elot u-Teshubot* ("Questions and Answers"), published in Venice in 1691 in which the altar of incense is placed just inside the door of the tabernacle at the opposite end of the room from the curtain concealing the Most Holy Place.[14] The conceptual location appears to be more important to Zahalon than the physical location.

The table below lists the major items in the tabernacle and a possible New Testament counterpart for each. It may be misleading to talk about a "tabernacle item" and its "New Testament counterpart" since Hebrews calls the old covenant a "copy" or "shadow" of that which is under Christ (8:5; 9:24; 10:1), not an "allegory" or a "parable." Nevertheless, our author's method would appear to be typlogical. It is probably also worth noting that, although some see the influence of Philo here, Hebrews actually parts company with Philo who appears to extend many of the features of the old covenant sacrificial system into a much more fully described heavenly counterpart.

Tabernacle Item	New Testament Counterpart
altar of burnt offerings	the cross and death of Jesus
basin	baptism and daily cleansing
Holy Place	the church
lamp	the Bible and the Holy Spirit
table	fellowship with God and man
bread	Lord's Supper
altar of incense	prayers
veil	Body of Christ
ark	presence of God
manna	provision of God
staff	leaders of God's choice
tablets	laws of God
cherubim	ministering angels of God
atonement cover	reconciliation to God

---

[14]Eduard Konig, "Tabernacle," *The Jewish Encyclopedia*, ed. by Isadore Singer, 11:655.

B. THE DAY OF ATONEMENT (9:6-10)

[6]When everything had been arranged like this, the priests entered regularly into the outer room to carry on their ministry. [7]But only the high priest entered the inner room, and that only once a year, and never without blood, which he offered for himself and for the sins the people had committed in ignorance. [8]The Holy Spirit was showing by this that the way into the Most Holy Place had not yet been disclosed as long as the first tabernacle was still standing. [9]This is an illustration for the present time, indicating that the gifts and sacrifices being offered were not able to clear the conscience of the worshiper. [10]They are only a matter of food and drink and various ceremonial washings — external regulations applying until the time of the new order.

9:6 When everything had been arranged like this, the priests entered regularly into the outer room to carry on their ministry.
Now that he has described the tabernacle and its furnishings, our writer turns his attention to the second element of that first covenant mentioned in 9:1 — the "regulations for worship" in the tabernacle. Yet he is not particularly interested in the day to day rituals for he summarizes them in short order (v. 6) and then devotes his attention to the central ceremony of tabernacle worship which also happens to form the heart of his description of Jesus' sacrifice: the annual Day of Atonement. The main activities of that ceremony are described in v. 7 and its significance in vv. 8-10. Nevertheless, this is a tightly integrated section for it represents one very long and extremely complicated sentence in the Greek text.

9:7 But only the high priest entered the inner room, and that only once a year, and never without blood, which he offered for himself and for the sins the people had committed in ignorance.
The author focuses on those parts of the ceremony which

are relevant for his argument, and many of the other, related activities are not expounded upon in any New Testament description of the atoning work of Christ. The rituals of the Day of Atonement (*Yom Kippur*), however, are fully described in Leviticus and can be summarized as follows:

Ritual of the Day of Atonement according to Leviticus 16

General Requirements

> The high priest may only enter the Most Holy Place on the Day of Atonement (v. 2)
>
> No one is to be in the Tent when the high priest enters the Most Holy Place (v. 17)
>
> On this day all Israelites must fast and do no work (vv. 29-31)

Clothes

> Remove ordinary priestly garb
>
> Bathe (v. 4)
>
> Put on special attire for the day of atonement (v. 4)
>
> Linen tunic, linen undergarments, linen sash, linen turban (v. 4)

Present offerings for the day: two goats for sin offering and ram for burnt offering (v. 5)

Offer bull as a sin offering for himself (vv. 6, 11-14)

> Slaughter it (and catch its blood; v. 11)
>
> Take censer with two handfuls of incense behind the curtain (vv. 12-13)
>
> Sprinkle bull's blood on and in front of the atonement cover (v. 14)

Two goat ceremony (vv. 7-8)

> Cast lots to choose: one for the Lord, one for a scapegoat (v. 8)

Offer goat as a sin offering for the people (v. 15)

> Slaughter it (and catch its blood; v. 15)
>
> Do as with bull's blood (take censer with incense, etc.; v. 15)
>
> Sprinkle goat's blood on and in front of the atonement cover (v. 15)

> (Explanation of the significance of these rituals — vv. 16, 17)

Cleansing of the sanctuary (vv. 16-19)

> Cleanse the tent of meeting with blood (v. 16)
>
> Cleanse the main altar with blood (vv. 18-19)

Scapegoat ceremony (vv. 20-22)

Lay hands on the goat and confess all Israel's sins (v. 21)

Send the goat away into the desert (v. 21)

The chosen man shall release the goat in the desert (v. 22)

Clothes

Remove special attire for the day of atonement (v. 23)

Bathe (v. 24)

Put on ordinary priestly garb (v. 24)

Present burnt offering for self and then for people (vv. 24, 25)

Hides, flesh and offal are taken outside the camp and burned (v. 27)

Finishing (vv. 26-28)

The man who released the scapegoat must wash clothes and self (v. 26)

The man who burned hides, flesh and offal must wash clothes and self (v. 28)

These two verses (9:6-7) are organized around a series of contrasts:

Day-to-Day Rituals	*Day of Atonement*
priests (plural)	the high priest only (singular)
regularly	once a year
outer room (lit., "first tent")	inner room (lit., "second [tent]")

Each of these contrasts can be seen as prefiguring the priestly ministry of Jesus: (1) he is unrivaled in his superiority, the one and only high priest of the believer (4:14; 7:26; 8:1), (2) his work is "once for all" (7:27; 9:12, 18), and (3) he takes us behind the curtain into the presence of God (4:14, 16; 6:20). Yet the final feature of our writer's description, which has no counterpart in the series of contrasts, will become the most significant feature in the parallel with Christ — it was "never without blood" that the high priest entered the inner room. We now read for the third time in the letter that the high priest had to offer sacrifices "first for his own sins, and then for the sins of the people" (5:3; 7:27; cf. Lev 9:7; 16:6). We have also read that, unlike previous high priests, Jesus had no need to offer a sacrifice for himself (7:27). However, this is the first explicit reference to "blood" (αἷμα, *haima*) in this connection.[15]

Haima appears no less than eighteen times in this letter[16] — eight times in 9:7-25 alone. The significant role of blood in both covenants will be described in subsequent verses and our writer's choice of the word here anticipates the approaching discussion. Two important observations can be made here nonetheless.

First, we see that the shedding of blood is a condition for any human to enter into the presence of God. The phrase "never without blood" translates a double negative — a particularly strong expression — in the Greek text. It was between the two cherubim, above the cover of the ark, where God had promised to meet his people (Exod 25:22).

Second, we see that the blood was shed for sin. Ἀγνόημα (*agnoēma*, "sins committed in ignorance") occurs only here in the New Testament. In the papyri, it is used in the sense of an "error" which is distinguished from a "crime" (e.g., in a proclamation of amnesty[17]). Our author has used the verb form in 5:2 (see comments on 5:2). The noun here (just as the verb in 5:2) probably refers to the "unintentional sin" described in Leviticus 4. The idea is probably not so much that any isolated instance of deliberate sin (since many of our sins involve an element of choice) cannot be covered by the blood sacrifice ("weakness" is accounted for in the sacrifice, 5:2-3) but that the kind of consistent, perpetual choice of a lifestyle of sin (such as the sort described by the customary present tense of 10:26) which indicates a deliberate disregard and disrespect for the sacrifice (10:29) removes one from the protection of his covenant relationship with God. For such, repentance is the missing element (6:1, 6).

---

[15]It appeared in 2:14 in reference to the human "flesh and blood" of Jesus' incarnation which, we understand, made it possible for him to offer his body as a blood sacrifice.

[16]It appears in 2:14; 9:7, 12, 18, 19, 20, 21, 22, 25; 10:4, 19, 29; 11:28; 12:4, 24; and 13:11, 12, 10.

[17]MM, p. 4.

9:8 The Holy Spirit was showing by this that the way into the Most Holy Place had not yet been disclosed as long as the first tabernacle was still standing.

Having described the unique dimensions of the priestly ministry on the Day of Atonement, our writer now proceeds to explain their greater significance. The "Holy Spirit" was responsible for the pattern provided by the old covenant. The similarities are no accident, no mere coincidence. God had planned them and made them in order to "show" us something. Δηλόω (*dēloō*, "make clear, show,"[18]) is also used in 12:27 ("indicate"). In both instances our author uses it of what can be "shown" from an Old Testament passage.

What the Spirit has shown us is that "the way into the Most Holy Place had not been disclosed." Even after the rituals performed on the Day of Atonement, the curtain would remain, separating the inner and outer rooms. No one would be permitted to enter. A year later, more sacrifices would be offered, yet the curtain would still remain. Nothing permanent was accomplished.

This was true "so long as the first tabernacle was still standing." Here, "first tabernacle" translates the identical phrase (*tēs prōtēs skēnēs*) translated "outer room" in v. 6. In verses 6-7, however, it was clear that our writer was describing the two different rooms inside of the old tabernacle ("outer" and "inner"). It is difficult to see how the phrase could carry the same meaning in the present context, however — the destruction of only the outer room would not remove the curtain which separated the Holy and Most Holy Places, even less affect any real change in our ability to enter God's presence. Here the phrase is best taken as the NIV renders it, as the earthly representation of the "true" tabernacle in heaven (8:1-2; 9:1). This is a sign argument: the need for and the continuation of both the tabernacle (and later the temple) and its ritual are proof that these are not enough to enable us to approach God.

---

[18]BAGD, p. 178.

9:9 This is an illustration for the present time, indicating that the gifts and sacrifices being offered were not able to clear the conscience of the worshiper. 9:10 They are only a matter of food and drink and various ceremonial washings — external regulations applying until the time of the new order.

Rather than providing a solution for our need, it served as "an illustration for the present time." "This" refers to "tabernacle" (v. 8)[19] and we read that it is a παραβόλη (*parabolē*, "comparison."[20] Our writer also uses this word in 11:19 to describe the "figurative" sense in which Abraham received Isaac back from the dead and the sense of "type" or "figure" seems to best describe our writer's method here as well. Elsewhere in the New Testament, the term is used (with one exception[21]) only in the Gospels of the parables told by Jesus. The term itself is used quite broadly, taking in a wide variety of comparative sayings — narrative parables, allegories, similitudes, types, symbols, proverbs, riddles and various figures of speech.[22]

The phrase "for the present time" translates a perfect participle which is somewhat ambiguous (KJV, "the time then present"). The NIV, RSV ("for the present age") and NASB ("for the present time") all represent a rendering more natural to the syntax of the sentence.[23]

How the phrase is rendered may make little difference, however, for the point indicated remains clear. The "gifts and sacrifices" (see comments on 5:1) offered under the old covenant were "not able to clear the conscience of the worshiper." The word translated "clear" is τελειόω (*teleioō*), usually translated "perfect." Its significance here must be under-

---

[19]Gender agreement (feminine) indicates the antecedent to the pronoun.

[20]BAGD, p. 612.

[21]Luke 4:23 would be the only exception, when Jesus suggests that those in his hometown would quote to him the "proverb," "Physician, heal yourself!"

[22]Grant R. Osborne, *The Hermeneutical Spiral: A Comprehensive Introduction to Biblical Interpretation* (Downers Grove, IL: InterVarsity, 1991), pp. 235-236.

[23]The ellipsis of ἐστιν in ἥτις παραβολὴ should probably be translated as present — "this *is* an illustration" (see MHT, III, p. 295, regarding the ellipse of ἐστιν).

stood in light of the key role the term plays throughout the letter (see comments on 6:1; 7:11, 19, 28). Most recently, in chapter seven, our writer elaborated upon how neither the Levitical priesthood nor the Law could make anything perfect, how the perfection of Jesus in his role as priest makes possible the perfection of believers, and the subsequent difference this makes in our ability to "draw near to God" (7:19). Here we see that the real barrier to our access to God has never been "external" (v. 10) but internal ("conscience," v. 9). The use of συνείδησις (syneidēsis, "moral consciousness"[24]) anticipates 9:14 (where we read that the blood of Christ can accomplish precisely what the old gifts and sacrifices could not) but here the word functions opposite "external." Its use with teleioō indicates that it is not merely the removal of our subjective feelings of guilt which enables our access to God, but the removal of that guilt which is an objective state, incurred by our sin ("acts that lead to death," cf. 9:14; Rom 6:23). Our "justification," made possible by the cross, can also set us free from the burden of guilty feelings. But, as we will read, it is the change in our standing before God accomplished by Jesus' sacrifice which enables us to draw near to God. This is the "new order" (διορθώσις, diorthōsis, "improvement," "reformation"[25]) ushered in by the cross.

C. JESUS' SACRIFICE CLEANSES OUR CONSCIENCE (9:11-14)

[11]**When Christ came as high priest of the good things that are already here,ᵃ he went through the greater and more perfect tabernacle that is not man-made, that is to say, not a part of this creation. [12]He did not enter by means of the blood of goats and calves; but he entered the Most Holy Place once for all by his own blood, having obtained eternal**

---

[24]BAGD, p. 786.
[25]Ibid., p. 199.

redemption. **¹³The blood of goats and bulls and the ashes of a heifer sprinkled on those who are ceremonially unclean sanctify them so that they are outwardly clean. ¹⁴How much more, then, will the blood of Christ, who through the eternal Spirit offered himself unblemished to God, cleanse our consciences from acts that lead to death,ᵇ so that we may serve the living God!**

ᵃ*11 Some early manuscripts are to come*   ᵇ*14 Or from useless rituals*

Now that our author has described that which is an "illustration for the present time" (9:9) — the tabernacle and rituals of the first covenant (9:1) — he now proceeds, in that light, to describe the superiority of Jesus' blood sacrifice. The remainder of the chapter is devoted to three major accomplishments of the shed blood of Christ: (1) the cleansing of our conscience (vv. 11-14), (2) the inauguration of the new covenant (vv. 15-22), and (3) our complete purification from sin (vv. 23-28).

9:11 When Christ came as high priest of the good things that are already here, he went through the greater and more perfect tabernacle that is not man-made, that is to say, not a part of this creation.
The KJV, RSV and NASB all begin with a conjunction — "But" — which is present in the Greek text but not translated by the NIV. What happened "when Christ came as high priest," then, is compared to what the other priests and high priests did "when everything had been arranged" in the earthly tabernacle (9:6).

It is difficult to say whether our writer refers to "good things that are already here" (NIV, cf. RSV "that have come") or to "good things to come" (KJV, NASB) since these different translations reflect a variant in the Greek text for which the manuscript evidence is not clear. Metzger defends the choice of that reading which is rendered by the NIV and RSV on the basis of (1) the age and diversity of the manuscripts which support it and (2) the likelihood that the variant rendered by the KJV and NASB was a copyist error influenced by the appearance of the same phrase in 10:1.[26] Just what the "good things" are is not clear but most probably this is a general reference to the superior accomplishments of the new covenant.

Jesus, too, entered the Most Holy Place through a tabernacle, but his was "not man-made, that is to say, not a part of this creation." Χειροποίητος (*cheiropoiētos*) is a compound word (χείρ, *cheir*, "hand" and ποιέω, *poieō*, "make" hence, "made with hands," KJV, RSV, NASB) which echoes 8:2 ("not [set up] by man") just as κτίσεως (*ktiseōs*, "creation") echoes 9:1 (κοσμικός, *kosmikos*, "earthly"). Earlier we read that Jesus was "a great high priest who has gone through the heavens" where "the throne of grace" is (4:14, 16) and who "sat down at the right hand of the throne of the majesty in heaven" (8:1). This is where he "serves in the sanctuary, the true tabernacle" (8:2) and thus it is in this sense that his tabernacle is "greater" (9:11). It is also "more perfect," a phrase which applies to the true tabernacle the same term so prominent in our writer's description of the believer's perfection (in a salvific sense) and the perfection of Jesus himself in his vocation as our high priest. The perfect high priest serves in a perfect tabernacle to make perfect those who believe in him.

The use of the title "Christ" may be more than a stylistic variation here since it appears more frequently in this chapter than in any other and is the exclusive manner of referring to Jesus in this chapter. Throughout, the Messianic expectation was an important dimension of our writer's exposition of Psalm 110:4 (see notes on 7:1-3, especially 7:2) and it may be that our writer considers the Messianic title most appropriate for his explanation of the role which Christ's death played in putting the new covenant into effect.

9:12 He did not enter by means of the blood of goats and calves but he entered the Most Holy Place once for all by his own blood, having obtained eternal redemption.

Following his description of the true and heavenly tabernacle, our writer turns to Christ's means of entry. On the Day of

---

[26]Metzger, p. 668.

Atonement, before the high priest could enter the Most Holy Place where God himself appeared in the cloud over the atonement cover, he had to offer two sacrifices: a young bull for a sin offering and a ram for a burnt offering (Lev 16:3). The bull was sacrificed to make atonement for the high priest and his household (Lev 16:6). Two goats were taken from the Israelite community (Lev 16:5). Lots were cast to choose one to be offered as a sin offering for the people (Lev 16:15) while the other was also used for making atonement in a different way — by being sent into the desert as a scapegoat (Lev 16:10). Hebrews says nothing about the scapegoat but the focus of our writer here is upon the use to which the blood was put. The blood of the bull, and then later that of the goat, were both to be taken into the Most Holy Place and sprinkled on and in front of the atonement cover (Lev 16:14). The blood was then to be applied to the tent itself and to the altar (Lev 16:16, 18-19). Even as the high priest entered the Most Holy Place to make atonement for his own sins, he was to enter with burning incense so that its smoke would conceal the atonement cover, lest he die (Lev 16:13). The blood of atonement was the difference between life and death when entering the presence of God.

Under the old covenant, the high priest entered the Most Holy Place "only once a year" (9:7) but Christ enters it "once for all" (9:12). Although it is true that he offered his life for all people (Rom 5:15-19; Heb 9:27), ἐφάπαξ (ephapax) denotes "once for all time."[27] The point of our writer is that Christ's single sacrifice was completely sufficient and did not need to be repeated as did those offered by the other priests (9:25-27; 10:11-12). The reason, of course, is that he presented "his own blood" and subsequent verses will explain the significance of the difference.

The RSV suggests that "eternal redemption" followed as a result ("thus securing an eternal redemption") whereas the

---

[27]Newman Barclay, *A Concise Greek-English Dictionary of the New Testament*, (London: United Bible Societies, 1971), p. 77.

KJV, NASB and NIV all suggest that it had been obtained previously ("having obtained"). The adverbial participle describes the relationship of "obtaining" to the act of "entering" rather than to the offering of the blood, and its tense (aorist) indicates that it preceded this act. Just as with the high priest on the Day of Atonement, the blood made atonement prior to the entry. Λύτρωσις (*lytrōsis*) means "ransom," "release" or "redeem."[28] In the papyri, this word and its cognates were used of the purchase money for manumitting slaves or for the redemption of property.[29] Our writer uses *apolytrōsis* in 11:35 to describe the "release" of those Old Testament heroes who were tortured for their faith. However, its use in the immediate context, where the NIV renders it with two terms ("ransom" and "set free," 9:15), is more determinative here. Christ's blood was a ransom price, paid to set us free from sin's guilt — finally and forever.

9:13 The blood of goats and bulls and the ashes of a heifer sprinkled on those who are ceremonially unclean sanctify them so that they are outwardly clean.

The thrust of the chapter to this point is now summed up in this lesser to greater argument. Verse 13 actually begins with εἰ (*ei*, "if") which is not translated by the NIV. The "how much more" of v. 14 provides the conclusion and completes the thought.

According to Numbers 19, the ashes of a heifer were to be mixed as needed with the water of cleansing which was applied to those who were unclean for their purification from sin (Num 19:9ff.). People became unclean by what they touched and made anything else they touched unclean as well (Num 19:22). The unclean person was to be sprinkled on the third and seventh days and then washed and bathed for cleansing on the seventh (Num 19:19). It is in this sense that they were cleansed "ceremonially" and "outwardly" (lit., "of the flesh," Heb 9:13).

---

[28]BAGD, p. 483.
[29]MM, pp. 382-383.

Άγιάζω (*hagaizō*, "sanctify") is sometimes translated "make holy" in the NIV[30] and is usually reserved for what could only be accomplished by the sacrifice of the blood of Jesus (in which "purify" could also be an acceptable translation[31]). Only here in Hebrews is it used in reference to the sacrifices of the old covenant and, for the sake of his lesser to greater argument, our writer admits that such rituals were effective for their intended purpose (outward and cermonial purity).

9:14 How much more, then, will the blood of Christ, who through the eternal Spirit offered himself unblemished to God, cleanse our consciences from acts that lead to death, so that we may serve the living God!

But "how much more" was accomplished by the blood of Christ! His sacrifice was able to do what the others could not (9:9) — "cleanse our consciences." Καθαρίζω (*katharizō*) is capable of a stronger translation, "purge" (KJV), but the object of the verb is the real point of contrast here. The effects of Christ's sacrifice were not merely "outward." It removed, in truth and fact, sin's guilt from our lives so that we now live with clean consciences. We no longer have to fear the consequences of "acts that lead to death" (lit., "dead works," see also the comments on 6:1). A footnote in the NIV offers "useless rituals" as an alternative translation but this does not fit the context. It is difficult to explain why one would have needed to be "cleansed from" these. They may have been ineffectual for the plight of the sinner yet created no guilt themselves for they had been commanded by God for their intended purpose.

What Jesus offered for our cleansing was "himself unblemished." Άμωμος (*amōmos*) is the same word used in the LXX to describe "the absence of defects in sacrificial animals" (Num 6:14; 19:2; etc.; see also Lev 22:19ff. where the defects which make a sacrifice unacceptable are described).[32] It is

---

[30]It is translated "make holy" in 2:11; 10:10, 14; and 13:12. It is translated "sanctify" in 9:13 and 10:29.

[31]BAGD, p. 9.

[32]Ibid., p. 46.

used nowhere else in Hebrews but Peter uses it in the same sense that our writer does here when he refers to "the precious blood of Christ, a lamb without blemish or defect" (1 Pet 1:19). Of course, the "unblemished" character of Jesus' sacrifice is of even greater significance since he was the only one who could have ever presented himself as an acceptable sacrifice. We know that he was without sin (4:15) while no other human has ever been (Rom 3:23) yet "God made him who had no sin to be sin for us, so that in him we might become the righteousness of God" (2 Cor 5:21).

D. JESUS' DEATH INAUGURATES THE NEW COVENANT (9:15-22)

[15]**For this reason Christ is the mediator of a new covenant, that those who are called may receive the promised eternal inheritance — now that he has died as a ransom to set them free from the sins committed under the first covenant.**

[16]**In the case of a will,**[a] **it is necessary to prove the death of the one who made it,** [17]**because a will is in force only when somebody has died; it never takes effect while the one who made it is living.** [18]**This is why even the first covenant was not put into effect without blood.** [19]**When Moses had proclaimed every commandment of the law to all the people, he took the blood of calves, together with water, scarlet wool and branches of hyssop, and sprinkled the scroll and all the people.** [20]**He said, "This is the blood of the covenant, which God has commanded you to keep."**[b] [21]**In the same way, he sprinkled with the blood both the tabernacle and everything used in its ceremonies.** [22]**In fact, the law requires that nearly everything be cleansed with blood, and without the shedding of blood there is no forgiveness.**

[a]*16 Same Greek word as *covenant*; also in verse 17   [b]*20 Exodus 24:8

9:15 For this reason Christ is the mediator of a new covenant, that those who are called may receive the promised eternal inheritance — now that he has died as a ransom to set them free from the sins committed under the first covenant.

We now read about the second of the three major accomplishments of the shed blood of Christ: the inauguration of the new covenant (vv. 15-22). Some suggest that "for this reason" may look backwards, i.e., grounding Christ's mediatorship in the thrust of vv. 11-14 — the ability of his shed blood to cleanse our conscience. There is no reason to protest this as a matter of fact, but the syntax of the sentence suggests that the phrase probably anticipates what will follow, since the phrase "that those who are called may receive the promised eternal inheritance" is a clause of purpose rather than result.[33]

On Christ as the mediator of the new covenant, see comments on 8:6. The remainder of the verse describes what we can receive under the new covenant, why we are able to receive it, and who is able to receive it.

Within the new covenant we "receive the promised eternal inheritance." As we have noted, inheritance terminology is frequent in Hebrews.[34] It last appeared in 6:17 as part of the forensic/legal terminology employed in our writer's description of the encouragement offered to believers by God's oath. Here, it anticipates the legal analogy of vv. 16-18, employed to demonstrate the necessity of Jesus' death for inaugurating the new covenant. Since the inheritance is described here as "eternal," the eschatological dimension of the believer's hope is probably more pronounced here than elsewhere (see comments on 6:17). In Hebrews, promise terminology is also prominent and encompasses the full scope of God's redemptive plan which began with his promises to Abraham as well as their typological, soteriological and eschatological significance for believers (see comments on "what is promised" in 8:6).

---

[33]This is the sense of ὅπως with the subjunctive (BAGD, p. 576; BDF, p. 186).

[34]1:2, 4, 14; 6:12, 17; 9:15; 11:7, 8; 12:17.

We are able to receive our promised eternal inheritance because Jesus "has died as a ransom" so that we might be "set free" from sin. The KJV ("by means of death") and the RSV, NASB ("since a death has occurred/taken place") offer slightly different readings of the adverbial participle (the former interprets it as modal, the latter as causal). The NIV offers the least interpretive rendering, indicating only the antecedent time relationship suggested by the aorist tense of the participle ("now that he has died"). There seems to be little difference between the modal and causal senses in the context, however, for it is clear from the preceding discussion that men can now receive what they formerly could not, and the difference is the death of Christ. Though our writer uses the word "death" rather than "blood" as in 9:12, the word here rendered "ransom" and "set free" by the NIV (ἀπολύτρωσιν, *apolytrōsin*) is a cognate of the same word rendered "redemption" (*lytrōsin*) in that verse and the idea is the same (see comments on 9:12 for a discussion of these words).

Finally, this verse indicates that Christ's death makes it possible for the entire community of faith, old and new, to receive this inheritance. Those whose sins were "committed under the first covenant" were set free not by the sacrifices and gifts of that covenant but only by the sacrifice of Jesus. Yet the inheritance can also yet be received by "those who are called" — the NIV employs the present tense to stress the abiding dimension of the Greek perfect tense which describes a past action continuing into the present.

9:16 In the case of a will, it is necessary to prove the death of the one who made it,

We have read that Christ's death makes it possible for us to receive the promised eternal inheritance. Now we read why his death was *necessary* to make it possible. For proof of the absolute necessity of Christ's death to inaugurate the new covenant, our writer first advances a parallel case argument and then returns to the Old Testament type for scriptural authority.

It is quite natural that the new covenant should be compared to a "will," since the word elsewhere translated "covenant" (διαθήκη, *diathēkē*, as recently as 9:15) was also the word used of a will (as it is translated here) in legal contexts. It can mean "last will and testament," "ordinance," "decree," "compact" or "contract."[35] In Hebrews it is used exclusively of God's redemptive covenants with men and an extensive discussion of its key role in the letter can be read in the comments on 8:6. The only exception is the present case in which it is nevertheless used to introduce an analogy to explain the relationship between the death of Christ and the new covenant.

9:17 because a will is in force only when somebody has died; it never takes effect while the one who made it is living.

In addition to *diathēkē*, the parallel case employs other terms frequent in legal contexts (βεβαίος, *bebaios*, "in force" — see 6:16 comments — and ἰσχύω, *ischyō*, "take effect"[36]). The central point of the comparison is still clear in the light of practices in our own day. A person might prepare and sign a legally binding will which names benefactors and assigns an inheritance. Unless changed, it is a promise which will be enforced by law. Until the testator dies, however, it remains no more than a promise for the future. Only the death of the testator changes the promised inheritance into a legal possession. Until then the will is only a piece of paper. Only then is it "put into force."

9:18 This is why even the first covenant was not put into effect without blood.

To supplement the analogy of vv. 16-17, our writer turns to the example provided by the first covenant and the tabernacle which has been expounded as a type of Christ's ministry as high priest. Whereas he employed the term "death" in

---

[35]BAGD, p. 183.
[36]MM, pp. 107, 308.

vv. 15-16, he now returns to the term "blood" introduced in v. 12. The rituals commanded for consecration of the tabernacle used the blood of the sacrifices and a cleansing power is accorded to blood (v. 22).

9:19 When Moses had proclaimed every commandment of the law to all the people, he took the blood of calves, together with water, scarlet wool and branches of hyssop, and sprinkled the scroll and all the people. 9:20 He said, "This is the blood of the covenant, which God has commanded you to keep."

Exodus 24 records the inauguration of the first covenant. When "Moses went and told the people all the Lord's words and laws" which had been told to him on Mt. Sinai, they agreed to do everything the Lord had said (v. 3). Burnt offerings were made and young bulls were sacrificed as fellowship offerings (v. 5). Moses then read the Book of the Covenant to the people and when they again pledged their obedience, Moses took the blood and sprinkled it on the people. Exodus makes no mention of the use of water or hyssop mentioned here or of Moses sprinkling the scroll. The silence does not prohibit the possibility, however, and there is thus no reason to question the accuracy of our writer's description. In Numbers 19 we read that the blood used for cleansing was mixed with water and hyssop and so this may well have been the customary practice.

9:21 In the same way, he sprinkled with the blood both the tabernacle and everything used in its ceremonies. 9:22 In fact, the law requires that nearly everything be cleansed with blood, and without the shedding of blood there is no forgiveness.

Some suggest that the Old Testament does not refer to the sprinkling of blood upon all the things mentioned by our writer in v. 21.[37] However, "in the same way" must anticipate an event which took place at a later time since the tabernacle

---

[37]Ellingworth, p. 470.

did not yet exist when the events of Exodus 24 transpired. When the tabernacle was set up, the tabernacle and everything in it was anointed with oil (Exod 40:6). Yet the Lord also commanded Moses to "consecrate it and all its furnishings and it will be holy" (40:9). Earlier, when the priests were consecrated, both blood and anointing oil were sprinkled upon them (29:21) and it is reasonable to assume that the rituals would have been similar.

The quote contained in verse 20[38] was echoed by the words of Jesus in the Gospels ("This is my blood of the covenant, which is poured out for many for the forgiveness of sins," Matthew 26:28; Mark 14:24; Luke 22:20). The precise significance of the genitive ("of") here is suggested by the context. Ellingworth suggests that is not merely "the blood associated with the covenant" but "the blood which seals" (TEV), "constitutes, or establishes the covenant, by virtue of the life poured out in sacrifice."[39] As to the relationship between blood, covenant and forgiveness suggested by Jesus himself, our writer describes it in a climactic expression: "without the shedding of blood there is no forgiveness." Ἀιματεκχυσία (*haimatekchysia*) is a compound word (αἷμα, *haima*, "blood" and ἐκχύννω, *ekchynnō*, "to pour out") which may have been coined by our writer to express "the surpassing potency of blood . . . for dealing with defilement."[40] Lane suggest that the term ἄφεσις (*aphesis*), used alternatively with καθαρίζω (*katharizō*, "cleanse," v. 22a and then again in v. 23, "purified"), "signals a definitive putting away of defilement or a decisive purgation" and "is a comprehensive term covering both the 'subjective' and 'objective' benefits of Christ's blood."[41]

---

[38]The wording here differs somewhat from the LXX which is a direct translation of the Hebrew (Ἰδοὺ τὸ αἷμα τῆς διαθήκης, ἧς διέθετο κύριος πρὸς ὑμᾶς περὶ πάντων τῶν λόγων τούτων).

[39]Ellingworth, p. 470.

[40]So Lane, p. 246. However, there are instances of the noun and verb occurring together (BAGD, p. 23).

[41]Lane, pp. 246-247.

E. JESUS' SACRIFICE WAS ONCE AND FOR ALL (9:23-28)

²³It was necessary, then, for the copies of the heavenly things to be purified with these sacrifices, but the heavenly things themselves with better sacrifices than these. ²⁴For Christ did not enter a man-made sanctuary that was only a copy of the true one; he entered heaven itself, now to appear for us in God's presence. ²⁵Nor did he enter heaven to offer himself again and again, the way the high priest enters the Most Holy Place every year with blood that is not his own. ²⁶Then Christ would have had to suffer many times since the creation of the world. But now he has appeared once for all at the end of the ages to do away with sin by the sacrifice of himself. ²⁷Just as man is destined to die once, and after that to face judgment, ²⁸so Christ was sacrificed once to take away the sins of many people; and he will appear a second time, not to bear sin, but to bring salvation to those who are waiting for him.

9:23 It was necessary, then, for the copies of the heavenly things to be purified with these sacrifices, but the heavenly things themselves with better sacrifices than these.
The word οὖν (*oun*, "then") is capable of being translated "therefore" (KJV, NASB) and serves to continue the parallel case begun in vv. 16ff., yet it also marks the transition from the other case (will) and the older example (old testament) to the new and present covenant. Once again, the tabernacle and its tools are described as "copies" (ὑπόδειγμα, *hypodeigma*) of what is in heaven (cf. 8:5). As before, it is an appropriate metaphor for describing his typological exegesis. The word translated "purified" (καθαρίζω, *katharizō*) is the same word translated "cleanse" in both v. 14 and v. 22. The repetition of the verbs makes the parallel more obvious in the Greek text. The better hope (7:7) offered by the better covenant (7:22; 8:6) looks forward to receiving better promises (8:6) because it was inaugurated by a better sacrifice (9:23).

9:24 For Christ did not enter a man-made sanctuary that was only a copy of the true one; he entered heaven itself, now to appear for us in God's presence.

Our writer now proceeds to delineate those differences which distinguish Christ's sacrifice as better. Christ did not enter the "man-made sanctuary" (*cheiropoiētos*, as in v. 11, cf. also 8:2), the "copy" (here ἀντίτυπος, *antitypos*, "antitype, representation"[42]), but the "true one" which is nothing less than heaven itself. Even as Solomon prayed for the temple he built, he had said, "But will God really dwell on earth? The heavens, even the highest heaven, cannot contain you. How much less this temple I have built!" (1 Kgs 8:27). No building could ever contain the presence of God and so there will be no more vain attempts. Christ is now in heaven itself, in the very presence of God.

9:25 Nor did he enter heaven to offer himself again and again, the way the high priest enters the Most Holy Place every year with blood that is not his own.

Christ is not forced to leave and return again for he is able to remain in God's presence. The difference is in the blood. Each former priest had entered with blood "not his own," a description which echoes the statement of v. 12 that Christ "entered the Most Holy Place once for all by his own blood" and anticipates the statement in v. 26 that "he has appeared once for all at the end of the ages to do away with sin by the sacrifice of himself."

9:26 Then Christ would have had to suffer many times since the creation of the world. But now he has appeared once for all at the end of the ages to do away with sin by the sacrifice of himself.

This is the climactic statement of the chapter. Its argument proceeds from contrary condition and turns on two contrasts: "many times" vs. "once" and "since the creation of the world"

---

[42]BAGD, p. 76.

vs. "at the end of the ages." If Christ's single sacrifice were not sufficient for atonement, he would have had to do exactly what the other, earthly priests had always done. But it was not required for him to do so. Thus his single sacrifice must have been sufficient.

Bruce suggests that the phrase "end of the ages" should be understood in the sense of "time of fulfilment."[43] It is true that Christ first came when "the time had fully come" for him to be sent (Gal 4:4) and the verb form of the word translated "end" (συντέλεια [synteleia], verb συντελέω [synteleō]) can also mean "fulfill."[44] Alternatively, αἰών can simply mean "a very long time"[45] and could be taken as referring to that period of time during which the old covenant was in effect. Christ put an end to it but lived through the end of it. Yet another possibility is that the phrase is similar in meaning to the nearly identical phrase used by Jesus in his parables about the weeds (Matt 13:39-40) and the net (Matt 13:49), in the Olivet discourse (Matt 24:3) and in the Great Commission (Matt 28:20) — all of which are usually understood in an eschatological sense. In this case, the phrase would reflect (1) the reference to Christ's second appearing in v. 28 and (2) an understanding on the part of the author that the "time" of Christ's coming encompasses both his first and second appearings as well as the interim period.[46]

Ἀθέτησις (athetēsis, "do away with") is a forceful term which appears in the technical legal formula of the papyri, meaning to "annul" or "cancel."[47] The cancellation of sin's debt (our death, Rom 6:23) by the ransom paid (Christ's death) is both forceful and final.

9:27 Just as man is destined to die once, and after that to face judgment, 9:28 so Christ was sacrificed once to take

---

[43]Bruce, p. 222.
[44]BAGD, p. 792.
[45]Ibid., p. 27.
[46]So Ellingworth, p. 484.
[47]MM, p. 12; cf. also comments on 7:18.

away the sins of many people; and he will appear a second time, not to bear sin, but to bring salvation to those who are waiting for him.

The "just as . . . so" construction suggests how incomprehensible it is that Christ would have ever suffered as the previous verse theorized. What is true for other men was also the case for Christ — like other men, he was "destined to die once." But this was enough to "take away the sins of many people." The complete sacrifice makes possible a complete salvation. Not only does our salvation reach into our past for the forgiveness of our sins; its consummation lies ahead in our future. He will not then need to bear sin, however. The sacrifice of his first appearing was sufficient for that purpose.

This verse contains both a promise and a warning. As Christians, we say "maranatha!" ("Come, Lord Jesus!" Rev 22:20) for we desire to be with him. Yet it is a matter of utmost importance that, in an age when people rarely expect to be held accountable for how they live their lives, two truths are yet certain. All men die. And all men will face judgment. On that day, only one decision will matter — whether we have embraced the Christ who sacrificed himself for our sins and our salvation.

HEBREWS 10

F. OLD COVENANT SACRIFICES COULD NOT TAKE AWAY SIN (10:1-4)

¹The law is only a shadow of the good things that are coming — not the realities themselves. For this reason it can never, by the same sacrifices repeated endlessly year after year, make perfect those who draw near to worship. ²If it could, would they not have stopped being offered? For the worshipers would have been cleansed once for all, and would no longer have felt guilty for their sins. ³But those sacrifices are an annual reminder of sins, ⁴because it is impossible for the blood of bulls and goats to take away sins.

10:1 The law is only a shadow of the good things that are coming — not the realities themselves. For this reason it can never, by the same sacrifices repeated endlessly year after year, make perfect those who draw near to worship.

The conjunction "for" (γὰρ, *gar*) connects this chapter to the end of chapter 9 although the NIV does not render it. To complete his discussion of the superiority of Christ's sacrifice, our writer returns to another part of the Jewish heritage, last mentioned in 8:4-5 and before that in 7:19 — "the law." In 7:19 we read, in a parenthetical statement, that "the law made nothing perfect," necessitating a better hope by which we could draw near to God. Our writer now enters into a fuller explanation of this truth.

The problem with the law — along with the sacrifices it prescribed — was that it was not this reality. It was "only a shadow" (lit., "The law has a shadow," see 8:5 on σκιά, *skia*) of "the realities themselves." Εἰκών (*eikōn*, "reality") appears only here in Hebrews but is the word Paul uses in Colossians to describe Jesus as "the *image* of the invisible God" (Col 1:15). By this Paul meant that in Jesus the very "fullness" of God dwelt in bodily form (Col 1:19; 2:9). Christ was not just a "likeness" or "similarity" but the "reality" itself. Similarly, though a shadow may resemble the form which casts it,[1] it is not the reality (cf. use of *skia* with σῶμα [*sōma*], "body," in Col 2:17). And so those sacrifices prescribed by the law could not clear the conscience of the worshiper because they could not perfect him. Because the worshiper could become clean from sin in neither fact nor conscience, he could not draw near to God. This is why we had need for the introduction of "a better hope . . . by which we draw near to God" (7:19).

There is a progressive relationship between (1) the believer's perfection, (2) the believer's conscience, and (3) the believer's ability to draw near to God. The word translated "perfect" (τελειόω, *teleioō*, v. 1) is the same word which has figured so prominently into our writer's description of the believer's salvation (which has past, present and future dimensions). In its past sense (justification), it describes the removal of sin's guilt from our lives. In its present sense (sanctification), it describes the gradual removal of sin's power from our lives as we grow daily to become more like Jesus. In its future sense (glorification), it describes the eschatological consummation of our holiness and hope.

10:2 If it could, would they not have stopped being offered? For the worshipers would have been cleansed once for all, and would no longer have felt guilty for their sins.

While "perfection" terminology in Hebrews most consistently refers to the fact of sin and the real guilt which it incurs for us (in an objective sense), our writer also recognizes the impact of such sin upon our "consciences" (9:9, 14) or the

---

[1]BAGD, p. 222.

subjective level at which we "feel guilty" for our sins (10:2). The word translated "cleansed" (of worshipers) in v. 2 (καθαρίζω, *katharizō*) is the same word used of the conscience in 9:14. However, in 9:9, when we read in the NIV about gifts and sacrifices which "were not able to clear the conscience of the worshiper," we noted that the word translated "clear" was *teleioō* (usually translated "perfect"). This is not mere coincidence. The lack of a *real* removal of the fact and guilt of sin is still felt in the *conscience* of the one who would "draw near to worship." Only a sacrifice which accomplishes *real* forgiveness can truly cleanse the *conscience* as well.

10:3 But those sacrifices are an annual reminder of sins,

The argument for the inadequacy of the law and its sacrificial system is framed by an *inclusio* in the Greek text.[2] The endless repetition of the sacrifices is offered as one sign of their inadequacy. If they had removed sin once for all, they would not have had to be repeated, but they were. Another sign of their inadequacy was the testimony of conscience. In their own hearts and minds, worshipers knew that they were not truly clean. As a result, the most that could be said for the Day of Atonement was that it was "an annual reminder of sins." Paul made the same observation about the Law itself (Rom 3:20; Gal 3:21-22). This is not an insignificant purpose for we need to become aware of our sin and our true situation before God. But it provides no remedy for the guilt and power of sin.

10:4 because it is impossible for the blood of bulls and goats to take away sins.

In its literal sense, ἀφαιρέω (*aphaireō*, "take away") is the same word used in the Gospels when we read that Peter drew his sword and "cut off" the ear of the high priest's servant (Matt 26:51; Mark 14:27; Luke 22:50). Here, of course, the

---

[2]The argument begins with κατ' ἐνιαυτὸν in v. 1b and is concluded by the phrase κατ' ἐνιαυτὸν at the end of v. 3.

word is clearly used in a metaphoric sense but may well retain a forceful sense of finality which is reinforced by the present tense of the verb which could be translated, "to *ever* take away sin."

G. CHRIST OFFERED HIS BODY TO MAKE US HOLY
(10:5-10)

[5]Therefore, when Christ came into the world, he said:
"Sacrifice and offering you did not desire,
but a body you prepared for me;
[6]with burnt offerings and sin offerings
you were not pleased.
[7]Then I said, 'Here I am — it is written about me in the scroll —
I have come to do your will, O God.'"[a]
[8]First he said, "Sacrifices and offerings, burnt offerings and sin offerings you did not desire, nor were you pleased with them" (although the law required them to be made). [9]Then he said, "Here I am, I have come to do your will." He sets aside the first to establish the second. [10]And by that will, we have been made holy through the sacrifice of the body of Jesus Christ once for all.

[a]7 Psalm 40:6-8 (see Septuagint)

10:5 Therefore, when Christ came into the world, he said: "Sacrifice and offering you did not desire, but a body you prepared for me; 10:6 with burnt offerings and sin offerings you were not pleased. 10:7 Then I said, 'Here I am — it is written about me in the scroll — I have come to do your will, O God.'"

 To accomplish what the sacrifices prescribed by the law of the old covenant could not ("therefore"), "Christ came into the world." To describe his mission, our writer appeals to Psalm 40:6-8 (actually the LXX of Psalm 39:7-8). Whereas the

Hebrew MT refers to "ear," the word "body" appears in the LXX. Many regard the LXX as an interpretive rendering in which what is true of the part (ear) is extended to the whole (body).[3] This interpretive rendering caused little concern for our writer, however, for the word "body" is precisely what he seizes upon to make his point from this passage (see v. 10 below).

The NIV supplies "Christ" as the subject — which is not explicitly identified in the Greek text. There is little reason to question this choice, however. Christ is clearly the one who "came into the world." Our writer clearly applies the words of the text, spoken in first person, to Christ (v. 10). As in other Messianic Psalms, the words of David prefigure those of the Messiah (cf. also the use of Ps 22:22 and Isa 8:18 in Heb 2:12-13). Ellingworth suggests that it is in this sense that Christ "speaks" these words, noting our writers use of present tense forms which can be taken as timeless.[4] Alternatively, there is no indication elsewhere in the New Testament that Christ ever spoke these words during his incarnation but this does not rule out the possibility.

10:8 First he said, "Sacrifices and offerings, burnt offerings and sin offerings you did not desire, nor were you pleased with them" (although the law required them to be made). 10:9 Then he said, "Here I am, I have come to do your will." He sets aside the first to establish the second.

The legal requirements for sacrifices and offerings are described in Leviticus 1-7. Here our writer is not concerned with particular details about them or fine distinctions between them but with their collective inability to satisfy God. The prophets had upbraided Israel for permitting a false confidence in their ritualistic cleanness to erode their sense of guilt or need for repentance (Hos 6:6; Isa 1:11-14; Micah 6:6-8; etc.). Jesus similarly criticized the Pharisees (Matt 9:13;

---

[3]Including Bruce (p. 232), Ellingworth (p. 500), and Morris (p. 98).
[4]Ellingworth, pp. 499-500.

12:7, cf. Mark 12:32-33). Why would readers want to return to a system which was not only ineffective in dealing with their sin but could well contribute to a spiritual apathy and false confidence which might blind them to their true spiritual condition?

The terms "first" and "second" are the same terms used throughout the letter to contrast the old and new covenants and they reveal our writer's method with the Psalm. He distinguishes between the sacrifices required by the law and the body prepared for the Messiah who came to do God's will. The first, identified with the older covenant, are "set aside." 'Αναιρέω (anaireō, "set aside"), a strong term which is almost always used of "killing" in the NT (of the attempt by Herod to kill the Christ-child, of the crucifixion of Jesus, of the martyrdom of James, etc.[5]). Hence, a stronger translation such as "destroy"[6] could well be justified. In the papyri, ἵστημι (histēmi) was commonly used in financial transactions, such as when a weighing was done to establish payment, and for the "setting up" of edicts in full view to be read by the public.[7]

10:10 And by that will, we have been made holy through the sacrifice of the body of Jesus Christ once for all.

Two words in the passage provide the basis for our writer's conclusion: "will" and "body." God's will had never been for believers to depend perpetually upon the repeated sacrifices offered under the old covenant. They were ineffective for removing sin and served only to remind us of our guilt (10:3-4). As in 7:11ff., we have read of yet another prophecy which indicated that, all along, God had planned for something better.

His plan was that the sacrifice of Christ's body would do what the other sacrifices could not — make us "holy"

---

[5]Matt 2:16; Luke 22:2; 23:32; Acts 2:23; 5:33, 36; 7:28; 9:23, 24, 29; 10:39; 12:2; 13:28; 16:27; 22:20; 23:15, 21, 27; 25:2; and 26:20. The only other exception is Acts 7:21 (when it is used to describe how Moses was "taken up" by Pharoah's daughter).

[6]BAGD, p. 54.

[7]MM, pp. 307-308.

(ἁγιάζω, *hagiazō*). This same word was used in 9:13 to describe how the blood of the animal sacrifices "sanctified" those who were ceremonially unclean. What Christ has done for us is more than ceremonial, however, for we also read in 9:14 that his offer of his "unblemished" self to God was able to "cleanse our consciences from acts that lead to death." His sacrifice accomplished in truth and reality what the others could accomplish only in ceremony.

Our author now employs ἐφάπαξ (*ephapax*, "once for all") for the third time (7:27; 9:12). More specifically, the word denotes "once for all time" (see 9:12) and here it occupies an emphatic position in the sentence.

H. OUR HIGH PRIEST NOW REIGNS (10:11-14)

[11]Day after day every priest stands and performs his religious duties; again and again he offers the same sacrifices, which can never take away sins. [12]But when this priest had offered for all time one sacrifice for sins, he sat down at the right hand of God. [13]Since that time he waits for his enemies to be made his footstool, [14]because by one sacrifice he has made perfect forever those who are being made holy.

10:11 Day after day every priest stands and performs his religious duties; again and again he offers the same sacrifices, which can never take away sins.

In chapter 5 (5:1ff.), our writer reasoned from what was true of "every high priest" to what is similarly true of Jesus our great high priest. Here he also begins by describing what is true of "every priest" but his point will rest in yet another significant difference between Jesus and every other priest. The other priests *stand* while Jesus *sits*. This frames the comparison.

The phrase "performs his religious duties" renders the same word which elsewhere is simply translated "serve" (the verb λειτουργέω [*leitourgeō*]; the noun λειτουργός [*leitourgos*] appears in 1:7 and 8:2; the adjective λειτουργικός [leitourgikos] in 1:14). The term denotes a service performed in some official capacity, whether political or religious.[8] The verb tenses suggest continuous, repeated action — "stands" renders a perfect tense (past action carrying into the present) and "performs his religious duties" a present tense participle (action simultaneous to the main event, i.e., also continual). The sacrifices are made *again and again* and they are always "the same." They can "never" take away sin. This last expression is emphatic (οὐδέποτε, *oudepote*, "never" followed by a present tense infinitive) and may even be translated, "never, ever take away sin."

10:12 But when this priest had offered for all time one sacrifice for sins, he sat down at the right hand of God.

But after Jesus offered his *one* sacrifice (here an aorist tense participle, rather than a present[9]) which was *for all time*, he "sat" (aorist tense — a decisive event of the past). The sacrifice of Jesus was singular, sufficient, permanent and decisive. *Where* he sat is significant as well, for he sat "at the right hand of God," by his throne which is in heaven (8:1). He was thus able to "draw near" to God, to enter his presence.

10:13 Since that time he waits for his enemies to be made his footstool,

Verse 13 actually completes the main clause of verse 12 (the NIV breaks up the sentence, although the rendering still captures the sense). Having completed this aspect of his priestly service, there are no more sacrifices to be made. He now reigns. Only the final victory awaits for the outcome has been determined. That victory is described with terms from a passage that by now is quite familiar to the readers — Psalm 110 (v. 4 figured prominently into chapter 5 and 7; here, our writer echoes v. 1, quoted in 1:13). At least some of the readers had suffered at the hands of persecutors (10:32-34). For

---

[8]BAGD, p. 471.

[9]The order is chiasmic: one "stood" (verb) and "served" (participle) and the other "offered" (participle) and "sat" (verb).

them, the "enemies" of Christ had faces and names and to know that they would be one day made his footstool was a promise of redemption and deliverance that was both physical and spiritual.

10:14 because by one sacrifice he has made perfect forever those who are being made holy.

In this verse we read why Jesus is able to sit and reign — the results of his "one sacrifice." The wording of the NIV may seem a bit confusing to us because it is actually more form-literal than the other major translations. Close attention to the verb forms employed by our writer and to the ways in which the terms have been used to this point in the letter are the key.

NIV	Greek Verb	Tense Form	Significance
"has made perfect forever"	τελειόω	Perfect	Past, Completed Action with continuing consequences
"are being made holy"	ἁγιάζω	Present	Durative, Incomplete Action of an event in progress

The significance of *teleioō* in our writer's theology of salvation has been described in detail elsewhere (7:11; 10:1 most recently) and the present verse is instructive as well. It could be argued that, elsewhere in the chapter, *hagiazō* is used in a manner roughly synonymous to his use of *teleioō* in reference to justification (10:10, 29).

Yet, throughout, it has been clear that the salvation of the believer is both an accomplished fact, an ongoing event, and a promise for the future. In the last section of chapter five and the first section of chapter six, "perfection" terminology figured prominently into our writer's challenge for his readers to "go on to maturity" (the ongoing dimension of our salvation in which our condition of life grows toward the holiness we have by virtue of being "in Christ"). We see here a similar use of *hagiazō* — i.e., our writer seems to use it in a manner similar to *teleioō* in this sense as well.

Only here, with the terms juxtaposed and formed in different tenses it seems clear that each describes a different dimension of the believer's salvation. In one sense, we "are

315

being made holy" (we "are being saved" as daily our lives become in fact more like Christ). Nevertheless, at the same time, we have already "been made perfect forever" (i.e., Jesus' sacrifice has purchased the forgiveness of our sins and our salvation does not depend on anything we could possibly add to God's plan by our own efforts). In this verse *teleioō*, then, describes our justification (the forgiveness for sin which we have as a result of our covenant relationship with God — the removal of sin's guilt) while *hagiazō* describes our sanctification (the process of spiritual growth through which, with the aid of God's Spirit, we someday attain to the fullness of the stature of Christ — the removal of sin's power).

I. THE WITNESS OF THE HOLY SPIRIT THROUGH JEREMIAH (10:15-18)

[15]The Holy Spirit also testifies to us about this. First he says:
   [16]"This is the covenant I will make with them after that time, says the Lord.
   I will put my laws in their hearts,
   and I will write them on their minds."[a]
[17]Then he adds:
   "Their sins and lawless acts
   I will remember no more."[b]
[18]And where these have been forgiven, there is no longer any sacrifice for sin.

[a]*16* Jer. 31:33   [b]*17* Jer. 31:34

10:15 The Holy Spirit also testifies to us about this. First he says:
For further "testimony" as to the sufficiency of Christ's sacrifice, our author returns to Jeremiah 31 which was first introduced in chapter 8 because it described the new covenant and proved that God had planned for this covenant from the beginning. There we read that "God said" these words (8:8)

and here that the "Holy Spirit also testifies" through them. Though they have come to us through the prophet Jeremiah, our author clearly recognizes the divine inspiration of Scripture, all of which is "God-breathed" (2 Tim 3:16; θεόπ-νευστος [*theopneustos*],[10] a compound word joining θεός [theos], "God" and πνεῦμα [*pneuma*], "spirit," "breath" or "wind"). Elsewhere Peter tells us that "no prophecy of Scripture came about by the prophet's own interpretation. For prophecy never had its origin in the will of man, but men spoke from God as they were carried along by the Holy Spirit" (2 Pet 1:20-21). Whether our author was acquainted with these letters we cannot know but he certainly held to the same view of Scripture. On this use of μαρτυρέω (*martyreō*) see comments on 7:8 and 7:17.

10:16 "This is the covenant I will make with them after that time, says the Lord. I will put my laws in their hearts, and I will write them on their minds." 10:17 Then he adds: "Their sins and lawless acts I will remember no more." 10:18 And where these have been forgiven, there is no longer any sacrifice for sin.

In comparison to his citation in chapter 8, our writer is now more selective in quoting from Jeremiah 31, citing only those portions of the passage which suit his purpose here. The first portion (from 31:33 in v. 16) identifies the new covenant as topic of the passage while the second portion (from 31:34 in v. 17) emphasizes a particular feature of that covenant — its provision for complete forgiveness of sin. Verse 18 frames this half of the chapter before the major transition in verse 19 by inverting the sign argument of 10:1-4. In the first four verses of the chapter, the endless repetition of the offerings of the old covenant are a sign of their inadequacy. Here, the absence of any further sacrifices within the new covenant is a sign of the sufficiency of the single sacrifice of Christ.

---

[10]A very rare word, occuring only once in the NT. J.N.D. Kelly, *Commentary on the Pastoral Epistles* (New York: Harper & Row, 1963), p. 203.

J. LET US DRAW NEAR TO GOD AND
SPUR ONE ANOTHER ON (10:19-25)

[19]**Therefore, brothers, since we have confidence to enter the Most Holy Place by the blood of Jesus, [20]by a new and living way opened for us through the curtain, that is, his body, [21]and since we have a great priest over the house of God, [22]let us draw near to God with a sincere heart in full assurance of faith, having our hearts sprinkled to cleanse us from a guilty conscience and having our bodies washed with pure water. [23]Let us hold unswervingly to the hope we profess, for he who promised is faithful. [24]And let us consider how we may spur one another on toward love and good deeds. [25]Let us not give up meeting together, as some are in the habit of doing, but let us encourage one another — and all the more as you see the Day approaching.**

The "therefore" which introduces verse 19 marks a major transition not only in this chapter but in the letter. As our author turns toward the faith and endurance which God expects from the new covenant community, he begins to address in a more specific manner the exigencies which have moved him to write his "short letter" — the suffering and persecution endured by his readers and their need for a "word of exhortation" which might encourage them to persevere (13:22). Though the burden of chapter 11 will be a definition of and illustration of faith, it is nevertheless set in the context of a stage of the document that becomes much more hortatory than doctrinal. In this section, our writer addresses three commands or exhortations to his readers.[11]

The first of these three commands or exhortations is found in v. 22: "let us draw near to God." In 7:19 our writer first referred to a "better hope . . . by which we draw near to

---

[11]In the Greek text, this section develops three statements which employ hortatory subjunctives as their main verbs προσερχώμεθα (v. 22), κατέχωμεν (v. 23) and κατανοῶμεν (v. 24).

God." Then in 7:25 we read that Jesus is able to "save completely those who come to God." Earlier in this chapter we read the opposite about the sacrifices of the old covenant — they "can never . . . make perfect those who draw near to worship" (10:1). Here, now, we are encouraged — even ordered[12] — to "draw near" to him. In one lengthy and complicated Greek sentence, we can identify the motive, manner and means of our approach to God within the new covenant.

10:19 Therefore, brothers, since we have confidence to enter the Most Holy Place by the blood of Jesus,

Our *motive* (i.e., that which would give us a reason to approach him) is twofold: "since we have confidence to enter the Most Holy Place by the blood of Jesus" (v. 19) and "since we have a great priest over the house of God" (v. 21). Both phrases translate objects of a present tense adverbial participle — the conditions described exist simultaneously with the act commanded by the main verb.

The necessity and efficacy of Christ's blood sacrifice was described in detail in chapter 9 and the reference to "blood" here should be understood in the light of that discussion. The "Most Holy Place" was where Jesus went on our behalf (6:19-20), by his own blood (9:12), and its use here is a typological reference to heaven (4:16; 8:1; 9:24). The statement in v. 19 echoes the command of 4:16, with its connection between that blood and the confidence of the believer, and signals the conclusion of this great discourse on the high priestly ministry of Jesus. "Confidence," however, may be a weak translation of παρρησία (*parrēsia*) which can also mean "courage," "boldness," or "fearlessness."[13] Lane suggests that the word lacks the subjective dimension suggested by "confidence" and suggests "authorization" or "permission" on the basis that the access to God was secured by Christ's sacrifice.[14] Our writer

---

[12]The first person plural subjunctive carries the imperative force (BDF, p. 183).

[13]BAGD, p. 630.

[14]Lane, p. 274, n. b.

has, however, addressed both the objective and subjective dimensions of sin's guilt (i.e., the clearing and cleansing of "conscience," 9:9,14; 10:2), and so Lane is also correct to point out that the subjective element is not completely absent here (although, he argues, it should not obscure the "objective character of the word."[15] Along the same lines, Ellingworth prefers either the TEV ("complete freedom") or the Jerusalem Bible ("right to enter").[16]

10:20 by a new and living way opened for us through the curtain, that is, his body,

The reference to Jesus' "blood" is supplemented with a reference to his "body" (σάρξ, "flesh").[17] Earlier, we read that Christ entered "behind" the curtain (6:19) but here a specific typological significance is accorded to the curtain itself. Our writer may thus have been acquainted with that element of the passion narratives which noted that, at the moment of Christ's death, "the curtain of the temple was torn in two from top to bottom" (Matt 27:51; Mark 15:38; Luke 23:45).

10:21 and since we have a great priest over the house of God,

The reference to Jesus here as "great priest" closely parallels the reference to him as "great high priest" in 4:14. The "house of God" is not a reference to the tabernacle or any other building. Our author has used this same phrase to refer to the community of believers in 3:6 ("Christ is faithful as a son over God's house. And we are his house if we hold on to our courage and the hope of which we boast"). Not only is he a son over God's house by virtue of who he is (1:2, 3, 5), not only our brother by virtue of his incarnation (2:11, 14), but now priest over us by virtue of his sacrifice and resurrection. Our sin notwithstanding, we have every reason to enter the presence of God with confidence.

---

[15]Ibid.
[16]Ellingworth, p. 517.
[17]BAGD, p. 743.

10:22 let us draw near to God with a sincere heart in full assurance of faith, having our hearts sprinkled to cleanse us from a guilty conscience and having our bodies washed with pure water.

Verse 22 describes the *manner* in which we are to draw near to God. First, we draw near "with a sincere heart." "Sincere" translates ἀληθινός (*alēthinos*), the same word used in reference to the "true" tabernacle (8:2; 9:24). The word may also be translated "dependable,"[18] hence Ellingworth's suggestion that it suggests "faithfulness and stability."[19] Καρδία (*kardia*) often means "heart" in the sense of "the seat of physical, spiritual and mental life" or "the center and source of the whole inner life."[20] Our writer seems to use the word in this sense in chapters 3 and 4 when, in several places, he warned his readers not to "harden" their hearts (3:8, 15; 4:7), to see to it that none had "a sinful unbelieving heart" (3:12). In 3:12, he observed that the word of God judges "the thoughts and attitudes of the heart." This fits the present context as well, although the recent references to "conscience" (9:9, 14 and perhaps 10:2) and the joining of "heart" with "conscience" later in this same verse suggest that this is the particular significance of the image here.

See also "draw near to God . . . in full assurance of faith." Πληροφορία (*plēroporia*, "full assurance," or "certainty,"[21] also appeared in 6:11 where the NIV translated it "to make [your hope] sure" (lit., "to the full assurance of the hope"). See comments on 6:11 for more on this word and the relationship between faith, hope and assurance. Here, the genitive ("of faith") is one of source or origin. Our assurance of our salvation — and hence our access to the presence of God — stems from our trust in what Jesus has done for us at the cross. We have confidence to approach God because we have confidence in the sufficiency of Christ's sacrifice.

---

[18]BAGD, p. 37.
[19]Ellingworth, p. 523.
[20]BAGD, p. 403.
[21]Ibid., p. 670.

The remainder of this verse describes *means* by which we draw near to God (i.e., what makes our approach possible). Two perfect tense participles describe events which precede our drawing near but the effects of which continue into the present, making our approach possible.

First, we draw near "having our hearts sprinkled to cleanse us from a guilty conscience." ῥαντίζω (*rhantizō*, "sprinkle, purify"[22]) is the same word used in chapter 9 in reference to the application of the blood of the old covenant sacrifices to unclean people (9:13, 19), the scroll (9:19), the tabernacle and everything used in its ceremonies (9:21).[23] The purpose was to make them outwardly and ceremonially clean (9:13). It remained for the sacrifice of Christ to provide the true and inner cleansing (9:14; 10:2) which has both objective and subjective dimensions (see comments on 10:1-4). The blood of Jesus, applied to our lives, removes from us the guilt of sin and the need for any guilty feelings which might cause us to refrain from entering the presence of God.

Second, we draw near "having our bodies washed with pure water." This complements the first means. The first statement refers to an inner cleansing of conscience. This statement refers to an outward act of purification. The word here translated "pure" (καθαρός, *katharos*) is a cognate of the word used to describe the "cleansing" or "purification" (καθαρίζω, *katharizō*) wrought by Christ's sacrifice of himself upon the conscience of the believer (9:14), by the blood of the animal sacrifices upon the tabernacle and its tools (9:22) and then that wrought by both (9:23). The blood used for cleansing under the old covenant was mixed with water and hyssop (9:21, cf. Num 19). The pairing of "body" with "heart," however, suggests an outward act of washing which coincides with the inner cleansing that takes place. Our writer has recognized the foundational role which baptism plays in initiating

---

[22]BAGD, p. 734.

[23]This exhausts the use of the word in the New Testament, although ῥαντισμός is used in 12:24 and 1 Peter 1:2 of the "sprinkled blood" of Jesus.

the new covenant relationship with God (6:1), and the New Testament includes clear evidence that immersion was practiced for the remission of sin (Acts 2:38). Paul, for one, had been baptized to "wash away" his sins (Acts 22:16). Both external (guilt) and internal (feelings of guilt) barriers to drawing near to God are removed by his sacrifice when it is applied to our lives and we trust in its sufficiency.

10:23 Let us hold unswervingly to the hope we profess, for he who promised is faithful.

Here is the second of the two commands or exhortations in the section. A quite literal translation might read, "hold on to the unwavering profession of the hope." The use of κατέχω (*katechō*, "hold fast, retain faithfully"[24]) echoes its appearance in 3:6 where the readers were exhorted to "hold on" to the courage and hope of which they boasted. A literal translation of 3:6 might well read, "hold on to . . . the boast of the hope" (hence 10:23 mirrors the syntax as well). Whereas 3:6 refers to the "boast" (καύχημα, *kauchēma*) of the hope, the present verse mentions the "profession" (ὁμολογία, *homologia*) of the hope. Our author has used the word in 3:1 and 4:14 in the sense of "confession" or an "acknowledgment that one makes"[25] — i.e., with a stress upon the content of what is professed rather than upon professing as an act. Our "hope" is the object of our confession. In Hebrews, ἐλπίς (*elpis*) likewise tends to refer to the thing expected/hoped for rather than the act of expecting (see comments on 6:11). This profession is to be "without wavering" (ἀκλινής, *aklinēs*[26]). This word does not occur elsewhere in the NT. It occurs in the papyri in reference to the "impartial" ears of one in authority.[27] The reason we are given for retaining an unchanging profession of what we hope for is that "he who promised is faithful."

---

[24]BAGD, p. 423.
[25]Ibid., p. 568.
[26]Ibid., p. 30.
[27]MM, p. 18.

On the whole, this verse reiterates from chapter 3 (3:1-6) the exhortation to courage and faithfulness in light of the faithfulness of Jesus, the apostle and high priest who is also God's Son. Now, however, his readers have received a more complete picture of that faithfulness — of the suffering which it demanded and of the victory which resulted. He has been faithful to us. We should be faithful to him. His victory is also ours. No threat of danger can cost us more or take away what we hope for — and already possess — in Christ Jesus.

10:24 And let us consider how we may spur one another on toward love and good deeds. 10:25 Let us not give up meeting together, as some are in the habit of doing, but let us encourage one another — and all the more as you see the Day approaching.

The NIV gives the impression that there are two separate commands in these verses yet there is only a single command in the single Greek sentence which comprises these two verses. The command is (literally), "consider one another." This same verb (κατανοέω, *katanoeō*) was translated "fix your thoughts upon" in 3:1. The specific matter we are to "fix" ourselves upon is "how we may spur one another on." Ellingworth notes that παροξυσμός (*paroxysmos*) refers to "intense emotion"[28] and this is reflected in Acts 15:39 where it is used of the "sharp contention" which arose between Paul and Barnabas. Although it can be used in a negative sense ("irritation"[29]), this does not seem to fit the present context. However, the intensity is probably not lacking and so our writer is probably encouraging his readers to take strong action to see that the results in mind are obtained.

Two ends, or results, are specified for this act of "spurring on." One is love. The other is "good works." The two are not unrelated, however. Ἀγάπη (*agapē*, "love") appears only one other time in the letter[30] — in 6:10 when our readers were

---

[28]Ellingworth, p. 527.
[29]BAGD, p. 629.
[30]Ἀγαπάω (the verb) appears in 1:9 and 12:6.

offered this assurance: "God . . . will not forget your work and the love you have shown him as you have helped his people and continue to help them." Works which help God's people are the expression of love — love for them and love for God. Our writer will soon refer to some of those works performed by the readers (vv. 32-34). They may be described as "good works" (καλῶν ἔργων, *kalōn ergōn*) to contrast them with the "acts that lead to death" (νεκρῶν ἔργων, *nekrōn ergōn*, lit., "dead works") referred to previously (6:1; 9:14).

What the NIV renders as a separate exhortation is actually a modal participle, i.e., one which describes the means by which the "spurring on" is carried out. Verse 25 might well begin, "by not giving up meeting together." Although the present tense of the participle need not carry the continual aspect, some see it here[31] — i.e., "don't ever give up meeting together." Ἐπισυναγωγή (*episynagogē*) is "scarcely to be differentiated from συναγωγή."[32] The latter was the technical term for the Jewish assembly (synagogue)[33] and never appears in Hebrews. Perhaps our writer, in his effort to dissuade his readers from reverting to Judaism, avoids this term purposely. Even so, assembling with others of like faith had enabled the Jewish faith to survive the dispersion and the importance of the public assembly would have been deeply embedded in their heritage. Nevertheless "some were in the habit of" neglecting meeting together. We are not told why. Perhaps it was for many of the same reasons that people in our own day fail to make and/or keep the same commitment.

What is stated negatively is then repeated in an affirmative manner. Instead, we are to encourage each other ("let us encourage" translates another modal participle which parallels the first). If people today fail to make or keep commitments to the public assembly for reasons similar to those of "some" in the early church, it is also true that the reasons

---

[31]So Ellingworth (p. 528) and Lane (p. 276, *nt*).
[32]BAGD, p. 301.
[33]Ibid., p. 782.

identified here for making and keeping that commitment are also valid today. It is God's plan for "spurring his people on" to love and good works. It is God's plan for providing the encouragement that his people need to remain faithful in a world which not only often fails to provide such encouragement but aggressively seeks to discourage it.

And there is one more reason that should be as important to us as it was to the first readers. We should do it "all the more" as we "see the Day drawing near." In the NT, "the Day" often refers to "the day of God's final judgment."[34] The reference to judgment and raging fire which will consume the enemies of God in v. 27 justifies understanding the term in an eschatological sense. On that day when Jesus appears a second time he will "bring salvation to those who are waiting for him" (9:28). But for those who "keep on sinning" he will bring judgment (10:26-27). How will we be found when Jesus returns? Whether we choose to avail ourselves of the encouragement of the assembly in the present will be a significant factor in whether we will remain faithful until that Day.

K. THE JUDGMENT OF GOD ON THOSE
WHO KEEP SINNING (10:26-31)

[26]If we deliberately keep on sinning after we have received the knowledge of the truth, no sacrifice for sins is left, [27]but only a fearful expectation of judgment and of raging fire that will consume the enemies of God. [28]Anyone who rejected the law of Moses died without mercy on the testimony of two or three witnesses. [29]How much more severely do you think a man deserves to be punished who has trampled the Son of God under foot, who has treated as an unholy thing the blood of the covenant that sanctified him, and who has insulted the Spirit of grace? [30]For we know him who said, "It is mine to avenge; I will repay,"[a] and

---

[34]Ἡμέρα, BAGD, p. 347.

again, "The Lord will judge his people."[b] [31]It is a dreadful thing to fall into the hands of the living God.

[a]*30* Deut. 32:35   [b]*30* Deut. 32:36; Psalm 135:14

10:26 If we deliberately keep on sinning after we have received the knowledge of the truth, no sacrifice for sins is left,

Having exhorted his readers to (1) draw near to God, (2) hold unswervingly to their hope and (3) spur one another on, our author now contemplates the alternative possibility. His description of the alternative includes two elements. First, "we deliberately keep on sinning." The NIV attributes the durative sense to the present tense participle here (just as some suggest the present participle in v. 25 should be translated; see comments on 10:25 above). As a result, it is not simply "sin" that threatens to disrupt our covenant relationship with God — forgiveness deals with this contingency. As shown by the context of 10:25, the author does not have in mind the Christian who becomes guilty of this or that particular sin. The person in view is the apostate who "gives up meeting" with the church and "deliberately keeps on sinning." Having abandoned the church, having purposely chosen a lifestyle of continual sin, the apostate spurns Jesus and his blood (10:29). Thus the apostate willfully forfeits the only source of salvation. As before, our writer may have in mind the same kind of "defiant sin" described in Numbers 15:30, which, in the case of the old covenant, caused one to be "cut off" from the covenant community.

As to the second element, this purposeful choice has been made "after we have received the knowledge of the truth." Bauer suggests that the word is to be understood in the definite sense here, as "the content of Christianity as the absolute truth."[35] This is what makes the deliberate and continual choice of sin so tragic — that it comes after our having understood and embraced what Christ has done for us. Calvin

[35]Ibid., pp. 35-36.

characterizes this as anyone who "knowingly and willingly throws away the grace which he had received."[36] This verse is quite reminiscent of the more extended warning of 6:4-8 in which we read of those "who have tasted the word of God" but fall away and refuse to repent, crucifying the Son of God all over again to their own loss.

Our writer is specific about the consequences of this purposeful choice of a lifestyle of deliberate and continuous sin. His first description pertains to what is lost: "no sacrifice for sins is left." This statement is a stark contrast to that in v. 18: "there is no longer any sacrifice for sin." The statement of v. 18 means that no additional sacrifices are necessary because Christ's sacrifice has made forgiveness available. The statement in the present verse, however, means that the forgiveness once possessed is now unavailable — "without the shedding of blood there is no forgiveness" (9:22). As Calvin noted, "If no salvation is to be found apart from Him, we should not be surprised that those who let go of Him of their own accord are deprived of every hope of pardon."[37]

The condition is not inherently irreversible, however. As in 6:6, the condition ("keep on sinning") is described by a present tense adverbial participle which places it in a coordinate time relationship to the main verb ("no sacrifice is left"). "If" does not represent the presence of such a participle in the Greek text but an interpretation of the relationship between the participle and the main verb. Here, also, the verse could just as well read, "so long as we keep on sinning," suggesting the possibility of repentance and a restoration of the covenant relationship. So long as we persist in this choice of deliberate and continual sin, however, no fate but the one described can be expected. There is no "middle ground" in our standing before God.

---

[36]Calvin, p. 146.
[37]Ibid.

10:27 but only a fearful expectation of judgment and of raging fire that will consume the enemies of God.

His second description pertains to what can be expected in its place. The expectation is "fearful." Φοβερός (*phoberos*) could even be translated "terrible" or "frightful."[38] The NIV renders the same word "terrifying" in 12:21 when describing how Moses trembled with fear when he saw the mountain burning with fire and when the people of Israel begged that God no longer speak to them for fear of their very lives (cf. Exod 20:19). What such people can expect is first described literally and then figuratively. In Hebrews, κρίσις (*krisis*, "judgment") appears elsewhere only in 9:27 where the term seems to refer of God's final judgment of all people (cf. 12:23 where God is described as "the judge [κρίτη, *kritē*] of all men"). Here, however, it carries the more frequent unfavorable sense of "sentence of condemnation . . . and the subsequent punishment."[39]

Figuratively, that judgment is described as a "raging fire." In 12:29 our writer will describe God himself as "a consuming fire." Jesus regularly spoke of final judgment and punishment in terms of "fire," "the fire of hell," a "fiery furnace," "eternal fire" and "the fire that never goes out."[40] Paul associates the second appearance of Jesus with "blazing fire" and the punishment of those who do not know God or obey the gospel (2 Thess 1:8). Peter observes that "the present heavens and earth are reserved for fire, being kept for the day of judgment and destruction of ungodly men" (2 Pet 3:7). Jude cites the fate of Sodom and Gomorrah "as an example of those who suffer the punishment of eternal fire" (7) and encourages his readers to "snatch others from the fire and save them" (23). In the book of Revelation, those who worship the beast "will be tormented with burning sulfur" (14:10) while the beast, the devil, death, and Hades are all thrown into "the lake of

---

[38]BAGD, p. 862.

[39]Ibid., p. 450.

[40]See Matthew 3:12; 5:22; 7:19; 13:40, 42, 50; 18:8, 9; 25:41; Mark 9:22, 43, 44, 45, 46, 47, 48; Luke 3:9; 12:49; John 15:6.

burning sulfur" (19:20; 20:9, 10, 14, 15) — it is the "second
death" (21:8). Such will be the inescapable fate of all of those
who are found to be "the enemies of God." And such will any
of us be should we persist in a purposeful choice of deliberate
and continual sin.

**10:28 Anyone who rejected the law of Moses died without
mercy on the testimony of two or three witnesses. 10:29 How
much more severely do you think a man deserves to be punished who has trampled the Son of God under foot, who has
treated as an unholy thing the blood of the covenant that
sanctified him, and who has insulted the Spirit of grace?**

Lest his readers doubt the absolute truth of his warning,
the author offers a lesser to greater argument ("how much
more") to further support the claim of vv. 26-27. The imposi-
tion of the death penalty on the testimony of at least two witnesses is recorded both in Numbers 35:30 (as punishment for
murder) and in Deuteronomy 17:6 (as punishment for idolatry). These are particularly heinous acts but the purposeful
choice of deliberate and continual sin is also described in the
most horrific terms.

First, such people have "trampled the Son of God under
foot." Jesus employed this same term (καταπατέω, *katapateō*)
to describe the fate of salt which has lost its saltiness: "It is no
longer good for anything, except to be thrown out and trampled by men" (Matt 5:13). On another occasion he warned his
disciples not to "throw your pearls to pigs. If you do, they
may trample them under their feet" (Matt 7:6). Those who
"deliberately keep on sinning" evidence the same attitude
toward the Son of God. They regard him as not good for anything and life in complete disregard for his worth.

Second, such people have "treated as an unholy thing the
blood of the covenant." Κοινός (*koinos*, "unholy") was used of
that which was "common,"[41] that is "unclean" (Mark 7:2; Acts
10:14, 28; 11:8; Rom 14:14). This is the exact opposite of what

---

[41]BAGD, p. 438.

should be the case for that blood had "sanctified" (ἁγιάζω, *hagiazō*, translated "make holy" in 10:10, 14) and "cleansed" him (καθαρίζω, *katharizō*, 9:14, 22, 23).

Finally, such people have "insulted the Spirit of grace." Ἐνυβρίζω (*enybrizō*, "insult") is capable of a stronger translation such as "outrage."[42] It appears only here in the NT. The cognate ὑβρίζω (*hybrizō*) was used by Luke to describe Jesus' scathing rebuke of the scribes and Pharisees (Luke 11:45) and is elsewhere associated with violent behavior. The servants were "mistreated" and killed in Jesus' parable of the wedding banquet (Matt 22:6). Jesus predicted that he would be mocked, "insulted," spit on, flogged and killed when he went to Jerusalem (Luke 18:32). Leading Jews and Gentiles in Iconium plotted to "mistreat" and stone Paul and Barnabas (Acts 14:5). And Paul was "insulted" in Philippi (1 Thess 2:2) where he was attacked by a crowd, stripped, flogged and thrown into prison (Acts 16:22-23). Bruce and Kistemaker see here a reference to the blasphemy of the Holy Spirit, a sin which Jesus said would not be forgiven (Matt 12:32; Mark 3:29).[43] As strong as the vocabulary of our writer here may be, both the use of the present participle in v. 26 (see comments above) and the specific blasphemous event in the Gospels to which Jesus made reference (attributing the work of the Holy Spirit to Satan) may not fit well into this view. It may be that our writer (1) focuses on the Son, his blood, and the Spirit since they are the essential and defining features of the new covenant and/or (2) has in mind the language of 9:14 ("How much more, then, will the blood of Christ, who through the eternal Spirit offered himself unblemished to God, cleanse our consciences from acts that lead to death").

The "greater" part of this lesser to greater argument is twofold. When the most extreme punishment under the old covenant is considered and compared to what people do to the Son, his blood and the Spirit when they "deliberately keep on

---

[42]Ibid., p. 270.
[43]Bruce, pp. 259-260; Kistemaker, p. 295.

sinning," it is clear that (1) they are even more deserving of punishment and (2) their punishment itself should be more severe. The syntax of v. 29 brings this out clearly. Quite literally, it might be translated, "by how much [more] do think they will be thought worthy of a worse punishment?" Since the "lesser" punishment was death, it is frightening to consider what punishment could possibly be worse than death itself (see "raging fire," v. 27). Again, the resemblance to 6:4-8 is striking.

10:30 For we know him who said, "It is mine to avenge; I will repay," and again, "The Lord will judge his people." 10:31 It is a dreadful thing to fall into the hands of the living God.

The lesser to greater argument is supplemented by an appeal to Scripture: Deuteronomy 32:35-36. These verses are not quoted in their entirety. Only the relevant phrases are cited. They amount to a promise of judgment which includes the punishment of evil. God himself claims the sole right to judge and our writer later refers to him as "the judge of all men" (12:23). And God himself will do the avenging and repaying.

The word translated "dreadful" is the same word translated "fearful" in v. 27 (see comments above). The terse statement of v. 31 is intimidating both because of what it conveys and the abruptness of the expression.

L. REMINDER OF EARLIER SUFFERING (10:32-34)

[32]Remember those earlier days after you had received the light, when you stood your ground in a great contest in the face of suffering. [33]Sometimes you were publicly exposed to insult and persecution; at other times you stood side by side with those who were so treated. [34]You sympathized with those in prison and joyfully accepted the confiscation of your property, because you knew that you yourselves had better and lasting possessions.

10:32 Remember those earlier days after you had received the light, when you stood your ground in a great contest in the face of suffering.

The persecutions faced by his readers are now introduced into the discussion and thus are set in the eschatological context of vv. 25-31. Christians may often wonder whether the present persecutions they endure for Christ's sake are a price they are willing to pay to remain faithful. However, evaluating the options requires an eternal frame of reference within which both the true rewards of perseverance and the frightening alternative can be considered. The readers must have had such a perspective on their sufferings for they accepted them "joyfully" (v. 34).

The author asks them to recall "those earlier days after [they] had received the light." The same word (φωτίζω, *phōtizō*) appeared in 6:4 when our writer referred to those "who have once been enlightened." Here, as there, it probably refers to "instruction"[44] or an "intellectual illumination that removes ignorance through . . . the preaching of the gospel"[45] since it parallels the phrase "after we have received the knowledge of the truth" in v. 26 (see n. 36 on 6:4-8 regarding the KJV rendering "illumination").

Our writer provides his own summary description of their sufferings. It was a "great contest" (ἄθλησις, *athlēsis*, which appears only here in the NT). The cognate ἀθλητής (*athlētēs*) refers to a "contender" or "athlete"[46] and the verb ἀθλέω (*athleō*) appears in 2 Timothy 2:5 when Paul encourages his readers to endure hardship and compares the believer to one "who competes as an athlete" to receive the victor's crown. The readers of Hebrews, just as all who endure suffering for the sake of Christ until his return, compete in the cosmic struggle which has already been decided. Whether we receive the victor's crown is conditioned only upon our ability to persevere in the struggle.

---

[44]Ellingworth, p. 320.
[45]Lane, p. 141.
[46]BAGD, p. 21.

10:33 Sometimes you were publicly exposed to insult and persecution; at other times you stood side by side with those who were so treated.

Their sufferings included "insult" (ὀνειδισμός, *oneidismos*). This is the same word used in 13:13 to the "disgrace" which Jesus bore as a result of his crucifixion. Yet Jesus had warned his disciples, "If the world hates you, keep in mind that it hated me first . . . If they persecuted me, they will persecute you also" (John 15:18-20). Yet we will soon read that Jesus "endured the cross, scorning its shame, and sat down at the right hand of God" (12:2-3). Only from such a standpoint can such "insults" be regarded as the compliments they in fact are. And no example can offer greater encouragement to endure than that of Jesus himself.

They also endured "persecution." Θλῖψις (*thlipsis*) literally means "pressing" or "pressure"[47] — Morris suggests "severe pressure."[48] How severe may be suggested by the fact that they were "publicly exposed" to both insult and persecution. The verb here is θεατρίζω (*theatrizō*),[49] a cognate of θέατρον (*theatron*, "theater"[50]) used for the place where public assemblies gathered. While 12:4 ("you have not yet resisted to the point of shedding your blood") suggests that the readers had yet to endure the most severe of Nero's persecutions,[51] they were probably experiencing the harbingers. Bruce[52] draws from Tacitus' *Annals* and I Clement to describe the public persecutions which were on the horizon:

> Their death . . . was made a matter of sport: they were covered in wild beasts' skins and torn to pieces by dogs; or were fastened to crosses and set on fire in order to serve as torches by night when daylight failed (Tacitus, *Annals*, xv.44).

---

[47]BAGD, p. 362.
[48]Morris, p. 110.
[49]As Morris notes, ibid.
[50]BAGD, p. 353.
[51]Evidence that the letter could not have been written much after AD 64.
[52]Bruce, p. 267.

[Christian women had to] enact the parts of Dirce and Danaus (I Clement 6:2).[53]

10:34 You sympathized with those in prison and joyfully accepted the confiscation of your property, because you knew that you yourselves had better and lasting possessions.
Lane cites several ancient sources which tell of false accusations of crime and vice, the impositions of heavy fines, confiscation of property and the looting of homes after their owners had been imprisoned or removed.[54] None of these forms of persecution seem far removed from what we read in these verses.

The cause of his reader's joy was that they knew they had "better and lasting possessions" (v. 34). Their true, eternal inheritance which God had promised them (9:15) yet awaited them. No earthly power or authority could take it away from them. They had learned not to "be afraid of those who kill the body but cannot kill the soul" and remained faithful to "the One who can destroy both soul and body in hell" (Matt 10:28). Their treasure was in heaven, not on earth "where moth and rust destroy and where thieves break in and steal" (Matt 6:19-20).

M. THE NEED TO PERSEVERE (10:35-39)

[35]So do not throw away your confidence; it will be richly rewarded. [36]You need to persevere so that when you have done the will of God, you will receive what he has promised. [37]For in just a very little while,

"He who is coming will come and will not delay.

---

[53]Both were tragic figures in Greek mythology. Dirce was the wife of the Theban king Lycus who was dragged to death by a wild bull (BAGD, p. 199). Danaus was the king of Libya whose daughters were punished forever in the underworld for murdering their husbands on their wedding nights (BAGD, p. 170).

[54]Lane, pp. 299-300.

³⁸But my righteous one^a will live by faith.
And if he shrinks back,
I will not be pleased with him."^b
³⁹But we are not of those who shrink back and are
destroyed, but of those who believe and are saved.

^a*38* One early manuscript *But the righteous*   ^b*38* Hab. 2:3,4

10:35 So do not throw away your confidence; it will be richly rewarded.

"So" (οὖν, *oun*) could be translated "therefore" to convey what is probably a stronger connective. Because they "had better and lasting possessions" (10:35), "therefore" they are commanded[55] not to "throw away" their confidence. Ἀπο–βάλλω (*apoballō*) may denote either "the (vigorous) action of throwing something away" or "a more passive process, as of a tree losing its leaves."[56] A case could be made for either sense in the present context, although on three separate occasions our writer has issued lengthy warnings against either a hardening of heart (3:7-4:11) or a decisive turn away from Christ (6:4-8; 10:26-31).

The word translated "confidence" (παρρησία, *parrēsia*) was translated "courage" in 3:6, when the author encouraged his readers to "hold on to" (vs. "throw away" here) their courage and hope. It also appeared in 4:16 and 10:19 of the "confidence" or "boldness" (KJV) with which we can now enter into God's presence as a result of Christ's sacrifice. Thus the word does not so much convey the idea of "trust" — although their faith in God's faithfulness to his promise must certainly have been the source of their confidence — so much as it conveys the idea of "courage," "boldness" or even "fearlessness"[57] in the face of the threats against them.

This "confidence" is the key to receiving the "rich reward"

---

[55]Μή with the subjunctive (ἀποβάλητε) carries an imperative force (BDF, p. 184).
[56]Ellingworth, p. 550.
[57]BAGD, p. 630.

that has been promised. The Greek syntax actually suggests a stronger tie between the two for it contains not future tense language but that of the present tense (lit., "your confidence which has a great reward"). μισθαποδοσία ("reward") can be used in reference to "payment of wages."[58] It was used earlier of the "just punishment" for violation and disobedience of that message spoken by angels (2:2). Whether the believer remains faithful or not, he will in either case receive his "just reward." It will be punishment for some and salvation for others.

10:36 You need to persevere so that when you have done the will of God, you will receive what he has promised.

"Perseverance" is needed to obtain the rich reward, however, and this is what the confidence enables. The use of the aorist participle ("when you have done the will of God") suggests a completion of this act — i.e., when one has persevered to the end in their obedience to the will of God. This is very similar to the lengthier discussion in chapter six pertaining to the relationship between our faith in God's promise, the patience with which we wait for it and the diligence which we must show to the very end to make our hope sure (6:11ff.).

10:37 For in just a very little while, "He who is coming will come and will not delay. 10:38 But my righteous one will live by faith. And if he shrinks back, I will not be pleased with him."

As he has done on more than one occasion, the author ends his appeal by turning to Scripture. The essence of this quote is taken from Habbakuk 2:3-4 in the LXX but the author has done some rearranging and interpreting.[59] Most significantly, the addition of a definite article before the participle "coming" offers a messianic reading of the passage (which now reads "*He who is* coming"). This was not a new

---

[58]Ibid., p. 523.
[59]So Ellingworth observes (p. 554).

idea. Morris mentions a rabbinic tradition which interpreted the passage messianically.[60] Our writer merely makes the connection more explicit. Also, the order of the wording has been altered so that the citation ends with that part of the passage which the author will apply to his readers ("shrink back"). The use of a single key word in the passage to establish a point of application for his readers is one of the author's prominent hermeneutical strategies (see Introduction).

10:39 But we are not of those who shrink back and are destroyed, but of those who believe and are saved.

The thrust of the citation is that (1) his (second) coming is certain and (2) two alternatives are available to those who wait. One can "live by faith" or "shrink back" (and be destroyed, v. 39). As in 6:9, our writer gives his readers a vote of confidence for their encouragement. Ἀπώλεια (apōleia, "destruction") appears only here in Hebrews and might also be translated "annihilation" or "ruin."[61] The word also appears in Revelation of the "destruction" of the beast (17:8, 11). The temptation to offer this verse in support an annihilation theory must be balanced against the use of "eternal" language to speak of the final punishment (see comments on 10:27).

---

[60]Morris, p. 111.
[61]BAGD, p. 103.

HEBREWS 11

VII. GOD EXPECTS US TO SHOW FAITH (11:1-40)

A. THE NATURE OF FAITH (11:1-3)

[1]Now faith is being sure of what we hope for and certain of what we do not see. [2]This is what the ancients were commended for.

[3]By faith we understand that the universe was formed at God's command, so that what is seen was not made out of what was visible.

The eleventh chapter of Hebrews is the famous chapter on faith. The last paragraph of chapter 10 (Heb 10:35-39) actually introduced the idea of faith with an OT quotation from Habakkuk 2:3-4, "My righteous one will live by faith." The first verse of the chapter gives a general description of faith. The second verse functions as a kind of heading for the eighteen πίστει (pistei, "by faith") statements of the chapter. In the NIV fifteen of these eighteen statements begin a new paragraph. Verses 9, 27 and 28 do not.

11:1 Now faith is being sure of what we hope for and certain of what we do not see.
The chapter begins with a general description of faith that is twofold. **Faith is** (1) the ὑπόστασις (hypostasis), the essence, the realization (NIV: "being sure") of what we hope for, and (2) the ἔλεγχος (elengchos), the proof, the conviction (NIV: "being certain") of what we do not see. The precise meaning of these two nouns has been widely discussed. The problem is

more difficult because of the infrequent use of both words in the NT. The word *hypostasis* occurs five times, three in Hebrews (1:3; 3:14; and here); while *elengchos* occurs only twice (2 Tim 3:16 and here).

Louw and Nida put the first word in the category of words that mean "nature, character" and the second in the group meaning of "true, false" suggesting that it means, "evidence that what we cannot see really exists."[1] Ellingworth summarizes the problem by saying that we understand these two nouns (a) objectively, something we have, for example a "guarantee" (NJB), or (b) subjectively, something we do or feel, for example "being sure" (NIV).[2]

G. Harder has a helpful discussion of the Hebrews passages which use *hypostasis*. On 11:1 he says its alternative translations are (i) "confidence, expectation; (ii) "pledge, security;" or (iii) "realization, actualization."[3] H.G. Link rejects a subjective (lacking doubt), hortatory (directing correction) or intellectual sense (meaning evidence) for *elengchos*, preferring "a strictly theological sense, as referring to conviction, about the power of the future world promised by God." He says it would then mean, "But faith is the pledge of things hoped for, the conviction of things we cannot see."[4] The NIV prefers the idea of the inner confidence about things which lack visible evidence.

11:2 This is what the ancients were commended for.

The ancients were commended by God for this faith in his promises and in the future which he held before them, even though there may have been no tangible proof of that future other than God's total truthfulness. The examples that finish the chapter show this confidence. Similar lists of honorable men of old may be found in Sirach 44-50; 4 Maccabees 16:17-23; 18:11-19 and M Taanith 2:4. Verse two begins with the

---

[1]LN, pp. 586, 673.
[2]Ellingworth, p. 564.
[3]NIDNTT, 1:712-714.
[4]Ibid., 2:142.

phrase, "in this" (ἐν ταύτῃ, *en tautē* — fem. sing. because "faith" is fem. sing.), thus setting up the structure of the following eighteen statements which begin with the phrase, "in faith" or "by faith" (*pistei*). The NIV hides this nice introductory touch of the author's pen when it translates, "This is what the ancients were commended for."

The first sixteen of these eighteen "by faith" statements only take us through Genesis and half of Exodus. In these first chapters of the Bible it is difficult to find good people not listed in Heb 11, but the list does not claim to be exhaustive.

It may be helpful to list the kinds of things people did "by faith." See the following table. The responses of faith include all kinds of things — construction, travel, worship and sacrifice, clear thinking, avoiding death; even miracles like having a son when past age, or describing an event hundreds of years before it happened, or crossing a sea on dry land, or making city walls fall, or leaving life without dying. The record of faith is a remarkable record.

VS	PERSONS	WHAT THEY DID "BY FAITH"
2	ancients	Were commended
3	"We"	Understand creation
4	Abel	Offered a better sacrifice
		*Was commended as a righteous man
		*Still speaks, though dead
5	Enoch	Avoided death
7	Noah	Built the ark
		*Condemned the world
		*Became heir of righteousness
8	Abraham	Left home for an unknown destination
9		Made his home in tents like a stranger in the promised land
11		Was enabled to become a father when past age
Summary statement:		
	("All these people"	**Were still living by faith when they died
		**Did not receive the things promised, but saw them from a distance
		**Longed for a better, a heavenly, country
17	Abraham	Offered Isaac as a sacrifice

19	(Abraham)	**Reasoned that God could raise the dead
		**Received Isaac back from death
20	Isaac	Blessed the future of Jacob and Esau
21	Jacob	Blessed Joseph's sons
		Worshiped
22	Joseph	Spoke of the exodus, instructing about his bones
23	Moses' parents	Hid baby Moses for three months
24	Moses	Refused to be known as the son of Pharaoh's daughter
		Chose to be mistreated with the people of God
		**Regarded disgrace for Christ greater than treasures of Egypt
27	Moses	Left Egypt
28		Kept the Passover and the sprinkling of blood
29	The people	Passed through the Red Sea
30		The walls of Jericho fell down, after the people marched around them
31	Rahab	Was not killed with those who were disobedient
+6	+ "the prophets"	+ 20 other deeds

Note: An asterisk (*) means the NIV text says "by faith," but the Greek text is not the formula *pistei.*

Note: A double asterisk (**) implies, but does not state, that the deed was based on faith.

11:3 By faith we understand that the universe was formed at God's command, so that what is seen was not made out of what was visible.

In his first example of faith, **we understand**, the writer draws his readers with himself into the company of the faithful. Ever so gently he stands alongside his readers. At several critical points in the epistle he uses the first person plural, "we" (2:1-3, 8; 3:6, 14; 4:1, 11, 14-16; etc.). It is the shepherd's heart that draws his flock close to himself so that he may impart some of his strength to them in their weakness. They worried him with their dangerously immature condition (Heb 5:11-6:8). In opening his Roman letter, Paul similarly expressed this desire to give strength to his readers (Rom 1:11-13). The mother of the seven Maccabean martyrs urged the last one to be faithful by reminding him that God who made everything, "did not make them out of things that existed" (2 Macc 7:28, NRSV). So here the first example encouraging us to staunch faith is an example of trusting that at God's command "what is seen was not made out of what was visible."

"By faith we understand that the universe was formed at God's command." The author of Hebrews agrees with the uniform perspective of biblical authors that God spoke the universe into a fully functioning system, including the sun, moon, stars and earth. Before he spoke there was nothing. After he said the words, instantly what he commanded became. Psalm 33:6-9 is typical:

> By the word of the LORD were the heavens made, their starry host by the breath of his mouth. He gathers the waters of the sea into jars; he puts the deep into storehouses. Let all the earth fear the LORD; let all the people of the world revere him. For he spoke, and it came to be; he commanded, and it stood firm.

No one was there when the universe began. Therefore, whether one believes that it generated itself or that God spoke it into existence is a matter of faith. Both those who believe in creation and those who believe in evolution hold a faith system. The question is simple. Which explanation best integrates all the data which we possess?

Whitcomb says the fundamental issue is:

> . . . whether one puts his trust in the written Word of the personal and living God who *was* there when it all happened, or else puts his trust in the ability of the human intellect, unaided by divine revelation, to extrapolate presently observed processes of nature into the eternal past (and future). *Which faith* is the most reasonable, fruitful, and satisfying? (Italics are his.)[5]

---

[5]John Whitcomb, *The Early Earth*, revised edition; (Grand Rapids: Baker, 1986), p.52.

The word "**formed**" (καταρτίζω, *katartizō*) points more toward earth as a finished product fully adequate for man's temporary home, rather than backward toward the nothingness out of which God made the earth. The latter idea would have been in the word κτίζω (*ktizō*, "to create"). The text here explicitly states that "what is seen was not made out of what was visible." It was all formed **at God's command** (lit., by the word of God). The word ῥῆμα (*rhēma*, "word") used here should be contrasted with the word λόγος (*logos*, "word"). *Rhēma* points more clearly to the spoken utterance of God, for example, "Let there be light." The most frequent verb of God's activity in Genesis 1 is speech.

B. FAITH ILLUSTRATED BY ABEL, ENOCH, AND NOAH (11:4-7)

⁴By faith Abel offered God a better sacrifice than Cain did. By faith he was commended as a righteous man, when God spoke well of his offerings. And by faith he still speaks, even though he is dead.

⁵By faith Enoch was taken from this life, so that he did not experience death; he could not be found, because God had taken him away. For before he was taken, he was commended as one who pleased God. ⁶And without faith it is impossible to please God, because anyone who comes to him must believe that he exists and that he rewards those who earnestly seek him.

⁷By faith Noah, when warned about things not yet seen, in holy fear built an ark to save his family. By his faith he condemned the world and became heir of the righteousness that comes by faith.

11:4 By faith Abel offered God a better sacrifice than Cain did. By faith he was commended as a righteous man, when God spoke well of his offerings. And by faith he still speaks, even though he is dead.

Jesus put Abel at the head of the list of righteous people whom the Jews had killed in their resistance of God's invitations to them:

> And so upon you will come all the righteous blood that has been shed on earth, from the blood of righteous Abel to the blood of Zechariah son of Berekiah, whom you murdered between the temple and the altar (Matt 23:35; Luke 11:51).

Abel is also the first hero of faith named in this list. His death, literally his blood, will be mentioned again in 12:24 in contrast with the blood of Jesus to which all Christians have come.

Cain is mentioned outside of Genesis 4 only three times in the Bible. In 1 John 3:12 he is held up as a bad example who belonged to the evil one and murdered his brother because his deeds were evil while his brother's were righteous. It becomes the basis for explaining that the wicked world will hate righteous people. Jude 11 mentions "the way of Cain" as one illustration of godless people who speak abusively against whatever they do not understand. They are "like unreasoning animals." Even after God confronted him, Cain invited Abel out to the field where he killed him. His anger certainly made him act "like unreasoning animals."

The point of this passage is that God **commended** Abel **as a righteous man** because his faith led him to do what God asked to be done. His obedience is held up before us as an example to be copied even though it eventually cost him his life. This is why **he still speaks, even though he is dead**. Cain and Abel may have talked about what God required as a sacrifice before either of them brought his sacrifice. Let Abel's determination to obey God whatever others would do be an encouragement to us.

In the face of the speculation about what made Abel's sacrifice better than that of Cain, our text simply explains that it was because of his faith. There is no suggestion that God required an animal which Cain refused, or that Cain did not bring the best from what he had. The very anger of Cain upon having his offering refused indicates an arrogant distrust of God (Gen 4:5). Cain knew better than God what he should offer! Faith is so important that Paul could say whatever does not originate in faith is sin (Rom 14:23). Jesus explained to the disciples that the reason the Holy Spirit would convict people of sin was because they *did not believe* in him (John 16:8-9). Disbelief is the central problem of sin. Belief is mandatory. Our author waits till after his third illustration of faith to explain this same concept that without faith it is impossible to please God (11:6).

11:5 By faith Enoch was taken from this life, so that he did not experience death; he could not be found, because God had taken him away. For before he was taken, he was commended as one who pleased God.

Enoch's faith led to a most unusual blessing. He was "translated," i.e., "**taken from this life** without dying." The word "translate" (μετατίθημι, *metatithēmi*), literally means "to convey to another place." It is often used in a nonliteral sense, simply "to change, alter" for example of changing one's mind (LS). Hebrews has three of its six NT uses. Acts 7:16 reported that when Jacob's family died their bodies were "brought back" (*metatithēmi*) to Shechem in Canaan. The Galatian believers "so quickly deserted" (*metatithēmi*) Christ and turned to another gospel that it astonished Paul (Gal 1:6). Certain men were "changing (*metatithēmi*) the grace of our God into a license for immorality" (Jude 4).

Hebrews usage adds the changing (*metatithēmi*) of the priesthood when Christ became our new high priest (7:12), and Enoch's being taken (*metatithēmi*) from this life (said twice in 11:5). The related noun μετάθεσις (*metathesis*, "removal, change") should also be considered. Its three appearances in the NT are all in Hebrews. Besides Enoch's "removal" (NIV: "before he was taken"), Hebrews mentions the "removal" of the law which accompanied the change of priesthood (7:12). In the other instance, the "removal" of what can be shaken is done so that what cannot be shaken may remain (12:27).

The tenses of three verbs in this verse are especially interesting. Enoch "could not be found" (ηὑρίσκετο, *hēurisketo,* imperfect tense; lit., "was not being found"), "was commended" (μεμαρτύρηται, *memartyrētai,* perfect tense), and "pleased" (εὐαρεστηκέναι, *euarestēkenai,* perfect tense). The first verb indicates that they kept looking for him unsuccessfully. Again and again they looked. It was not like Enoch to wander off with no explanation. They cared for him. Their continued looking shows that they did not know that he was "translated." Perhaps Moses was the first to receive this information from God by inspiration. If so, it would elevate the magnitude of Abraham's faith when he reasoned that God would resurrect Isaac from the dead. See further discussion of this in the notes on verses 17-19.

The other two verbs are both perfect tenses. Blass and DeBrunner call the perfect tense "a condition or state as the result of a past action" and illustrates by explaining, "ἕστηκεν 'he placed himself there and stands there now.'"[6] In our verbs, this means that God became pleased with Enoch and the new status and enjoyment of this new bliss should be borne in mind. One of these new conditions is God's open endorsement of Enoch's character, for he gave a witness, and a new state of endorsement existed.

The special description of Enoch in the Hebrew text of Genesis 5:24 is that he "**walked with God.**"[7] The LXX, which our author consistently follows, reads that he "pleased God." While the wording is different, the thought is not. To "walk" with God obviously implies a close companionship on a spiritual plane, which would mean that God was pleased with Enoch.

---

[6]BDF, p. 166.

[7]The Hebrew word for "walked" (*halach*) is very common in the OT; but the Hithpael form (*hithhalach*) is not. Gesenius says the Hithpael form "more often indicates an action less directly affecting the subject, and describes it as performed with regard to or for oneself, in one's own special interest." E. Kautzsch and A.E. Cowley, eds., *Gesenius' Hebrew Grammar* (Oxford: Clarendon Press, 1963 [from second English edition, 1910]), p.150.

11:6 And without faith it is impossible to please God, because anyone who comes to him must believe that he exists and that he rewards those who earnestly seek him.

Like a clever homiletician our author began his stories of faith before he had fully explained the role and necessity of faith. Now that he has indicated that Enoch was "one who pleased God," he expands on this feature of faith, i.e., faith pleases God. He says, "**Without faith it is impossible to please God**." Two facets of faith are necessary for anyone to be able to come to God. (1) He must believe that God exists. (2) He must believe that God rewards those who earnestly seek him. It would be reasonable to expect to find both of these traits in each example of faith laid before us.

Some may not believe that God exists. There are many more who believe that God exists, but who do not **believe that he rewards** those who **earnestly seek** him. In a crisis they prayed, and God did not do what they asked of him. Therefore they conclude that God is at least unresponsive, if not wicked; and they turn away from him. They "know" God does not reward those who seek him. Such people could very profitably examine the examples of faith in this chapter. The tense of two verbs may help here. Both participles, "one who comes" (προσερχόμενον, *proserchomenon*) and "who earnestly seek" (ἐκζητοῦσιν, *ekzētousin*) are present tenses. This indicates continual coming and continual seeking. God does not respond to the occasional seeker. One must keep coming as a lifestyle. One must keep seeking as a regular, habitual predominant way of life. A single cry never indicates the real nature of our heart. A perpetual cry does.

11:7 By faith Noah, when warned about things not yet seen, in holy fear built an ark to save his family. By his faith he condemned the world and became heir of the righteousness that comes by faith.

Noah's expression of faith consisted of a construction project. He built an ark, a huge boat 450 feet long. Until 1858 the largest boat besides the ark was the P&O liner called

"Himalaya," which was barely half as long as the ark! In that year Filby says, "Isambard Brunel launched the Great Eastern, 692 feet by 83 feet by 30 feet . . . five times the tonnage of any ship then afloat."[8] It was another forty years before a boat was built bigger than the Great Eastern.

When **warned** by God, Noah acted on things which could not be seen (cf. v. 1). He trusted the truth of the message given him by God. Though God is not named here as the source of the warning, it is so sure an inference that translators generally insert the word "God" with no special marking that it has been added. See notes on the word "warned" (χρηματίζω, chrēmatizō) at 8:5.

Jude gave one general clue of God's coming judgment on the ungodly, but his words seem to point to the second coming rather than the flood.

> Enoch, the seventh from Adam, prophesied about these men: "See, the Lord is coming with thousands upon thousands of his holy ones to judge everyone, and to convict all the ungodly of all the ungodly acts they have done in the ungodly way, and of all the harsh words ungodly sinners have spoken against him" (Jude 1:14-15).

Unless one gives an early date for Pseudepigraphical books, which no one seems to even suggest, there is no known information before this warning by which Noah could have anticipated the coming of a flood of the magnitude which the Bible describes. Only God's plans for this gigantic boat undergirded his pronouncement, "I am going to put an end to all people, for the earth is filled with violence because of them. I am surely going to destroy both them and the earth. So make yourself an ark . . ." (Gen 6:13-14).

The warning from God moved Noah "**in holy fear**" (εὐλα–βέομαι, eulabeomai). The verb appears in the NT elsewhere only where the Pharisees and Sadducees so strongly argue

---

[8]Frederick Filby, *The Flood Reconsidered* (Grand Rapids: Zondervan, 1971), pp. 92-93.

about the resurrection that the commander "was afraid" Paul would be torn to pieces by them (Acts 23:10). Bauer describes the adjective εὐλαβής, (*eulabēs*, "devout") as "in our lit. only of relig. attitudes *devout, God-fearing*" and the noun *eulabeia* ("reverent awe") as "in our lit. prob. only of reverant *awe* in the presence of God, *fear of God.*" The former is only in Luke 2:25; Acts 2:5 and 8:2 in the NT. Both NT occurrences of the latter are in Hebrews (5:7; 12:28). Louw and Nida suggest the verb means here "to obey, with the implication of awe and reverence for the source of a command," and would translate, "he obeyed (God) and built an ark."[9] One should be cautious about criticizing the use of fear in motivating people to respond to the gospel. Here God himself used fear to motivate Noah. It would result in saving his family.

The Genesis account said Noah "found favor in the eyes of the Lord" and that he was "a righteous man, blameless among the people of his time, and he walked with God" (Gen 6:8-9). Indeed, he was the first man in Genesis to be called "righteous." See Gen 6:9; 7:1; and Ezek 14:14,20. The verse reminds us that this righteousness came because he clung tenaciously to God. His was the righteousness that comes by faith. Noah acted on God's word alone, without any other "evidence" of the impending flood. Our text, like Genesis, applauds the character of Noah, not that of his family. Still, the family enjoyed the benefits of Noah's labors born out of his faith. Their own faith must have been greatly strengthened by the faith of their grand patriarch. Evidently there were no grandchildren till after the flood (Gen 11:10).

Noah is called "a preacher of righteousness" in 2 Peter 2:5, which must indicate some kind of open stand and clear message against the evil of his day. Mankind was so wicked the text says, "Every inclination of the thoughts of his heart was only evil all the time" (Gen 6:5). The NIV says, "By his faith (lit., "by which") he condemned the world." Technically the "which" could refer to salvation or the ark. But Ellingworth is

---

[9]LN, p. 467.

right that it is much better to relate the phrase "to the dominant theme of faith, as in v. 4."[10]

Thus the text says that by faith Noah did three things: (1) he built an ark; (2) he condemned the world; and (3) he became heir of the righteousness that comes by faith.

C. FAITH ILLUSTRATED BY ABRAHAM (11:8-19)

[8]By faith Abraham, when called to go to a place he would later receive as his inheritance, obeyed and went, even though he did not know where he was going. [9]By faith he made his home in the promised land like a stranger in a foreign country; he lived in tents, as did Isaac and Jacob, who were heirs with him of the same promise. [10]For he was looking forward to the city with foundations, whose architect and builder is God.

[11]By faith Abraham, even though he was past age — and Sarah herself was barren — was enabled to become a father because he[a] considered him faithful who had made the promise. [12]And so from this one man, and he as good as dead, came descendants as numerous as the stars in the sky and as countless as the sand on the seashore.

[13]All these people were still living by faith when they died. They did not receive the things promised; they only saw them and welcomed them from a distance. And they admitted that they were aliens and strangers on earth. [14]People who say such things show that they are looking for a country of their own. [15]If they had been thinking of the country they had left, they would have had opportunity to return. [16]Instead, they were longing for a better country — a heavenly one. Therefore God is not ashamed to be called their God, for he has prepared a city for them.

[17]By faith Abraham, when God tested him, offered Isaac as a sacrifice. He who had received the promises was about

---

[10]Ellingworth, p. 579.

to sacrifice his one and only son, [18]even though God had said to him, "It is through Isaac that your offspring[b] will be reckoned."[c] [19]Abraham reasoned that God could raise the dead, and figuratively speaking, he did receive Isaac back from death.

[a]*11 Or By faith even Sarah, who was past age, was enabled to bear children because she*   [b]*18* Greek *seed*   [c]*18* Gen. 21:12

This chapter gives more space to discussing the faith of **Abraham** than of anyone else, vv. 8-19. This is proper, for he is held up before Christians as the main model of faith in Romans 4:1-25; Galatians 3:6-9 and James 2:20-24. Three main illustrations from Abraham's life are chosen here to display his faith. (1) He obeyed God's call to go to a new unknown land. (2) He became able to have a son when he was too old. (3) He was willing to offer his only son Isaac.

11:8 By faith Abraham, when called to go to a place he would later receive as his inheritance, obeyed and went, even though he did not know where he was going.

Abraham was so important to the Jews that they said he was one of five possessions God took to himself in his world: the Law, heaven and earth, Abraham, Israel, and the Temple (M Aboth 6:10). They said Abraham had performed the whole Law before it was given (M Kidd. 4:14). Several works in varying amounts embellish the Biblical data relating his struggles with the surrounding idolatry and his teaching people various subjects, especially the laws of God. Josephus tells the story of Abraham in *Antiquities,* I.vi.5-xvii.1 (I.148-256) in which he includes citations from numerous ancient sources that describe Abraham, but are no longer extant. Of the three incidents presented in Hebrews, Josephus gives the greatest space to the sacrifice of Isaac.[11]

---

[11]Kaugmann Kohler, "Abraham — In Apocryphal and Rabbinical Literature," *The Jewish Encyclopedia;* I:85-87.

The Muslim faith also gives great honor to Abraham. Gottheil says, "Of all the Biblical personages mentioned in the Koran, Abraham is undoubedly the most important." He says further that Mohammed claimed "that Abraham was the real founder of the religion that he himself was preaching; that Islam was merely a restatement of the old religion of Abraham and not a new faith now preached for the first time;" and that Mohammed even went so far as to assert that Abraham built Kaaba, the holy house of Islam in Mecca, and that the son he offered was Ishmael, not Isaac.[12]

The first illustration in Hebrews of Abraham's faith concerns his original call by God. The Greek text gives a sharp contrast by putting both of the first two verbs at the beginning of the sentence, "By faith, being **called**, Abraham obeyed . . ." His obedience was immediate. Even the present participle encourages this idea of immediacy, "While he being called," not "After he was called," as the aorist participle would have suggested. Genesis gives the same impression of immediate obedience. The very next words after God's call and promise are, "So Abram left, as the Lord had told him" (Gen 12:4). At this point he did not know the country, the distance, not even the exact direction of his destination. Attridge suggests that he learned what land God had in mind for him only after arriving in Canaan.[13] He simply obeyed God's call.

11:9 By faith he made his home in the promised land like a stranger in a foreign country; he lived in tents, as did Isaac and Jacob, who were heirs with him of the same promise.

Even when he arrived in the promised land, Abraham lived in tents, **like a stranger in a foreign land**. It is ironic for the owner of the land to have to live in temporary quarters.

---

[12]Richard Gottheil, "Abraham — In Mohammedan Legend," *The Jewish Encyclopedia*; I:87-90.

[13]Harold Attridge, *The Epistle to the Hebrews* (Philadelphia: Fortress Press, 1989), p.322. There is some uncertainty in the Bible text as to whether his call came while in Ur of Chaldees, as Acts 7:2-4 indicates, or when he had already arrived at Haran with his father, as Gen 11:31-12:4 indicates.

Acts 7:5 says, "He gave him no inheritance here, not even a foot of ground. But God promised him that he and his descendants after him would possess the land, even though at that time Abraham had no child." In a similar situation Paul described an adolescent heir, treated like a slave while a minor, though he owned the whole estate (Gal 4:1-2). Several words in this chapter show Abraham's lack of connection with the land. He "made his home" (παρῴκησεν, *parōkēsen*, lit., "live as a stranger") in the promised land like a "stranger" (ἀλλοτρίαν, *allotrian*).

The first of these words appears only here and in Luke 24:18, where the two disciples heading for Emmaus find Jesus so out of touch with current events about the Messiah's death that they conclude that Jesus must only "live as a stranger" [BAGD definition] in Jerusalem. The NIV omits the "stranger" idea by translating, "Are you the only one living in Jerusalem . . ." The noun form παροικία, (*paroikia*, "a sojourn in a strange place") is only used of the Jews in Egyptian bondage (Acts 13:17) and of Christians in this world (1 Pet 1:17). The noun form πάροικος, (*paroikos*, "stranger, alien") describes Moses in Egypt (Acts 7:29), Jews in Egypt (Acts 7:6), Christians in the world (1 Pet 2:11) and Gentiles who through Christ are no longer "foreigners" and "aliens" (*paroikoi*) of God's people.

Part of the reason God repeatedly directed the Jews to deal kindly with the aliens among them was that they had been aliens in Egypt. So Exodus 23:9; Leviticus 19:33-34; 25:35; Deuteronomy 10:18-19 and 23:17. For additional Scriptures on the special treatment he required for aliens see Exodus 22:21; Leviticus 23:22; Deuteronomy 24:14-21 and 26:11-13. There is an additional reminder of earth as a temporary residence of God's people in Leviticus 25:23, "The land must not be sold permanently, because the land is mine and you are but aliens and my tenants."

The idea of Canaan as the **inheritance** of Abraham, and by extension, the Jewish people, must be modified by what was said in Hebrews 3-4 about the people's not entering God's rest. Their early and perpetual breaking of the covenant must also preclude any claim to the offer God made in the covenant. Jews who resisted Jesus fell from this inheritance. Only a remnant remained. All believers became participants in this inheritance, and most of these were Gentiles (Rom 9-11).

11:10 For he was looking forward to the city with foundations, whose architect and builder is God.

Jesus has been appointed heir of all things (Heb 1:2). Abraham was destined to share in Jesus' inheritance. Though God gave him the land replacing the seven nations who were there before him (Acts 13:19), Abraham knew that this was not the best part of the inheritance. The **promise** God gave to Abraham made him look forward to "a city with foundations, whose architect and builder is God."[14] He also knew that the promise was not obtainable by law but by faith. "Abram believed the Lord, and he credited it to him as righteousness" (Gen 15:6). See also Romans 4:15ff. Galatians 3:18 adds, " If the inheritance depends on the law, then it no longer depends on a promise; but God in his grace gave it to

---

[14]Here God is called an "architect" (τεχνίτης, *technitēs*) and "builder" (δημιουργός, *dēmiourgos*). Silversmiths (Acts 19:24, 25, and variant in 38) and potters (2 Clement 8:2) were also called "architects" (BAGD, 814). Rev 18:22 makes a broad application, "no craftsman of any craft will ever be found in you again." Lampe (V,1392) includes makers of perfumes, haridressers, cooks, astrologers, copyists of scriptures and surgeons. He finds it often used of God as the architect of the universe and supreme artist.

The second word only appears here in the NT and in the LXX only in 2 Macc 4:1. Its cognate verb, δημιουργέω (*dēmiourgeō*, "to be a workman"), though not in the NT, is in the LXX in Wisdom 15:11; 2 Macc 10:2; and 4 Macc 7:8. The word becomes tainted in Gnosticism as a term for an "inferior or evil creator" (Lampe, II,341). Theologians and church historians transliterate it as "Demiurge."

The words are such close synonyms with τέκτων (*tektōn*, "carpenter") that LN can hardly differentiate. "There is every reason to believe that in biblical times one who was regarded as a *tektōn* would be skilled in the use of wood and stone and possibly even metal" (LN 1:520). Jesus, the Son of God, was a carpenter (Mark 6:3), known as the son of a carpenter (Matt 13:55), while on earth.

Abraham through a promise." Even the birth of a son, the second incident used here to show Abraham's faith, was the result of a promise (Gal 4:23).

The beauty of the offer of God through the gospel is that Christians become heirs with Abraham of this grand promise from God. " If you belong to Christ, then you are Abraham's seed, and heirs according to the promise" (Gal 3:29). Even Gentiles can participate equally with Jews as "fellow citizens with God's people and members of God's household" (Eph. 2:19). This is the mystery of the gospel that had been made especially plain to Paul (Eph 3:1-21). The end result is that all of God's children are "heirs of God and co-heirs with Christ" (Rom 8:17) in "an inheritance that can never perish" (1 Pet 1:4).

Abraham's real expectation is a divinely built city, not a wind-blown country. Bengel reminds us that "a tent has no foundations."[15] In the ancient world cities were places of permanence and culture, of refuge and commerce. Pygmy city-states and giant empires had a city as their center. God, indeed, "has prepared a city for them" (11:16), "the heavenly Jerusalem, the city of the living God" (12:22). This is what the readers had already acknowledged as their "better and lasting possessions" (10:34). It is natural for Jerusalem and its location on Mt. Zion to become the terminology of promise for the people of God. The most famous description of this future city of God is found in Revelation 21-22. The most widely known extrabiblical description of this city is probably Augustine's *The City of God*.[16] McCown explains that "whereas Judaism and the gospels had a distinctly agricultural background, Christianity almost immediately gravitated toward the city. . . . No book in the Bible is more thoroughly bound to the city than the book of Revelation."[17]

---

[15]Cited by Ellingworth, p. 584.

[16]Random House has one common edition, for example, Saint Augustine, *The City of God*, translated by Marcus Dods (New York: Random House, The Modern Library), 1950.

[17]C.C. McCown, "City," in *The Interpreter's Dictionary of the Bible* (Nashville: Abingdon Press), IV,632-638, p.637.

11:11 By faith Abraham, even though he was past age — and Sarah herself was barren — was enabled to become a father because he considered him faithful who had made the promise.

The second incident used to express Abraham's faith is his miraculous return to fertility, accompanied by Sarah's rejuvenation. Both Abraham and Sarah were "barren," "**past age.**" Yet through faith God enabled them to have the promised son, Isaac. Faith in this instance was trusting that God was faithful, when all the physical evidence pointed the other way. Paul said God "is able to do immeasurably more than all we ask or imagine, according to his power that is at work within us" (Eph 3:20). In this instance, by faith Abraham and Sarah reached out into that capability beyond where others could see and knew that God would do the impossible thing, because he had said he would.

This was not a virgin birth, but it was definitely a miraculous birth. What could not happen did happen "because he (or she) considered him faithful who had made the promise." There is a textual difficulty here. The NIV margin more closely follows the established Greek text, "Or: *By faith even Sarah, who was past age, was enabled to bear children because she.*" Abraham's ability to have the promised son was dependent on Sarah's fertility. Thus whether Sarah alone was "past age," or both of them were, makes no difference in the final outcome.

11:12 And so from this one man, and he as good as dead, came descendants as numerous as the stars in the sky and as countless as the sand on the seashore.

The NIV expression, "as good as dead," which it also uses for the same form in Romans 4:19, is so soft it is misleading if not plainly erroneous. Νενεκρωμένος (*nenekrōmenos*, "having died") is a perfect participle. It means he had died with all its effects including barren childlessness and an evidently thwarted promise. Both passages also speak of Sarah's deadness. If there is something in genetics by which women come past age and men do not, it is not indicated by the text.

The promise was that, "I will surely bless you and make your descendants as numerous as the stars in the sky and as the sand on the seashore" (Gen 22:17). See also Genesis 15:5; 26:4; 32:12. Moses told the people of Israel as they were about to enter Canaan that they had become as numerous as the stars and the sand, i.e., the promise was fulfilled (Deut 1:10; 10:22; 28:62). Eventually, the addition of Gentile believers to Abraham's seed would expand this number even more. Isaiah challenged those who sought the Lord to "look unto the rock whence ye are hewn, and to the hole of the pit whence ye are digged. Look unto Abraham your father, and unto Sarah that bare you: for I called him alone [Or: "when he was but one" NIV first edition, 1975], and blessed him, and increased him (Isa 51:1-2, KJV).

It is ironic that physical genealogical descent from Abraham which came about through faith would later come to be used as a substitute for faith. See Matt 3:9; Luke 3:8; Matt 8:10-12; John 8:39; Rom 2:28-29; 4:11-12; 9:6.

11:13 All these people were still living by faith when they died. They did not receive the things promised; they only saw them and welcomed them from a distance. And they admitted that they were aliens and strangers on earth.

The author pauses for a parenthetical admiration of these giants of faith. **"All these people were still living by faith when they died."** He has been urging his readers to be faithful "till the end" (3:14) or "till the very end" (6:11). See also 4:9-11; 5:11-6:6; 9:27 and 10:26-31. Now he shows that the "greats" of faith kept the faith and died still waiting for the unfulfilled promises. He will remind them again at the end of the chapter (v. 39) that "none of them received what had been promised." Faith sharpened their vision and strengthened their commitment to God's future provisions for them.

They **"saw"** and **"welcomed"** the promises **"from a distance."** Abraham "rejoiced at the thought of seeing my day; he saw it and was glad" (John 8:56). Moses "regarded disgrace for the sake of Christ [i.e., the Messiah] as of greater value than the treasures of Egypt, because he was looking ahead to his reward" (11:26). Peter says of the prophets in general,

> Concerning this salvation, the prophets, who spoke of the grace that was to come to you, searched intently and with the greatest care, trying to find out the time and circumstances to which the Spirit of Christ in them was pointing when he predicted the sufferings of Christ and the glories that would follow. It was revealed to them that they were not serving themselves but you, when they spoke of the things that have now been told you by those who have preached the gospel to you by the Holy Spirit sent from heaven. Even angels long to look into these things (1 Pet 1:10-12).

"Seeing what was ahead, he [David] spoke of the resurrection of the Christ" (Acts 2:31). Isaiah saw so many things about Jesus and the whole Messianic era which he brought that he has been called "the fifth Evangelist."[18] Jesus told his disciples that others knew enough about the coming days of the Messiah but that they "longed to see what you see but did not see it, and to hear what you hear but did not hear it" (Matt 13:17).

The word for "welcomed" (ἀσπάζομαι, *aspazomai*) is normally used of greeting people, and the NT often uses it in this way. The end of Hebrews has this normal use twice (13:24). Ellingworth thinks that "The unusual, apparently impersonal object here suggests that for the author, the heavenly city is primarily a community."[19] **They admitted that they were aliens** (ξένοι, *xenoi*) **and strangers** (παρεπίδημοι, *parepidēmoi*) **on earth**. This is the perspective God had taught them in Leviticus 25:23 when he prohibited permanent land sales. The words "on earth" clearly contrast with the "heavenly" country (v. 16) for which they are longing. Christians join the patriarchs in this feeling of anticipation. This world is not our

---

[18]Albert Barnes, *Notes on the Old Testament: Isaiah* (Grand Rapids: Baker, n.d. Reprinted from the 1851 edition published by Blackie & Son, London), volume 1, p. 2.

[19]Ellingworth, p. 594.

home. We are looking for "the city that is to come" (13:14),
"the kingdom that cannot be shaken" (12:28). In their early
days of faith the readers had held their possessions of this
world very lightly (10:32-34).

**11:14 People who say such things show that they are looking
for a country of their own. 11:15 If they had been thinking
of the country they had left, they would have had opportunity to return.**

This admission[20] of a temporary status also confirmed the
fact they they were looking for another country which they
could call their own. This was certainly not Ur of Chaldees
from which they had come. They could have returned at any
time, but Abraham made his servant swear (Gen 24:4-9) that he
would not let Isaac return to the country they "left," ἐκβαίνω
(*ekbainō*). This word appears nowhere else in the NT. Here the
structure is, "If (but they were not) . . ." as in 4:8; 8:4 and 7.

**11:16 Instead, they were longing for a better country — a
heavenly one. Therefore God is not ashamed to be called
their God, for he has prepared a city for them.**

For this faith in the future which God had in mind, God **is
not ashamed to be called their God**. Stated positively, God is
proud to be called their God. We met the same idea in 2:11
where Jesus is not ashamed to call those who are made holy,
"brothers." Beginning in Genesis 17:7-8 the OT has numerous statements of God's offer to be their God and they his
people. Leviticus 26:12 says it succinctly, "I will walk among
you and be your God, and you will be my people" (Lev
26:12). This same relationship is repeated in the new
covenant as was already mentioned in Hebrews 8:10 quoting
Jeremiah 31:33, "I will be their God, and they will be my people." In addition one should consider the hundreds of

instances where God is simply called "their God" or "the Lord your God."

God's **preparation of a city** for them is a promise very much like Jesus' promise to the disciples in John 14:1-3. Since the father and the son had worked very closely together in the preparation of this world, it is fitting that they would both be involved in the preparation of the next. God had "prepared" the land of Canaan for his people (Exod 23:20). The LXX used the same word as in Hebrews. God has "prepared" a dinner (Matt 22:4), a kingdom (Matt 25:34), indeed, many things (1 Cor 2:9) for his people. God "prepared" a "place" to escape the dragon for the woman who bore a son (Rev 12:6). The holy city which descends from heaven has been "prepared" as a bride adorned for her husband (Rev 21:2).

11:17 By faith Abraham, when God tested him, offered Isaac as a sacrifice.

The third illustration of Abraham's faith concerns his offering of Isaac as a sacrifice. Our text says, "God tested him." James says God tempts no one; rather one's own evil desire tempts him (James 1:13-14). Does God generally not tempt people, but broke the general rule on this occasion? That is not very palatable. Did a Demiurge tempt him, i.e., some intermediate angel? This is even weaker. Should we say a "testing" to let one's true character become known is not the same as a "tempting" which would lure one into sin? James' discussion continues in this direction (James 1:13-18).

The Rabbis taught that Abraham faithfully withstood ten temptations, of which this one was the greatest (M Avoth 5:3).[21] The Midrash Rabbah on Numbers (XVII.2) says when

---

[21]J. Israelstam has included a list of these ten temptations with his translation of "Aboth," in *The Talmud*, Edited by I. Epstein (London: The Soncino Press, 1935), Avoth, p. 59, n. 6. "I ARN Ch. XXXIII amplifies: Two trials at the time he was bidden to leave Haran, two with his two sons, two with his two wives, one in the wars of the Kings, one at the covenant 'between the pieces' (Gen XV), one in Ur of the Chaldees (where, according to a tradition, he had been thrown into a furnace whence he came out unharmed).

the test with Isaac was finished, Abraham asked God never to put him to any test again, because it almost destroyed him. After discussing this trial another midrash asks the penetrating question, "Can you do what Abraham did?" (Midrash Rabbah on Genesis LV.1).

He who had received the promises was about to sacrifice his one and only son,

The word προσφέρω (*prospherō*, "offered . . . as a sacrifice") appears twice in verse 17. The first time is a perfect tense drawing the deed plus its consequences before our eyes. The second is an imperfect tense showing that he was in the midst of doing the sacrifice. The NIV translates "**was about to sacrifice.**" Although adding the words "about to" may be an accepted way of translating an imperfect tense, in my judgment it appears unnecessarily interpretive here. This would narrowly limit the sacrifice to killing the victim. If the preparation for sacrificing is also viewed as part of the "bringing near" of a sacrifice, then Abraham would be already in the process of sacrificing when God stopped him.[22] Turner calls this verb in Hebrews 11:17 "a conative or Desiderative imperfect, of incomplete or interrupted action" and translates, "*tried to offer.*"[23]

Strangely, Louw and Nida give no hint that any meaning of this verb falls in domain # 53, "Religious Activities" or that it is used for bringing a sacrifice to God. The LXX uses the

---

II ARN Ch. XXXVI speaks of ten trials, but names only nine: (i) at Ur; (ii) *Get thee out of thy land* . . . (Gen. XII, 1); (iii) The famine when he left Haran (Ibid. v. 10); (iv) Sarah at Pharaoh's palace; (v) Sarah at Abimelech's; (vi) Circumcision; (vii) The covenant '*between the pieces*'; (vii) With Isaac; (ix) With Ishmael. P.R.E. contains numbers II, III (the latter as two separate trials), IV, VI-IX of the above list and adds his hiding underground from Nimrod for thirteen years, and the wars of the Kings (including the plight of Lot)."

[22]The NIV uses the expression "about to" twenty-nine times in the NT, in Hebrews only here and 8:5. Most of these use the word μέλλω (*mellō*, "be about to") or some similar expectation of anticipated beginning.

[23]Nigel Turner, *Syntax*, Volume III, in James Moulton's *A Grammar of New Testament Greek*, p. 65.

verb dozens of times in describing the sacrifices in the book
of Leviticus, half of its OT appearances. Vorlander recognizes
this "connection with the OT sacrifice system."[24] Upon reading the book of Hebrews one should notice the connection of
this verb with sacrificing in 5:1, 3; 8:3, 4; 9:7, 9, 14, 25, 28;
10:1, 2, 8, 11, 12; 11:4 and here). Once it is of "offering"
prayers to God (5:7). Only once in Hebrews is the verb not
used in the sense of an offering to God (12:7).

The editors of the Greek text make verses 17-19 a single
sentence. The following indentation may help clarify this
interconnectedness which is diminished in the NIV by dividing it into three separate sentences:

"By faith Abraham offered Isaac
    while he was being tested;
and he was offering his only [son] —
    [i.e.,] the one who had received the promises [was offer-
        ing his only [son]]
    [i.e., the one] to whom it was said that 'In Isaac your off-
        spring will be reckoned' —
        after he had reasoned that God was also able to
        raise him from the dead
            from whence he also received him figuratively."

Abraham **had received the promises**. This was already
said of Abraham in 6:13-15 and 7:6. The heirs also held these
promises (Heb 6:17; 9:15; 10:36; 11:9, 17, 33). Yet 11:13 and
39 said they did not receive the promises. The NIV aims to
solve this problem by translating "promise" as "what was (or:
has been) promised" or "things promised" (6:15, 17; 10:36;
11:13, 33, 39). Though the same word is used in each
instance, this differentiates between the word given, and the
deed fulfilled. Abraham knew what God said would happen,
but it had not yet been done. Hebrews is full of such forward-
looking expectation of God's rewards that are still future.

In one sense Isaac was not Abraham's **one and only son**.
He had Ishmael; and after Sarah died, by Keturah he had six

---

[24]NIDNTT, 2:41.

more sons named in Genesis 25:1-2. The phrase "one and only" is an attempt to express in more comfortable English an old phrase "only begotten" for the word μονογενής (*monogenēs*). BAGD translates the word "only, unique." The lineage of the Messiah would pass uniquely through Isaac. Christians are most familiar with this word from John 3:16, "For God so loved the world that he gave his **one and only** Son, that whoever believes in him shall not perish but have eternal life" (NIV). The word is used of the only son of a widow, whom Jesus raised to life (Luke 7:12), of Jairus' daughter (Luke 8:42), of the boy with convulsions (Luke 9:38), and of Isaac (Heb 11:17). Usually the NT uses this word to show Jesus' unique relation to God (John 1:14, 18; 3:16, 18; 1 John 4:9).

11:18 even though God had said to him, "It is through Isaac that your offspring will be reckoned."

The words **"even though"**are added by the NIV to express the unusual contrast between verses 17 and 18. The verse quotes Genesis 21:12. While Abraham did have another son, Ishmael, it is not this son of the slave woman through whom Abraham's covenant descendants would come. God's choice fell on Isaac to be the son of the covenant. God stopped Abraham from taking Isaac's life as Genesis 22 dramatically relates.

11:19 Abraham reasoned that God could raise the dead, and figuratively speaking, he did receive Isaac back from death.

Both were from God: both the promise of future children through Isaac and the requirement to offer him as a human sacrifice. That put Abraham in a dilemma. (1) The boy must die. (2) This boy must have future children. (3) The only conclusion that fit both of these was for God to raise Isaac back to life again after he died as a sacrifice.

There is no record that Abraham had ever seen a resurrection or had information about resurrection from the dead. The lack of our information does not prove that he did not have this information. It is hard to imagine that the ancients never knew anything but those things which we are sure they knew. Perhaps the translation of Enoch was the nearest thing to a resurrection that had happened up to Abraham's lifetime. But Moses may have been the first one to learn from God what had happened to Enoch. Abraham believed God could do anything. In the current dilemma he **reasoned** that God would do this unprecedented thing. Since Abraham reasoned that Isaac would die and God would raise him back to life, in his mind **he did receive Isaac back from death**. Our author says this can be called "figuratively speaking" he received him back from death.

D. FAITH ILLUSTRATED BY ISAAC, JACOB, AND JOSEPH (11:20-22)

[20]**By faith Isaac blessed Jacob and Esau in regard to their future.**
[21]**By faith Jacob, when he was dying, blessed each of Joseph's sons, and worshiped as he leaned on the top of his staff.**
[22]**By faith Joseph, when his end was near, spoke about the exodus of the Israelites from Egypt and gave instructions about his bones.**

11:20 By faith Isaac blessed Jacob and Esau in regard to their future.

Very briefly Isaac, Jacob and Joseph are presented as heroes of faith. **Isaac blessed Jacob** (Gen 27:27-29) **and Esau** (Gen 27:39-40). The whole story of deception by which Jacob stole the special blessing from Esau and had to flee for his life consumes Genesis 27. Their reunion is reported in Genesis 32-33. In Hebrews the term for the **future**, "the coming things" (μελλόντων, *mellontōn*) usually is used for spiritual things concerning the salvation which Christ brought (1:14; 9:11 variant; 10:1), if not the future world (2:5; 6:5; 13:14). There is no hint in Isaac's words in Genesis that he was talking about anything more than physical prosperity of Jacob's descendants and their being honored by surrounding peoples. The blessing for Esau has only physical prosperity and eventually throwing off his brother's yoke.

11:21 By faith Jacob, when he was dying, blessed each of Joseph's sons, and worshiped as he leaned on the top of his staff.

Jacob is credited with two deeds of faith. He **blessed each of Joseph's sons** (Gen 48:1-22), and he **worshiped** on his staff (Gen 47:29-31). The Genesis account indicates that Jacob knew very well what he was doing when he crossed his arms and elevated Ephraim above Manasseh, although this displeased Joseph. Jacob himself had been elevated above his older twin Esau. And Joseph had been favored above his eleven brothers, though not with the blessing of the lineage. The touching with the right hand is the only indication that Ephraim is preferred. There is only one blessing recorded. Jacob asks God to "bless *these boys*. May *they* be called by my name . . . and may *they* increase greatly." One might almost expect the fuller blessings of all the tribes to be noted here from Genesis 49. By the singling out of the proper grandson for preeminence, Jacob was exercising remarkable faith.

Jacob called Joseph to him and made him take an oath that he would bury him back in Canaan where "my fathers" were buried. Then he "worshiped as he leaned on the top of his staff." His heart was in the promised land. His orientation was still looking toward the future that God had promised even when he was in the midst of the comforts and safety provided for his family in Egypt. It is a strong evidence of faith when adequate care for one's family does not dim the anticipation of the better blessings which God has promised for the future.

11:22 By faith Joseph, when his end was near, spoke about the exodus of the Israelites from Egypt and gave instructions about his bones.

Joseph **spoke about the exodus of the Israelites from Egypt** (Gen 50: 24-26). He referred back to the oath God had given Abraham that after four hundred years in Egypt he would bring his descendants back to the land of Canaan (Gen 15:13-21). Then he made his brothers swear an oath that when they returned they would bring **his bones** up with them out of Egypt. Moses brought Joseph's bones with him when Israel came out of Egypt (Exod 13:19). They were eventually buried in Shechem in the land which Jacob bought from the sons of Hamor (Josh 24:32). It is easy to forget that they carried his bones around with them during the forty years in the desert. It is also easy to forget that they were kept somewhere in somebody's house during the four hundred years in Egypt.

E. FAITH ILLUSTRATED BY MOSES (11:23-28)

[23]By faith Moses' parents hid him for three months after he was born, because they saw he was no ordinary child, and they were not afraid of the king's edict.

[24]By faith Moses, when he had grown up, refused to be known as the son of Pharaoh's daughter. [25]He chose to be mistreated along with the people of God rather than to enjoy the pleasures of sin for a short time. [26]He regarded disgrace for the sake of Christ as of greater value than the treasures of Egypt, because he was looking ahead to his reward. [27]By faith he left Egypt, not fearing the king's anger; he persevered because he saw him who is invisible. [28]By faith he kept the Passover and the sprinkling of blood, so that the destroyer of the firstborn would not touch the firstborn of Israel.

Five incidents of faith are chosen from Moses' life. Actually three are his. His parents' hiding him at birth is reported almost as an introduction to his life of faith. The people's passing through the Red Sea then would be almost a conclusion of these examples. Moses lived another forty years of great faith after these events. Perhaps his faith is best expressed by the faith-deeds of the people he led to trust

God. By faith Moses himself (1) refused the privileges of being a royal son, (2) left Egypt, and (3) kept the Passover and the sprinkling of blood.

11:23 By faith Moses' parents hid him for three months after he was born, because they saw he was no ordinary child, and they were not afraid of the king's edict.

Moses' birth is a nice change after dealing with the deaths of Jacob, Isaac (twice seen dying) and Abraham, whose body was dead. What did Moses' parents see in their baby that "he was no ordinary child?" What made them preserve him from the mandated death? There must have been something more than a mother's natural love for her baby or the Nile River would have been filled with babies in baskets whom caring parents were trying to save. Let us address three subjects: the meaning of the word "ordinary," the involvement of God, and the involvement of the whole family. First, what does the phrase "**no ordinary child**" mean? The Hebrew in Exodus 2:2 simply called him טוֹב (*tōv*, Hebrew for "good"), which is about as ambiguously general as a word could be. The LXX used a rare word to describe the baby, ἀστεῖος (*asteios* "good"). This same rare word is in the NT only in Acts 7:20 and Hebrews 11:23, both of baby Moses. In the LXX this word describes baby Moses (Exod 2:2), Eglon, King of Moab (Judg 3:17 – the Hebrew calls him "fat"), Judith (Judith 11:23), Susanna (Daniel LXX Susanna 2 or 7), and the "good" resolve of Eleazar not to renounce the law (2 Macc 6:23). Balaam's road/way in resisting God was "not good" (Num 22:32).

Second, Acts 7:20 ties God to the description of the baby. The Greek phrase there is ἀστεῖος τῷ θεῷ (*asteios tō theō*), literally "good to God," i.e., good with relation to God. BAGD explains the use in this verse as an ethical dative, "*in the sight of God,* hence with superlative force . . . *very.*"[25] The NIV

---

[25]The Hebrew language has a similar ethical dative. BDB (p. 42) reminds us that in the Hebrew language the word "God" may be used, "as characterizing mighty things in nature." Thus mountains, cedars or stars "of God" would be "*mighty mountains,*" etc.

translates Acts 7:20 simply, "he was no ordinary child." The NIV margin shows more precisely how the Greek text of Acts 7:20 relates this goodness to God by translating, *"was fair in the sight of God."*

Third, he was hidden by "**his fathers.**" In the NT, like the book of Hebrews, the word "fathers" commonly means one's ancestors (Heb 1:1; 3:9; 8:9). Exodus had only said his mother hid him. In some way this three month effort to conceal the baby must have involved the whole family — mother, father, brother, sister, grandparents, great grandparents, neighbors, aunts and uncles. In this time of crisis births would be more certainly noticed, especially births of baby boys. The Egyptians were not dumb. It would be hard to hide from them any signs of a pregnant woman or a newborn child. One slipup by any Israelite would have betrayed their precious secret to the Egyptians. How would a mother feel when she knew that the community was protecting the baby of her sister or cousin and they had not protected her baby from death? Surely God helped them.

We know the edict of death had just recently been given because Moses had an older brother Aaron who escaped the fresh decree that newborn baby boys must die (Exod 1:11-22). The midwives feared God rather than the king and let the boys live. Similar divine protection later surrounded the birth of the Messiah in the face of Herod's murderous intentions. God led the wise men to directly disobey Herod's command (Matt 2:8-12, 16). Joseph also eluded Herod's plot by using the recently received rich gifts in order to hire the fastest transportation possible in the nighttime escape to Egypt (Matt 2:13-14).

A second evidence of the faith of Moses' parents was that **they were not afraid of the king's edict.** It is hard to believe that there was no fear in their hearts when this terrible pronouncement was made, but fear did not determine their actions. Hence it could be said that they were not afraid of the king's edict. Moses himself displayed this same courage in the second illustration of his faith, his departure from Egypt (v. 27).

11:24 By faith Moses, when he had grown up, refused to be known as the son of Pharaoh's daughter.

Moses is first introduced as a baby (v. 23). Now his adult decisions of faith are sampled. When he **refused to be known as the son of Pharaoh's daughter**, he turned his back on the fabulous personal wealth of a Pharaoh, the national wealth of the mightiest nation on earth, and the tremendous treasures of its culture, influence and prestige. And he is commended for it. The examples of this chapter are certainly not presented as foolish choices of faith. It is difficult for Christians of the western world to appreciate this kind of decision. Over and over people are praised for seeking and using positions of power and wealth to enhance Christianity. Yet at a deeper level all understand Paul's words,

> I consider that our present sufferings are not worth comparing with the glory that will be revealed in us. The creation waits in eager expectation for the sons of God to be revealed. For the creation was subjected to frustration, not by its own choice, but by the will of the one who subjected it, in hope that the creation itself will be liberated from its bondage to decay and brought into the glorious freedom of the children of God (Rom 8:18-21).
>
> For our light and momentary troubles are achieving for us an eternal glory that far outweighs them all. So we fix our eyes not on what is seen, but on what is unseen. For what is seen is temporary, but what is unseen is eternal (2 Cor 4:17-18).

11:25 He chose to be mistreated along with the people of God rather than to enjoy the pleasures of sin for a short time.

Was Moses masochistic? Did he just like suffering? No. He saw something in God's future for God's people that was a far greater reward than Pharaoh's future apart from God. The word "suffer with" (συγκακουχέω, *synkakoucheō*) is only here in the NT, never in LXX, rare in the church fathers. Even without the prefix "*syn*" (with) it appears only in Hebrews 11:37 and 13:3 in the NT, but three times in the LXX (3 Kings

[=English 1 Kings] 2:26 [twice] and 11:39, and rarely in the church fathers. The readers had made a similar choice of "co-suffering" with those in prison (10:34). The exact word in that verse is συμπαθέω (*sympatheō*) from which the English word "sympathy" is derived. BAGD even translates the word *"sympathize with, have* or *show sympathy with."* This word appears in the NT elsewhere only in Hebrews 4:15, where Jesus is said to "sympathize with our weaknesses."

Moses chose against **the pleasures of sin**. His position in Egypt would let him explore many of the indulgences Solomon had examined — pleasure, laughter, wine, great projects, horticulture, money, a harem, learning, work (Eccl 2). There was a certain "pleasure" in them all. But like Solomon, Moses also found them quite unfulfilling, "meaningless," "vanity." The imperfect tense of the verb ἀπέβλεπεν (*apeblepen,* **"was looking ahead"**) in verse 26, indicates that he kept looking off into the future again and again. Finally he made a decision. Both verbs **"chose"** (ἑλόμενος, *helomenos*) and **"regarded"** (ἡγησάμενος, *hēgesamenos*) are aorist tenses showing a single decisive event.

11:26 He regarded disgrace for the sake of Christ as of greater value than the treasures of Egypt, because he was looking ahead to his reward.

As Moses examined the faith of "these slaves of ours," he found something far more significant and satisfying than anything Egypt could offer. There were some ancient roots they had that reached farther back than Egypt's history, and some expectations that reached much farther forward than Egypt's anticipations. There was a reward much larger and clearer than the foggy sayings of Egyptian soothsayers. There was something about a "Messiah" (Hebrew for "Christ" v. 26) sent from the single god over all gods, who simply spoke and everything came to be. Moses was drawn to that. He could see the difference between being "rich in this present world" and putting one's hope in God, "who richly provides us with everything for our enjoyment" including a rich full future reward (1 Tim 6:17). What would Alexander the Great at his zenith, or other great men of the world, have done if confronted with such a message?

Ellingworth reminds us that Psalms 69:9 and 89:51 discuss the same "reproach" (ὀνειδισμός, *oneidismos*, v.26) which David found against those who choose for God. He enumerates the many times the NT uses these two Psalms.[26]

The text of Exodus tells the story of Moses' punishing the cruel Egyptian taskmaster at the time of the critical break with his position of favor in Egypt (Exod 2:11-15). It does not explain as fully as this NT text all that went into his decision. Nor does the NT text tell what incident first expressed his decision "to be mistreated along with the people of God rather than to enjoy the pleasures of sin." How did this additional information rise? Was it (1) from the creative insight of our author? Or (2) from some extrabiblical text, whether apocryphal, pseudepigraphical, rabbinic, Egyptian, etc.? Or (3) from some non-written oral tradition embellished with each retelling? Or (4) from God himself giving the author of Hebrews information he could not otherwise have known? How did the Gospel writers know what Jesus prayed when he was alone in the garden of Gethsemane (Matt 26:36-46 and parallels)? How can Peter tell us how this universe will end (2 Pet 3:10)? How could Moses know that the great flood covered "all the high mountains under the entire heavens" (Gen 7:19), or that God created the world by speaking it into existence (Gen 1:3, 6, 9, 11, 14, 20, 24, 26, 29; so Ps 33:9)? How could the author of Hebrews know what Jesus did in heaven (Heb 9:11-14, 24-28; 10:12-14)? There is a far more significant source here than astute scholarship or creative writing, or we are all in deep trouble.

11:27 By faith he left Egypt, not fearing the king's anger; he persevered because he saw him who is invisible.

Moses' second great deed of faith was also prompted by

---

[26]Ellingworth, p. 614.

his vision. This is probably Moses' second departure at the time of the Exodus. At his first departure he killed the Egyptian who was beating an Israelite. Exodus says, "When Pharaoh heard of this, he tried to kill Moses, but Moses fled from Pharaoh" (Exod 2:15). Although the text does not directly say Moses feared the Pharaoh, the account looks like he did. There could have been other motives besides fear which mingled in his rapid exit.

Forty years later he returned at God's direction, led in causing the ten plagues, and appeared always in command of the situation. When Moses left Pharaoh upon announcing the last plague, it was Moses who was angry (Exod 11:8). During the night when death struck, Pharaoh summoned Moses and told them to leave, and he added, almost timidly, "And also bless me" (Exod 12:32). The Egyptians also urged them to leave expressing their own fear that "otherwise we will all die!" Further the text relates the generous gifts the Egyptians gave the Israelites and explains, "The Lord had made the Egyptians favorably disposed toward the people" (Exod 12:31-36; so 11:3). The LXX adds the phrase "and by Pharaoh" to the Hebrew text of Exodus 11:3, "The LORD made the Egyptians favorably disposed toward the people, and Moses himself was highly regarded in Egypt by Pharaoh's officials and by the people [LXX "and by Pharaoh"]."

The word "persevered" (καρτερέω, kartereō) and its cognate forms appear only about a dozen times in the LXX, nowhere else in the NT. If this departure is his second, Moses took all the Israelites with him in departing. His persevering must have included convincing them all to start the Passover celebration, to leave the only home they knew, and not to collapse when trapped between the Egyptian army and the Red Sea. The last of these is expanded into its own statement of faith in the next verse. Perhaps one should paraphrase verse 27, "By faith Moses led two million slaves to march boldly out of the grip of the mightiest nation on earth, fearlessly plundering them as they went; and they were able to persevere in this daring deed primarily because of the persistent vision of one man who kept looking at the God who is invisible."

The NIV puts the word "because" in an odd place. Its grammatical structure more naturally relates the word *gar* ("because") to the whole second half of the verse, not just to the adverbial participle "seeing." It appears that NIV has ignored the conjunction ("because"), which it often does,[27] and interpreted the adverbial participal as a causal participal. The following structure may suggest a better translation:

> "By faith he left Egypt
>> not fearing the king's anger;
>
> for
>> as one seeing him who is invisible
> he persevered."

The present tense of the participle "seeing" indicates that he kept looking at the invisible one, over and over again. A sound vision continually held before us will strengthen us to do our finest deeds. When that perpetual vision is of the invisible God who can only be seen on earth with the mind's eye of faith, wonderful things happen. This is how to build faith. This was how Moses built his own faith that helped him overcome a hostile environment. This was how Moses' faith could turn a land full of crying, groaning slaves into a people whom God could use for his glory. HE "left Egypt." Indeed! Look at the train who followed in the wake of his faith. It is no accident that our author urges his readers to "fix your thoughts on Jesus" (3:1). "Let us fix our eyes on Jesus" (12:2). The book of Hebrews is full of looking at Jesus.

11:28 By faith he kept the Passover and the sprinkling of blood, so that the destroyer of the firstborn would not touch the firstborn of Israel.

Moses' third deed of faith was **keeping the Passover** and

---

[27]The NIV ignores 46 of the 91 occurrences of γάρ (*gar*, "because") in Hebrews. See the note at 2:5.

its attendant **sprinkling of blood** (v. 28). This was more than just "doing" the Passover. The verb is a perfect tense of ποιέω (*poieō*, to do). What he did had lasting consequences. It may be translated "instituted" the Passover. It was to be "a lasting ordinance" (Exod 12:24), "a day you are to commemorate; for the generations to come you shall celebrate it as a festival to the Lord — a lasting ordinance" (Exod 12:14). Its permanence is prescribed throughout the Pentateuch.

This first Passover was accompanied by the **sprinkling of the blood** of the Passover lamb on the top and both sides of the doorframe (Exod 12:21-23). When the Lord went through the land at midnight and struck dead the firstborn of every home and animal, he would not enter any house with the blood on the doorframe. No one knows how well Moses persuaded the people. No one knows how many Israelite families left their firstborn dead in Egypt that night because of their disobedient disdain of blood on their doors. No one knows how many Egyptians decided that night, like Moses had decided long before, to join the people of God in their privations rather than remain in wealthy, mourning Egypt. The text simply reports, "Many other people went up with them" (Exod 12:38).

The covenant at Mt. Sinai was confirmed by sprinkling blood on the people (Exod 24:3-8). Hyssop is mentioned in connection with various offerings (Exod 12:22; Lev 14:4-6, 49-52; Num 19:6 and 19). Blood was to be sprinkled as part of the ceremony in various offerings, purifications and consecrations. The most notable may be the original entrance into the covenant agreement, the consecration of new priests, the endless sacrifices of lambs, and the ceremonies on the Day of Atonement. The Passover ceremony, celebrated on the same night in which all of Egypt's firstborn died, knit the Israelites into a single mobile family. Before this Passover night, they were slaves. After it, they were a free people leaving Egypt. That freedom allowed them to worship God *as he directed*, i.e., there would be an endless sprinkling of blood under his Sinai covenant.

Because of the blood sprinkled around their doorframes, **the destroyer of the firstborn** would not hurt them. The NIV tries to make the text perfectly clear by ending verse 28 with the phrase, "the firstborn of Israel," instead of the slightly ambiguous "them." The word **"firstborn"** is neuter here probably because it included animals with people. Surely far more animals than people died in the tenth plague. The word for "destroyed" (ὀλοθρεύω, *olothreuō*) appears only here in the NT. Exodus only said the destroyer would not enter their houses and strike them down. Hebrews says he would not even touch them.

By naming three great deeds of Moses and Abraham, they are honored more than any others in this list of the faithful. Only by anticipation did Abraham's deeds which are reported here touch more than a very few people. On the other hand, Moses' exercise of faith immediately changed the lives of thousands. He led the people in leaving Egypt and in keeping the Passover. The next three examples of faith express deeds which Moses largely stimulated by his faithful leadership.

F. FAITH ILLUSTRATED IN ISRAEL (11:29-38)

[29]**By faith the people passed through the Red Sea[a] as on dry land; but when the Egyptians tried to do so, they were drowned.**

[30]**By faith the walls of Jericho fell, after the people had marched around them for seven days.**

[31]**By faith the prostitute Rahab, because she welcomed the spies, was not killed with those who were disobedient.[b]**

[32]**And what more shall I say? I do not have time to tell about Gideon, Barak, Samson, Jephthah, David, Samuel and the prophets,** [33]**who through faith conquered kingdoms, administered justice, and gained what was promised; who shut the mouths of lions,** [34]**quenched the fury of the flames, and escaped the edge of the sword; whose weakness was turned to strength; and who became powerful in battle and**

routed foreign armies. ³⁵Women received back their dead, raised to life again. Others were tortured and refused to be released, so that they might gain a better resurrection. ³⁶Some faced jeers and flogging, while still others were chained and put in prison. ³⁷They were stoned^c; they were sawed in two; they were put to death by the sword. They went about in sheepskins and goatskins, destitute, persecuted and mistreated — ³⁸the world was not worthy of them. They wandered in deserts and mountains, and in caves and holes in the ground.

ᵃ29 That is, Sea of Reeds   ᵇ31 Or *unbelieving*   ᶜ37 Some early manuscripts *stoned; they were put to the test;*

Three more specific examples of faith yet remain. None of them are by people who would normally be classed as giants of faith. The Israelites cross the Red Sea in terror at the pursuing Egyptians. The walls of Jericho fall down after Israel has simply marched around them for seven days. Rahab sees an invincible people approaching and stays alive by joining them. These are not so much illustrations of great depth of faith, but of the fact that faith does something.

11:29 By faith the people passed through the Red Sea as on dry land; but when the Egyptians tried to do so, they were drowned.

In the previous two illustrations of faith (vv. 27-28), Moses' faith carried the people of Israel along with him. In this illustration of faith (v. 29) the people have risen to their own trust in God. **"By faith the people passed through the Red Sea."** The account is in Exodus 13:17–15:21. The path of the people on leaving Egypt which led to their militarily vulnerable position beside the sea was directly dictated by God. After giving his verbal direction, he led them with the pillar of cloud by day and the pillar of fire by night (13:17-22). Looking back on what happened is almost humorous. It was not humorous for them. Israel was "marching out boldly" until they saw the

Egyptian chariots coming. Immediately "they were terrified" (v. 10). But when the Israelites had crossed the sea and saw the pursuing Egyptians dead on the shore, "the people feared the LORD and put their trust in him and in Moses his servant" (Exod 14:29-31). To say that it was "by faith" that the people passed through the Red Sea can only mean that faith is there when there is obedience. However small, however full of fear, it is still faith, if there is obedience. They certainly did not feel calm, or even "trusting" before the crossing. They were "terrified."

A few words must be said about the place of crossing. At all twenty-six occurrences of the phrase "the Red Sea" the NIV margin prefers, "Sea of Reeds." It is fashionable for many texts and atlases to locate Israel's "crossing" at some marshy area north of the deep water. The text of Hebrews makes four points about their crossing: (1) It was done "by faith." (2) They passed "through" the Red Sea. (3) They did it "on dry ground." (4) The Egyptians were drowned when they tried to follow. It would be hard to drown all the Egyptians if Israel did not cross at some deep water. The biblical picture of a deep water crossing is quite certain.

11:30 By faith the walls of Jericho fell, after the people had marched around them for seven days.

The second general expression of the effect of faith involves all the people at the conquest of Jericho (v. 30). **"By faith the walls of Jericho fell."** The only thing it said they did was march around the city for seven days. This is not a very deep level of faith. Nevertheless, there is the clear element of DOING what God required, even if it is doing what the crowd does, as long as it is what God said should be done. A messenger from God, an angel (?), called "a man" and "the commander of the Lord's army" met Joshua before the attack and told him that the method of attack would be by marching around the city in this unusual way (Josh 5:13-6:5). The whole story is told in Joshua 5-7.

11:31 By faith the prostitute Rahab, because she welcomed the spies, was not killed with those who were disobedient.

The story about **Rahab** also teaches the value of obedience even if it is a small deed (v. 31). Certainly she knew the risk of helping the spies, worse, of concealing them. She was especially aware at the inn of the travelers' talk about the approaching Israelites. She would later tell them, "All who live in this country are melting in fear because of you. We have heard how the LORD dried up the water of the Red Sea for you when you came out of Egypt, and what you did to Sihon and Og, the two kings of the Amorites east of the Jordan, whom you completely destroyed" (Josh 2:9-10).

There was more in her heart. She had seen the frustrating impotence and degrading immorality of the gods around her. The stories coming from spies and travellers who kept an eye on the Israelites suggested that their God was a far different kind of god, a good god. She knew little more than his name. Perhaps she had heard some of the very fair laws of this god.[28]

Suddenly two strange men appeared at her inn. Guessing that they were Israelite spies she had to make a quick decision. Should she help them and risk death herself, or expose them and become a heroine in Jericho? For what? Jericho could not stand against them if Egypt could not. There was no time to inquire about their god now. She had only a few moments to decide and to act. She hid them quickly. One last time she approached them just before they lay down for the night, and she blurted out the growing confidence in her

---

[28]Deut 4:5-8 anticipated that various nations would admire Israel's righteous laws, "See, I have taught you decrees and laws as the LORD my God commanded me, so that you may follow them in the land you are entering to take possession of it. Observe them carefully, for this will show your wisdom and understanding to the nations, who will hear about all these decrees and say, 'Surely this great nation is a wise and understanding people.' What other nation is so great as to have their gods near them the way the LORD our God is near us whenever we pray to him? And what other nation is so great as to have such righteous decrees and laws as this body of laws I am setting before you today?"

heart, "The LORD your God is God in heaven above and on the earth below" (Josh 2:11).

From tiny bits of information came enough faith to do one little thing. It was enough to show where her heart was. Faith without accompanying deeds is a useless thing. With them it is powerful. James uses both Abraham's offering of Isaac and Rahab's helping the spies as evidence that faith must do something to be real (James 2:17-26). In Hebrews the only evidence presented of her faith is that she did not "perish with, be destroyed with" (συναπόλλυμι, *synapollymi*) those who were disobedient. The word occurs nowhere else in the NT, and is not very frequent in the LXX. In this instance Rahab's faith helped her leave the group.

As it did in verse 27 the NIV adds the word "because" as an interpretation of an adverbial participle. The Greek text does not require "welcoming the spies" to be seen as the reason that she escaped death. It may as correctly be translated simply "after she welcomed the spies." Nothing is mentioned here about her saving her whole family, nor about the scarlet cord which was the means of this preservation. A small deed, done quickly with little advance notice, built on a general fear of dire consequences, was all she had available. It was all she needed. By that one little deed she won for herself a place in the hall of fame of the faithful and in the lineage of the Messiah (Matt 1:5).

These concrete examples show that faith always looks to God. It seeks him out and aims to please him by doing whatever he says to do. God is trusted to be the designer, the builder and the host of a better city in a better country with better people. In honoring this faith God guides the steps, enlightens the mind and enlarges the influence. Faith gives strength to do what men in their weakness could not do. Faith knows that if its own strength fails, God will assist, even if he must do a miracle. When faith seizes the moment, it seizes God.

Though faith leads to new places, new privileges, new privations, it never leads away from God. Faith expects a better future full of God's own rewards. Faith keeps the eyes on heaven while driving the nails on earth. Faith sees the end past long costly projects or large luring pleasures.

A believer draws others along in his train. He aims to save his family. He works to save the world. He leaves a clear voice when he has gone. God commends the faithful.

11:32 And what more shall I say? I do not have time to tell about Gideon, Barak, Samson, Jephthah, David, Samuel and the prophets,

To the eighteen examples of faith already given our author appends a few names and a large list of wonderful deeds that this faith has stimulated (vv. 32-38). The previous examples are enough to demonstrate that those with faith do not "shrink back" but "persevere." They "will be richly rewarded" (10:35-39). Faith gives confidence and improves the understanding of what cannot be seen. Westcott capsulizes this summary in Hebrews, "In part (a) they wrought great things (32-35a): in part (b) they suffered great things (35b-38)." Then he draws attention to the "remarkable symmetry" of the nine phrases in vv. 33-34.[29] The first triplet has only two accents in each phrase; the second and third triplets have three.

In 11:32 the author lists four judges, then David, Samuel, and "the prophets," explaining, "I do not have time to tell about them." How did each of these exercise faith? **Gideon** seemed very reluctant to respond to God's call to save Israel. He wanted a sign before each major event to which God called him. When God had him tear down his father's altar to Baal and its accompanying Asherah pole, he did it at night, because he was afraid; but because he believed, he did it. Later, with only 300 men holding trumpets and torches, he attacked and routed the army of Midianites, Amalekites and other eastern people who were "thick as locusts" having camels that "could no more be counted than the sand on the

---

[29]Westcott, pp. 376-377.

seashore" (Judg 7:12). His faith seemed very timid, but he did what God directed him to do.

Barak defeated Sisera the Canaanite and his 900 iron chariots. Barak refused to go to battle until Deborah the prophetess agreed to go with him. She "was leading Israel at that time" (Judg 4:4). In the Bible text Deborah is always mentioned before Barak.

Samson has little evidence in the Bible text that he trusted God. His parents raised him as a Nazirite as the angel had directed when he explained that "he will begin the deliverance of Israel from the hands of the Philistines" (Judg 13:5). Four times are recorded that "the Spirit of the Lord came upon him," once when a lion attacked him (Judg 14:9), twice to fight Philistines (Judg 14:19; 15:14). See also Judges 13:25. His whole life seemed to be an expression of trusting God for superhuman strength as a Nazirite until Delilah lured him to uncover his vow. The clearest expression of his faith came at the end of his life. Taunted as a prisoner in the temple of Dagon, he prayed for his strength to return. With it he pulled down the temple killing more Philistines at his death than during his life. Evidently, faith may return when one repents and asks to be used again by God.

Jephthah's remarkable faith is seen in keeping a careless vow, even though it was very costly to him (Judg 11:29-40). He made a solemn agreement with God before the battle. God kept his part and helped him win, so Jephthah determined to keep his part. The vow may have been foolish. The faith in God was not. Scholars offer different interpretations of whether Jephthah kept his vow by killing or by banishing his daughter. Either way, Jephthah's faith is indeed remarkable.

David is the only person whom God calls "a man after my own heart" (Acts 13:22 based on 1 Sam 13:14). His life is so full of deeds of faith that anyone interested in pursuing this feature of his life should read 1 Samuel 16-31; 2 Samuel; 1 Kings 1-2; 1 Chronicles 11–29 and the many Psalms bearing his name. In addition, there are many indications of David's faith in the character and writings of his son Solomon. One caution must be taken in examining every one of these models of faith. Great faith does not mean perfect life or character.

Samuel marks the transition from judges to kings and prophets. He was the last of the judges (1 Sam 7:6, 15-17; etc.) and the first of the prophets (1 Sam 3:20; 2 Chr 35:18; especially Acts 3:24 and 13:20). His deeds of faith, like David's, are numerous, and may be read at leisure in 1 Samuel 1-19 and Jeremiah 15:1.

The faith of "**the prophets**" is generally seen as they deliver God's messages in the face of difficulties of all kinds. It may be almost a rule of thumb that the only prophets who have no recorded difficulty because of delivering their messages are those of whom no narrative at all is recorded. The book of Hebrews began by noticing "the prophets" (1:1). At this point, after mentioning the prophets, Hebrews simply lists numerous afflictions and achievements of the faithful (vv. 33-38).

The most prominent judges who appear in the book of Judges are selected in Hebrews 11:32, two who are earlier and two later. The names can been seen as pairs, though the grammatical structure of the Greek text does not suggest pairing except for David and Samuel.[30] The chronological order within each of the three pairs is reversed. This may reflect their relative importance in the pair. Attridge thinks it is more likely that "the systematic departure from a strict scriptural sequence is a part of the attempt to create an image of a vast horde of exemplars of faith."[31] That impression had

---

[30]Only the last two names are joined with any conjunction, *Dauid te kai Samouhl*, "David and Samuel." LS says the word *te* ("and") usually connects clauses, but it may connect individual words or whole sentences. It often occurs preceding the word *kai* ("and"), in which case the pair of words is simply translated "and." Half of the eighteen times the word appears in Hebrews it has the structure "A *te kai* B." Three times *te* appears alone. Sometimes it is in a longer string, i.e., *te* A [Or: A *te*] *kai* B *kai* C *kai* D. Two items are joined thus in 2:11 and 9:19; three items in 9:2; and four items in 2:4. Here in 11:32 the pair of words *te kai* appears simply to mean "and" and does not serve grammatically to divide the six names into pairs.

[31]Attridge, p. 347.

begun by the time the author got to these names. Three of
these judges are mentioned with Samuel in 1 Samuel 12:11 as
examples of those whom God sent to deliver Israel when they
cried out for mercy from their oppression, "Then the LORD
sent Jerub-Baal [also called Gideon], Barak, Jephthah and
Samuel, and he delivered you from the hands of your enemies on every side, so that you lived securely."

The Bible makes Joshua a transition figure between Moses
and the judges in much the same way Samuel was a transition
figure between judges and kings. Samuel himself became in a
sense the first of the prophets (1 Sam 3:20; 9:9; Acts 3:24;
13:20-21). Technically, there were "prophets" before
Samuel,[32] but with him the emphasis shifted from the inde-
pendent rule of individual judges to the sustained rule of a
succession of kings assisted by prophets. The author of
Hebrews appears to notice this transition with "David and
Samuel" being followed simply by "the prophets." Samuel and
David are very closely related in Scripture. For example, in
setting up the order of worship and the personnel for the
temple, the gatekeepers were "assigned their positions of
trust by David and Samuel the seer" (1 Chr 9:22).

**11:33 who through faith conquered kingdoms, administered
justice, and gained what was promised; who shut the
mouths of lions,**

The conquering (ἀγωνίζομαι, *agōnizomai*) of kingdoms
probably means literal warfare, not spiritual warfare or sports,
although the word is used of all three. Many of those already
named in the chapter conquer kingdoms — Barak (Judg 4:24);
Gideon (Judg 7, here the conquest is especially ascribed to
God); Jephthah (Judg 11); Samson (Judg 16). David conquered

---

[32]Abraham was called a "prophet" (Gen 20:7 [cf. Ps 105:15]) as were other
early people: Moses (Deut 18:15-19 [cf. Ex 7:1]); Miriam (Ex 15:20); the sev-
enty elders (Num 11:25-29); Deborah (Judg 4:4 [cf. 6:8]); even Saul (1 Sam
18:10). The term was used of others as well (Deut 18:20-22; 34:10; 1 Sam
10:5-13; 28:6, 15).

Philistines, Moabites, Zobah, Damascus, Hamath, and others (2 Sam 8).

"Administering justice" (lit., "worked righteousness") may be said of individuals (as Acts 10:35; 1 John 2:29 and 3:7) or especially of judges or rulers who cause righteousness, then uphold it (as Isa 58; Amos 1-2). In the OT righteousness is predominantly a quality of God. In the NT it is predominantly a gift of God to believers. It may be seen both in Joseph's fleeing the advances of Potiphar's wife and in saving Egypt's food and overseeing its proper use. Hebrews shows that Jesus loves righteousness (1:8), in fact, he is "king of righteousness" like Melchizedek (7:2). By faith he permits believers to inherit his righteousness (11:7).

It was specifically said of Abraham in 6:15 that he **gained** or "received (ἐπιτυγχάνω, *epityngchan ō*) **what was promised.**" It is the only other place in Hebrews where this verb is used, and it happens to be used with "receiving" the promise. The OT verse quoted in 6:14 is Genesis 22:17 immediately after Abraham has "offered" Isaac on the altar. God's response to this trusting obedience of Abraham was, "Now I know that you fear God because you have not withheld from me your son, your only son" (Gen 22:12). See notes on 11:17-19.

What Israel sought so earnestly they did not "receive" and became hard; while the elect, i.e., those who believed, did receive it (Rom 11:9). In the only other NT use of this verb, James 4:2-3 says some things are not received because we do not ask God for them or because we have wrong motives in our requests. One of its two LXX uses describes Joseph "prospering, gaining" in Potiphar's house (Gen 49:2).

Daniel was saved in the den of lions by God's angel coming to **"shut the mouths of the lions"** (Dan 6:22). Daniel's accusers were immediately devoured by the lions when they were thrown into the den. Similarly by faith Samson overpowered a lion (Judg 14:5-6), and David killed both lions and bears (1 Sam 17:34-37).

Benaiah, one of David's valiant warriors, also overcame a lion, though the OT text does not state that it was because of his faith (2 Sam 23:20; 1 Chr 11:22). On two occasions young men of God were killed by lions because they disobeyed God (1 Kgs 13:24-26; 20:35). The foreigners who entered Samaria after the deportation of the northern kingdom were plagued by lions because they did not live for God (2 Kgs 17:25-26). Isaiah used the picture of transforming the violent nature of lions as a strong indication of the power of the Messiah to change the character of people (Isa 11:6-7).

11:34 quenched the fury of the flames, and escaped the edge of the sword; whose weakness was turned to strength; and who became powerful in battle and routed foreign armies.

The three Hebrew lads in Babylon may be the first to come to mind. Refusing to worship the ninety foot statue of the king, they chose rather to be thrown into the fiery furnace. They emerged unsinged and unscented by the fire that was heated seven times hotter than usual. The fire was so hot it killed the men who threw them into the furnace (Dan 3). Westcott quotes an observation of Theophlet that it does not say they **quenched the fire**, but the power of the fire, which is even greater.[33]

Others died by fire because they did not trust God: Nadab & Abihu (Lev 10:1-2); Korah and the 250 men with him (Num 16:35); and the two groups of fifty military men sent to capture Elijah (1 Kgs 1:10, 12, 14). If the idea is understood figuratively, then passages like Isaiah 43:2 should be considered.

Some **escaped the edge of the sword**, literally a plural word "mouths" of a sword. The plural here may indicate the same as the "two-edged sword" of 4:12; or it may be plural to match the plural "mouths" of lions in v. 33.

If this phrase means to avoid being killed with a literal sword, as in war, then there are numerous examples of individuals and whole armies where faith achieved this end. Moses held up his hands in an act of faith by which Israel

---

[33]Westcott, p. 378.

defeated the Amalekites (Exod 17:8-16). By faith David escaped Goliath's sword (1 Sam 17). By faith Jehoshaphat was saved from a huge army from the east (1 Chr 20). Cf. Luke 21:24. The sword was so widely used in the ancient world that Liddell and Scott say it sometimes "stands for violent death" of any kind or even for war.[34]

Sometimes physically weak persons **became strong** through faith. Samson became weak like ordinary men because of breaking his trust with God about his hair. He became super-strong again at the end of his life when he prayed and trusted God once again (Judg 16). Elijah beat the 450 prophets of Baal. Then weakened by fear of Jezebel, and fleeing for his life, he became strong enough to travel for forty days and forty nights on the strength of two successive meals (1 Kgs 19:1-9).

Sometimes people were strengthened when weak in some other way. Abraham was weak in lying to Pharaoh to save his life (Gen 12:10-20), but he became courageous enough to risk his life to rescue Lot (Gen 14:1-24). Gideon was overly timid when called by God, but then routed an army far outnumbering his own (Judg 6-7).

It may indicate strength of character. Micaiah stood up against the uniform voice of the king's prophets (1 Kgs 22). Jeremiah faced the threats of his own family (Jer 11:21-23). Ezekiel described the faithful prophet's heart, "Whether they listen or fail to listen — for they are a rebellious house — they will know that a prophet has been among them" (Ezek 2:5).

When the Spirit of the Lord came on Othniel (Judg 3:10), and later Jephthah (Judg 11:29), they went out to victorious war. Young David's military prowess entered the lyrics of songs in ancient Israel, "Saul has slain his thousands, and David his tens of thousands" (1 Sam 18:7). He conquered Philistines, Moabites, Zobah, Damascus, Hamath, Edom, Ammon and Amalek (2 Sam 8). Israel's enemies were God's enemies. Ellingworth says that this is the only place in the NT

---

[34]LS, p. 496.

where faith is associated with military conquest. Contrast
Matthew 5:44f. Jesus will eventually make all the kingdoms of
this world become the kingdom of our Lord (Rev 11:15).
Zechariah used this imagery of the increased strength of
those who follow God, "On that day the LORD will shield
those who live in Jerusalem, so that the feeblest among them
will be like David, and the house of David will be like God,
like the Angel of the LORD going before them" (12:8). To the
exploits of Othniel, Gideon, Jephthah, David and
Jehoshaphat, which are given above, many more could be
added throughout the history of God's people.

**11:35 Women received back their dead, raised to life again.
Others were tortured and refused to be released, so that
they might gain a better resurrection.**

It is significant that **women** are mentioned as **receiving
their dead back to life**. They were more vulnerable than men
in the event of the death of a spouse or an only son. Widows
are often grouped with aliens and the fatherless as needing
special kindness and receiving God's careful attention (Exod
22:22-24; Deut 14:29; 24:19-21; Isa 1:23; etc.) They were sup-
ported in part together with the Levites, aliens and fatherless
by the third tithe, taken from every wage-earner every third
and sixth year of the seven year cycle (Deut 14:28-29; 26:12-
13). De Vaux claims that "the social and legal position of an
Israelite wife was . . . inferior to the position a wife occupied
in the great countries round about [i.e., Egypt or Babylon].
. . . Judith was a rich widow. More commonly widows, especially those with children to support, were in a piteous condition."[35]

Elijah gave a son back to the widow of Zarephath (1 Kgs
17:7-24; Sir 48:5). Elisha brought the Shunammite's son back
to life (2 Kgs 4:8-37). Jesus resurrected an only child and gave
him back to his widowed mother (Luke 7:12-17). In Lazarus'

---

[35]Roland de Vaux, *Social Institutions,* Volume 1 of *Ancient Israel* (New York:
McGraw-Hill Book Company, 1965), p.40.

resurrection account we only read of the two sisters left in the family, Martha and Mary (John 11).

There were other resurrections. When Jesus sent his disciples on a mission to the lost sheep of the house of Israel, part of their assignment was to "raise the dead" (Matt 10:8). The fact that the people were raised from the dead was part of Jesus' proof to John that he was the Messiah who was to come (Matt 11:5; Luke 7:22). There was a general expectation among the populace in Jesus' day that there could be resurrection from the dead (Matt 27:64). Herod thought John the Baptist had risen from death when he heard about Jesus' works (Mark 6:14, 16; Luke 9:7). Many people were resurrected when Jesus died. Matthew reports that "The tombs broke open and the bodies of many holy people who had died were raised to life. They came out of the tombs, and after Jesus' resurrection they went into the holy city and appeared to many people" (Matt 27:52-53).

During the intertestamental period there was an awareness of resurrection. When the seven famous martyr brothers were executed, the second brother said as he approached death, "You dismiss us from this present life, but the King of the universe will raise us up to an everlasting renewal of life, because we have died for his laws" (2 Macc 7:9, NRSV). The fourth brother, while being tortured said, "One cannot but choose to die in the hands of mortals and to cherish the hope God gives of being raised again by him. But for you there will be no resurrection to life" (2 Macc 7:14, NRSV). Judas and his men went to take up the bodies of Jews fallen in battle. Finding sacred tokens of the idols of Jamnia under each fallen man's tunic, Judas collected money for a sin offering for them and sent it to Jerusalem. They were commended in 2 Maccabees 12:43-44,

> In doing this he acted very well and honorably, taking account of the resurrection. For if he were not expecting that those who had fallen would rise again, it would have been superfluous and foolish to pray for the dead. But if he was looking to the splendid reward that is laid up for those who fall asleep in godliness, it was a holy and pious thought (NRSV).

Mothers, in 2 Esdras 2:15-16, are urged to bring up their children with gladness, for God has promised, "I will raise up the dead from their places, and bring them out of their tombs, because I recognize my name in them" (NRSV). They are further encouraged to help widows, orphans, the needy, the old, etc., "When you find any dead, commit them to the grave and mark it, and I will give you the first place in my resurrection" (2 Esdras 2:20-24, NRSV).The OT had already begun this expectation of resurrection (Job 19:25-26; Ps 16:8-11; 17:15; 49:12-15; 73:24; 102:25-28; Isa 53:10-12; Dan 12:2).

Part of the **torture** was the offer of **release** at any moment during the torture if some token would be given of renouncing the Jewish law. See 4 Maccabees 11:9-11 for one method of torture. BAGD defines τυμπανίζω (*tympanizō*) as "*torture with the* tympanon, a certain kind of instrument of torture," citing 2 Maccabees 6:19, 28; or "*torment, torture* generally" adding "The compound *apotump.* in the same sense" and citing 3 Maccabees 3:27; Josephus *Contra Apion* 1,148; and others. Liddell and Scott says it means "*to beat a drum*" or "generally, *to beat with a stick, bastinado.*" Its other words built on the same root are associated with drums and sticks. In the Greek OT *tympanon* is customarily used for the Hebrew *toph*, ("a drum"), but in 2 Maccabees 6:19 and 28 it is evidently an instrument of torture. NRSV in these two verses says "the rack."

Many suffered faithfully to **"gain a better resurrection."** This shows an awareness of both the fact of resurrection and a differentiation in that resurrection. Resurrection was known to Daniel (Dan 12:2-3), to Isaiah (Isa 53: 10, 12) and to Abraham (Heb 11:17-19), and probably the Psalm writers (Ps 22:29; 49:12-15; 73, especially v. 24; 102:25-28). See Job 19:25-27 and Jeremiah 31:15-17.

11:36 Some faced jeers and flogging, while still others were chained and put in prison.

Jeers and flogging appear together in the NT only when describing Jesus' abuse. The first noun **"jeers"** (ἐμπαιγμός, *empaigmos*) occurs only here in the NT, although its cognate verb, ἐμπαίζω (*empaizō*, "to ridicule, mock") is used thirteen times. The second noun **"flogging"** (μάστιξ, *mastix*, "lashes" or "torment"), on the other hand, appears six times in the NT, while its cognate verbs, μαστιγόω (*mastigoō*, "to whip, flog, scourge") and μαστίζω (*mastizō*, "to strike with a whip"), appear respectively seven times and only in Acts 22:25.

In the NT these words appear together only when Jesus predicts his mistreatment in Jerusalem. Matthew records "mock, flog and crucify" (20:19); Mark and Luke add "spit" (Mark 10:34; Luke 18:32-33); and Luke further adds "insult." The word "mock" is used almost exclusively of Jesus' abuse, either being predicted or carried out (Matt 27:29,31,41; Mark 15:20,31; Luke 22:63; 23:11, 36). The only two exceptions are the wise men mocking Herod by not returning to tell him about the baby king (Matt 2:16) and the mocking of the man who only half built a tower (Luke 14:29).

Upon the death of Judas Maccabee, the Syrian leader Bacchides sought out the friends of Judas and "mocked" them, taking vengeance on them (1 Macc 9:26). Saul feared this abuse at the hands of the Philistines and prefered death (1 Sam 31:4; 1 Chr 10:4). The torture and slow death of the seven martyr brothers is called "mocking" or "sport" (2 Macc 7:10). The general "mocking" of the the people of God is mentioned in Isaiah 33:4; Ezekiel 22:3; Zechariah 12:3 and 2 Maccabees 8:17.

The claim that "still others **were put in prison**," should perhaps be better translated with the rough addition, "and even fetters and prison." This would match the striking Greek syntax where the genitive forms seem to couple with the genitives of the previous phrase. Verse 36 would then read more literally, "And others received a trial of mockings and of lashes, and even of fetters and of prison."

These two words are never joined as a pair like this anywhere else in the NT or LXX, although many were bound and imprisoned for their faith, for example, Joseph (Gen 39:6-20), Hanani (2 Chr 16:7-10), and Paul (Acts 16:22-24). God broke Israel's "bond" of slavery in Egypt (Lev 26:13;

Ps 107:14). Many others were put in prison or in bonds for their faith in God.

11:37 They were stoned; they were sawed in two; they were put to death by the sword. They went about in sheepskins and goatskins, destitute, persecuted and mistreated —

The Bible record tells of several people who were **stoned** for their faith: Naboth (1 Kgs 21:13-15); Zechariah, son of Jehoiada the priest (2 Chr 24:19-22); Stephen (Acts 7:59); Paul (Acts 14:19; 2 Cor 11:25). Jesus was attacked by stoning (John 10:31-33). Moses and Aaron were nearly stoned (Exod 17:4; Num 14:10), as was David (1 Sam 30:6). Jesus' parable was not foreign to real life when he described wicked men's stoning the messengers and the heir of a vineyard-owner to get possession of a vineyard (Matt 21:33-44).

Stoning was the prescribed death penalty for a number of crimes: worshipping other gods (Deut 17:1-7); tempting people to turn away from God (Deut 13:1-11); offering children to Moloch (Lev 20:2); wizardry or having a familiar spirit (Lev 20:27); blasphemy (Lev 24:10-16, 23); gathering wood on the Sabbath (Num 15:32-36); being a rebellious son (Deut 21:18-21); not penning up a goring ox (Exod 21:28-32); adultery or even slandering a new wife (Deut 22:13-24). Montefiore reminds us that the land of Israel was full of stones which could be used for this purpose.

The verb "**sawed in two**" may be from πρίζω (*prizō*) or πρίω (*priō*), both of which Liddell and Scott defines as "to saw." Their fuller discussion is given under πρίω, "*to saw, saw asunder; sever, cut in twain;* II *to grind* or *gnash the teeth,* esp. with rage; generally *to bite;* III. *to seize as with the teeth, grip.*" There is some textual uneasiness since this word occurs only here in the NT. BAGD makes *prizō* primary over *priō*. The sin of Damascus was seen at its worst when "she threshed (ἔπρι–ζον, *eprizon*) Gilead with sledges having iron teeth" (Amos 1:3). Here the LXX adds "the pregnant women (of Gilead)." The verb appears a second time in the apocryphal Daniel (Sus, 59) where Daniel told the second evil judge who wrongfully condemned Susanna that the angel of God was waiting with his sword to "saw him in two so as to destroy them both." He told the first judge (Daniel, Sus, 55) that the angel of God would "cut him in two" (σχίζω, schizō, "to split, cleave; generally, to part asunder").

The death of Isaiah is frequently presented as the clearest example of a believer who was sawed in two. In one place the Talmud says that in Babylon 2 Kings 21:16 is interpreted to mean that Manasseh killed Isaiah (Sanh. 103b[36]). In another account the story says that Isaiah pronounced the unpronounceable Name of God and was swallowed up by a cedar. The cedar, however, was brought and sawn asunder. When the saw reached his mouth he died. This was his penalty for having said, 'And I dwell in the midst of a people of unclean lips.' (Yeb. 49b[37]). Rist presents the version in the Jerusalem Talmud (Sanh 10) that Isaiah, fearing Manasseh, hid in a cedar-tree. Seeing the fringes of his garment which were not hidden, Manasseh caused the tree to be sawn in half.[38] The Ascension of Isaiah, a pseudepigraphical work, said Isaiah made some dire predictions about Manasseh. Belchira, a false prophet, then offered Isaiah his freedom if he would renounce his prophecies as lies. Isaiah refused and died bravely.[39]

"Put to death by the sword" is the expression ἐν φόνῳ μαχαίρης ἀπέθανον (en phonō machairēs apethanon, lit., "in murder of a sword they died"). BAGD translates, "*(by being murdered) with the sword.*"[40] [they died]. This exact expression occurs in Exodus 17:13 of Joshua's routing the Amalekites; in Numbers 21:24 of Israel's destroying Sihon, king of the Amorites; in Deuteronomy 13:15 of Israel's destroying any

---

[36]Soncino 1935 edition, p. 702.

[37]Ibid., p. 324.

[38]Isaac Broyde, "Isaiah — In Rabbinical Literature," in *The Jewish Encyclopedia*; 6:636.

[39]See more details in Martin Rist, "Isaiah, Ascension of," in *The Interpreter's Dictionary of the Bible*, 2:744-746.

[40]BAGD, p. 864.

idolatrous city of Israelites; and in Deuteronomy 20:13 of killing all the men of a city which refused to make peace with Israel.

A list of good people who died by the sword because they were trusting people must include the people of Nob who helped David (1 Sam 22:19), the prophets of God killed by Jezebel (1 Kgs 18:4; 19:10, 14); James (Acts 12:2), perhaps Uriah (2 Sam 12:9), perhaps even Abner and Amasa (1 Kgs 2:32). The Apocrypha reported several people who died by the sword in the Maccabean era because they adhered to God's laws: Jonathan and his men (1 Macc 12:46), the people of Jamnia (1 Macc 15:38), the people of Jerusalem (2 Macc 5:23, 26), and numerous unnamed Jews (2 Macc 6:1-7).

The sword was widely used because it was such an effective and inexpensive weapon of death. Examples of death by the sword could be multiplied. As the final statement in a list of many different kinds of suffering, death by the sword could representative of many other kinds of violent death which believers endured. See, for example, Numbers 20:18; 21:24; 1 Chronicles 21:12, 16, 27, 30; 2 Chronicles 20:9; 36:20 and Psalm 22:20. *Foxe's Book of Martyrs* records many kinds of extreme torture used against believers in the beginning church.[41]

Our author moves now from extreme physical abuse to economic abuse and privation. They wore **sheepskins and goatskins**. Either they were barred from labor to earn money or barred from shops to spend money to purchase normal clothing. In either case they would have homemade clothes. Driven from ordinary society, "they wandered in deserts and mountains, and in caves and holes in the ground." It appears that many of them had to make their own clothing directly from animal products. So these were not top quality leather luxuries, but crude, homemade necessities. The phrase is

---

[41]Marie Gentert King, editor, *Foxe's Book of Martyrs* (New York: Pyramid Books, 1968), pp. 11-33.

included here in a list of things which people suffered because of their faith.

The two phrases, "in sheepskins" (ἐν μηλωταῖς, *en mēlōtais*) and "goatskins" (ἐν αἰγείοις δέρμασιν, *en aigeiois dermasin*), should be taken together. The first phrase is used "of the cloak worn by prophets" (BAGD), specifically of Elijah's mantle (1 Kgs 19:13, 19; 2 Kgs 2:8) which subsequently came into Elisha's possession (2 Kgs 2:13-14). Liddell and Scott gives the classical Greek meaning as "a sheep's skin." The word appears nowhere else in the Greek Bible. Lampe defines the word as used by the church fathers as *"sheepskin, hence rough hairy cloak* worn by monks."[42] Ahab's messengers observed that Elijah "was a man with a garment of hair and a leather belt[43] around his waist" (2 Kgs 1:8; cf. Matt 3:4). Elijah's mantle, then, may have been (1) an additional leather ("sheepskin") garment he occasionally wore over his usual "garment of hair" to display his prophetic role. This fits Myers' idea of a "mantle of distinction" (אדרת, *'addereth*) which kings and prophets wore.[44] It may have been (2) a "sheepskin" in the modern sense of the skin of a sheep dressed with the fleece still on it. There is no direct indication that Elijah had to wear this kind of clothing because of privation or punishment. Levites shared the third tithe along with the very poor (Deut 14:28-29; 16:11, 14), but they were never associated directly with the prophets. John the Baptist wore clothes made of camel's hair and a leather belt. His fare of locusts and wild honey suggests privation. Motyer says the

---

[42]G.W.H. Lampe, *A Patristic Greek Lexicon* (Oxford: Clarendon Press, 1965), 4:868.

[43]Owen and Barabas claim that "the leather girdle or belt was from two to six inches wide, and . . . was worn by soldiers, by men of the desert, and by countrymen who tended cattle or engaged in the rougher pursuits of life." G. Frederick Owen and Steven Barabas, "Dress," in *The Zondervan Pictorial Bible Dictionary*, p. 226.

[44]Jacob M. Myers, "Dress," in *The Interpreter's Dictionary of the Bible*, Vol. 1, p. 870.

"curds and honey" of Isaiah 7:15 is "the food of poverty. . . . The divine child is to be born into the poverty of his people."[45]

They were **"destitute, persecuted and mistreated."** The word ὑστερέω (*hystereō*) means "to be in need of, to lack." The prodigal son had spent everything. He was **"destitute"** in a distant country when the famine came. He began "to be in need." His condition was so poor he wanted to eat what he fed to the pigs (Luke 15:14-16). The word describes how far beneath the glory of God the lives of men may fall. "All have sinned and *fall short of* the glory of God" (Rom 3:23). The cognate noun ὑστέρημα (*hysterēma*, "need, deficiency") describes the poor widow who out of her "need, poverty" gave two very small copper coins to God. While others gave out of their wealth, this was "all the living that she had"(Luke 21:1-4). Though "destitute" of the world's goods, in a sense these believers lacked nothing when following God, for he provides for his own (Neh 9:21; Ps 23:1 and Luke 22:35).

The ten NT references of θλίβω (*thlibō*, "to press together, oppress") help focus the meaning of **"persecution."** The "way" which Jesus' followers much walk is "narrow, confined," the opposite of the broad way which others preferred (Matt 7:14). Jesus told the disciples to have a boat ready to keep people from "crowding, pressing upon" him (Mark 3:9). Paul was often persecuted in his work (2 Cor 1:6; 4:8; 7:5; 1 Thess 3:4). Sometimes relief would come from a courageous believer (1 Kgs 18:3-4; 1 Tim 5:10; Heb 10:32-34).

This is the word the LXX uses to describe the persecution of the Jews by various nations in the period of the judges (Judg 4:3; 6:9; 8:34; 10:8,9,12; 11:7 and summary 1 Sam 10:18). It is a common term of warfare. The oppression is usually of the whole nation, not of individuals, as here. It is also usually because of sin, not because of mistreatment for being faithful to God. Wicked enemies are often called

---

[45]J. Alec Motyer, *The Prophecy of Isaiah* (Downers Grove, IL: InterVarsity Press, 1993), p. 86.

"oppressors." Isaiah said the Messianic influence would bring
an end to oppressing one another (Isa 11:13). In its summary
of the oppression of the people of God, Psalm 107 (106 LXX)
itemizes traits like those in Hebrews 11:37.

The word for **"maltreated,"** κακουχέω (*kakoucheō*, "to mal-
treat, torment"), appears only twice in the NT, both in
Hebrews (here and 13:3). It is also rare in the LXX, and found
only a few times in other OT Greek versions. BAGD says it is
used in marriage contracts. Perhaps that is why marriage is discussed immediately after this rare word in Hebrews 13:3.

**11:38 the world was not worthy of them. They wandered in
deserts and mountains, and in caves and holes in the
ground.**

These believers were clinging to God in faith. They were
fugitives and outcasts, the displaced persons of the world.
Accepted by no one, treated like "the scum of the earth, the
refuse of the world" (1 Cor 4:13), these homeless wanderers
longed to be home in heaven. Their citizenship was in heaven
(Phil 3:20). All they had left on earth was the promise of God.
To this they clung as they **wandered** about **in deserts and
mountains, in caves and holes in the ground.**

Israel hid in caves from the Midianites (Judg 6:2) and later
from the Philistines (1 Sam 13:5). David escaped from Saul by
hiding in the caves of Adullam and Engedi (1 Sam 22:1; 24:3).
Obadiah kept 100 prophets alive in caves to escape the murderous apostasy of Ahab and Jezebel (1 Kgs 18:3-4, 13). Upon
recapturing the temple after three years of absence the
Maccabees "celebrated it for eight days with rejoicing, in the
manner of the festival of booths, remembering how not long
before, during the festival of booths, they had been wandering in the mountains and caves like wild animals" (2 Macc
10:6; see 6:7-11). Montefiore says the description in Hebrews
"suits the freedom fighters against the Seleucids (1 Macc. ii.
31; 2 Macc. v. 27; vi. 11; x. 6)," then adds,

> Israel abounds in uninhabitable territory with excellent hiding-
> places for fugitives and outcasts, and these were later used in

guerrilla warfare against Herod (cf. Josephus, *Bell. Jud.* I. 16. 4) and against Rome (cf. P. Benoit and others, *Discoveries in the Judaean Desert*, II (Oxford, 1961), and Y. Yadin and others, *Judaean Desert Caves*, I and II (Jerusalem, 1961 and 1962).[46]

The "world" here means the world "as that which is hostile to God," the seventh definition BAGD gives for κόσμος (*kosmos*). Ironically, the world rejected as unworthy the very ones of whom **the world** itself **was not worthy**. Men of faith were the ones **commended** by God (cf. vv. 4 and 5). "Man looks at the outward appearance, but the Lord looks at the heart" (1 Sam 16:7).

G. GOD PLANNED TO MAKE THEM PERFECT WITH US (11:39-40)

[39]**These were all commended for their faith, yet none of them received what had been promised. [40]God had planned something better for us so that only together with us would they be made perfect.**

They were all commended for their faith. In discussing the word "commended" (μαρτυρηθέντες, *martyrēthentes*) BAGD defines the active voice, "*bear witness, be a witness;*" and the passive voice, "*be witnessed, be well spoken of.*" Six of the seven appearances of this word in Hebrews are in the passive voice, four are in this chapter (7:8, 17; 11:2, 4, 5, 39). Only 10:15 is active, where it says the Holy Spirit bears witness to us, then quotes an OT passage which is that witness. Melchizedek was "declared to be living" (7:8). Jesus was "declared" to be "a priest forever in the order of Melchizedek" (7:17). In this chapter the ancients are commended for their faith (11:2), Abel was commended as a righteous man (11:3), and Enoch was commended as one who pleased God (11:5). Then, all the

---

[46]Montefiore, p. 211.

people of the chapter "were commended for their faith" (11:39).

Though **commended for their faith**, these heroes and others like them only had the promise that good things were coming if they remained faithful. They had not received the things promised. God's plan was to join believers of the Old Covenant with believers of the New Covenant, redeem them all with the blood of Christ and place them together in his blessed future city. There is something better for us than our current abundant blessings in the church.

Before he ever created the world, God made the plan and the commitment that Jesus would die for fallen man (1 Pet 1:18-21; Rev 13:8). He evidently planned then the things that are described in Hebrews 5-7 about Jesus' being our high priest and the things described in Hebrews 9-10 about Jesus' being our perfect sacrifice for sins, hence also Jesus' high priestly activities in the "greater and more perfect tabernacle," i.e., "heaven itself" (Heb 9:11-14, 23-25). Other NT writers reveled in this glorious future God is preparing for man (Rom 8:18-39; Eph 2-3; Rev 21-22).

The only other place in the LXX or NT where the word προβλέπω (*problepō*, "to plan, foresee") is Psalm 37:13 (LXX 36:13), where the Lord laughs at the wicked, for he "plans or foresees" what their future holds. To balance the scales of right and wrong, the future holds heavy blessings for those faithful to God and heavy punishment for those who oppose him. Jesus said, "A time is coming when all who are in their graves will . . . come out — those who have done good will rise to live, and those who have done evil will rise to be condemned" (John 5:28-29). The Son of Man will sit on his throne and divide all nations, rewarding some and punishing others appropriately (Matt 25:31-46; Rev 20:11-15). It is this blessed future heavenly country for which the patriarchs longed (11:17).

The previous paragraph assumes that the perfecting of verse 40 is to be future for us. The perfecting may be done now. Jesus has already died for us. Upon accepting him anyone becomes perfected. There is no condemnation for those who are in Christ (Rom 8:1). Sins are forgiven (Acts 2:38; 1:3; 2:17; 7:27; 8:12; 9:28). "By one sacrifice he [Jesus] has made perfect forever those who are being made holy" (Heb 10:14). Hebrews 12:22-23 points the same direction. The believing readers have already come "to Mt. Zion, to the heavenly Jerusalem, . . . to the spirits of *righteous men made perfect.*" This is the perfecting which the Law could not achieve (Heb 7:19; 9:7, 9; 10:1). "He has died as a ransom to set them free from the sins committed under the first covenant" (Heb 9:15).

There is a third sense of "perfection" as growing to maturity, but this is not in the author's mind as he finishes the chapter on faith. See Colossians 1:28; 4:12; Hebrews 5:14; 6:1; James 1:4. It is not clear whether Philippians 3:12 points to maturing in Christ or to the final end.

Here, the best sense is probably the current perfection of forgiveness given to all through the sacrifice of Jesus. It is in the church that he has purposed to create in himself one new man out of people from various backgrounds and times; "in this one body he reconciles both of them to God through the cross" (Eph 2:15-16). They were not perfected apart from us. We are not perfected apart from them. While on earth Jesus promised that there would be one flock and one shepherd (John 10:16; Isa 19:23-25; 49:6; Joel 2:28, 32; Amos 9:11-12; Mic 4:1-3; etc.). Paul said he was "confident of this, that he who began a good work in you will carry it on to completion until the day of Christ Jesus" (Phil 1:6).

It is strange that in this concluding paragraph the readers are not asked to copy the faith of the believers who are on the list. They had been asked *not* to follow the unbelievers discussed in chapter three (4:1). They will be asked to "imitate the faith" of their leaders (13:7), like they had been asked to "imitate those who through faith and patience inherit what has been promised" (6:12). In the introduction to this section on faith (10:35-39) they were asked not to throw away their "confidence," but to "persevere." Then they were almost assumed into the circle of the faithful with the words, *"we are* not of those who shrink back and are destroyed, but of those who believe and are saved." Though they believed, they, too, like these heroes of faith, had not received the final reward. They must keep believing till the very end. Perhaps their faith felt tiny like the faith of Rahab. Maybe they felt their faith brought mistreatment like the faith of Moses. Whatever the size or nature of their faith, it was faith. The size of their faith did not matter. It was the presence of faith that knit them to Enoch and Noah and Abraham. God's plan was that believers of all ages, OT and NT, would one day be joined together and rewarded together. The text says, "together with us they would be made perfect" (11:40).

The readers will be asked to fix their eyes on Jesus (12:1-3), as they had been urged to fix their thoughts on him (3:1). It was this fixing of his vision on the Messiah that helped Moses make his decision of faith (11:24-26). He kept looking off at him who is invisible (11:27).

None **received what was promised**. Let us briefly trace the connection between God's promise and his covenant. At his call God made a promise (ἐπαγγελία, *epangelia*) to Abraham that consisted of several parts: (1) God would make him into a great nation; (2) he would make his name great; (3) he would bless those who blessed Abraham and curse those who cursed him; and (4) all peoples on earth would be blessed through him (Gen 12:1-3). The promise was formalized into a covenant with accompanying sacrifices (Gen 15). Then circumcision was added as "a sign of the covenant" (Gen 17:11). Isaac was singled out as the child through whom the covenant would be established (Gen 17:17-21; 21:13; 22:15-18). It was confirmed to Isaac (26:1-6). It was for this covenant with Abraham, Isaac and Jacob that God brought the Israelites out of Egypt (Exod 2:24-25). The land of Canaan was given as part of this covenant (Exod 6:4). God offered to make Israel his "treasured possession" when he gave them the law at Mt. Sinai, "Now *if* you obey me fully and keep my covenant, then out of all nations you will be my treasured possession" (Exod 19:5, emphasis added). When they heard the laws of God, they agreed to do all that God said. This further advance in their relationship was sealed with blood,

> Then he [Moses] took the Book of the Covenant, and read it to the people. They responded, "We will do everything the LORD has said; we will obey." Moses then took the blood, sprinkled it on the people, and said, "This is the blood of the covenant that the LORD has made with you in accordance with all these words" (Exod 24:7-8).

In Exodus 34 Moses was allowed to see a limited vision of God. At that time God was making a covenant that he would drive out the nations of the land of Canaan before Israel; *but* they should be careful to destroy their altars, make no treaty with them, plus, plus. The condition of obedience is repeated that was given in Exodus 19:5. The ten commandments are called "the words of the covenant" (Exod 34:28; see Deut 4:13).

What began as a promise to Abraham of posterity and honor from God, who is always faithful to his word, was expanded into a formal covenant agreement including a sign, laws, sacrifices, protection and blood confirming the covenant. What began as a response from Abraham, who trusted God, was expanded into a lifetime of expectation, privation and even heavy abuse for a whole group of people whose eye was on God and his future reward as being far superior to anything this world could offer.

HEBREWS 12

VIII. GOD EXPECTS US TO ENDURE DISCIPLINE (12:1-29)

A. A CALL TO PERSEVERANCE (12:1-3)

¹Therefore, since we are surrounded by such a great cloud of witnesses, let us throw off everything that hinders and the sin that so easily entangles, and let us run with perseverance the race marked out for us. ²Let us fix our eyes on Jesus, the author and perfecter of our faith, who for the joy set before him endured the cross, scorning its shame, and sat down at the right hand of the throne of God. ³Consider him who endured such opposition from sinful men, so that you will not grow weary and lose heart.

12:1 Therefore, since we are surrounded by such a great cloud of witnesses, let us throw off everything that hinders and the sin that so easily entangles, and let us run with perseverance the race marked out for us.

"Therefore" connects what is to come with the previous chapter. We will now read the "so what" of the famous "faith chapter" (Heb 11). Again there is a brief return to the "we" language — a language of identification — which has surfaced regularly throughout the letter (2:1ff.; 4:14ff.; 6:1ff.; 8:1; 10:19ff.; 10:39).

There is a single command[1] within verses 1 and 2: "let us

---

[1] A first person plural subjunctive which carries the force of an imperative (τρέχωμεν, trechōmen).

run with perseverance the race marked out for us" (v. 1).
Perseverance is the key idea of this section since forms of this
word (ὑπομονή, *hypomenē*) occurs no less than three times in
these three verses ("endured" the verb ὑπομένω [*hypomenō*] in
both v. 2 and v. 3). The word conveys the idea of "standing
one's ground" or "holding out" in times of trouble and afflic-
tion.[2] These were certainly such times for the readers and
helping them persevere is the immediate purpose of the letter
(see introduction).

Three participles describe events which attend our efforts
to persevere. First, we do it while "surrounded" by "a great
cloud of witnesses." Their proximity in the context clearly
suggests that the witnesses are those heroes of faith which
have been presented for our consideration in chapter 11. The
image our writer constructs here is one of an athletic competition (a race) taking place within a stadium — cf. his reference
to the "great contest" in which his listeners "stood [their]
ground" (*hypomenō*, 10:32). Considering the tendency of
Hebrews to use μαρτυρέω (*martyreō*) in the sense of "testimony," however, Bruce is probably correct to suggest that they
are "witnesses" not in the sense of being our spectators but in
the sense that the endurance of their lives bears testimony "to
the possibilities of the life of faith" — "it is not so much they
who look to us as we who look to them — for encouragement."[3]

Second, we see that to run this race we need to "throw off
everything that hinders and the sin that so easily entangles."
Whereas the other two participles are present tense, this one
is aorist which suggests that it must be done before the race
begins. Morris points out that the word translated "everything
that hinders" (ὄγκος, *ongkos*) was sometimes used of the extra
body weight that an athlete would shed during training.[4] This
metaphor describes the effect that sin (as well as the feelings

---

[2]BAGD, p. 845.
[3]Bruce, p. 346.
[4]Morris, pp. 133-134.

of guilt which accompany it, cf. 9:9, 14; 10:2) has on the Christian's ability to persevere or endure until the end of the "race."

12:2 Let us fix our eyes on Jesus, the author and perfecter of our faith, who for the joy set before him endured the cross, scorning its shame, and sat down at the right hand of the throne of God.

Finally, it is so important that we "fix our eyes on Jesus" that the NIV translates this participle as if it were a main verb. This is not the same word used in the similar exhortation of 3:1 but the thought is the same and thus this exhortation frames the greater part of the epistle. Jesus is the "author" (ἀρχηγός, *archēgos*, "originator, founder, one who begins something"[5]) and "perfecter" of our faith. Τελειόω (*teleioō*) has been a key soteriological term in the letter (see comments on 7:11) and the thought of Jesus' "perfection" in his role as priest and his "perfection" of the believer may not be wholly absent here. However, it is more probable that, in this instance, the word functions opposite *archēgos* to convey the idea that Jesus completed or finished what he began.

12:3 Consider him who endured such opposition from sinful men, so that you will not grow weary and lose heart.

Two aspects of his example can encourage us to "not grow weary and lose heart" — the fact that he endured worse than the readers had (since he endured the cross while they had not yet resisted to this point, v. 4) and that he, too, endured (even "scorned") shame (just as they were "exposed to insult," 10:33). Even in this, he was "made like his brothers in every way" (2:17). Yet, because he endured, Jesus sat down at the right hand of God. His example is proof to the readers that if they, too, endure, they will also be "richly rewarded" (10:35).

---

[5]BAGD, p. 112.

B. THE WORD OF ENCOURAGEMENT (12:4-6)

[4]In your struggle against sin, you have not yet resisted to the point of shedding your blood. [5]And you have forgotten that word of encouragement that addresses you as sons:
　"My son, do not make light of the Lord's discipline,
　and do not lose heart when he rebukes you,
　[6]because the Lord disciplines those he loves,
　and he punishes everyone he accepts as a son."[a]

[a]6 Prov. 3:11,12

12:4 In your struggle against sin, you have not yet resisted to the point of shedding your blood.

Ἀνταγωνίζομαι (*antagōnizomai,* "struggle") continues the imagery of the athletic competition[6] verse 4 echoes the description of the reader's sufferings in 10:33-34 (see comments there). However, the struggle is here said to be against "sin," rather than their human oppressors. This could mean the temptation to sin (by renouncing Christ) presented by the persecutions and their sufferings, but in the immediate context it probably anticipates the equation of their hardship with the discipline of God which is intended to produce holiness and righteousness in them (12:7, 10, 11).[7]

12:5 And you have forgotten that word of encouragement that addresses you as sons: "My son, do not make light of the Lord's discipline, and do not lose heart when he rebukes you, 12:6 because the Lord disciplines those he loves, and he punishes everyone he accepts as a son."

Our writer offers his readers a "word of encouragement"

---

[6]It occurs only here in the NT but was used in the papyri of gymnastic performers (MM, p. 46).

[7]The phrase "you have not yet resisted to the point of shedding your blood" supports the dating of the document proposed in the introduction. At the height of the Neronian persecutions, many Christians were martyred (including Paul and Peter according to tradition) hence the letter was probably written just before then.

from Proverbs 3:11, 12. He thus appeals to Scripture to suggest that (1) his readers see the disciplining hand of the Lord in their struggles and (2) their struggles are a sign of God's love for them. It also introduces the parent-child analogy which will be elaborated upon in the verses which follow.

C. GOD DISCIPLINES HIS CHILDREN (12:7-11)

[7]Endure hardship as discipline; God is treating you as sons. For what son is not disciplined by his father? [8]If you are not disciplined (and everyone undergoes discipline), then you are illegitimate children and not true sons. [9]Moreover, we have all had human fathers who disciplined us and we respected them for it. How much more should we submit to the Father of our spirits and live! [10]Our fathers disciplined us for a little while as they thought best; but God disciplines us for our good, that we may share in his holiness. [11]No discipline seems pleasant at the time, but painful. Later on, however, it produces a harvest of righteousness and peace for those who have been trained by it.

12:7 Endure hardship as discipline; God is treating you as sons. For what son is not disciplined by his father? 12:8 If you are not disciplined (and everyone undergoes discipline), then you are illegitimate children and not true sons.

The word "hardship" is not present in the Greek text. The preposition translated "as" by the NIV (εἰς, *eis*) is somewhat ambiguous in the context. It could be taken to indicate that discipline is the object of the verb, i.e., "endure discipline." Or it could be taken to indicate the goal or end of the action, i.e., "endure for/as discipline."[8] Παιδεία itself foregrounds the result which the action has in mind for it can also be

---

[8]As to the former alternative, Bauer notes that the predicate accusative is sometimes replaced by εἰς with the accusative under Semitic influence (p. 230). The NIV takes it in reference to "the vocation, use or end indicated (BAGD, p. 229).

translated "upbringing, training, instruction" and a παιδευτής (*paideutēs*) was an "instructor" or "teacher."[9] The term παι-δάριον (*paidarion*) was used of a child or a youth[10] and so neither is the role of the parent far removed from the idea. It is clearly what our writer has in mind for he tells us that "God is treating you as sons." Earlier we read that even Jesus, "although he was a son," endured "days of the flesh" along with the temptations and sufferings that accompany them (see comments on 5:8).

12:9 Moreover, we have all had human fathers who disciplined us and we respected them for it. How much more should we submit to the Father of our spirits and live!

Hence, from the Scriptures, our writer draws an analogy to help us understand God's role in our suffering — that of a father's "tough love." The logic of the argument runs from lesser (human) to greater (divine) but the very use of the analogy suggests that what we think of God may first be shaped by what we think of our fathers. When verse 9 says, "we have all had human fathers who disciplined us and we respected them for it," it speaks to first century Mediterranean cultures rather than to twentieth century America. Unfortunately, neither discipline nor respect are a part of the experience of most children of today. Fewer and fewer have human fathers who discipline with a consistent, character-building goal in mind and our culture with near unanimity degrades such fathers. Blessed is the child whose father cares enough to draw careful, clear rules for right living and then justly punishes infractions. Such fathers imitate God in this grace, for we have a heavenly Father who cares enough to do just that for his children.

The ends of God's discipline can also be found in these verses. One is life: "How much more should we submit to the Father of our spirits and live!" (v. 9). The training of his disci-

---

[9]BAGD, p. 603.
[10]Ibid.

pline is designed to make us tough enough to last, strong enough to endure so that we can receive our rich reward (10:35), our promised eternal inheritance (9:15) rather than the judgment and raging fire which those who fail to persevere can expect (10:26-27).

12:10 Our fathers disciplined us for a little while as they thought best; but God disciplines us for our good, that we may share in his holiness.

Another is holiness. Ἁγιότητος (*hagiotētēs*) is a cognate of ἁγιάζω (*hagiazō*), a key term in the letter for our sanctification — i.e., that spiritual growth process by which our lives become more and more holy now that we have been justified (put right in God's mind) by Jesus' sacrifice (see comments on 10:14). The discipline which we endure is a part of this growth process.

12:11 No discipline seems pleasant at the time, but painful. Later on, however, it produces a harvest of righteousness and peace for those who have been trained by it.

Finally, the author mentions "a harvest of righteousness and peace for those who have been trained by it." The agricultural imagery suggests that righteousness and peace are a natural outgrowth of our endurance. The reference to "righteousness and peace" anticipates the exhortation in v. 14 (see comments below). Δικαιοσύνη (*dikaiosynē*), when used in a moral and religious sense, refers to "the characteristic required of men by God."[11] In the Greek text, εἰρηνικός (*eirēnikos*, "peaceable, peaceful"[12]) actually describes the "fruit" of righteousness (NASB, "afterwards it yields the peaceful fruit of righteousness"). This could be an inner peace which we experience now that our consciences have been cleansed (9:14), but the immediate context suggests that

---

[11]Ibid., p. 196.

[12]Ibid., p. 228; cognate of εἰρήνη (*eirēnē*), "peace" or "harmony," ibid., p. 227.

it means living peacefully with others (12:14). Paul similarly described peace as a part of the fruit of the Spirit (Gal 5:22).

Thus we see the worth of the discipline for "those who have been trained by it." The literal sense of γυμνάζω (*gymnazō*) is to "exercise naked"[13] and the term continues the athletic imagery which frames this portion of the chapter (12:1-11). The exercise which leads to spiritual strength is similar to that exercise which leads to physical strength: no pain, no gain.

D. PRACTICAL ACTIONS (12:12-17)

[12]**Therefore, strengthen your feeble arms and weak knees.** [13] **"Make level paths for your feet,"[a] so that the lame may not be disabled, but rather healed.**

[14]**Make every effort to live in peace with all men and to be holy; without holiness no one will see the Lord.** [15]**See to it that no one misses the grace of God and that no bitter root grows up to cause trouble and defile many.** [16]**See that no one is sexually immoral, or is godless like Esau, who for a single meal sold his inheritance rights as the oldest son.** [17]**Afterward, as you know, when he wanted to inherit this blessing, he was rejected. He could bring about no change of mind, though he sought the blessing with tears.**

ᵃ*13* Prov. 4:26

12:12 Therefore, strengthen your feeble arms and weak knees. 12:13 "Make level paths for your feet," so that the lame may not be disabled, but rather healed.

"Therefore" indicates that what follows is a practical application of the "word of encouragement" drawn out of Proverbs 3:11-12. The application is twofold. On one hand, the readers are encouraged to address their own situation.

---

[13]BAGD, p. 167.

The command (an imperative verb is used) to "strengthen [their] feeble arms and weak knees" grows out of the exercise imagery of v. 11. Παραλελυμένα (*paralelymena*, "weak," from *paralyō*) can even mean "disabled" or "paralyzed" (and it is sometimes translated this way in the NIV, e.g., Luke 5:24; Acts 8:7). On the other hand, they are encouraged to consider the welfare of others as well. The quotation is taken from Proverbs 4:26 and is applied to the responsibility which the community of faith must take upon itself to care for its weaker, struggling members and help them along the way lest they become casualties.

12:14 Make every effort to live in peace with all men and to be holy; without holiness no one will see the Lord.

The main thrust of this section is conveyed in v. 14: "without holiness no one will see the Lord." This echoes v. 10 which suggested that holiness was one of the ends of God's discipline. The word translated "holiness" here is ἁγιασμός (*hagiasmos*, cf. *hagiotēs* in v. 10) and its significance here is probably best understood in light of the comments on 10:14 where we read that "by one sacrifice he has made perfect (τελειόω, *teleioō*) forever those who are being made holy (*hagiazō*)." Since in the present context "holiness" has been identified with the outcome of our spiritual growth, i.e., as we endure God's discipline, it is most likely that here (as in 10:14), the term refers primarily to our "sanctification" — that present, ongoing, dimension of our salvation the end of which is a holy condition of life, the removal of sin's power as well as its guilt. If we are to "see the Lord" (the future tense of the verb suggests eschatological consummation), what was begun at the cross must be completed in our lives. This is not to suggest that salvation is based on works but only to recognize that "he who began a good work in you will carry it on to completion until the day of Christ Jesus" (Phil 1:6) so that, perfectly holy and completely free from sin, we enter into the presence of God.

Holiness, however, requires a strong effort of cooperation

on our part, for our writer exhorts his readers to "make every effort." Διώκω (diōkō) can also be defined as "press on" or "strive for"[14] and so the strong rendering of the NIV is a fair translation. "Effort" is required in two directions, however, which reflect the pairing of "righteousness" (a requirement of God) and "peace" (actually the "peaceable fruit of righteousness," i.e., its manifestation in harmonious relationships with others — see comments on 12:11).

On one hand, we are to put effort into the pursuit of our own holiness of life. The "holiness" referred to by hagiazō and its cognates is what "consecrates" or "sets [us] apart" for God.[15] On the other hand, we are to put effort into living "in peace with all men." Here we see both the "vertical" and "horizontal" dimensions of our salvation. The redemption and reconciliation which we experience in our relationship with God places at our disposal the spiritual resources necessary to redeem and experience reconciliation in our relationships with others as well. No example in the Bible illustrates this better than the opening chapters of Genesis. The breaking of fellowship with God has consequences for every other relationship in the life of the sinner — self, creation, spouse, siblings, and others. The alienation which exists in our relationship with our Creator manifests itself in all of our other relationships. Only through the restoration of that primary relationship with God can we experience a restoration of the possibilities for God's will in those other relationships. Peace with God enables peace between men.

12:15 See to it that no one misses the grace of God and that no bitter root grows up to cause trouble and defile many.

As proof for his contention that "without holiness no one will see the Lord," our writer presents examples. The first is alluded to, the second explained. The word translated "miss" (NASB, "fall short") is the same word which our writer used

---

[14]BAGD, p. 201.
[15]Ibid., pp. 8-9.

in 4:1 to apply the example of Israel to his listeners, warning them, "Be careful that none of you be found to have fallen short of it [the rest promised by God]". Although πικρία (*pikria*, "bitterness") occurs nowhere else in Hebrews it is consonant with our writer's description of the "hardening" of the Israelites (3:7, 12-13; 4:7). The Israelites who died in the wilderness did not pursue holiness but practiced chronic disobedience and a lack of faith. They neither entered the promised land nor experienced the rest it offered. They continually wandered in the wilderness for forty years and died there.

12:16 See that no one is sexually immoral, or is godless like Esau, who for a single meal sold his inheritance rights as the oldest son. 12:17 Afterward, as you know, when he wanted to inherit this blessing, he was rejected. He could bring about no change of mind, though he sought the blessing with tears.

Those who are "sexually immoral" (see comments on 13:4) and the "godless" have no part in holiness. An example of the latter is Esau, whose sin nevertheless consisted in preferring fleshly gratification to his commitment to the God of his fathers. The reference to his "inheritance rights" recalls our writer's frequent use of inheritance terminology to describe the hope of the believer (9:15, etc.). His end was rejection. This was not because his sin was unforgivable or that God was unwilling to forgive but due to his lack of repentance. The NIV uses "change of mind" to render μετανοία (*metanoia*) which is elsewhere translated "repentance" (6:1, 6). This is the same principle described in chapter 6. Apart from repentance there is no restoration. Esau's outward tears were no substitute for a lack of change in his heart and mind. This is how one "misses the grace of God" (v. 15).

E. TERRIFYING MT. SINAI (12:18-21)

[18]You have not come to a mountain that can be touched
and that is burning with fire; to darkness, gloom and storm;
[19]to a trumpet blast or to such a voice speaking words that
those who heard it begged that no further word be spoken
to them, [20]because they could not bear what was commanded: "If even an animal touches the mountain, it must be
stoned."[a] [21]The sight was so terrifying that Moses said, "I
am trembling with fear."[b]

[a]*20* Exodus 19:12,13   [b]*21* Deut. 9:19

**12:18 You have not come to a mountain that can be touched
and that is burning with fire; to darkness, gloom and storm;**

As on previous occasions, our writer follows a stern warning with an uplifting word of assurance (6:9ff.; 10:35ff.). What
we read in these verses is the first half of a contrast between
two mountains. One, our writer says, "You have not come to"
(v. 18), but the other "you have come to" (v. 22; the NIV
brings out the close parallelism in the Greek text).

The first mountain is not named but this is not necessary
for the readers would have immediately recognized the
description of Sinai. We can read it in Exodus 19-20. When
our writer describes this mountain as one "that can be
touched" he is not saying that the Israelites had permission to
approach the mountain and touch. He is merely acknowledg-
ing that it was a material, earthly mountain that could be
touched as opposed to the "heavenly" nature of the second
mountain (v. 22).

**12:19 to a trumpet blast or to such a voice speaking words
that those who heard it begged that no further word be spoken to them, 12:20 because they could not bear what was
commanded: "If even an animal touches the mountain, it
must be stoned."**

The description includes two signs of how "terrifying" the
experience was. (Φοβερός [*phoberos*] is the same word translat-

ed "fearful" in 10:27 and "dreadful" in 10:31 where the author depicted the judgment of God.) One is the response of the Israelites. When they heard God speak they were so frightened that they begged Moses to speak to them on God's behalf instead (Exod 20:19).

12:21 The sight was so terrifying that Moses said, "I am trembling with fear."

The other indication of how terrifying the situation was is the response of Moses himself. His words are not recorded in Exodus and this exact statement is found nowhere in Scripture, although Moses mentioned the fear he felt on that day in Deuteronomy 9:19. Even Moses, the one with whom God would speak "face to face, as a man speaks with his friend" (Exod 33:11), trembled with fear. The imagery ("fire," "darkness," "gloom," "storm") of the passage adds to the effect — not in that the description is fabricated (for these are verified in the Exodus narrative) but in that they are foregrounded in our writer's description.

F. MT. ZION, THE HEAVENLY JERUSALEM (12:22-24)

²²**But you have come to Mount Zion, to the heavenly Jerusalem, the city of the living God. You have come to thousands upon thousands of angels in joyful assembly, ²³to the church of the firstborn, whose names are written in heaven. You have come to God, the judge of all men, to the spirits of righteous men made perfect, ²⁴to Jesus the mediator of a new covenant, and to the sprinkled blood that speaks a better word than the blood of Abel.**

12:22 But you have come to Mount Zion, to the heavenly Jerusalem, the city of the living God. You have come to thousands upon thousands of angels in joyful assembly,

Verse 22 introduces the second half of the contrast begun in verse 18 (cf. the parallelism between v. 18 and v. 22) — the positive counterpart of the new covenant. Mt. Zion was the site which David captured to claim Jerusalem. He took up residence in the fortress there and called it the "City of David" (2 Sam 5:6-10). There "the Lord God Almighty was with him" (2 Sam. 5:10), there the temple was later built (1 Kgs 6:1ff.; 2 Chr 3:1ff.) and the Psalms are replete with references to Mt. Zion as the dwelling place of God and Jerusalem as the city of God. In the book of Revelation, Mt. Zion is where the throne of God is located (14:1-3). Paul contrasts these same two mountains (Sinai and Zion) in Galatians 4:24-26 but our writer makes no reference to the allegory there.

Instead, our writer offers his customary typological interpretation of the places, persons and institutions of the old covenant. It is interesting that he employs the perfect tense here rather than the future: "you have come to Mount Zion" (v. 22). The heavenly reward of the believer may become complete at the consummation but we can begin to experience it in the present.

What or who do we come to when we come to the heavenly Jerusalem? Several particulars are specified. First, we come to "thousands upon thousand of angels in joyful assembly." Μυριάς (myrias, "myriad"), as an exact number, means ten thousand but may simply mean "a very large number, not exactly defined."[16] The role(s) which angels play in the lives of believers is never specified clearly in Scripture although they are mentioned as active servants and messengers of God throughout the entire canon. The reference to the "joyful assembly" here reminds us of the "rejoicing of the angels in the presence of God over one sinner who repents" (Luke 15:7, 10).[17]

---

[16]BAGD, p. 529.

[17]There is some disagreement as to whether the dative πανηγύρει (panēgyrei, "assembly") should be taken with the preceding reference to the angels or with the subsequent reference to the church ("to the assembly and the church"). The placement of καὶ throughout vv. 23-24 supports the decision of the NIV.

12:23 to the church of the firstborn, whose names are written in heaven. You have come to God, the judge of all men, to the spirits of righteous men made perfect,

We also come "to the church of the firstborn, whose names are written in heaven." It is tempting to see in "the firstborn" a reference to Jesus as the head of the church (see Col 1:15, 18). However, the use of a plural here (i.e., those who are firstborn vs. the one firstborn) makes this unlikely. It is more likely the term hearkens back to (1) 2:10-17 where we read that we are "of the same family" as Jesus the Son who "is not ashamed to call [us] brothers" (2:10-11) and (2) to the OT concept of the firstborn as belonging especially to God (Exod 13:13; 34:20; Num 18:15).[18] Earlier we learned the importance of active participation in a congregation of other believers (see comments 10:24-25). Here is another reminder that life in the new covenant is not merely a private or individual experience. It is God's will that those individuals who come to him in faith find fellowship within the church, that setting within which both the vertical and horizontal dimensions of our salvation can grow (see comments on 12:14). Jesus had referred to "names [which] are written in heaven" (Luke 10:20). Paul also referred to "the book of life" (Phil 3:4) which is mentioned several times in Revelation (3:5; 20:12; 20:15; 21:27).

We also come to "God, the judge of all men." He has previously been described as "him to whom we must give account" (4:13). Eschatological punishment has figured prominently into our writer's warnings (6:8; 10:26-27, 30-31, 39, cf. also 12:29) although the terminology of hope, promise, inheritance and reward have made the positive counterpart of judgment (9:27-28) even more pronounced.

We have come "to the spirits of righteous men made perfect." Lane points out that this expression is an idiom for the godly dead in Jewish apocalyptic literature[19] and this makes

---

[18]So Ellingworth suggests (p. 679).
[19]Lane, p. 470.

sense in the context of the reference to names written in heaven and the judgment of God. Some suggest that the reference is to the spirits of the pre-Christian believers such as those mentioned in chapter 11.[20] Others suggest that the phrase refers to departed Christian saints.[21] The suggestion of 11:40 — that the ancients who were commended for their faith are made perfect together with us — may support the former position, but otherwise it is difficult to say with certainty which (if not both) may be the case. We can fairly say that there is a fellowship which joins the heavenly community and transcends both time and space. All of God's saints — past, present and future — whether on earth or in heaven, share a common experience of God's grace and faithful response to his word.

12:24 to Jesus the mediator of a new covenant, and to the sprinkled blood that speaks a better word than the blood of Abel.

Finally, our writer notes that we come to Jesus who is, now for the third time, described as "the mediator of a new covenant" (8:6; 9:15). The "sprinkled blood" was his own and it was shed for our forgiveness (9:14, 22). This brief description neatly summarized both dimensions of his priestly ministry which is the heart of the new covenant — his sacrifice and his intercession (see 8:6 on "mediator"). When God confronted Cain for the murder of his brother Abel, he said to him, "Your brother's blood cries out to me from the ground" (Gen 4:10). Our author has pointed out that Abel "still speaks even though he is dead" (Heb 11:4). The word which Abel's blood speaks is that of sin, death and punishment. Christ's blood speaks of grace, forgiveness and salvation.

---

[20]E.g., Bruce, p. 378.
[21]E.g., Morris, p. 142.

G. A KINGDOM WHICH CANNOT BE SHAKEN (12:25-29)

[25]See to it that you do not refuse him who speaks. If they did not escape when they refused him who warned them on earth, how much less will we, if we turn away from him who warns us from heaven? [26]At that time his voice shook the earth, but now he has promised, "Once more I will shake not only the earth but also the heavens."[a] [27]The words "once more" indicate the removing of what can be shaken — that is, created things — so that what cannot be shaken may remain.

[28]Therefore, since we are receiving a kingdom that cannot be shaken, let us be thankful, and so worship God acceptably with reverence and awe, [29]for our "God is a consuming fire."[b]

[a]26 Haggai 2:6   [b]29 Deut. 4:24

12:25 See to it that you do not refuse him who speaks. If they did not escape when they refused him who warned them on earth, how much less will we, if we turn away from him who warns us from heaven?

Verse 25 reminds us of the opening warning of the letter (2:1-3). Thus the main portion of the document both begins and ends with a call to hear the message spoken. In chapter 2, our writer had in mind that "salvation which was first announced by the Lord" (2:3). Here he refers to "him who speaks" (12:25). There, readers were warned that they would not escape if they ignored that salvation (2:3). Here, that they would not escape if they refuse the one who warns them (12:25).

12:26 At that time his voice shook the earth, but now he has promised, "Once more I will shake not only the earth but also the heavens."

Who is the one who "speaks" in 12:25? The answer is found in v. 26. His voice shook the earth "at that time" (at

Sinai, Exod 19:19 cf. Heb 12:18-21) and his words are recorded in Haggai. He is none other than "the LORD Almighty"
(Hag 2:6). The Israelites "refused him" and "did not escape"
(v. 25). The same Israelites who were so frightened of God at
Sinai were the ones who later hardened their hearts (as
Pharaoh had done before them) and rebelled in the desert
(3:8).

The argument precedes from lesser to greater although
the NIV gives the opposite impression ("how much less"
whereas the Greek text employs the same phrase which has
heretofore been rendered "how much more," cf. 9:14; 12:9),
although this is perhaps the best way to capture the meaning
of the verse in English. If their punishment was deserved,
ours will be that much more deserved for we have refused a
much greater gift.

**12:27 The words "once more" indicate the removing of what
can be shaken — that is, created things — so that what cannot be shaken may remain.**

The words of the Lord recorded in Habakkuk 2:6 are read
as a promise which is yet to be fulfilled. Our writer interprets[22]
the words "Once more" as suggesting a comparison between
the events of Sinai and another cataclysmic intervention of
God yet to come. The reference to both "the earth" and "the
heavens" resembles the promise of God, recorded in Isaiah
66:22, to make "new heavens" and "a new earth" which will
endure. In his Revelation, John "saw a new heaven and a new
earth, for the first heaven and the first earth had passed
away" (21:1; cf. v. 27 here which refers to a "removing of what
can be shaken — that is, created things — so that what cannot
be shaken remains"). This would seem, then, to be yet another of our writer's references to the final consummation — "the
Day" (10:25) when Jesus "will appear a second time" (9:27).

---

[22]Lane suggests that this is an example of "parenetic midrash" which is an
exposition of Scripture for a hortatory purpose (p. 481). See section on our
writer's "Use of the Old Testament" in the Introduction.

12:28 Therefore, since we are receiving a kingdom that cannot be shaken, let us be thankful, and so worship God acceptably with reverence and awe, 12:29 for our "God is a consuming fire."

Those who are being persecuted in the kingdoms of the present world will someday receive "a kingdom that cannot be shaken." All other kingdoms will pass away and someday only that kingdom will remain. The appropriate response to that sure promise is described in v. 28. The main verb is "let us be thankful" and it carries the force of a command.[23] Our gratitude for the victory which God has won and will win for us is to carry over into "worship" (lit., "through which we might worship"). This is probably an acceptable translation of λατρεύω (*latreuō*) although it has typically been translated as "serve" throughout the letter, since the "service" to which it refers is that of the priests within the context of the rituals of tabernacle worship. Deuteronomy 4:24 is cited and reminds us of the terrible image of 10:27 and explains the presence of "reverence" and "awe" in our worship.

---

[23]The rendering of ἔχωμεν χάριν (*echōmen charin*) by the NIV as "let us be thankful" is consistent with Bauer's recommendation for an idiomatic rather than form-literal translation (BAGD, p. 878). The first person plural subjunctive carries the imperative force.

HEBREWS 13

IX. CONCLUDING EXHORTATIONS (13:1-25)

As chapter thirteen begins, the main body of argument has passed and the benediction and closing greetings approach. At the outset, the practical exhortations of chapter twelve continue. Gradually the turn is made to what F.F. Bruce calls "the usual assortment of ethical and practical admonition and personal information with which New Testament epistles tend to close."[1] The rhetorical engagement which began in a manner quite different than a letter clearly ends like one.

A. KEEP LOVING EACH OTHER (13:1-3)

[1]Keep on loving each other as brothers. [2]Do not forget to entertain strangers, for by so doing some people have entertained angels without knowing it. [3]Remember those in prison as if you were their fellow prisoners, and those who are mistreated as if you yourselves were suffering.

13:1 Keep on loving each other as brothers.
Literally, verse 1 reads "let brotherly love remain." The verb, which is in the imperative mood and carries the force of command, is μένω (*menō*) which also appeared in 12:27. Brotherly love, then, belongs to that which "cannot be shaken" and thus "may remain." It is the same verb Paul employs in 1 Corinthians 13:13 when he notes that "these three remain: faith, hope and love. But the greatest of these is love."

---

[1]Bruce, p. 386.

13:2 Do not forget to entertain strangers, for by so doing some people have entertained angels without knowing it.

These verses indicate two ways to practice this "brotherly love." One way is to "not forget to entertain strangers." The compound word φιλοξενία (*philoxenia*) can also be translated "hospitality"[2] and its close relationship with the compound word translated "brotherly love" (φιλαδελφία, *philadelphia*) is seen in the word which they share (φιλία, *philia*, "friendship, love").[3] Our writer's observation about possibly entertaining angels reminds us of the words of Jesus recorded in Matthew 25:35 ("I was a stranger and you invited me in"). In 6:10 our writer observed that helping God's people is a demonstration of our love for God himself. Again, this is as Jesus had said ("whatever you did for one of the least of these brothers of mine, you did for me," Matt 25:40).

13:3 Remember those in prison as if you were their fellow prisoners, and those who are mistreated as if you yourselves were suffering.

Another way to practice brotherly love is to remember the prisoners and the mistreated. Again, we here echoes of the words of Jesus ("I was in prison and you came to visit me," Matt 25:36) but there is an interesting parallel in Paul's letter to the Philippians when he writes "whether I am in chains or defending and confirming the gospel, all of you share in God's grace with me" (1:7). Their concern for him, expressed in tangible ways (Phil 4:14ff.), is one of the reasons Paul was able to write the "joy letter" while in prison. Remembering the mistreated may well encompass the remainder of Jesus' words in Matthew 25:31ff (caring for the hungry, the thirsty, the naked and the sick), but again we see the breadth of the significance attached to such acts of kindness when Paul reminds the Corinthians of an important truth about practicing what it means to be the body of Christ: "If one part

---

[2]As in the NASB; see BAGD, p. 860.
[3]BAGD, p. 859.

suffers, every part suffers with it" (1 Cor 12:26). Taken together, these expressions of brotherly love amount to nothing less than the golden rule (Matt 7:12).

B. STAY PURE (13:4-6)

[4]Marriage should be honored by all, and the marriage bed kept pure, for God will judge the adulterer and all the sexually immoral. [5]Keep your lives free from the love of money and be content with what you have, because God has said,

"Never will I leave you; never will I forsake you."[a]
[6]So we say with confidence,

"The Lord is my helper; I will not be afraid.

What can man do to me?"[b]

[a]5 Deut. 31:6   [b]6 Psalm 118:6,7

Whereas verses 1-3 specified virtuous practices which we should pursue, verses 4-6 identify behaviors which mar our holiness and should be guarded against. The first is sexual immorality and the description here takes in the scope of illicit relationships.

13:4 Marriage should be honored by all, and the marriage bed kept pure, for God will judge the adulterer and all the sexually immoral.

The institution of marriage itself, as the God-provided context for sexual joy and fulfillment, should be "honored" (τίμιος, *timios*, "valuable" or "precious").[4] It appears only here in Hebrews but elsewhere in the NT it is used of precious metals and stones (1 Cor 3:12; 1 Pet 1:7; Rev 17:4; 18:12, 12, 16; 21:11, 19). Peter uses it to describe the "precious blood of Christ" (1 Pet 1:19). We are exhorted to place the highest possible value on the sanctity of the marriage relationship.

---

[4]Ibid., p. 818.

Marriage itself is honored by keeping "the marriage bed . . . pure" (v. 4). Κοίτη (*koitē*, "bed," especially "marriage bed") is a euphemism for sexual intercourse.[5] God himself — "a consuming fire" (12:29) — will judge the adulterer.

God will also judge those otherwise "sexually immoral." The word here is πόρνος (*pornos*, "fornicator"[6]), the more general word for sexual sins of all kinds. Morris observes that "this was a novel view to many in the first century" because "for them chastity was an unreasonable demand to make."[7] This description is all too contemporary. Blessed are those who are raised in homes and communities where their parents, educators and elected officials believe that they can and will remain sexually pure if provided with the necessary guidance and held accountable for their choices.

13:5 Keep your lives free from the love of money and be content with what you have, because God has said, "Never will I leave you; never will I forsake you."

Another lust which can mar our holiness is greed. This truth is first stated negatively and then positively. First, we must keep our lives "free from the love of money." Ἀφιλάργυρος (*aphilargyros*) is a rare word. It does not appear outside of the NT and there only in the present verse and in 1 Timothy 3:3. Cognates appear seldom as well. Luke describes the Pharisees as *philargyros* ("lovers of money," 16:14). Paul says that φιλαργυρία (*philargyria*, "the love of money") is "a root of all kinds of evil" (1 Tim 6:10, cf. also 2 Tim 3:2). Jesus pointed out the power of greed to corrupt our commitment to him when he told his disciples, "it is easier for a camel to go through the eye of a needle than for a rich man to enter the kingdom of God" and there could have been no better example for them than the rich young ruler who had just asked Jesus how to get eternal life but, when he

---

[5]BAGD, p. 440.
[6]Ibid., p. 693.
[7]Morris, p. 147.

had been told to sell his possessions, "went away sad because he had great wealth" (Matt 19:16-24).

The alternative for the believer is to "be content with what you have." Paul said that he had "learned the secret of being content in any and every situation, whether well fed or hungry, whether living in plenty or in want" (Phil 4:12). What our writer offers his readers are two promises to trust in.

First he cites Deuteronomy 31:6. The context of that passage is a promise by the Lord to Joshua and the Israelites as they prepared to cross the Jordan and enter the promised land that he would never leave them. Our writer applies it to his readers. It is a promise of God's *presence*. Jesus has made the same promise for us to claim as well (Matt 28:20; John 14:18).

13:6 So we say with confidence, "The Lord is my helper; I will not be afraid. What can man do to me?"

Next our writer cites Psalm 118:6, 7. This is a promise of God's *provision*. God is with us. God will help us. What more would we desire? Jesus reminded his disciples that our heavenly Father knows what we need before we even ask him (Matt 6:8) and promised that, if we seek first his kingdom and his righteousness, all that we need will be given to us (Matt 6:33). Trusting in God's promise is the key to contentment.

B. REMEMBER YOUR LEADERS (13:7-8)

⁷Remember your leaders, who spoke the word of God to you. Consider the outcome of their way of life and imitate their faith. ⁸Jesus Christ is the same yesterday and today and forever.

13:7 Remember your leaders, who spoke the word of God to you. Consider the outcome of their way of life and imitate their faith.

Ἡγέομαι (*hēgeomai*, "lead, guide") was used of men in any

leading position[8] and does not indicate specifically what kind of leaders are in mind here. What we do know about those referred to as "leaders" is that they "spoke the word of God," which probably means that they labored in the ministries of preaching and teaching. Since this verb form ("spoke") is aorist, it may be describing a particular event in the past — i.e., the initial presentation of the gospel to the readers — and so the ministry of evangelism, not to be separated from the above, may have been a part of their leading as well. The NT is clear that the ministry of God's word is at the heart of both the evangelistic and equipping ministry of the church (2 Tim 3:16-17).

These verses also indicate *how* leaders are to be "remembered": their faith is to be imitated. The best compliment to be paid to a leader is to strive to become like them. Some suggest that the word "outcome" indicates that the author is referring to leaders who have died[9] but Morris is probably correct to point out that this stretches the meaning of the word too far.[10] The same word (*hēgeomai*) is also used to describe their leaders in v. 17 and v. 24 where it is clear that they are living.

13:8 Jesus Christ is the same yesterday and today and forever.

The reference to Jesus should remind us that he is our ultimate model. What all Christians strive for is to "become mature, attaining to the whole measure of the fullness of Christ" (Eph 4:13). This is why, even though Paul wanted the Corinthians to follow his example, he wrote them, "Follow my example as I follow the example of Christ" (1 Cor 11:1). The author will resume his discussion of leaders in v. 17.

---

[8]BAGD, p. 343.

[9]Bruce (pp. 394-395), Westcott (p. 434), and Moffatt (pp. 230-231) among them.

[10]Morris, p. 148.

D. COUNTERPARTS TO OLD COVENANT PRACTICES
(13:9-16)

⁹Do not be carried away by all kinds of strange teachings. It is good for our hearts to be strengthened by grace, not by ceremonial foods, which are of no value to those who eat them. ¹⁰We have an altar from which those who minister at the tabernacle have no right to eat.

¹¹The high priest carries the blood of animals into the Most Holy Place as a sin offering, but the bodies are burned outside the camp. ¹²And so Jesus also suffered outside the city gate to make the people holy through his own blood. ¹³Let us, then, go to him outside the camp, bearing the disgrace he bore. ¹⁴For here we do not have an enduring city, but we are looking for the city that is to come.

¹⁵Through Jesus, therefore, let us continually offer to God a sacrifice of praise — the fruit of lips that confess his name. ¹⁶And do not forget to do good and to share with others, for with such sacrifices God is pleased.

Once more our writer returns to his typological reading of old covenant practices. Only now does he identify his concern for his readers with "all kinds of strange teachings" which, as his extended argument suggests, may have been part of the temptation for them to return to their old ways. Hence, a few more last minute observations are made. In these verses we can identify at least three different old covenant practices which have counterparts in the new covenant.

13:9 Do not be carried away by all kinds of strange teachings. It is good for our hearts to be strengthened by grace, not by ceremonial foods, which are of no value to those who eat them.

(1) We draw strength from God's grace, not ceremonial foods. The KJV, RSV and NASB all read simply "foods." The NIV reads "ceremonial foods" but there is no adjective in the Greek text. As a result, this should probably not be taken as a

reference to the priests' portions of the sacrifice or the communal meals which accompanied some of the sacrifices. A more straightforward reading of the text would see here a general reference to the food regulations (i.e., the distinguishing between clean and unclean foods) specified under the covenant (Lev 11). Earlier our writer observed that such regulations were merely "external" (9:10). As to their ability to atone for sin, they have "no value to those who eat them." Only grace is able to save us from our sins.

13:10 We have an altar from which those who minister at the tabernacle have no right to eat.

The priests were allotted a portion of some of the offerings (Lev 6-7). There is no such right within the new covenant for we have a different type of sacrifice (the sacrifices of the old covenant were burnt on an altar; Exod 38:1ff.). There is no material altar at all in the new covenant, for the sacrifice was that of Christ's body on the cross. Food portions are entirely irrelevant within the scheme of the "new order" (9:10) of the new covenant which "has made the first one obsolete" (8:13).

13:11 The high priest carries the blood of animals into the Most Holy Place as a sin offering, but the bodies are burned outside the camp. 13:12 And so Jesus also suffered outside the city gate to make the people holy through his own blood.

(2) We bear the disgrace of Jesus, not the ashes of burnt offerings. Under the old covenant it was necessary to bear the remains of the animal offerings outside the camp to be burnt in a wood fire on the ash heap (Lev 4:11-12). Similarly Jesus was crucified outside the city gate. We know from the Gospels that he was crucified at Golgotha (Mark 15:22) which must have been outside the gate for we read that Simon of Cyrene, who was forced to bear the cross of Jesus, "was passing by on his way *in* from the country" (Mark 15:21) while "they were going out" (Matt 27:32).

13:13 Let us, then, go to him outside the camp, bearing the disgrace he bore. 13:14 For here we do not have an enduring city, but we are looking for the city that is to come.

Going to him there means bearing his disgrace, for crucifixion was not only a horrible death but one reserved for slaves, thieves, assassins and other criminals. Jews considered one crucified to be cursed (Deut 21:23; Gal 3:13; 1 Cor 1:23). Jesus was crucified as a traitor and a criminal. Through their sufferings, which included insult and persecution (see comments on 10:33), the readers were bearing his disgrace. Their reward was that they were made holy through his blood. It is an eternal perspective which places present suffering and disgrace in its true context (10:34), and the reminder here (v. 14) is reminiscent of the example of Abraham (11:10).

13:15 Through Jesus, therefore, let us continually offer to God a sacrifice of praise — the fruit of lips that confess his name.

(3) We offer sacrifices of praise and good deeds, not the sacrifices of animals. In 10:28 we read of "worship" as an appropriate response to what God has promised us. Here we read that "praise" is the appropriate response to what God has accomplished for us (through the blood of Jesus, v. 12). The phrase "fruit of lips" can be found in Hosea 14:2 where it describes Israel's response to the grace of God and the forgiveness of their sins.

13:16 And do not forget to do good and to share with others, for with such sacrifices God is pleased.

The Psalms are replete with examples of Jewish worship which praised God by reciting his saving acts. The mention of "doing good" and "sharing with others" echoes 6:10; 10:24; and 13:1-3. These are the "sacrifices" that please God within the new covenant.

E. OBEY YOUR LEADERS AND PRAY FOR US (13:17-19)

¹⁷**Obey your leaders and submit to their authority. They keep watch over you as men who must give an account. Obey them so that their work will be a joy, not a burden, for that would be of no advantage to you.**

¹⁸**Pray for us. We are sure that we have a clear conscience and desire to live honorably in every way. ¹⁹I particularly urge you to pray so that I may be restored to you soon.**

13:17 Obey your leaders and submit to their authority. They keep watch over you as men who must give an account. Obey them so that their work will be a joy, not a burden, for that would be of no advantage to you.

In v. 7 the readers were exhorted to "remember" their leaders by following their example. Now they are exhorted to "obey" them. This is same word for "leader" which appeared in v. 7 so it is clear that the writer has returned to the subject of leaders within the church and that this is not an exhortation pertaining to civic leaders.

Participating in leadership ministry within the church is not easy. It is time consuming and emotionally demanding. Those who are to be led can make the job either a "joy" or a "burden." To lead God's church is to be entrusted with the care of the spiritual well-being of God's flock. And God holds leaders responsible, not only for their own lives but for their watchful care over the church. James suggested to his readers that "Not many of you should presume to be teachers, my brothers, because you know that we who teach will be judged more strictly" (3:1). Leading the church is an awesome responsibility and a demanding task. But it is also the greatest privilege in the universe.

For the church to be effectively led, however, efforts to provide leadership must be reciprocated by members who accept their responsibilities. They have responsibilities to God, to their leaders and to themselves. First, obedience and submission to God-chosen leadership has been commanded by God. To disregard this responsibility is to disregard the authority of God. Also, members also have the responsibility to make the job of leadership easier, not more difficult. No one can lead without followers. Finally, it is to their own advantage for members to work with leadership. They are seeking our spiritual well-being. The word translated "keep watch" (ἀγρυπνέω, *agrypneō*) literally means to "keep oneself awake."[11] God will hold them accountable if they fall asleep on the job and many a leader has lost sleep serving the best interests of his charge. It is God's plan for our spiritual growth to provide leaders who can help us. If we frustrate their efforts, we are the ones who lose.

13:18 Pray for us. We are sure that we have a clear conscience and desire to live honorably in every way.

Prayer is also an important means of supporting leadership in the church as well as our brothers and sisters in Christ, and so the writer asks his readers to pray for him. The present tense imperative could just as easily be translated "keep on praying for us," suggesting that (1) his readers had already made it their custom to pray for him and (2) the writer was convinced of his ongoing need for prayers on his behalf. Yet he does not ask only for prayers for himself. Timothy apparently had been and would soon again be joining his party (v. 23) which also included some from Italy (v. 24). The matter for prayers on their behalf was to be twofold. First, prayer was needed for their lifestyle. They were confident about their past ("we have a clear conscience") but not so much that they were overconfident about the future.

13:19 I particularly urge you to pray so that I may be restored to you soon.

Second, prayer was needed for their restoration. This should not be taken to mean that the writer was in prison as Timothy had recently been since he was planning to come

---

[11]BAGD, p. 14.

soon (v. 23). The restoration he desired was to be reunited with his readers.

F. BENEDICTION AND CLOSING EXHORTATIONS
(13:20-22)

[20]May the God of peace, who through the blood of the eternal covenant brought back from the dead our Lord Jesus, that great Shepherd of the sheep, [21]equip you with everything good for doing his will, and may he work in us what is pleasing to him, through Jesus Christ, to whom be glory for ever and ever. Amen.

[22]Brothers, I urge you to bear with my word of exhortation, for I have written you only a short letter.

13:20 May the God of peace, who through the blood of the eternal covenant brought back from the dead our Lord Jesus, that great Shepherd of the sheep,

The reference to "the God of peace" in this benediction resembles a common feature in Paul's letters (a tendency to refer to "the God of peace" as the end of the letter approaches, Rom 15:33; 2 Cor 13:11; Phil 4:9; 1 Thess 5:23; 2 Thess 3:10 [Lord of peace]). The reference to Jesus as "great Shepherd" is also similar to Peter's reference to him as the "Chief Shepherd" (1 Pet 5:4).

The benediction itself rehearses, one final time, the two key Christological events of the new covenant: the cross ("the blood of the eternal covenant") and the resurrection ("brought back from the dead").

13:21 equip you with everything good for doing his will, and may he work in us what is pleasing to him, through Jesus Christ, to whom be glory for ever and ever. Amen.

The prayer which the benediction expresses includes two elements as well, both of which refer to our appropriate response to what God has done for us in Christ. In regard to his readers, he prays that God may "equip" them "with every-thing good for doing his will." Similarly, for his own party, he prays that God may "work in" them "what is pleasing to him." The syntax suggests that both are accomplished "through Jesus Christ." Seeking to please him is the only appropriate response to what he has done for us. And even this we can only do through him.

13:22 Brothers, I urge you to bear with my word of exhortation, for I have written you only a short letter.

In verse 22 we read the writer's own description of his document. It is intended as a "word of exhortation" (παρακλήσις, *paraklēsis*) and this is clear from the prominent hortatory sections in the letter. This phrase may be used to describe messages which are either oral or written. It was used of oral messages presented in the synagogue (e.g., in Acts 13:15 where Paul was invited to speak in the synagogue at Pisidian Antioch). Here it is used of Hebrews; our writer also used *paraklēsis* to describe Proverbs 3:11-12 when he cited it in chapter 12 (12:5). The role of such a message (preaching or the reading of a letter) may not be altogether absent from the exhortation in 10:25 to meet together and "encourage" one another since this translates the verb form (παρακαλέω, *parakaleō*). Our writer also describes this as a "short letter" — literally, "I have written to you briefly" (NASB; ἐπιστέλλω, *epistellō*, "inform or instruct by letter"; cf. ἐπιστολή, *epistolē*, "letter, epistle").[12] This reflects the lack of firm distinction between written and spoken rhetoric in the age (see the discussion on Form and Structure in the Introduction).

G. PERSONAL GREETINGS (13:23-25)

[23]I want you to know that our brother Timothy has been released. If he arrives soon, I will come with him to see you.

---

[12]BAGD, p. 300.

²⁴**Greet all your leaders and all God's people. Those from Italy send you their greetings.**
²⁵**Grace be with you all.**

13:23 I want you to know that our brother Timothy has been released. If he arrives soon, I will come with him to see you.

The reference to Timothy's "release" may mean that he had been imprisoned but not necessarily. In Acts, this word (ἀπολύω, *apolyō*) is used both of releasing Paul from jail (Acts 16:35) and of simply releasing someone from a charge made against them (Jesus in Acts 3:13; Paul, Acts 26:32). It can simply mean to be "dismissed" or "sent away" from an assembly or some place.[13] However, it would be no surprise if he had been imprisoned. It would then be yet another indication of the persecution facing Christians at the time when this letter was written. The author described the suffering of his readers in chapter 10 (vv. 32-34).

13:24 Greet all your leaders and all God's people. Those from Italy send you their greetings.

All that we know about the rest of the author's party is that it was comprised of or included some who were from Italy. This supports the hypothesis that the letter was written to Jewish Christians who were suffering in Rome.

13:25 Grace be with you all.

Whether Paul was the author or not is difficult to say (see discussion of Authorship in the Introduction). "Grace be with you all," however, is a typical closing for Paul which is present in each of his epistles in the NT (Rom 15:20; 1 Cor 16:23; 2 Cor 13:14; Gal 6:18; Eph 6:24; Phil 4:23; Col 4:18; 1 Thess 5:28; 2 Thess 3:18; 1 Tim 6:21; 2 Tim 4:22; Titus 2:15; Phlm 25).

---

[13]BAGD, p. 96.